World
or Me

Story by Be-PaPas Art by Chiho Saitou

Volume 1

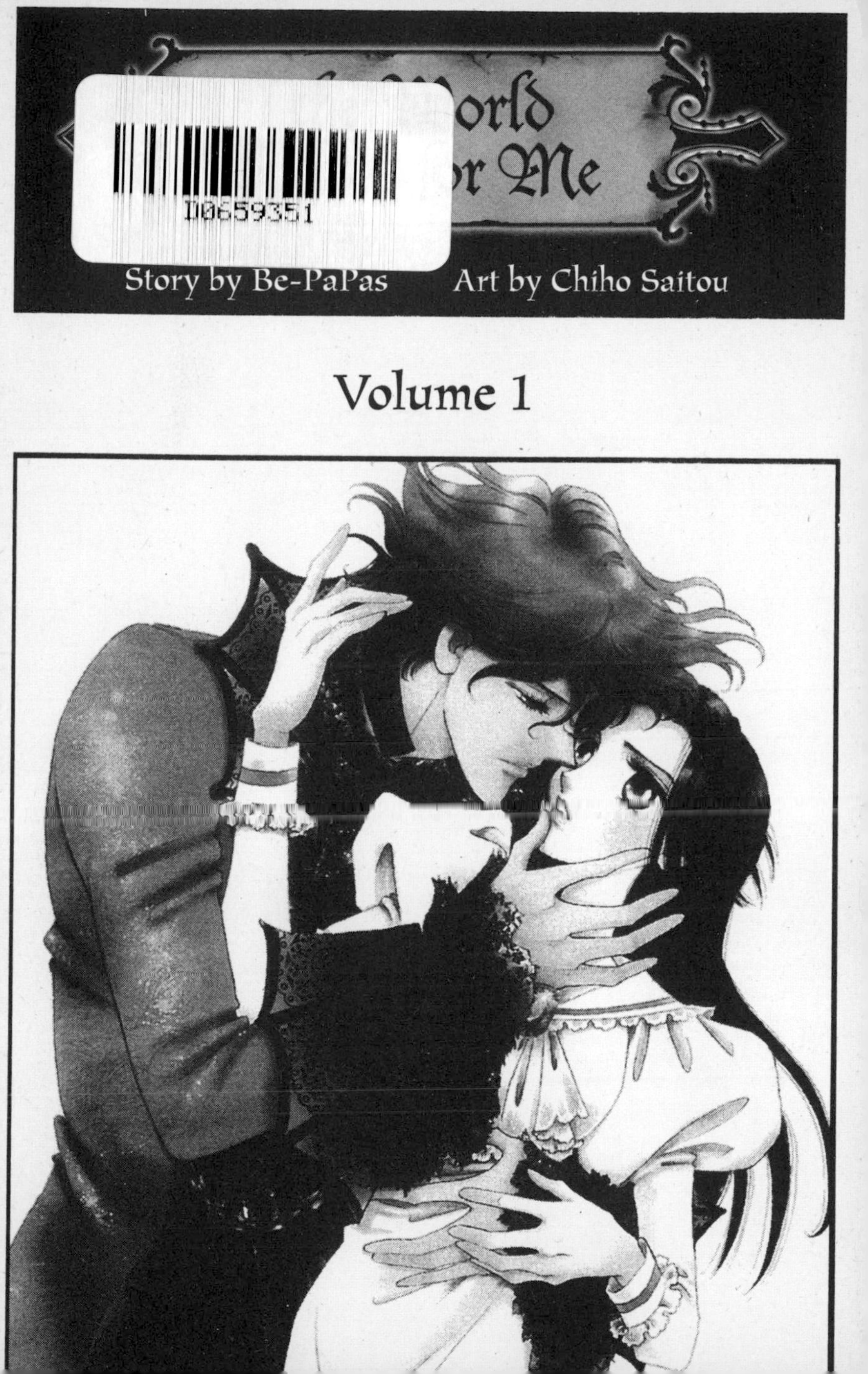

The World Exists For Me Vol. 1
Story by Be-PaPas
Art by Chiho Saitou

Translation - Shirley Kubo
English Adaptation - Suzanne Waldman
Copy Editors - Peter Ahlstrom and Hope Donovan
Retouch and Lettering - James Lee
Production Artist - Rafael Najarian
Cover Design - Thea Willis

Editor - Rob Tokar
Digital Imaging Manager - Chris Buford
Production Managers - Jennifer Miller and Mutsumi Miyazaki
Managing Editor - Lindsey Johnston
VP of Production - Ron Klamert
Publisher and E.I.C. - Mike Kiley
President and C.O.O. - John Parker
C.E.O. - Stuart Levy

A  Manga

TOKYOPOP Inc.
5900 Wilshire Blvd. Suite 2000
Los Angeles, CA 90036

E-mail: info@TOKYOPOP.com
Come visit us online at www.TOKYOPOP.com

ISBN: 1-59816-034-6

First TOKYOPOP printing: December 2005
10 9 8 7 6 5 4 3 2 1
Printed in the USA

the World Exists for Me

Volume 1

Story by
Be-PaPas

Art by
Chiho Saitou

HAMBURG // LONDON // LOS ANGELES // TOKYO

the World Exists for Me

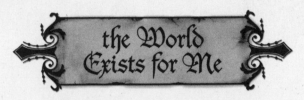

CONTENTS

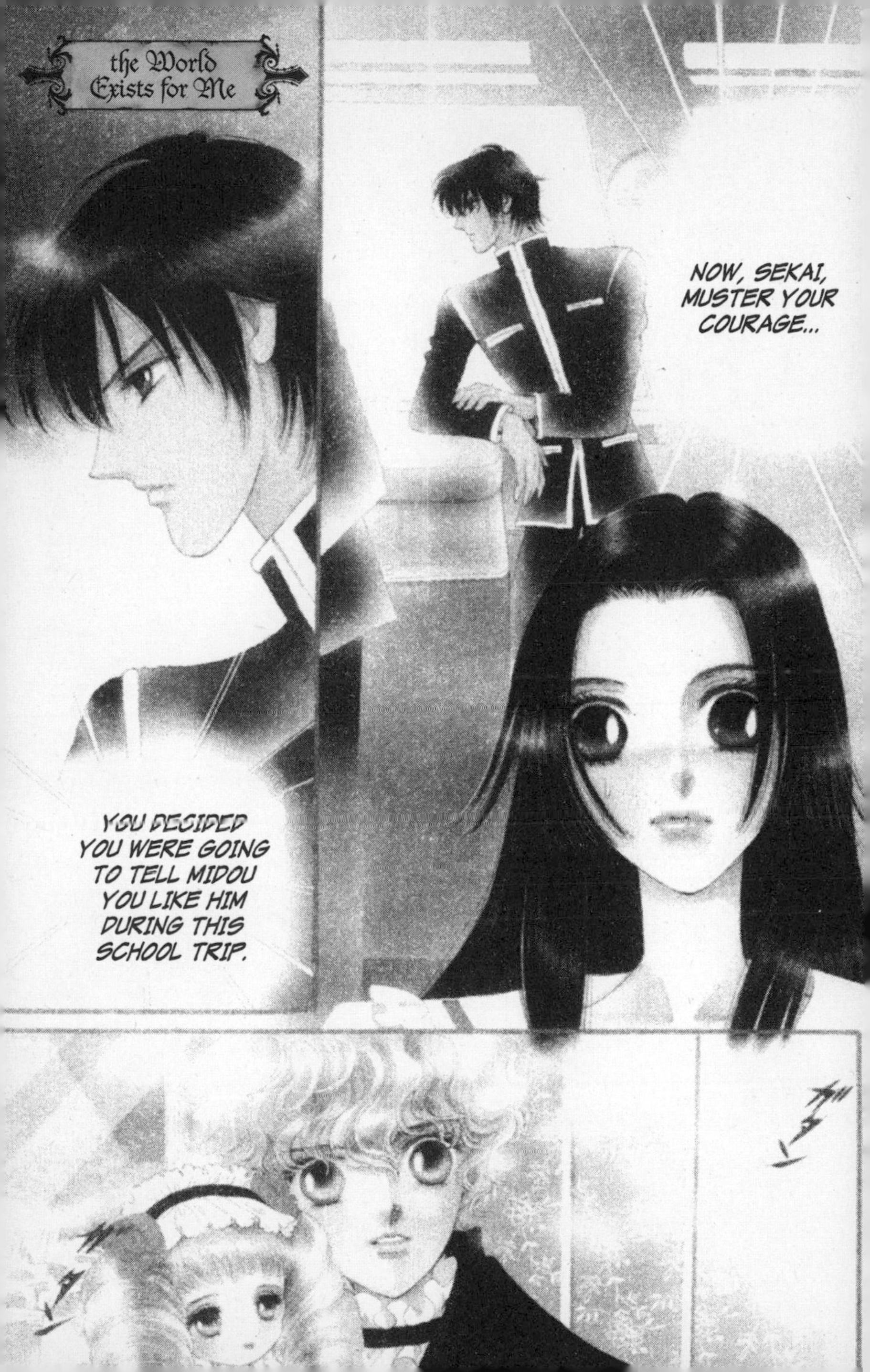
NOW, SEKAI, MUSTER YOUR COURAGE...
the World Exists for Me
YOU DECIDED YOU WERE GOING TO TELL MIDOU YOU LIKE HIM DURING THIS SCHOOL TRIP.

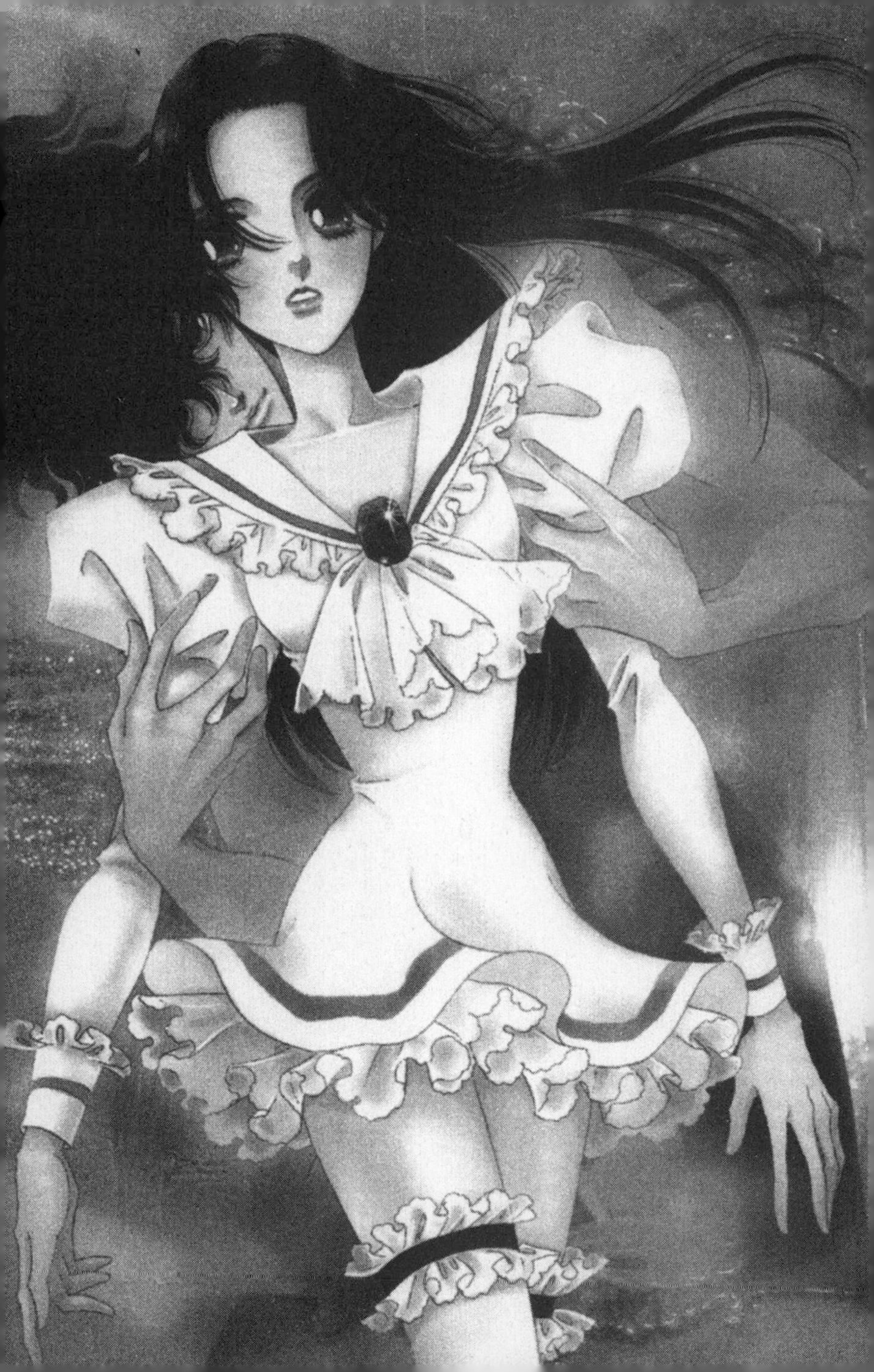

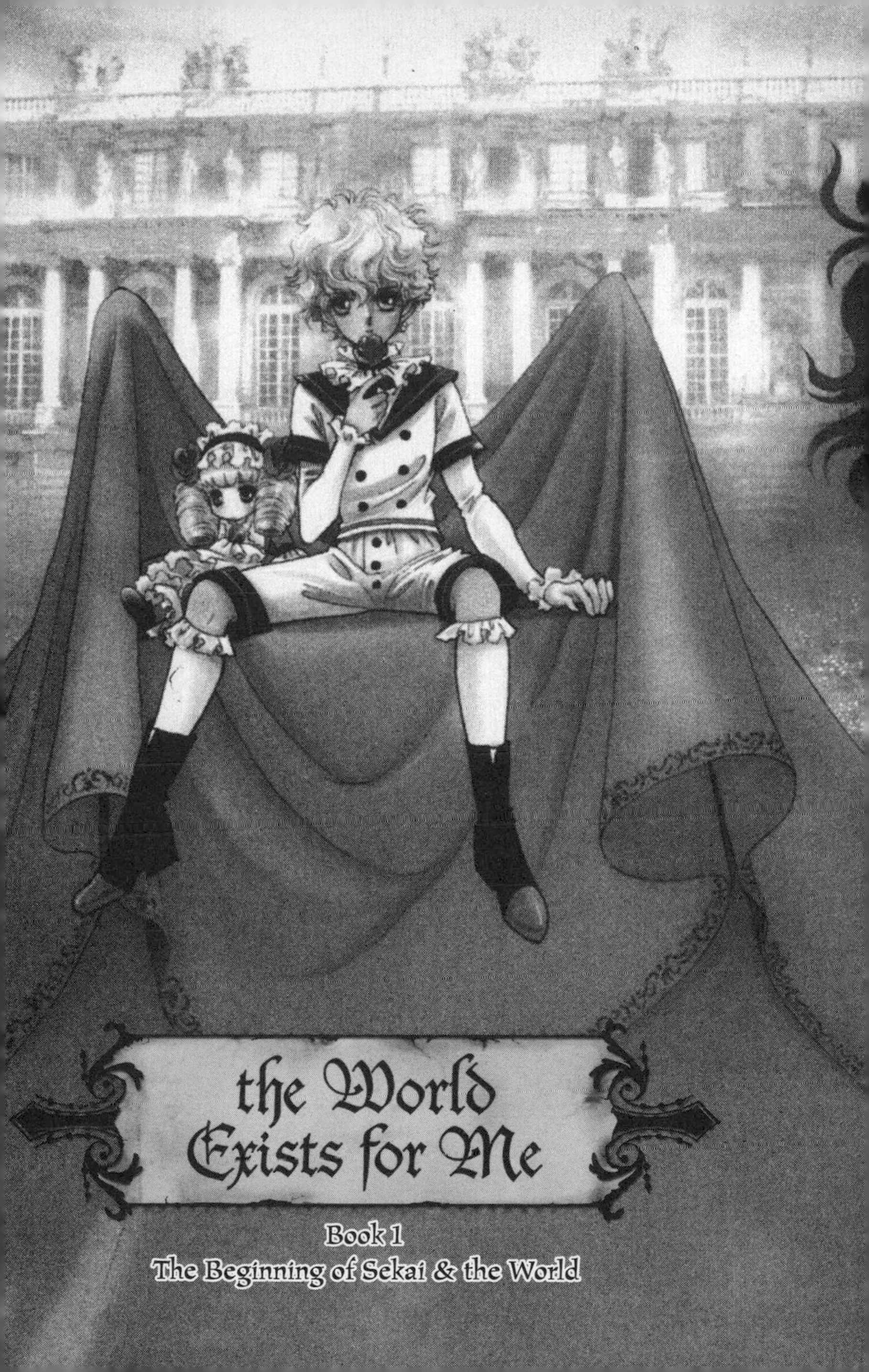
the World Exists for Me
Book 1
The Beginning of Sekai & the World

BE-PAPAS Presents

"WORLD OF THE S&M"

MANGA BY CHIHO SAITOU STORY BY KUNIHIKO IKUHARA
And SEINOSUKE ITO

Associate costume designer:KIWA TAKADO

Distributed by KADOKAWASHOTEN

"The world exists for me"

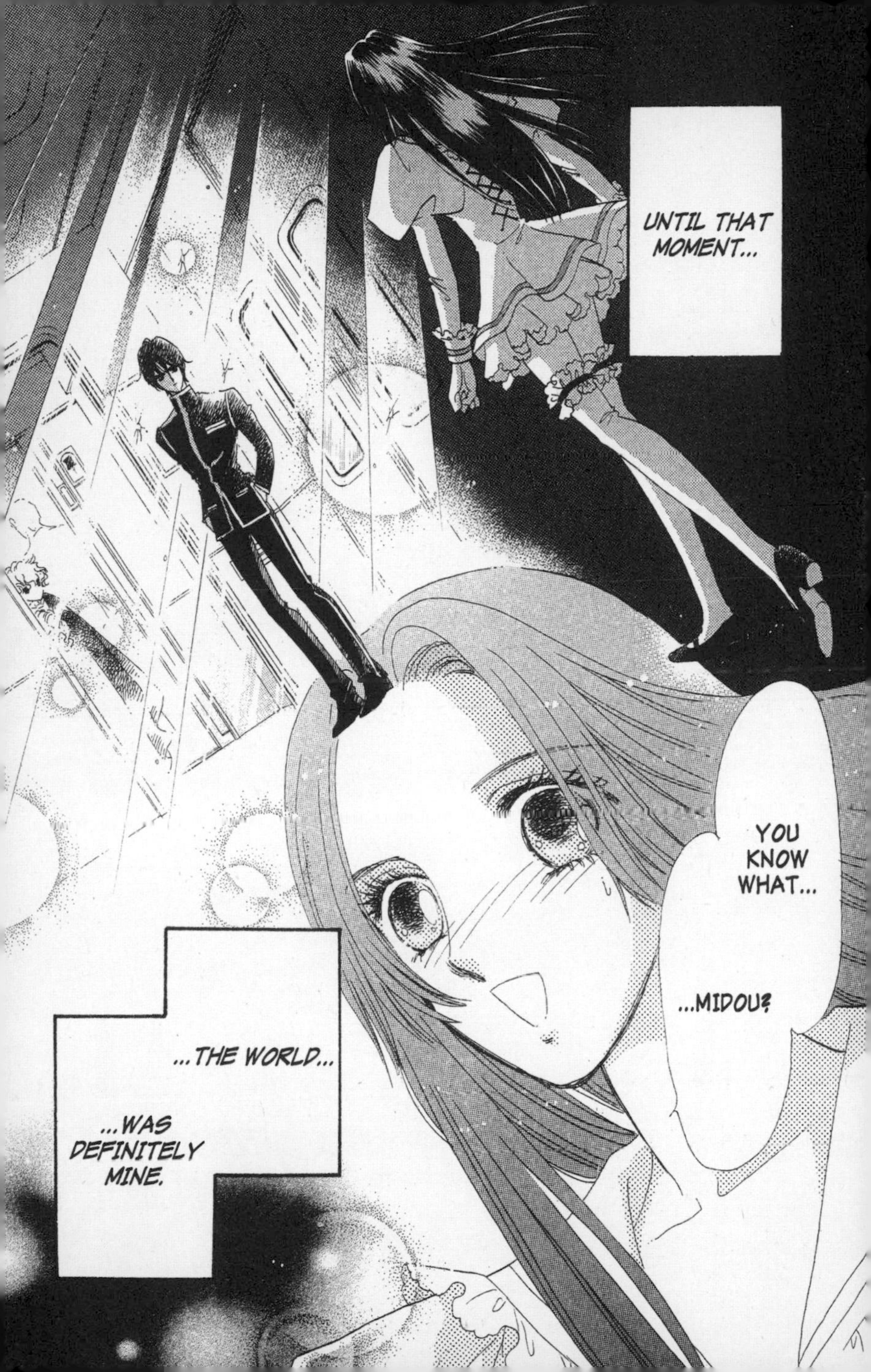
UNTIL THAT MOMENT...
YOU KNOW WHAT...
...MIDOU?
...THE WORLD...
...WAS DEFINITELY MINE.

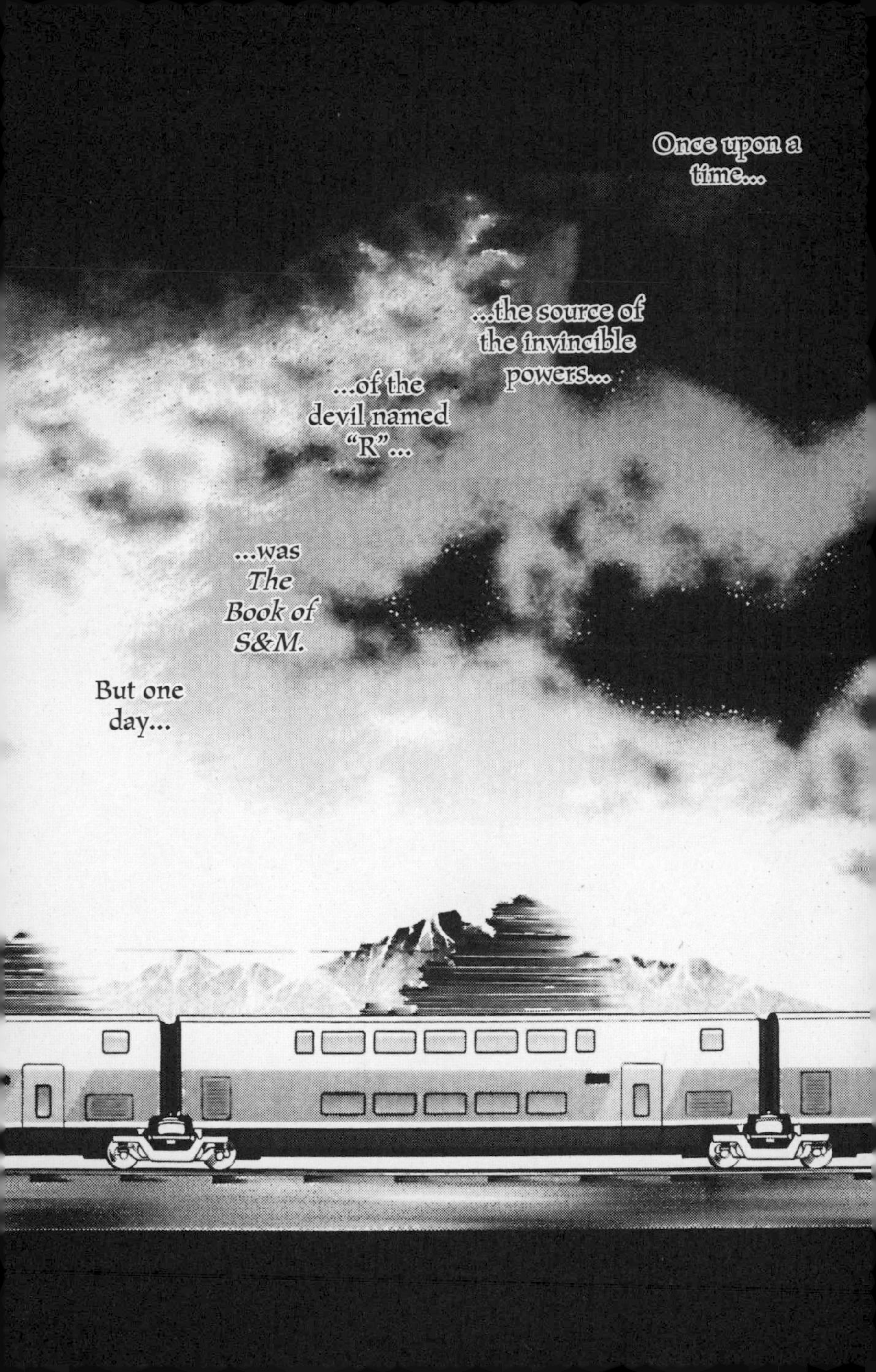
Once upon a time...
...the source of the invincible powers...
...of the devil named "R"...
...was *The Book of S&M.*
But one day...

...a young man
swiped the
book without
knowing what
it was...

...cut it
up into
strips...

...and
created a
girl doll
called
"S"...

...and a boy
doll called
"M" out
of papier-
mache.

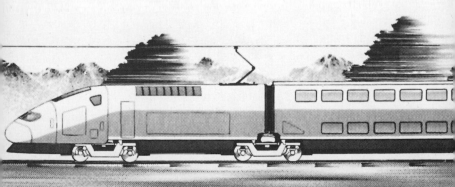

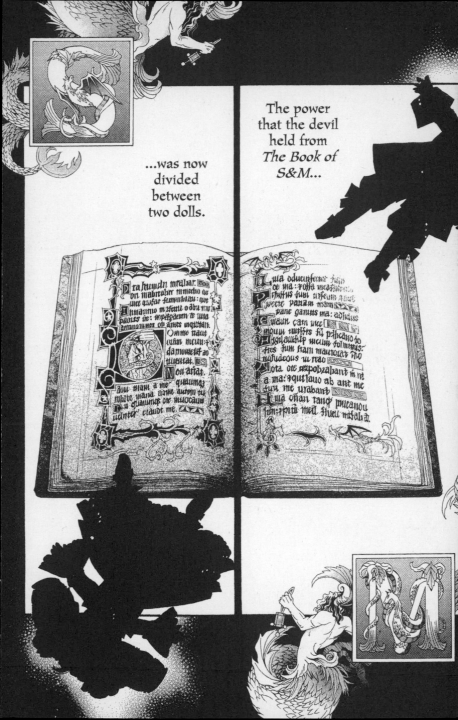

The power
that the devil
held from
*The Book of
S&M...*

...was now
divided
between
two dolls.

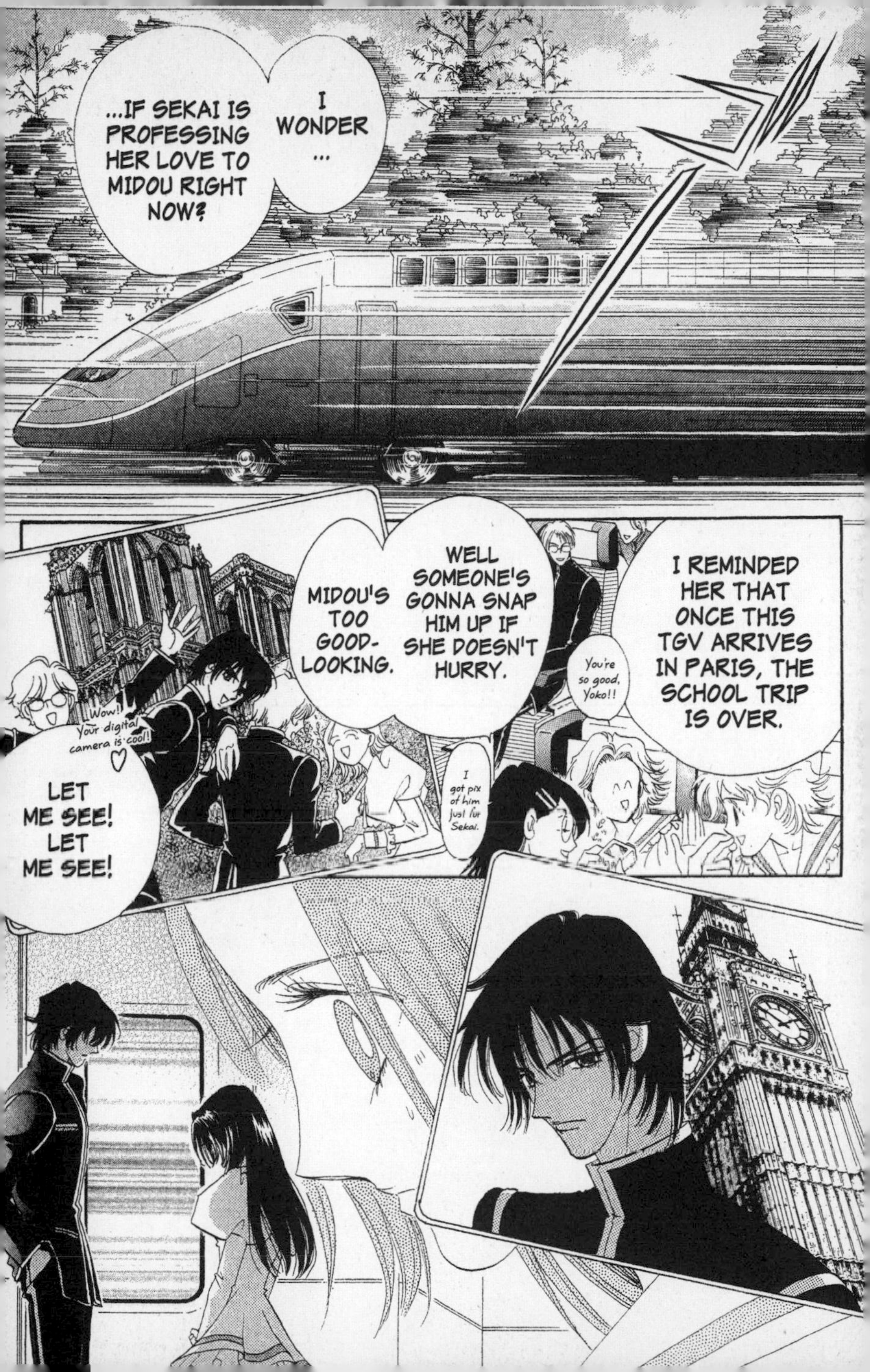
I WONDER ...
...IF SEKAI IS PROFESSING HER LOVE TO MIDOU RIGHT NOW?
I REMINDED HER THAT ONCE THIS TGV ARRIVES IN PARIS, THE SCHOOL TRIP IS OVER.
You're so good, Yoko!!
I got pix of him just for Sekai.
WELL SOMEONE'S GONNA SNAP HIM UP IF SHE DOESN'T HURRY.
MIDOU'S TOO GOOD-LOOKING.
Wow! Your digital camera is cool! ♡
LET ME SEE! LET ME SEE!

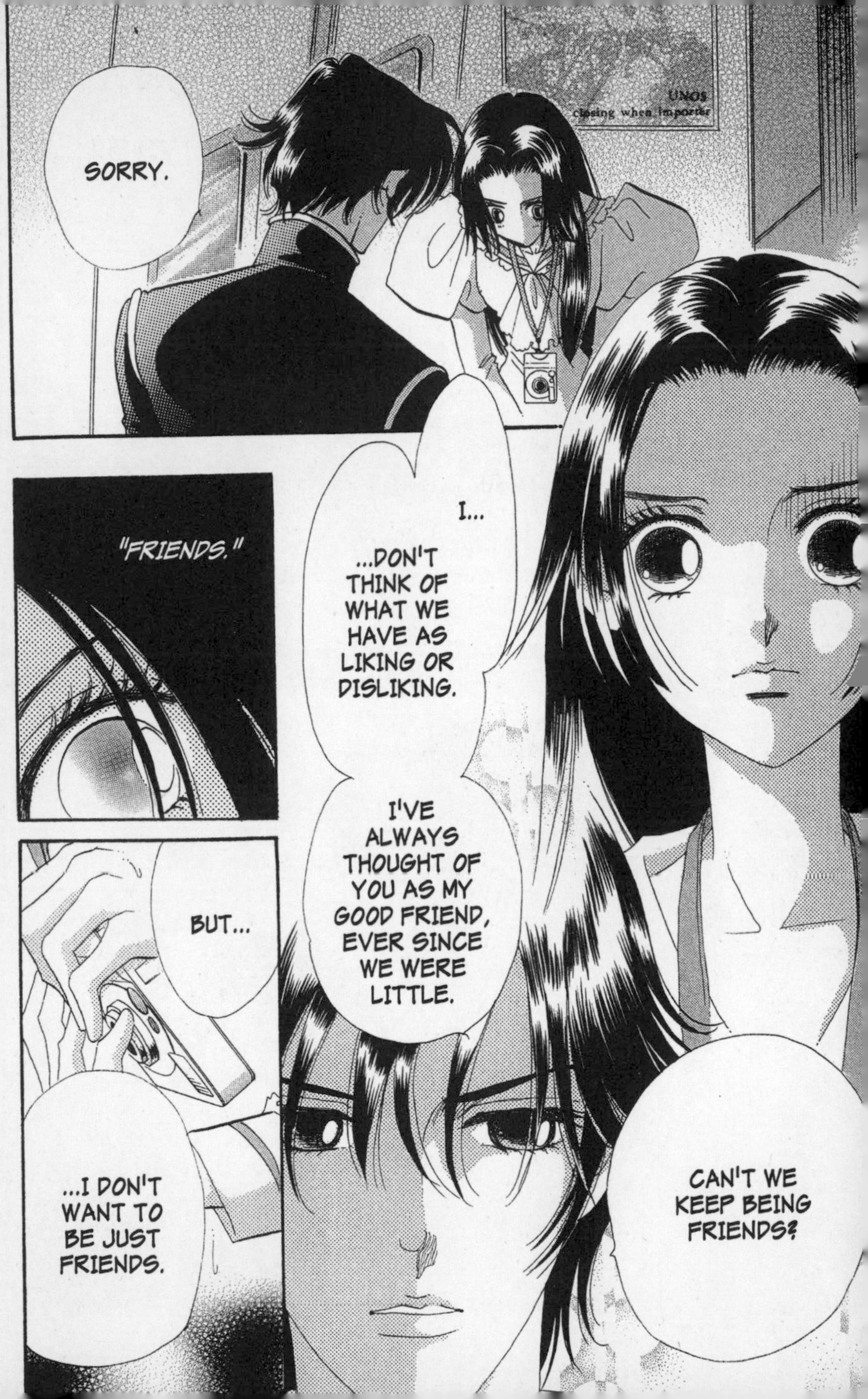
UNOS
closing when importer
SORRY.
I...
...DON'T THINK OF WHAT WE HAVE AS LIKING OR DISLIKING.
I'VE ALWAYS THOUGHT OF YOU AS MY GOOD FRIEND, EVER SINCE WE WERE LITTLE.
CAN'T WE KEEP BEING FRIENDS?
"FRIENDS."
BUT...
...I DON'T WANT TO BE JUST FRIENDS.

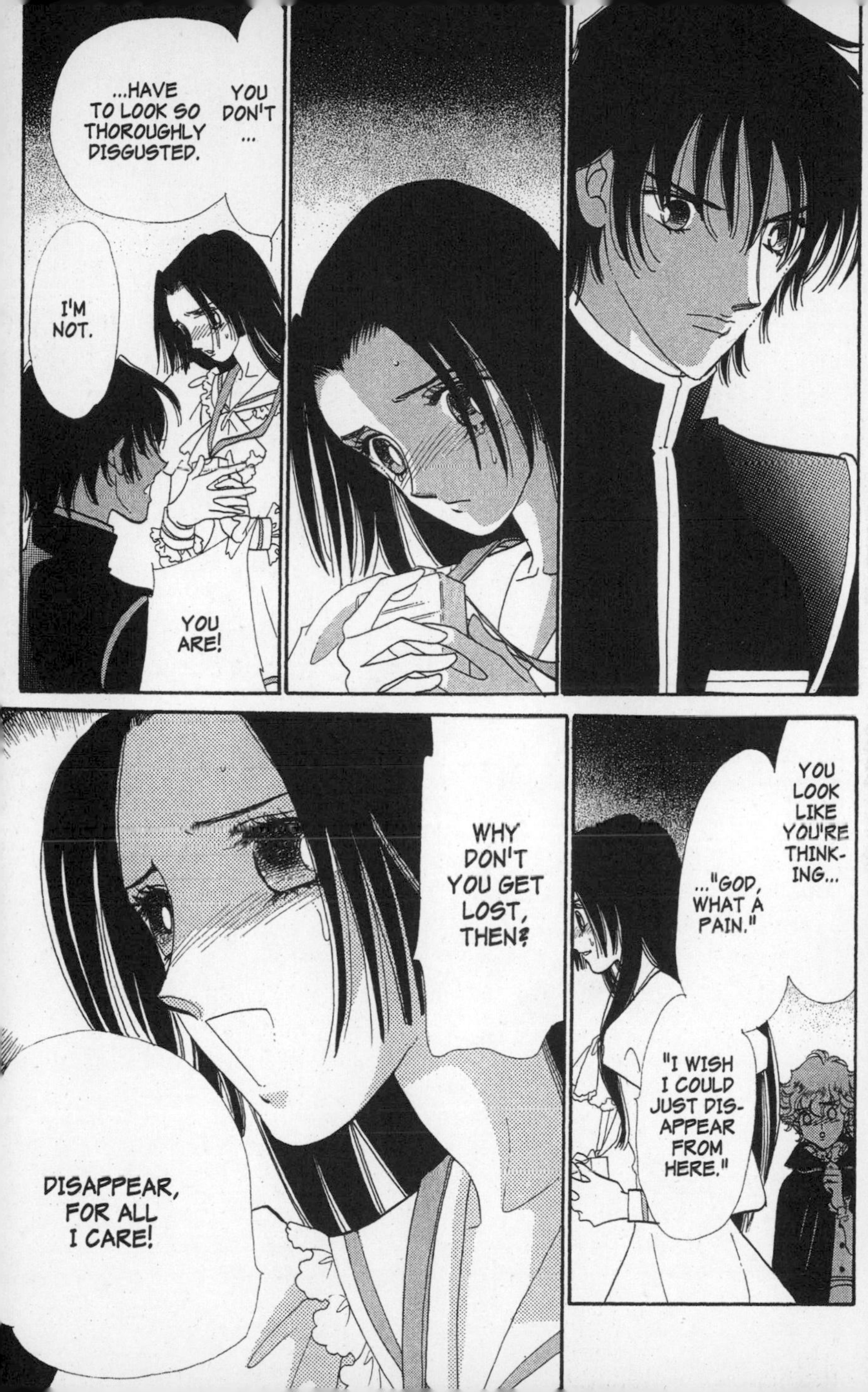
YOU DON'T ...
...HAVE TO LOOK SO THOROUGHLY DISGUSTED.
I'M NOT.
YOU ARE!
YOU LOOK LIKE YOU'RE THINKING...
..."GOD, WHAT A PAIN."
"I WISH I COULD JUST DIS-APPEAR FROM HERE."
WHY DON'T YOU GET LOST, THEN?
DISAPPEAR, FOR ALL I CARE!

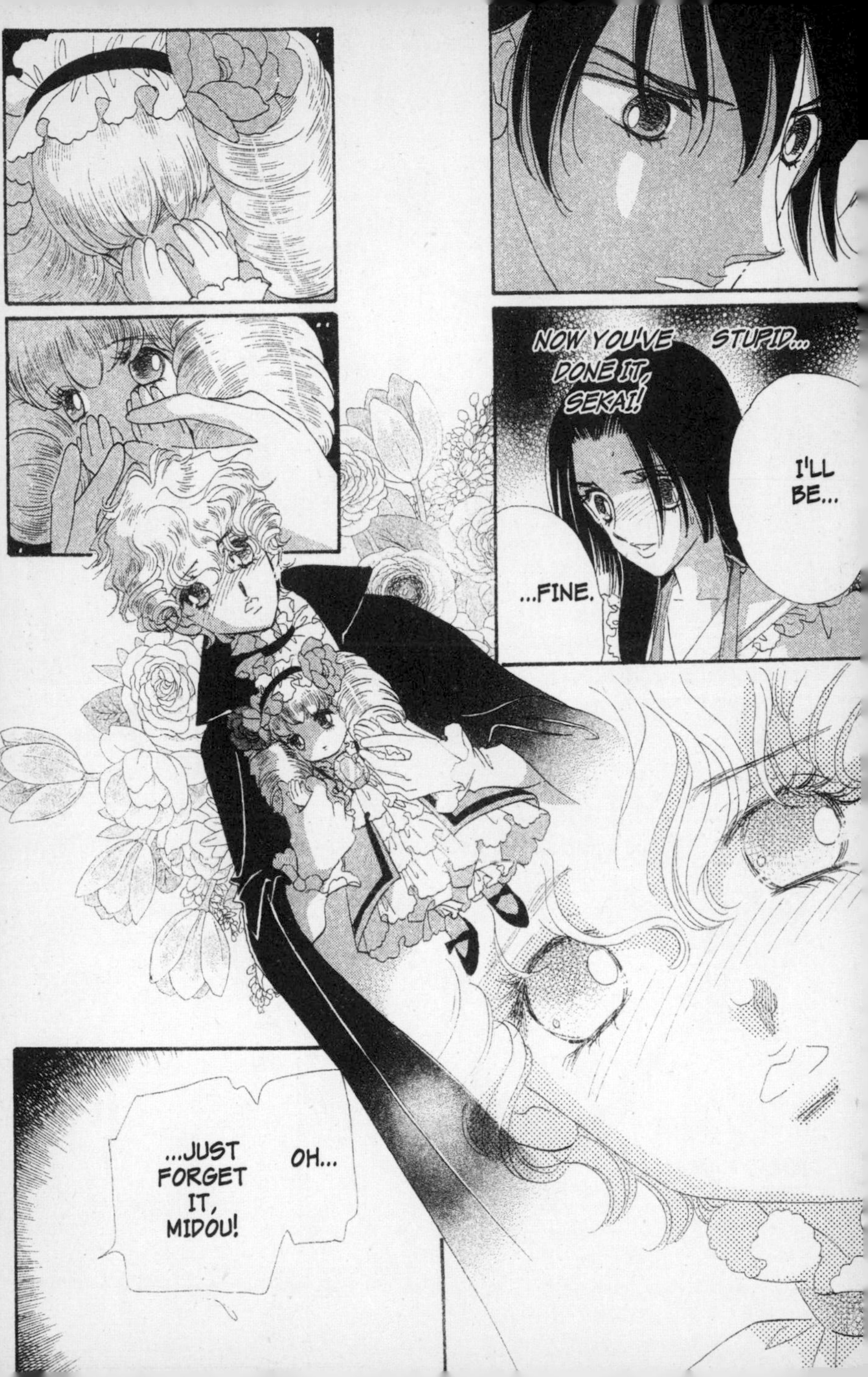
STUPID...
NOW YOU'VE DONE IT, SEKAI!
I'LL BE...
...FINE.
OH...
...JUST FORGET IT, MIDOU!

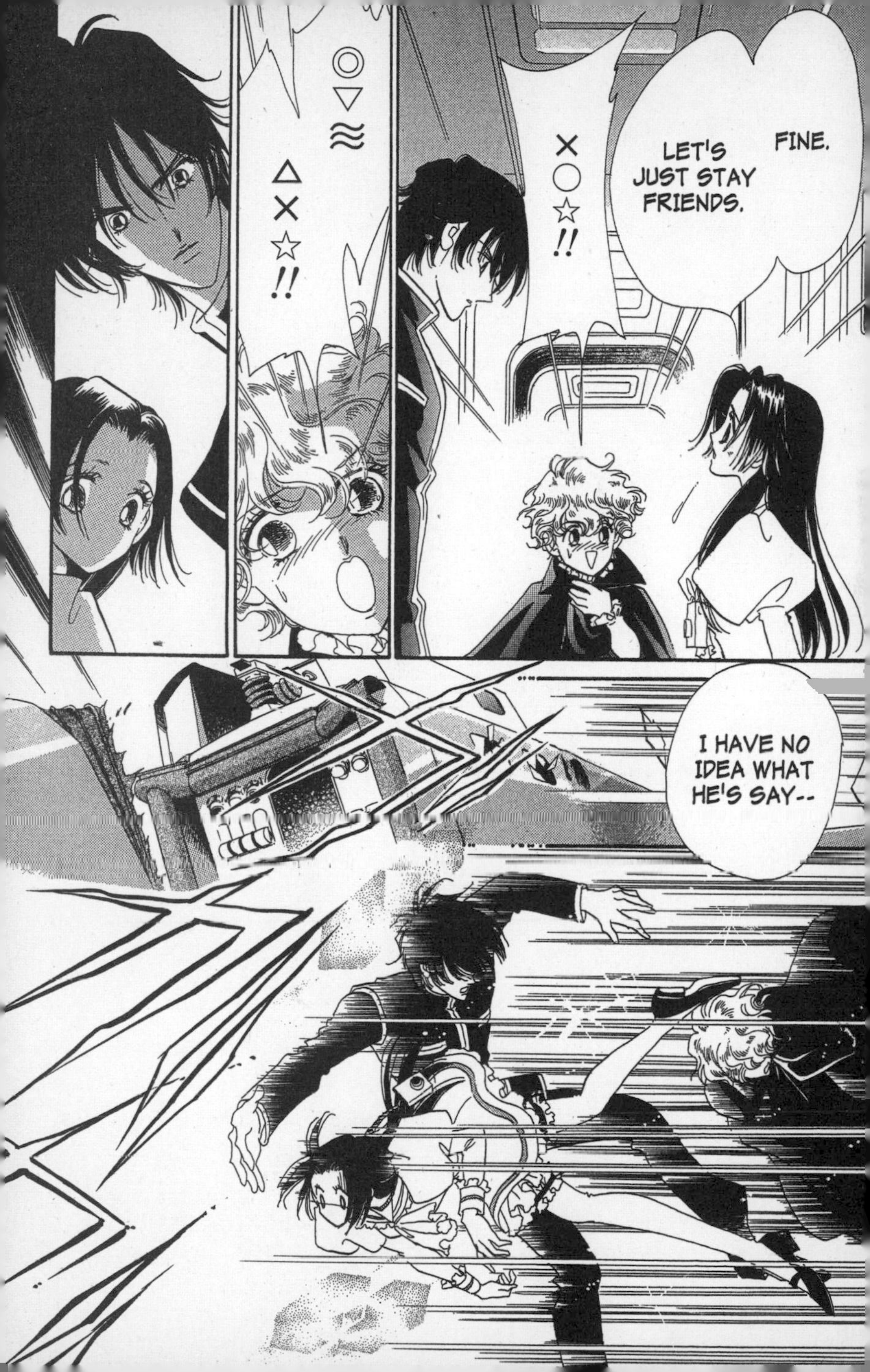

FINE.
LET'S JUST STAY FRIENDS.
×○☆!!
◎▽≈△×☆!!
I HAVE NO IDEA WHAT HE'S SAY--

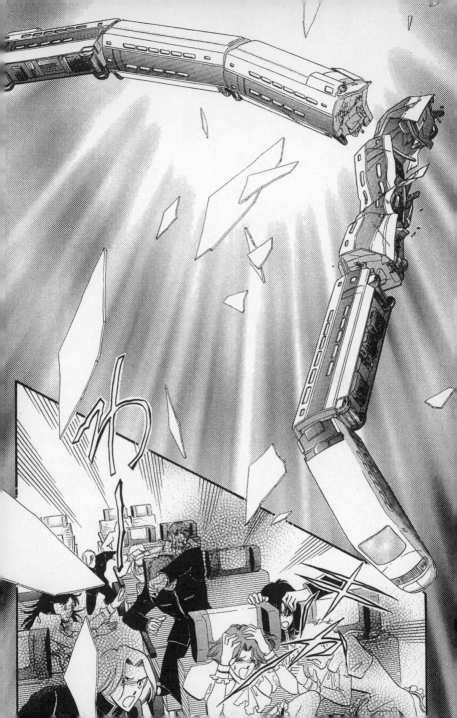

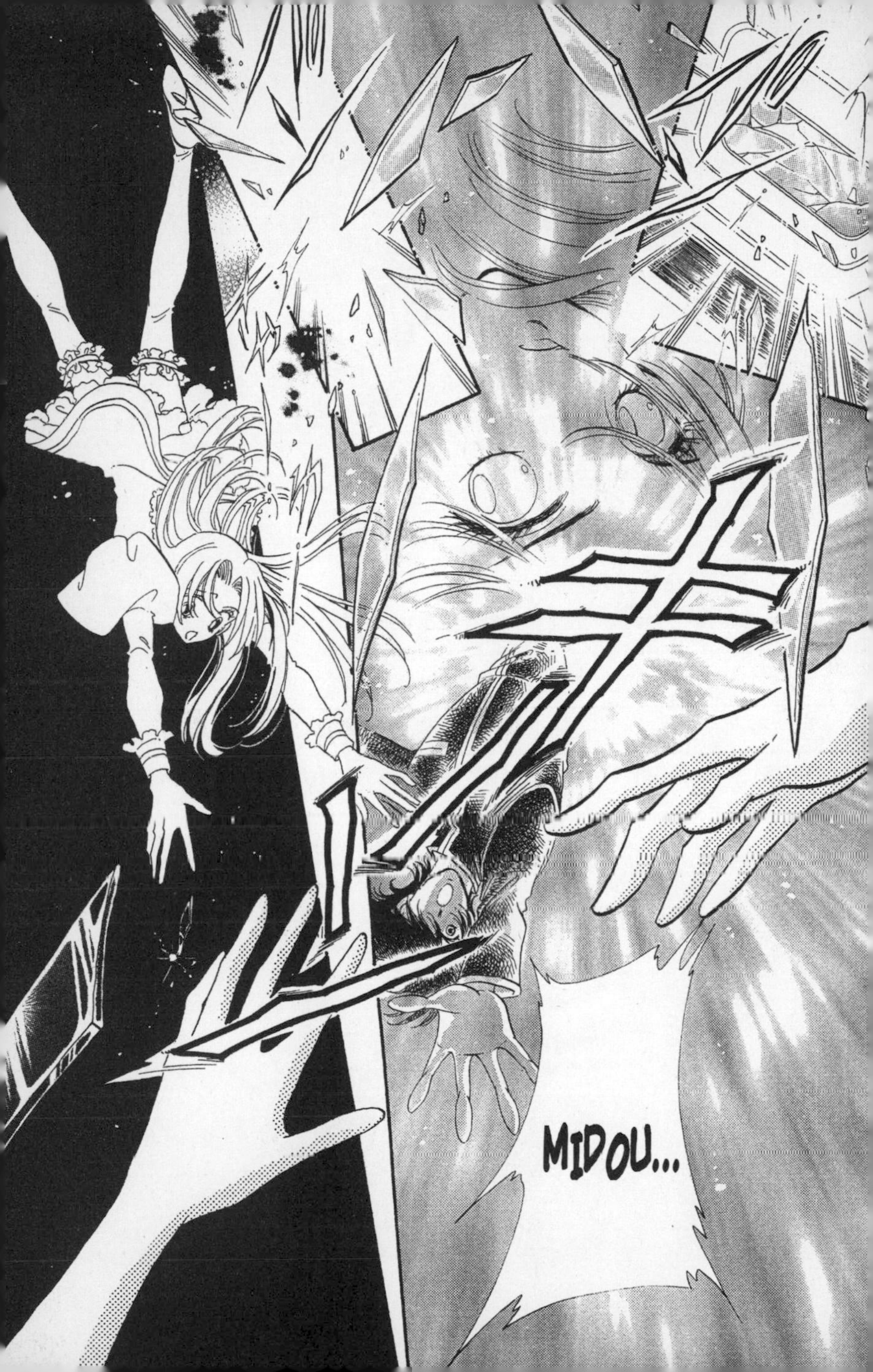
MIDOU...

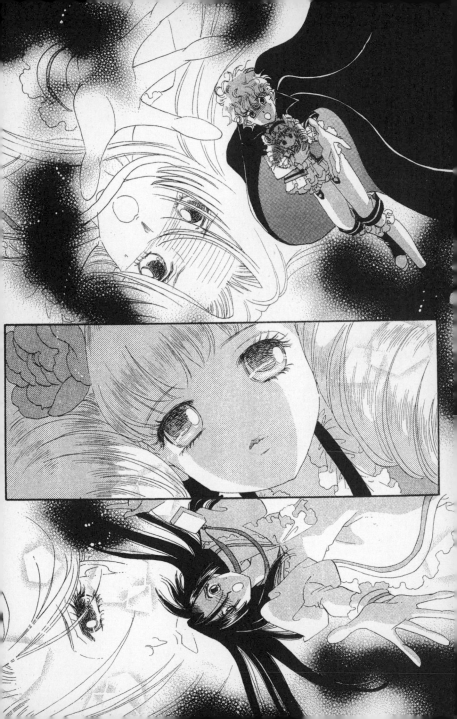

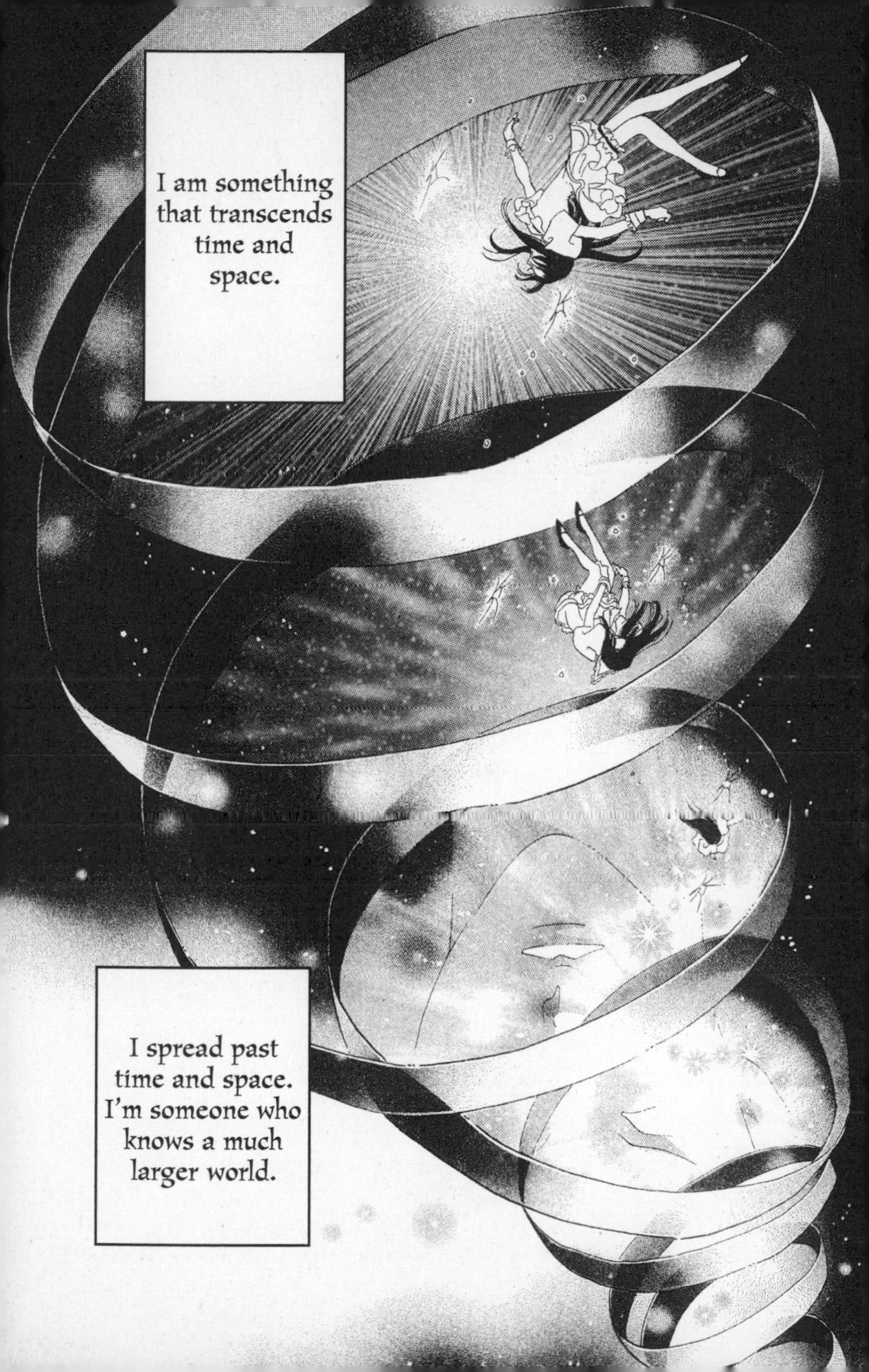
I am something that transcends time and space.
I spread past time and space. I'm someone who knows a much larger world.

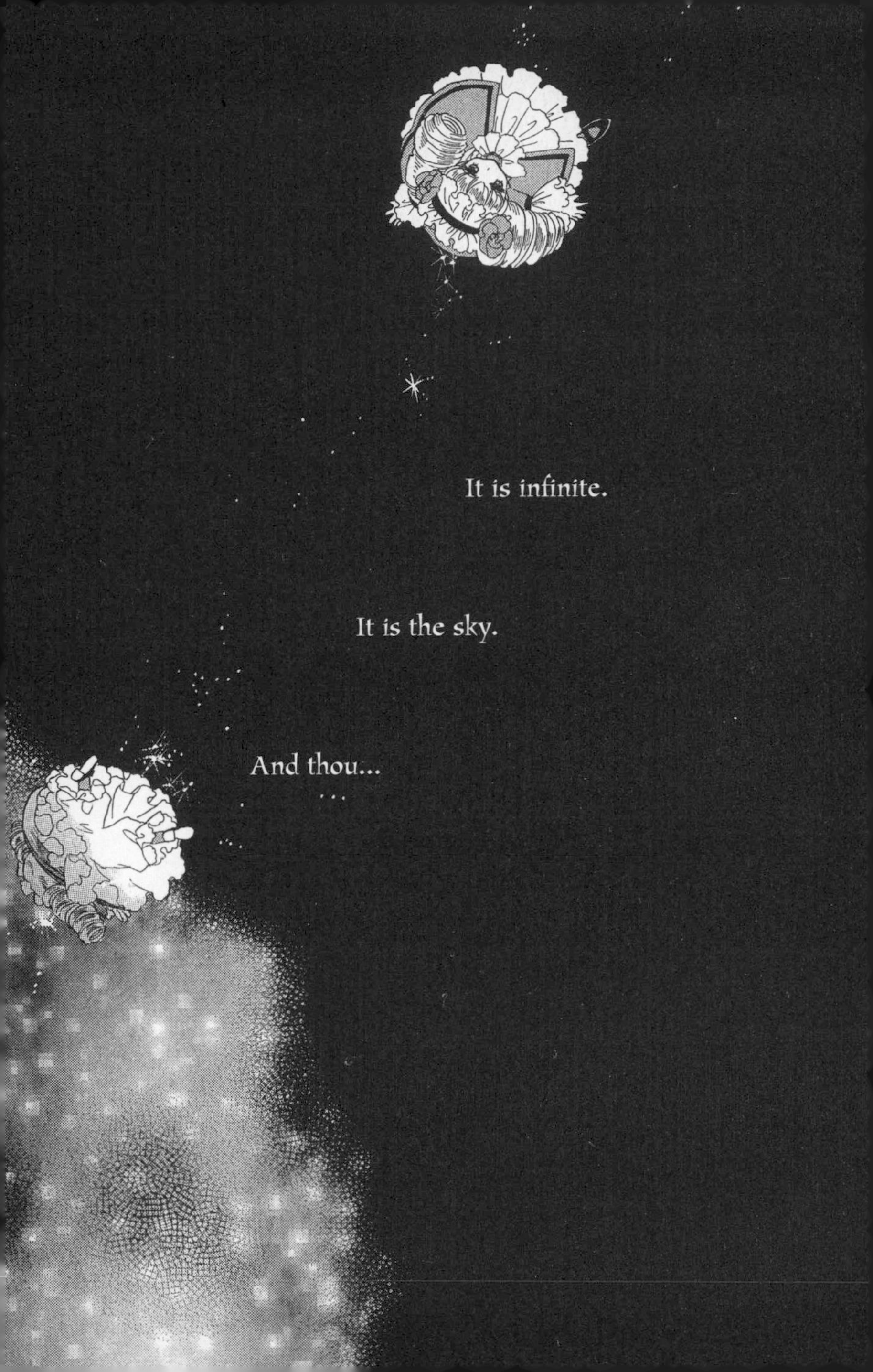
It is infinite.
It is the sky.
And thou...

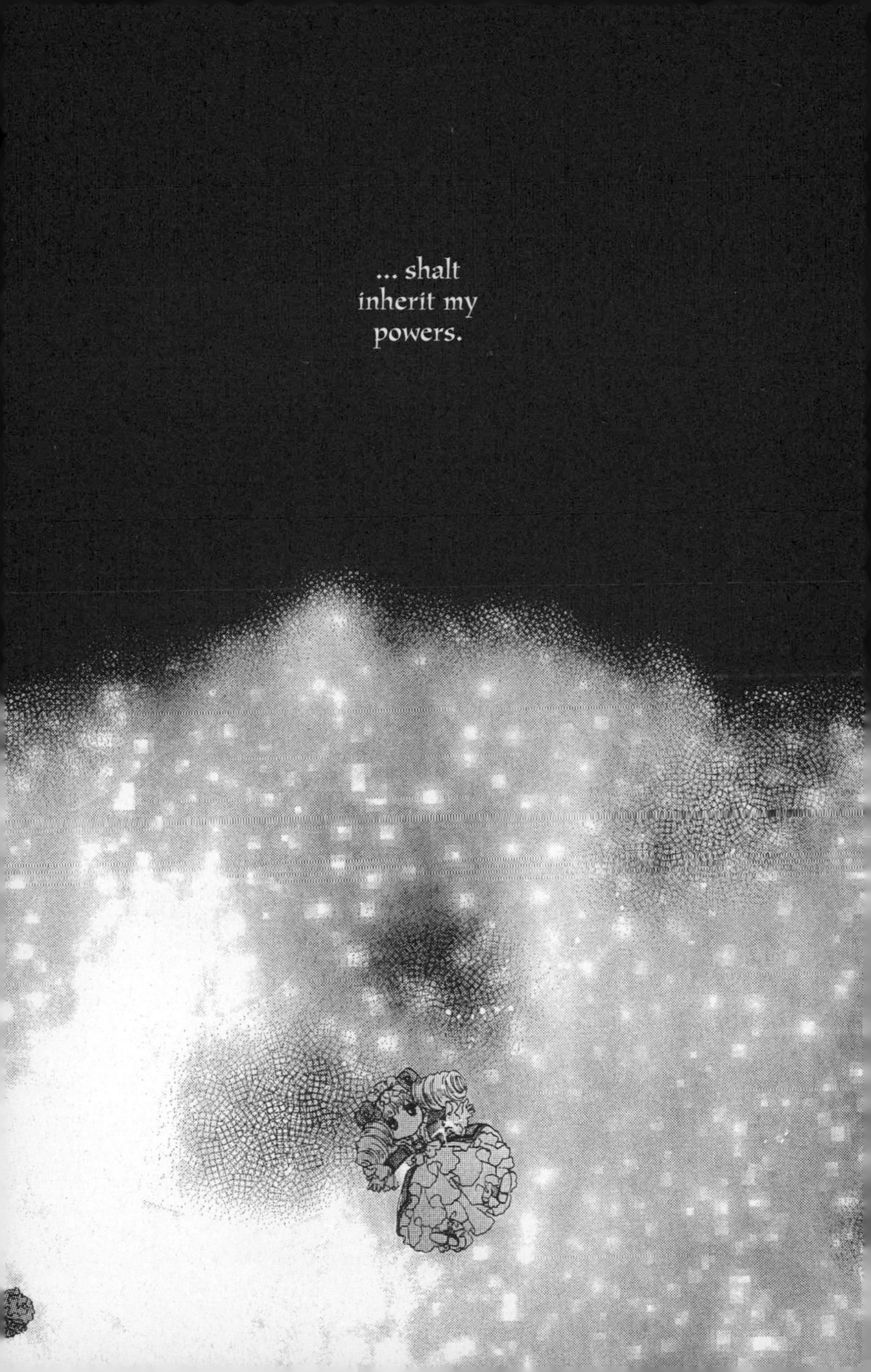
... shalt inherit my powers.

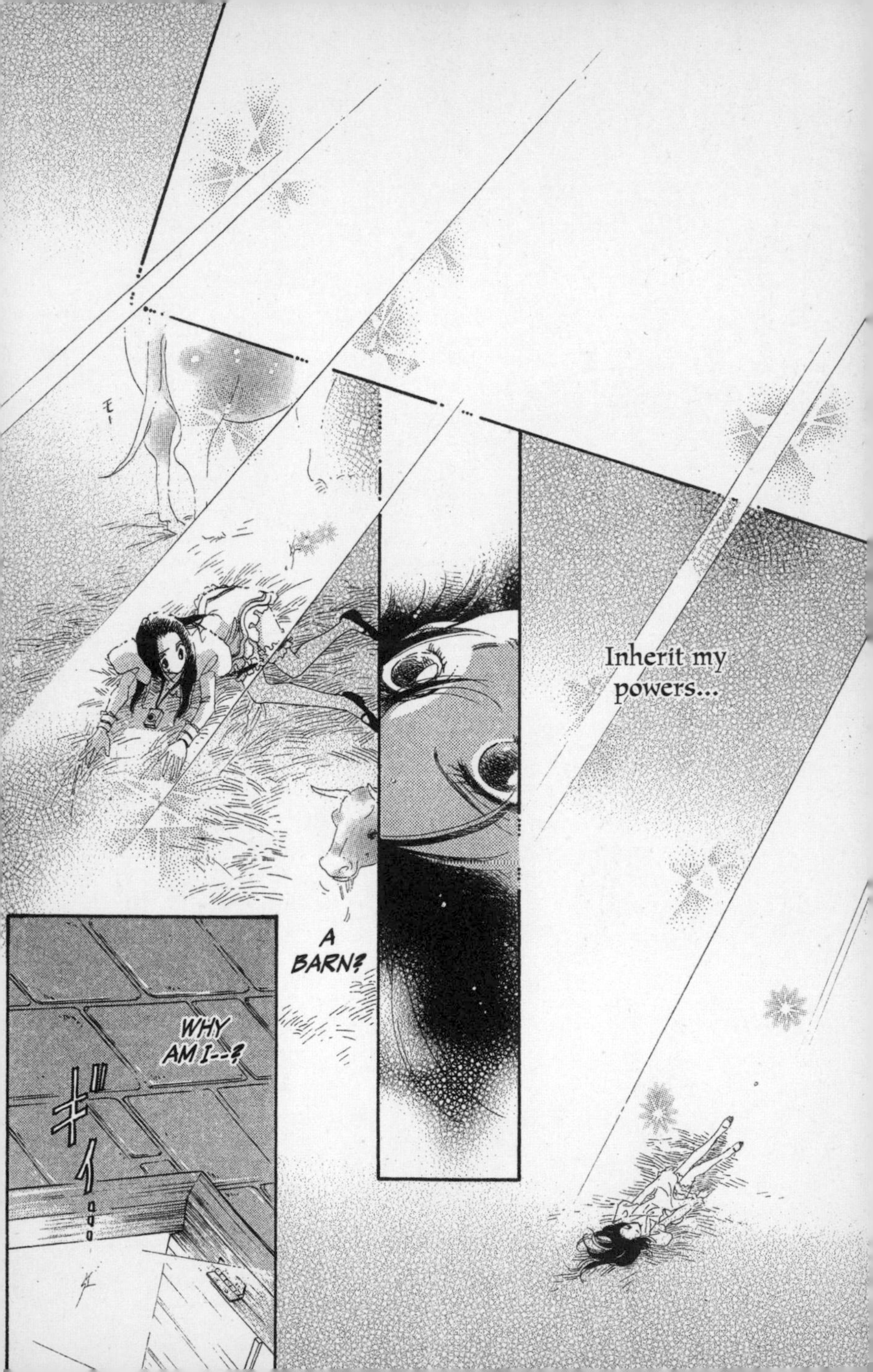
Inherit my powers...
A BARN?
WHY AM I--?
ギィ…

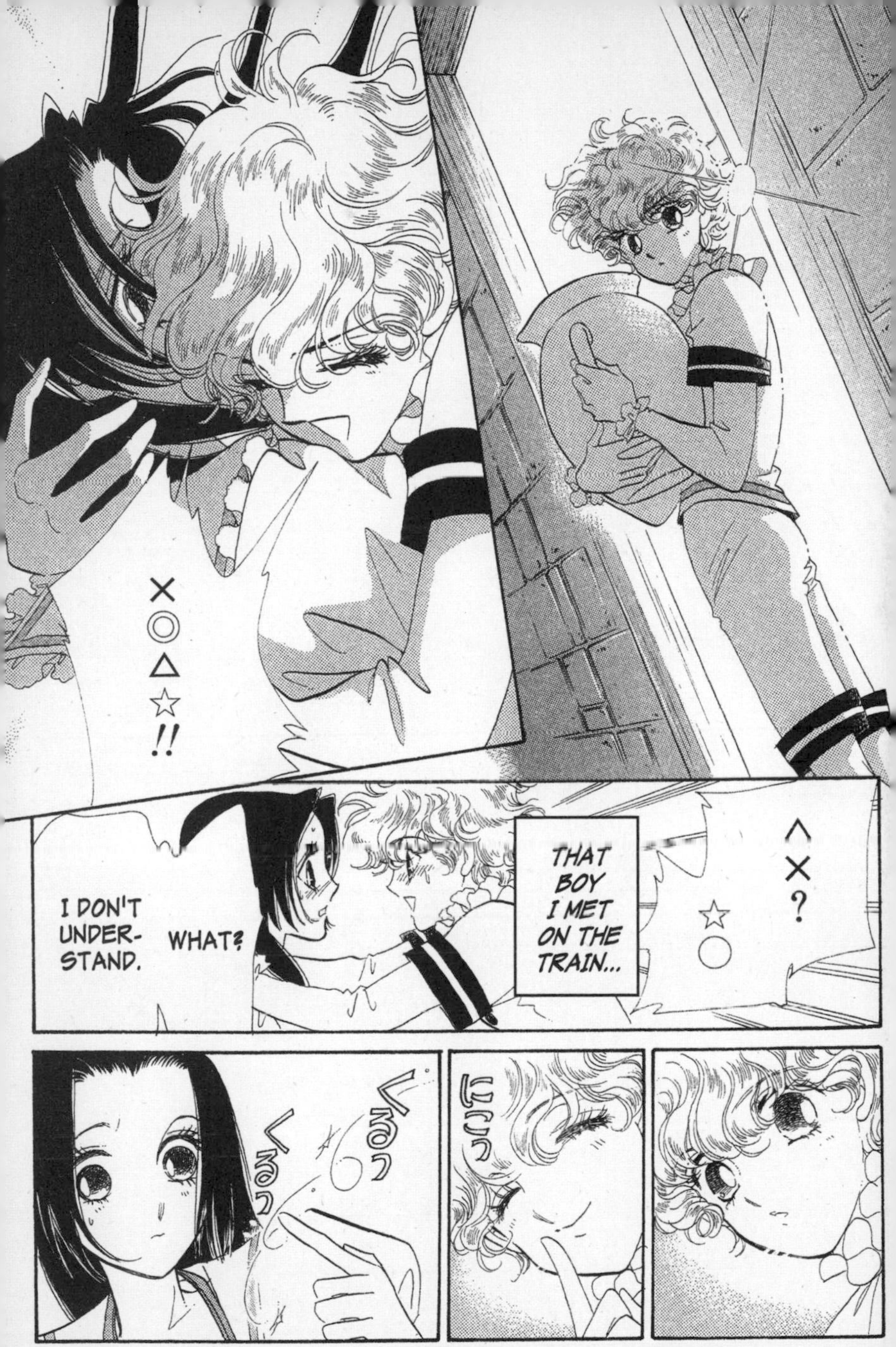
×○△☆!!
^×?
☆○
THAT BOY I MET ON THE TRAIN...
WHAT?
I DON'T UNDER-STAND.
にこっ
くるっ
くるっ

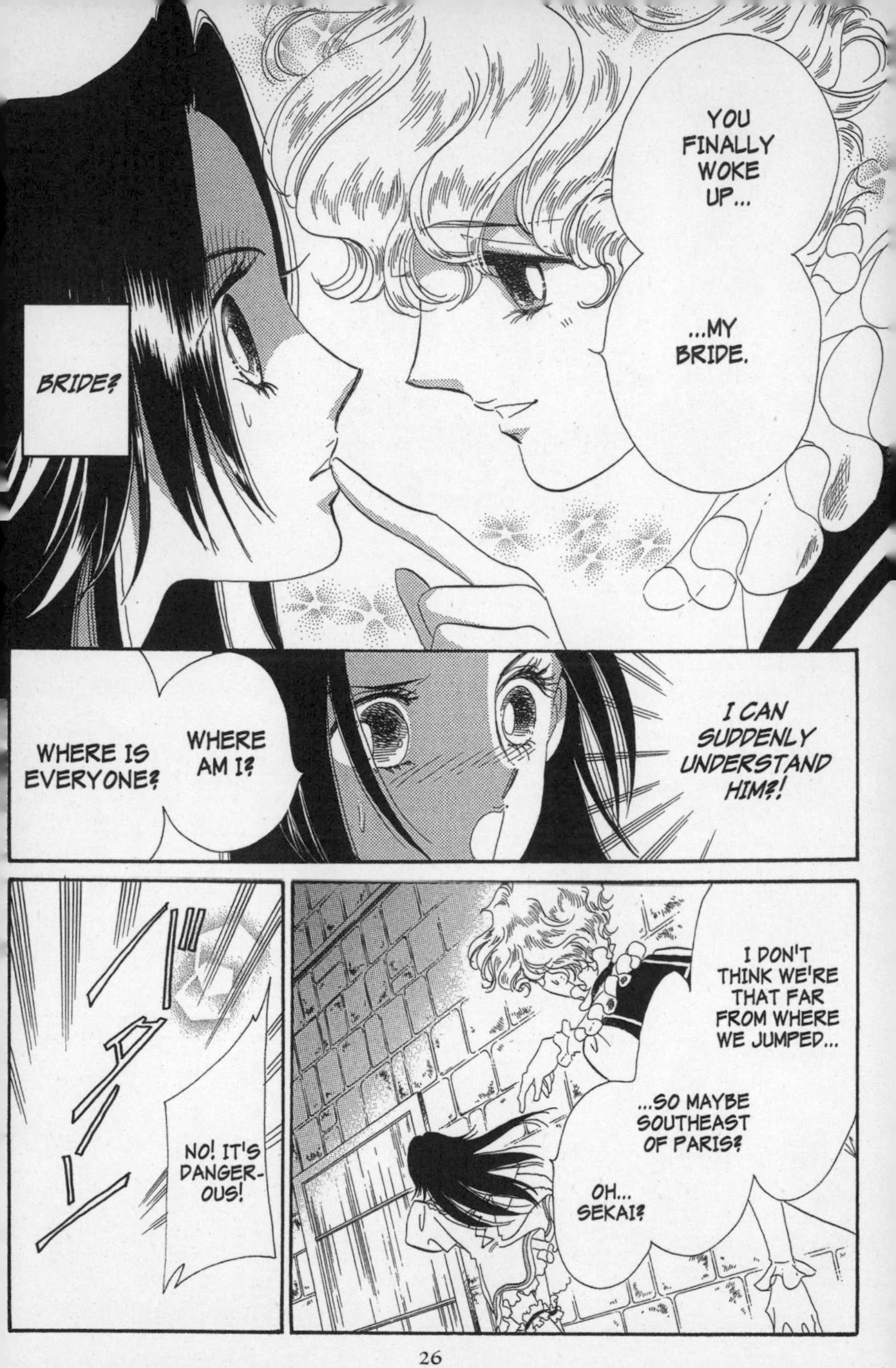
YOU FINALLY WOKE UP...
...MY BRIDE.
BRIDE?
I CAN SUDDENLY UNDERSTAND HIM?!
WHERE AM I?
WHERE IS EVERYONE?
I DON'T THINK WE'RE THAT FAR FROM WHERE WE JUMPED...
...SO MAYBE SOUTHEAST OF PARIS?
OH... SEKAI?
NO! IT'S DANGER-OUS!

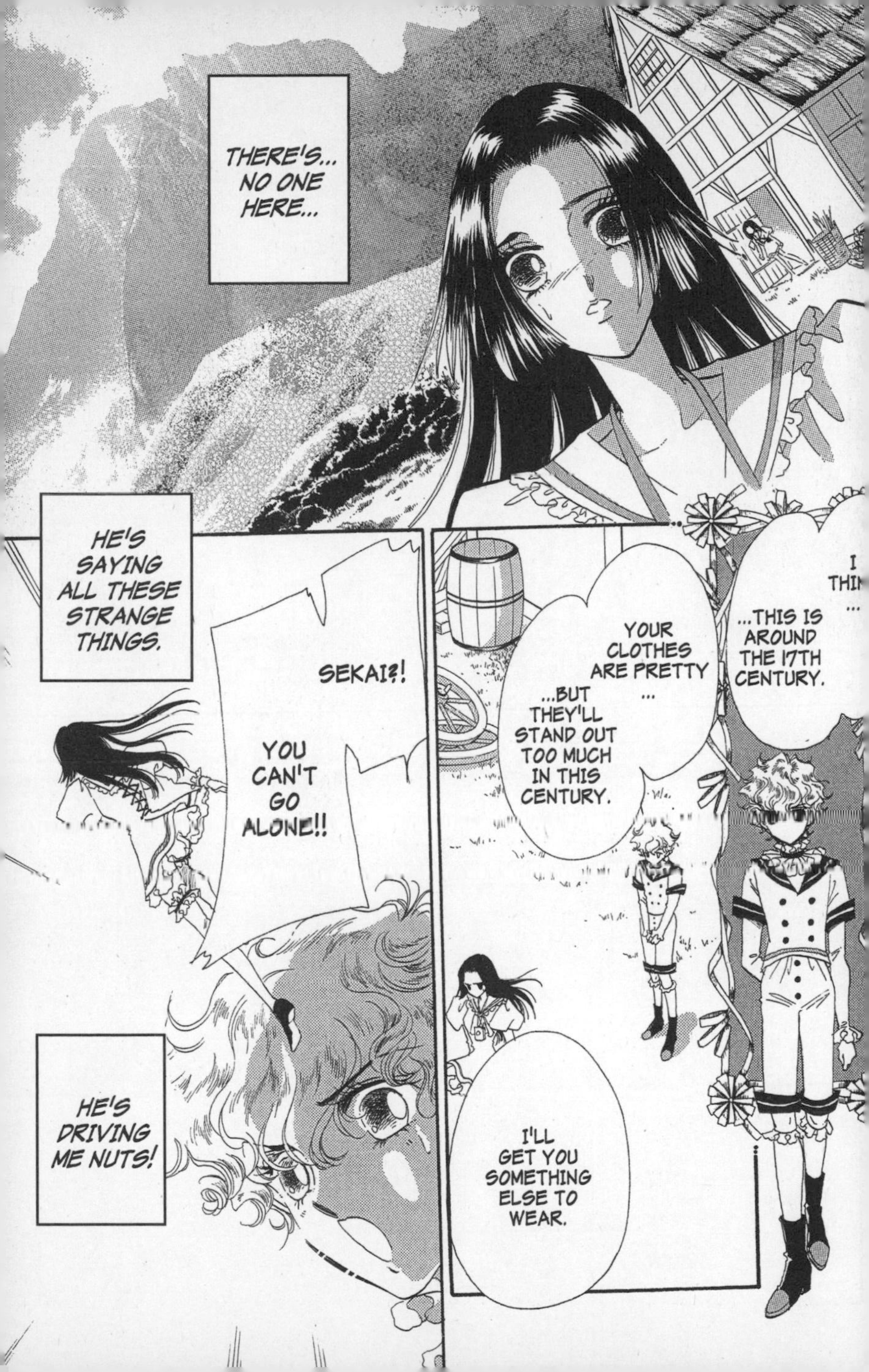
THERE'S... NO ONE HERE...
...THIS IS AROUND THE 17TH CENTURY.
YOUR CLOTHES ARE PRETTY ...
...BUT THEY'LL STAND OUT TOO MUCH IN THIS CENTURY.
I'LL GET YOU SOMETHING ELSE TO WEAR.
HE'S SAYING ALL THESE STRANGE THINGS.
SEKAI?!
YOU CAN'T GO ALONE!!
HE'S DRIVING ME NUTS!

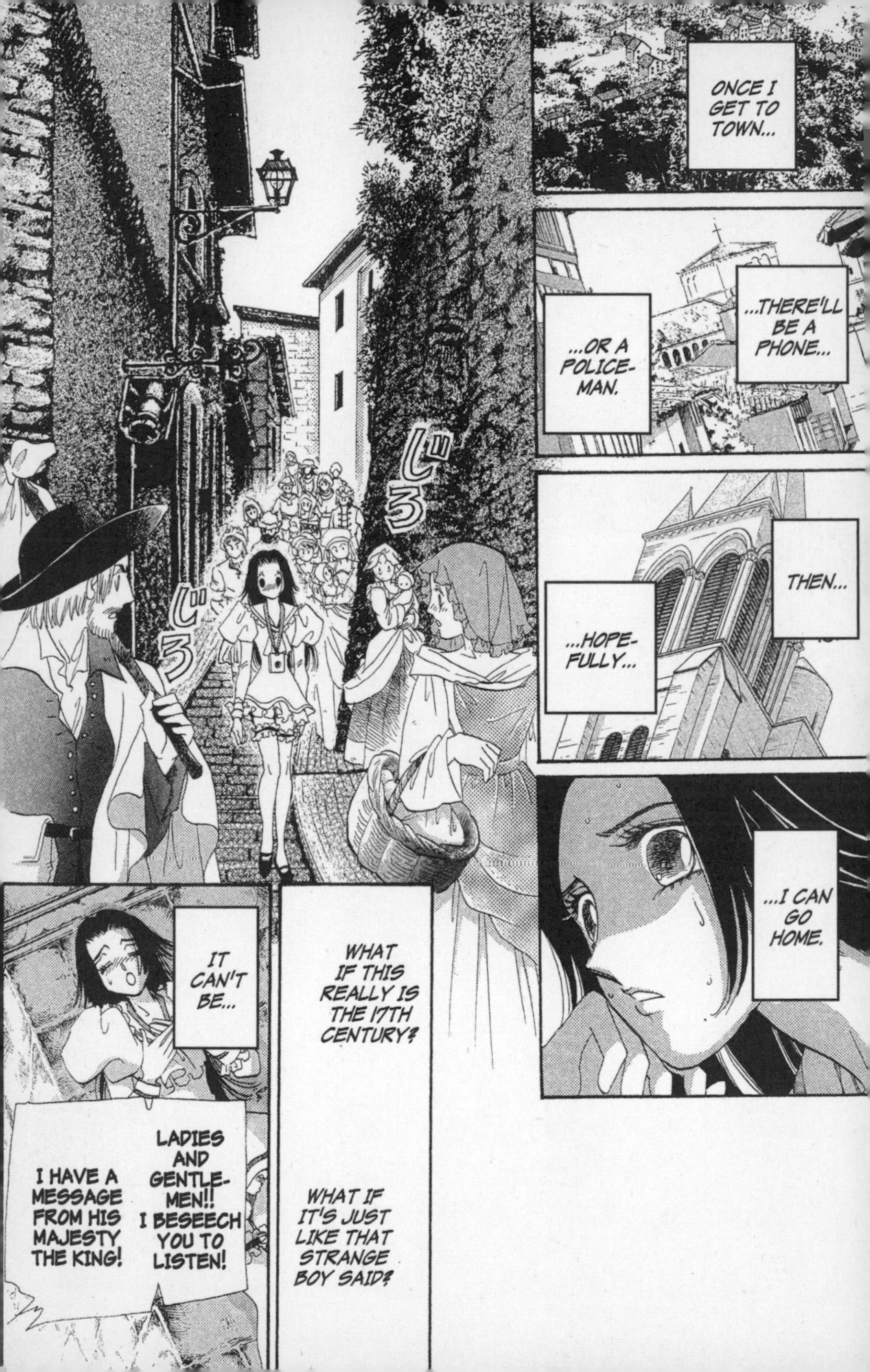
ONCE I GET TO TOWN...
...THERE'LL BE A PHONE...
...OR A POLICEMAN.
THEN...
...HOPEFULLY...
...I CAN GO HOME.
じろ
じろ
WHAT IF THIS REALLY IS THE 17TH CENTURY?
WHAT IF IT'S JUST LIKE THAT STRANGE BOY SAID?
IT CAN'T BE...
LADIES AND GENTLEMEN!! I BESEECH YOU TO LISTEN!
I HAVE A MESSAGE FROM HIS MAJESTY THE KING!

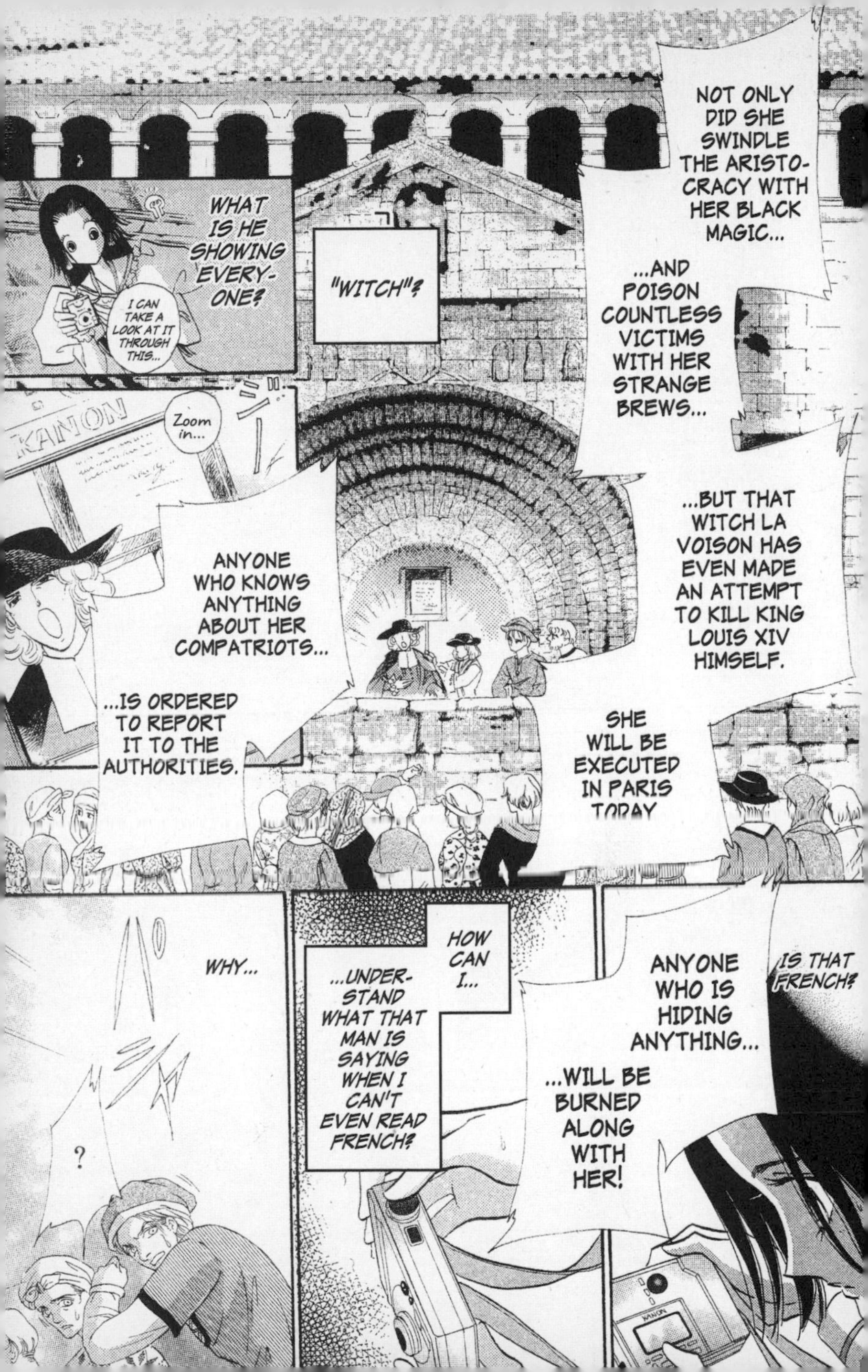
NOT ONLY DID SHE SWINDLE THE ARISTO-CRACY WITH HER BLACK MAGIC...
...AND POISON COUNTLESS VICTIMS WITH HER STRANGE BREWS...
"WITCH"?
WHAT IS HE SHOWING EVERY-ONE?
I CAN TAKE A LOOK AT IT THROUGH THIS...
...BUT THAT WITCH LA VOISON HAS EVEN MADE AN ATTEMPT TO KILL KING LOUIS XIV HIMSELF.
SHE WILL BE EXECUTED IN PARIS TODAY
ANYONE WHO KNOWS ANYTHING ABOUT HER COMPATRIOTS...
...IS ORDERED TO REPORT IT TO THE AUTHORITIES.
KANON
Zoom in...
IS THAT FRENCH?
ANYONE WHO IS HIDING ANYTHING...
...WILL BE BURNED ALONG WITH HER!
HOW CAN I...
...UNDER-STAND WHAT THAT MAN IS SAYING WHEN I CAN'T EVEN READ FRENCH?
WHY...
?

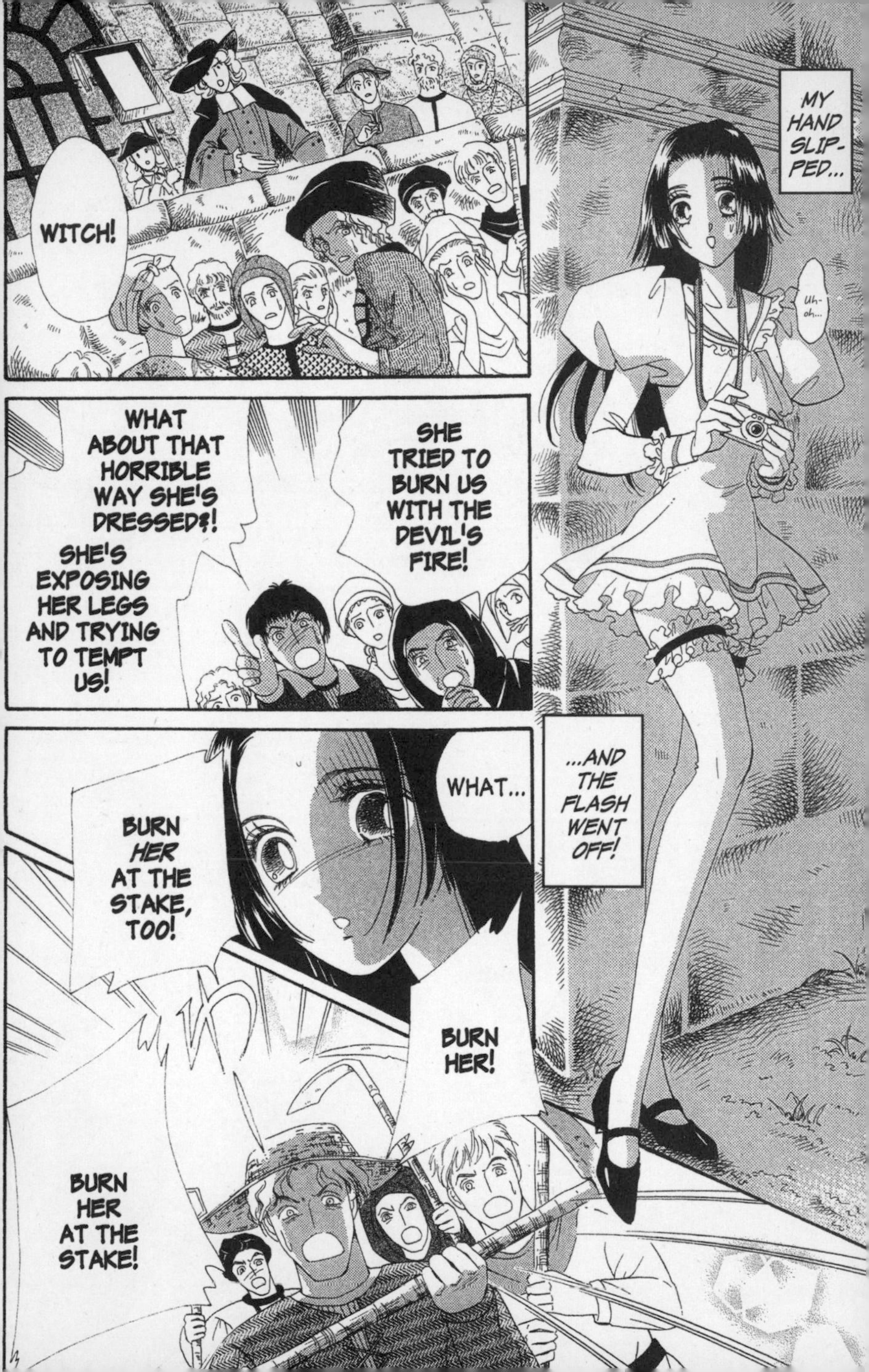
MY HAND SLIPPED...
Uh-oh...
...AND THE FLASH WENT OFF!
WITCH!
SHE TRIED TO BURN US WITH THE DEVIL'S FIRE!
WHAT ABOUT THAT HORRIBLE WAY SHE'S DRESSED?!
SHE'S EXPOSING HER LEGS AND TRYING TO TEMPT US!
WHAT...
BURN *HER* AT THE STAKE, TOO!
BURN HER!
BURN HER AT THE STAKE!

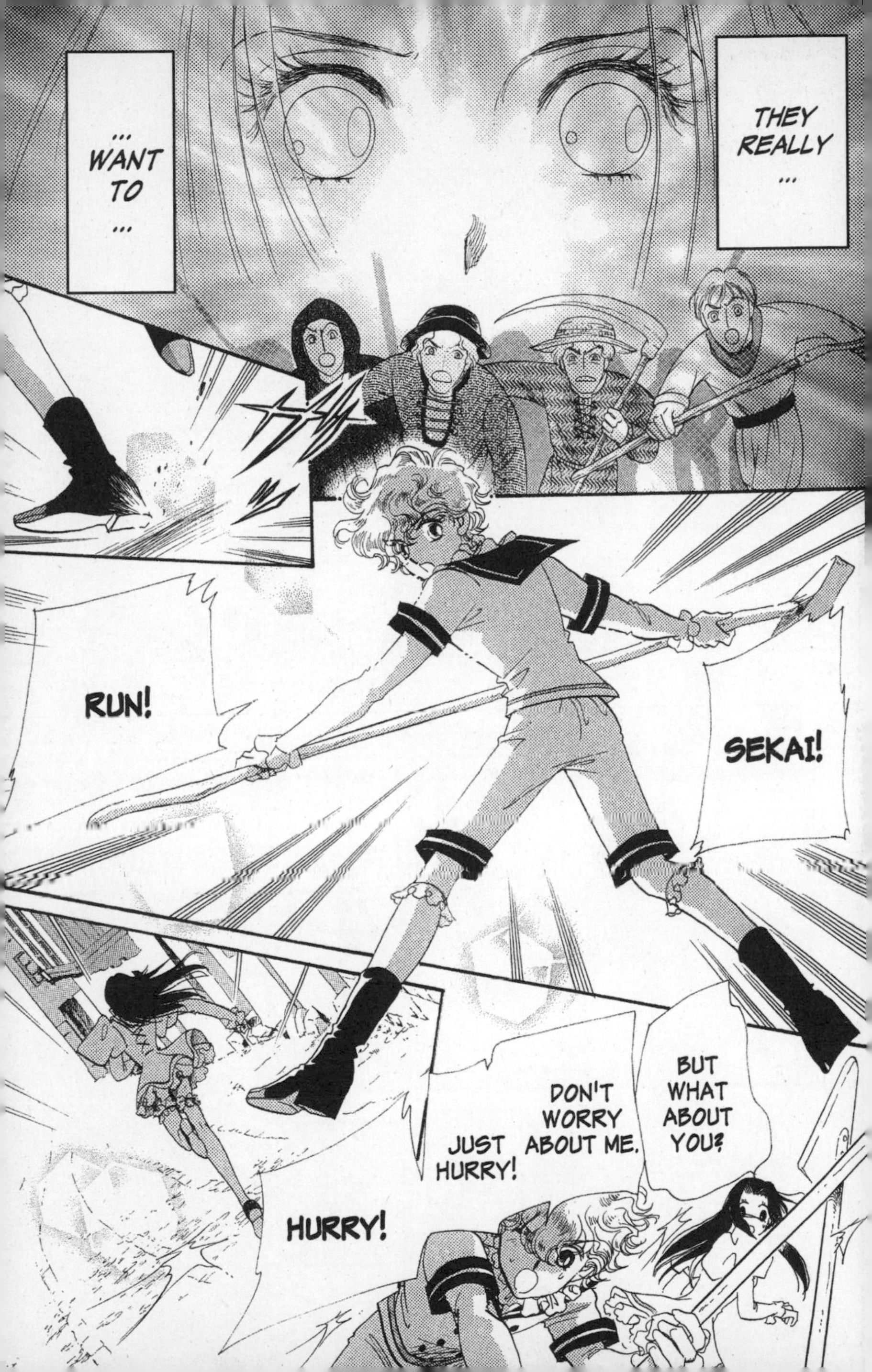
THEY REALLY ...
... WANT TO ...
SEKAI!
RUN!
BUT WHAT ABOUT YOU?
DON'T WORRY ABOUT ME.
JUST HURRY!
HURRY!

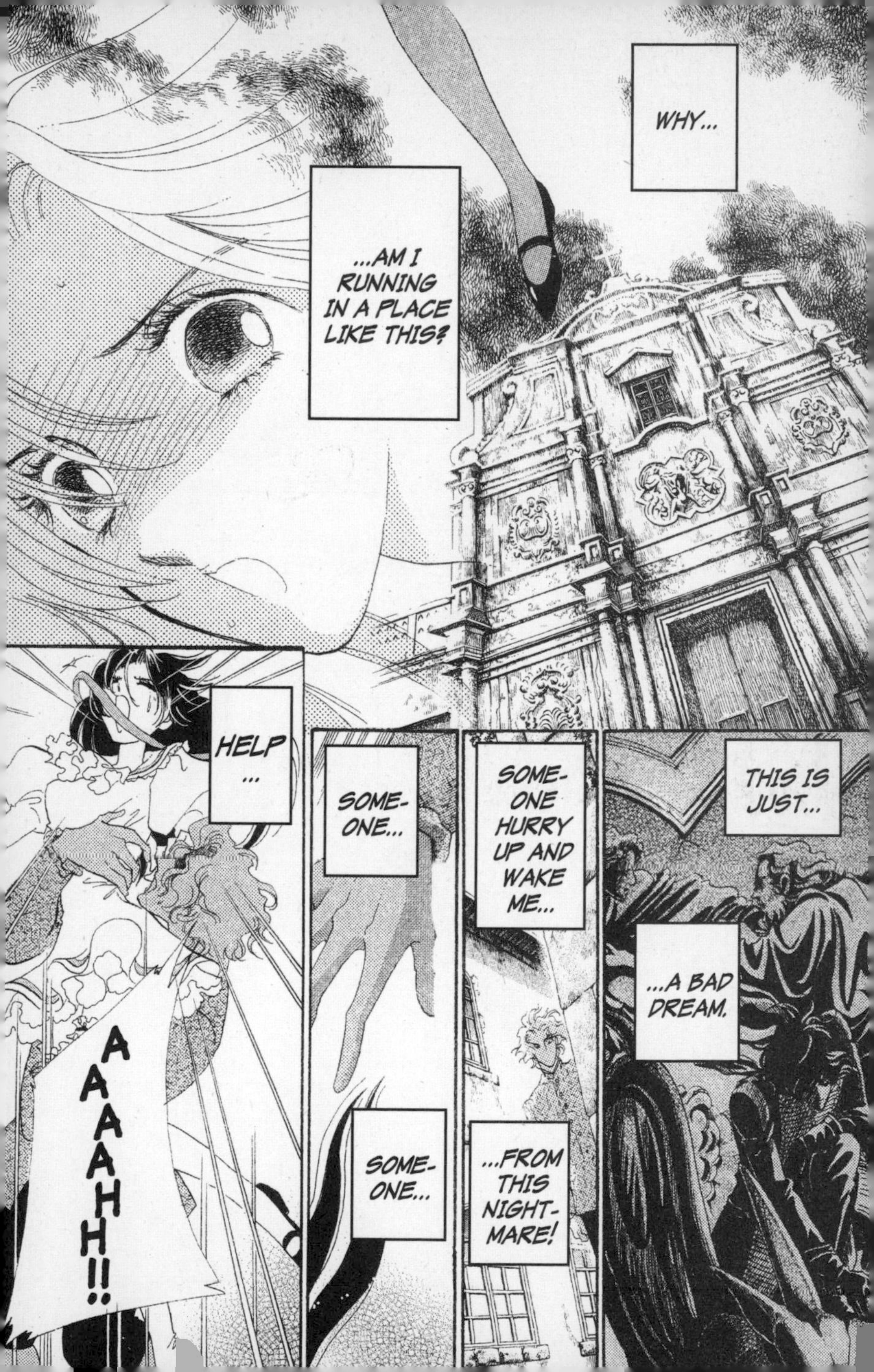
WHY...
...AM I RUNNING IN A PLACE LIKE THIS?
THIS IS JUST...
...A BAD DREAM.
SOMEONE HURRY UP AND WAKE ME...
...FROM THIS NIGHTMARE!
SOMEONE...
SOMEONE...
HELP...
AAAAH!!

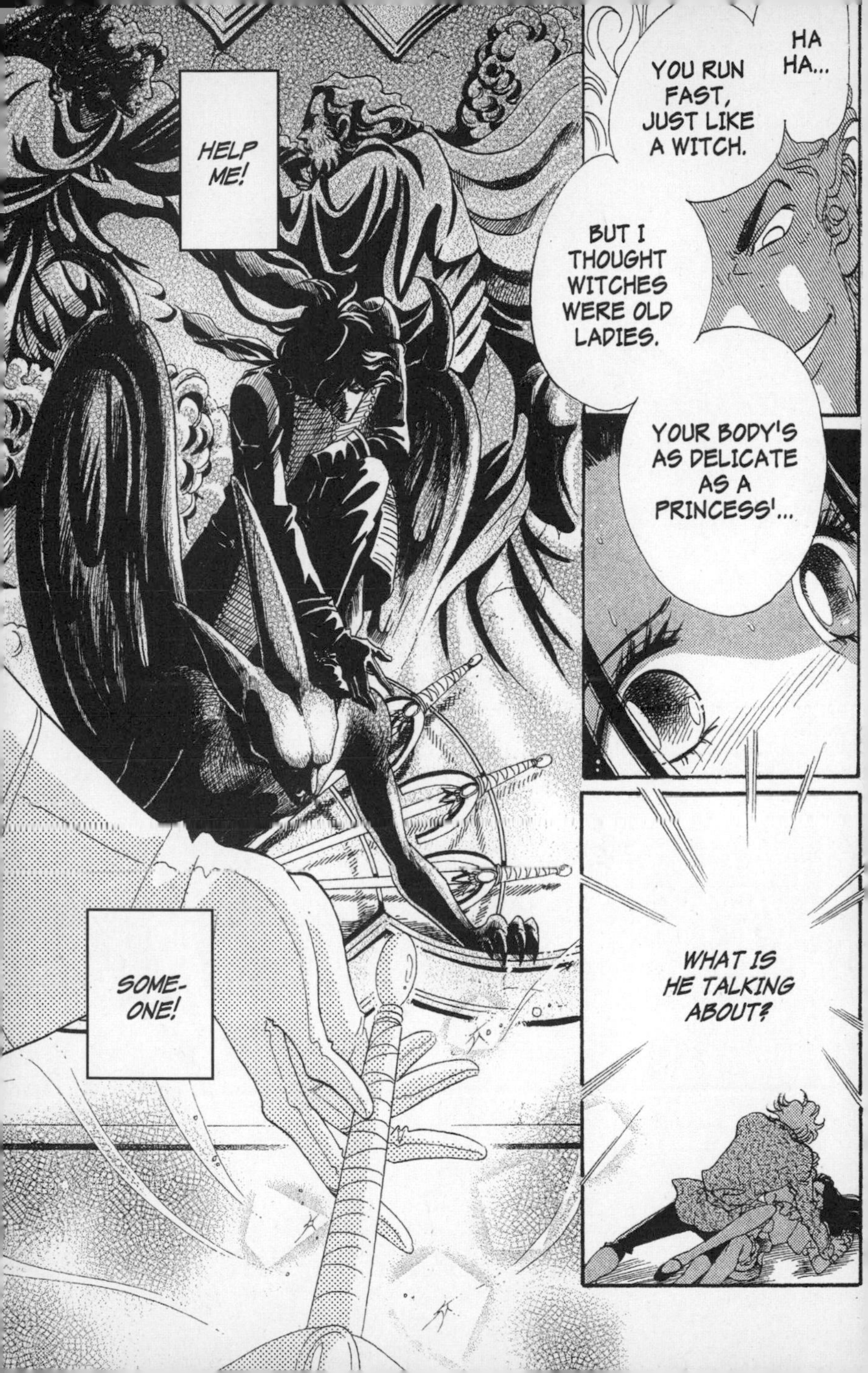
HA HA...
YOU RUN FAST, JUST LIKE A WITCH.
BUT I THOUGHT WITCHES WERE OLD LADIES.
YOUR BODY'S AS DELICATE AS A PRINCESS'...
WHAT IS HE TALKING ABOUT?
HELP ME!
SOME-ONE!

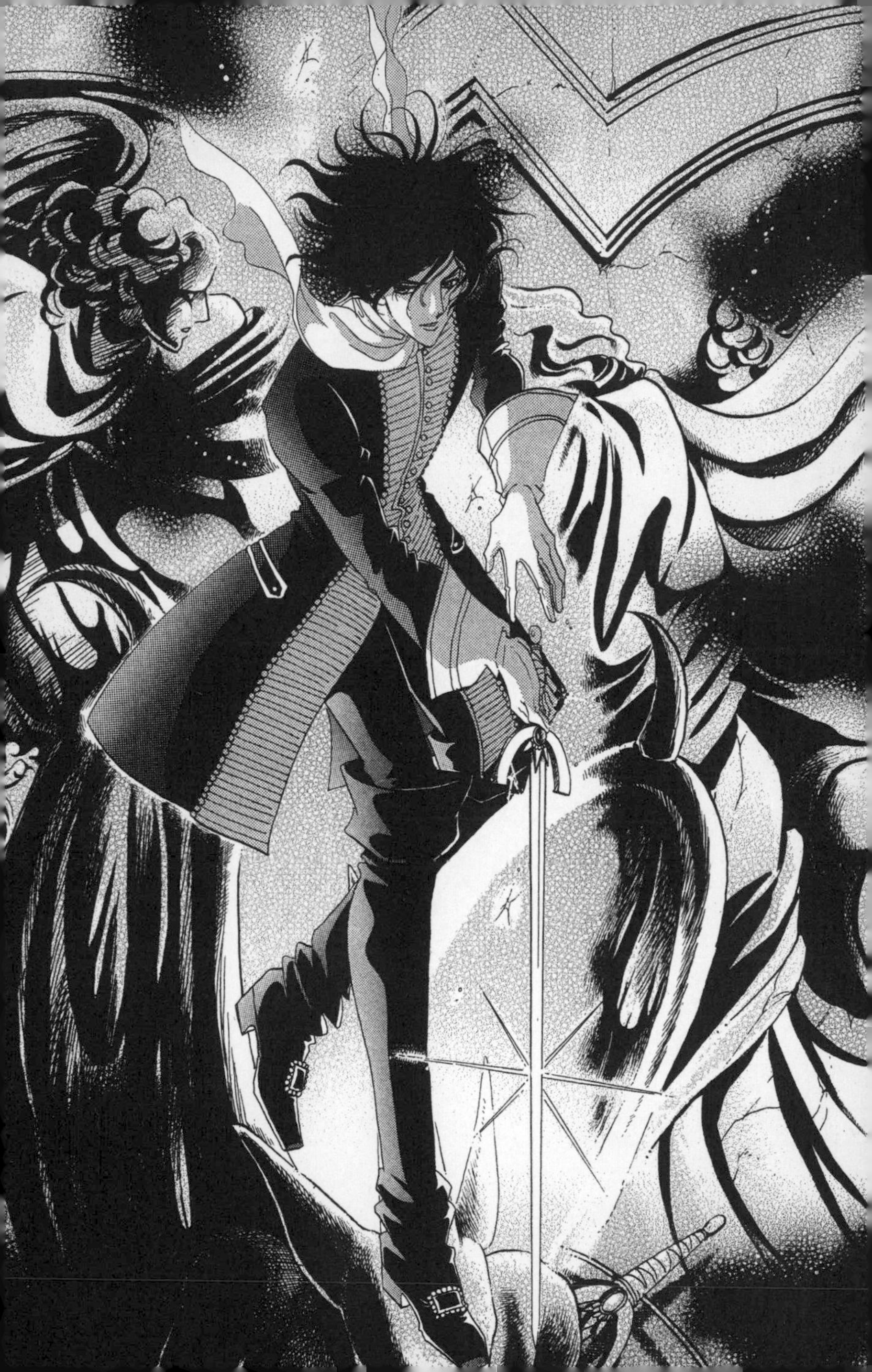

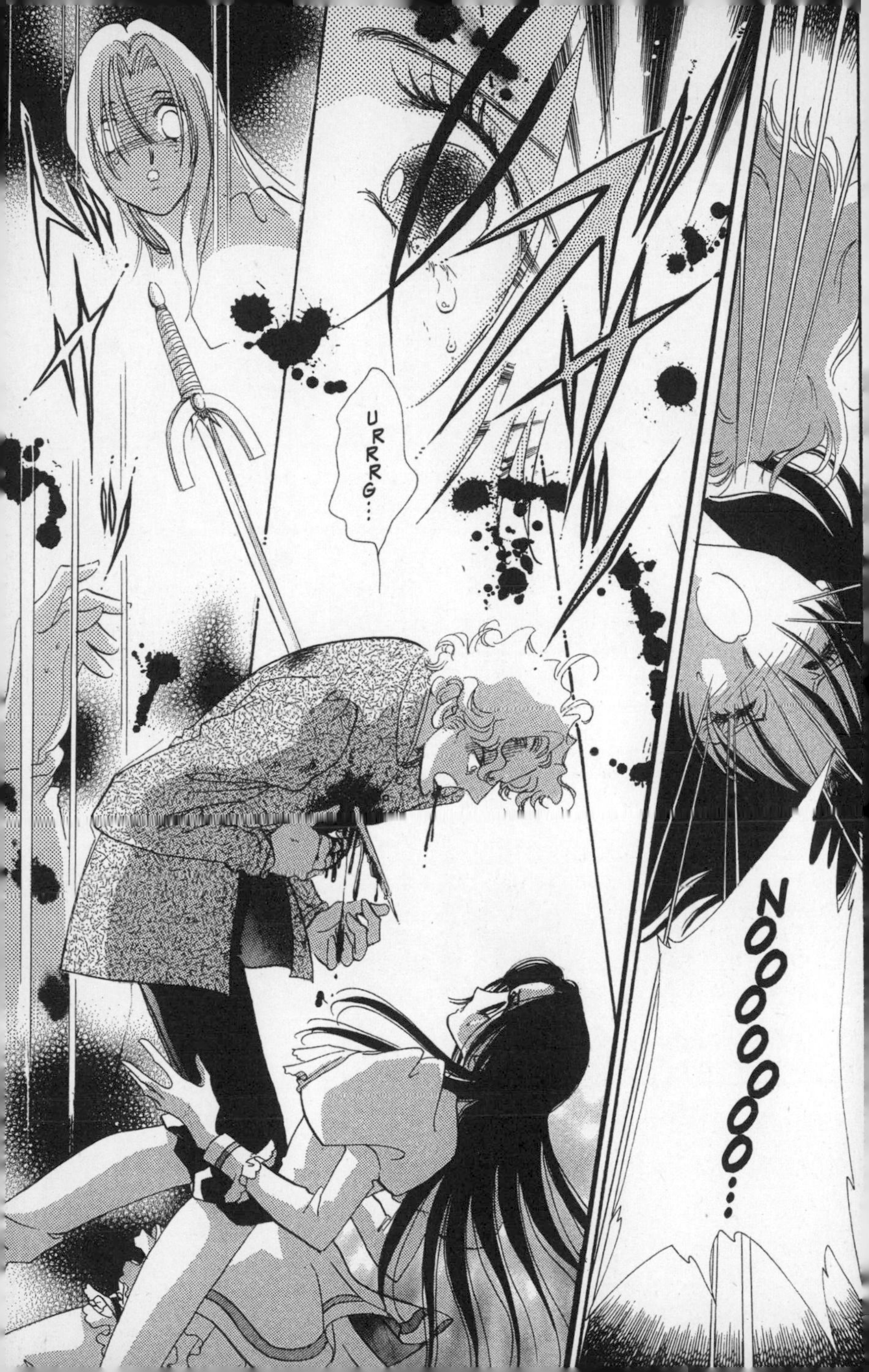
NOOOOOOOO...
URRRG...

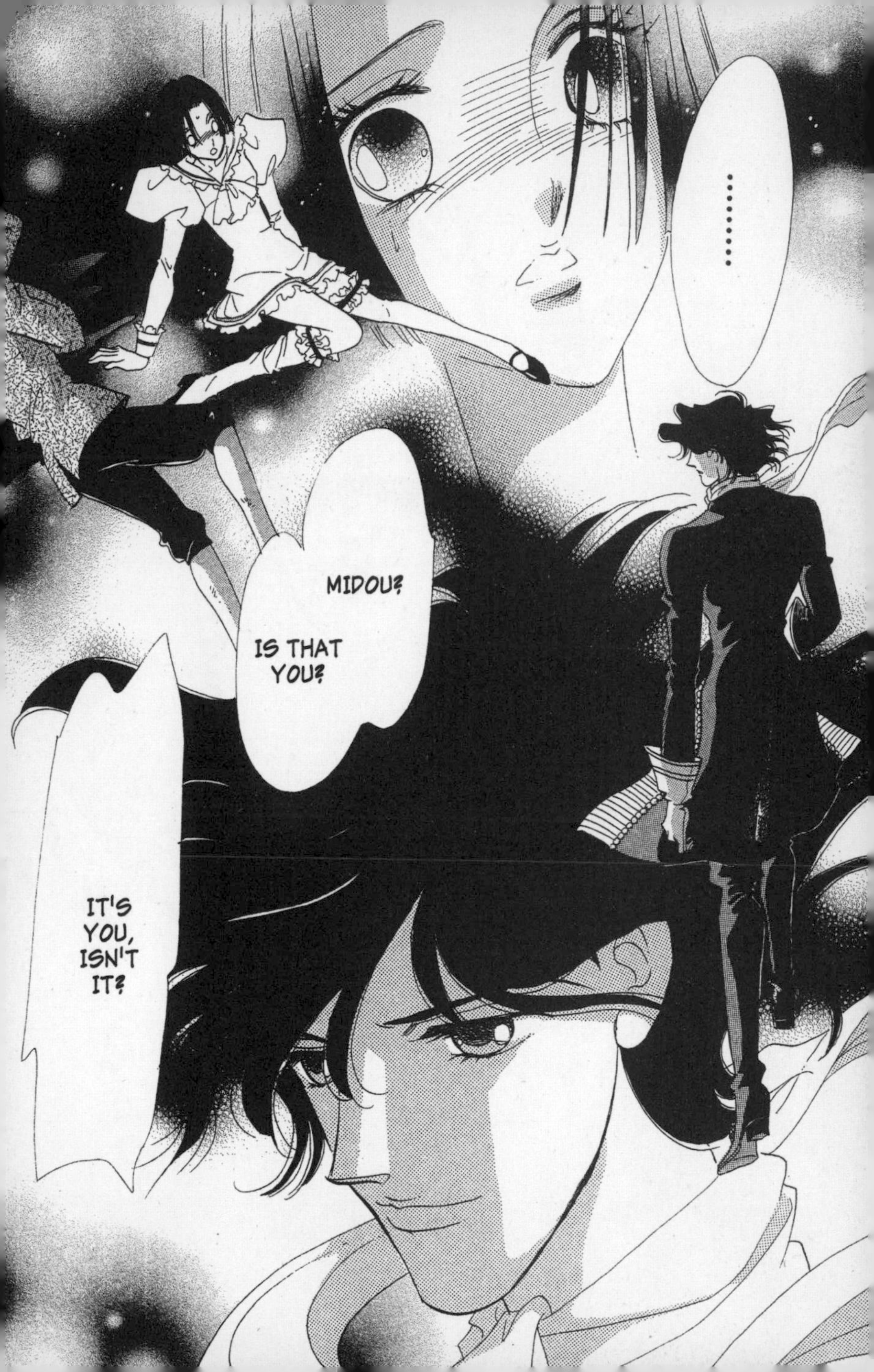
......
MIDOU?
IS THAT YOU?
IT'S YOU, ISN'T IT?

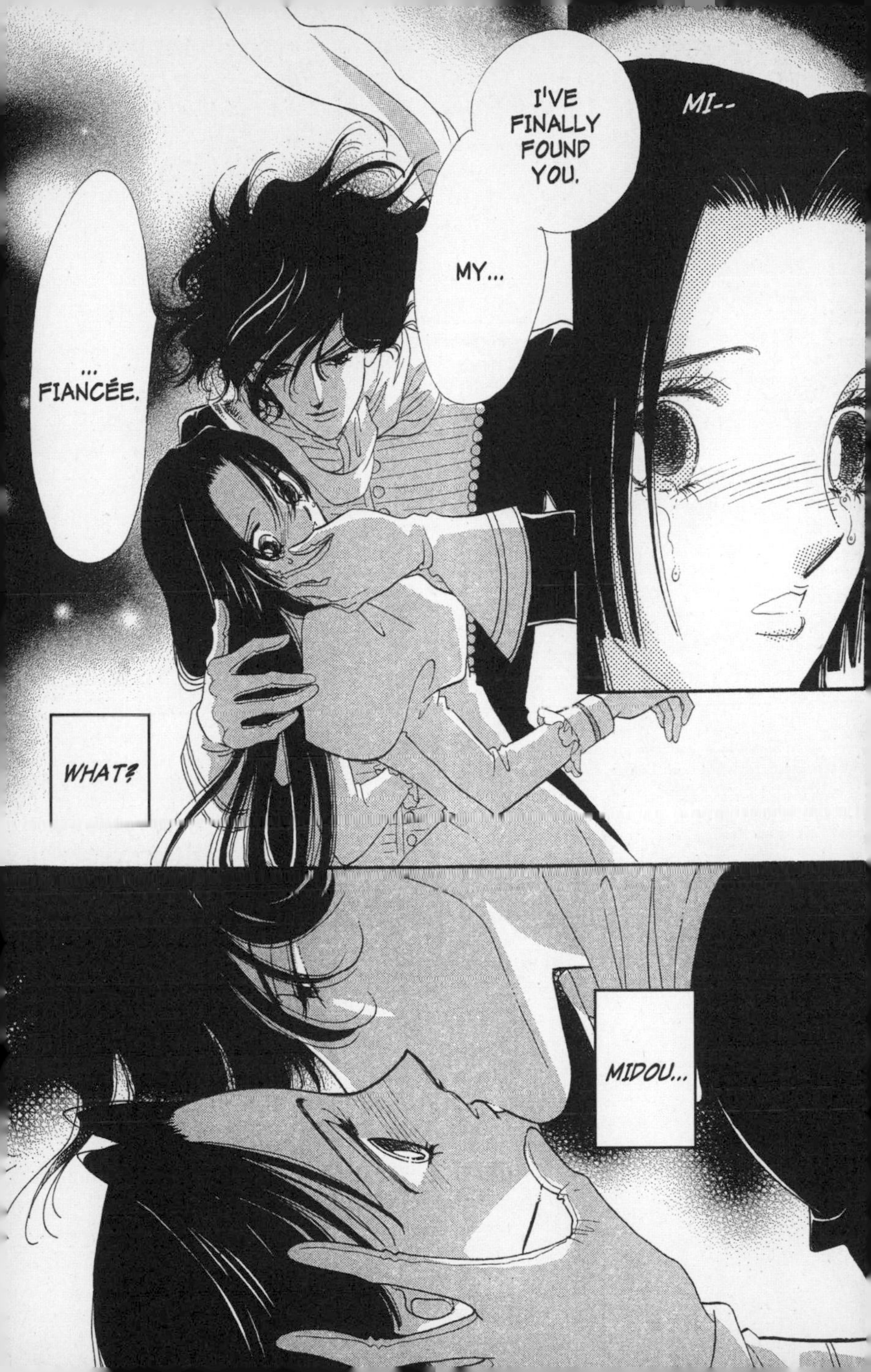
MI--
I'VE FINALLY FOUND YOU.
MY...
...FIANCÉE.
WHAT?
MIDOU...

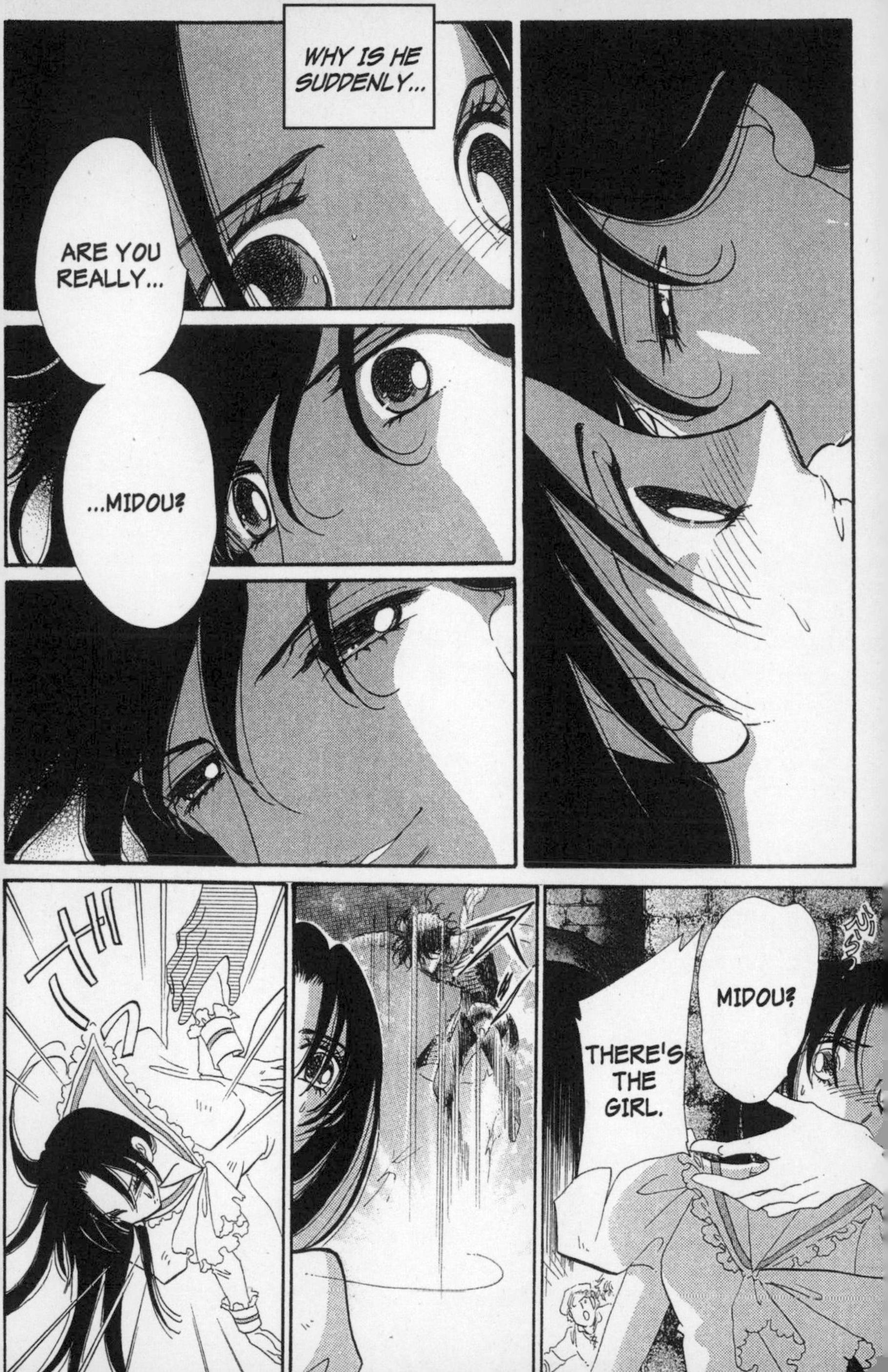
WHY IS HE SUDDENLY...
ARE YOU REALLY...
...MIDOU?
MIDOU?
THERE'S THE GIRL.

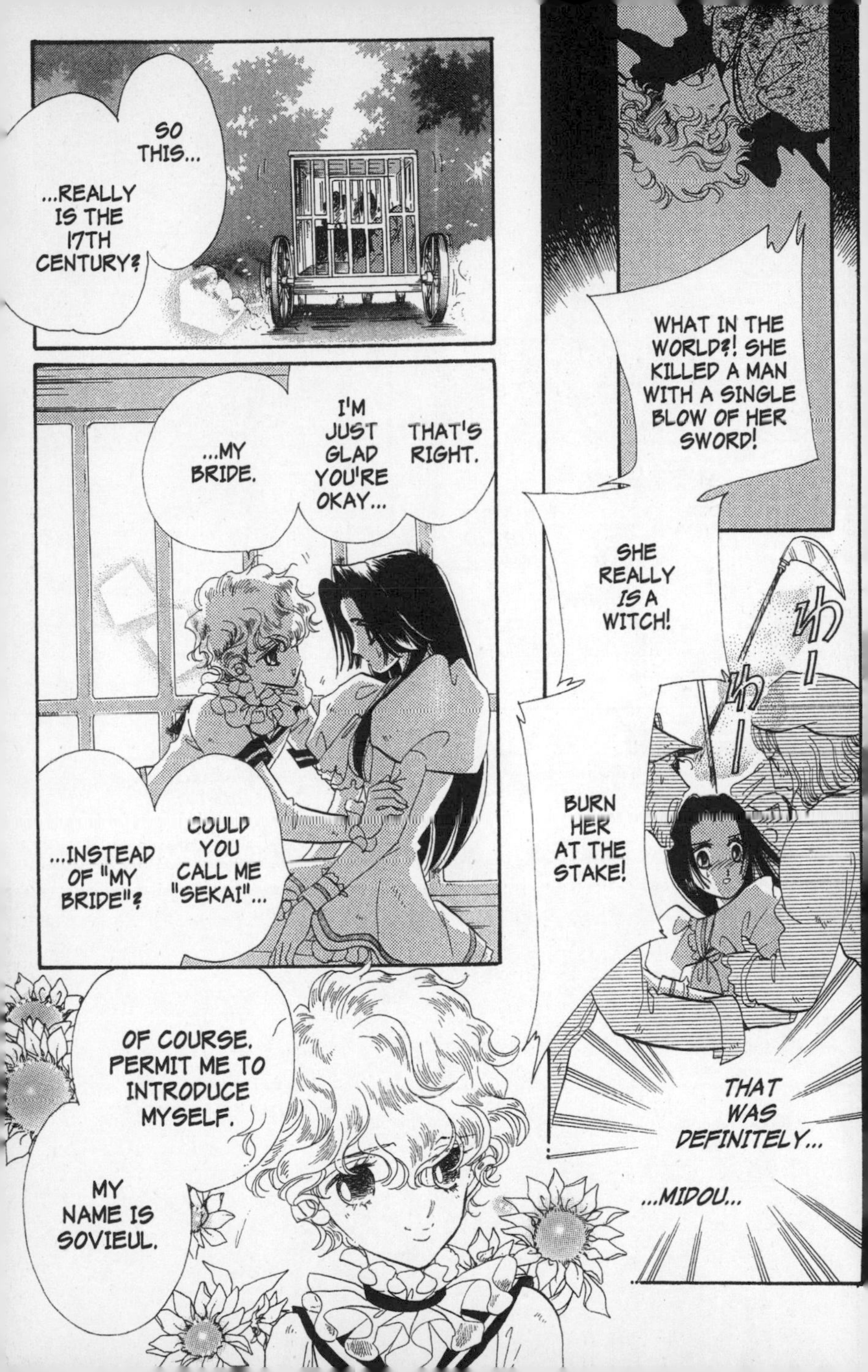
WHAT IN THE WORLD?! SHE KILLED A MAN WITH A SINGLE BLOW OF HER SWORD!
SHE REALLY *IS* A WITCH!
わー
わー
BURN HER AT THE STAKE!
THAT WAS DEFINITELY...
...MIDOU...
SO THIS...
...REALLY IS THE 17TH CENTURY?
THAT'S RIGHT.
I'M JUST GLAD YOU'RE OKAY...
...MY BRIDE.
COULD YOU CALL ME "SEKAI"...
...INSTEAD OF "MY BRIDE"?
OF COURSE. PERMIT ME TO INTRODUCE MYSELF.
MY NAME IS SOVIEUL.

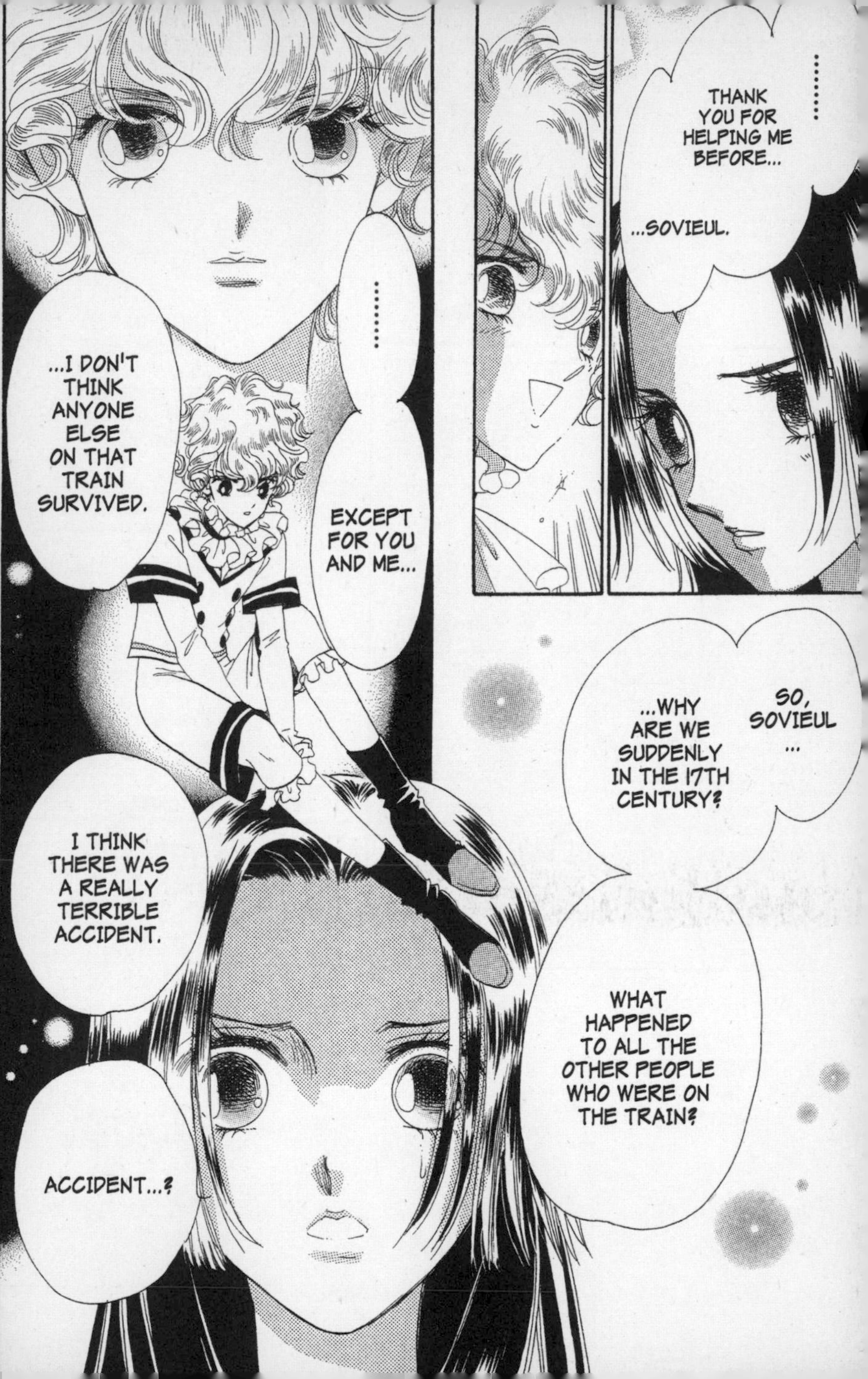
......
THANK YOU FOR HELPING ME BEFORE...
...SOVIEUL.
SO, SOVIEUL ...
...WHY ARE WE SUDDENLY IN THE 17TH CENTURY?
WHAT HAPPENED TO ALL THE OTHER PEOPLE WHO WERE ON THE TRAIN?
......
EXCEPT FOR YOU AND ME...
...I DON'T THINK ANYONE ELSE ON THAT TRAIN SURVIVED.
I THINK THERE WAS A REALLY TERRIBLE ACCIDENT.
ACCIDENT...?

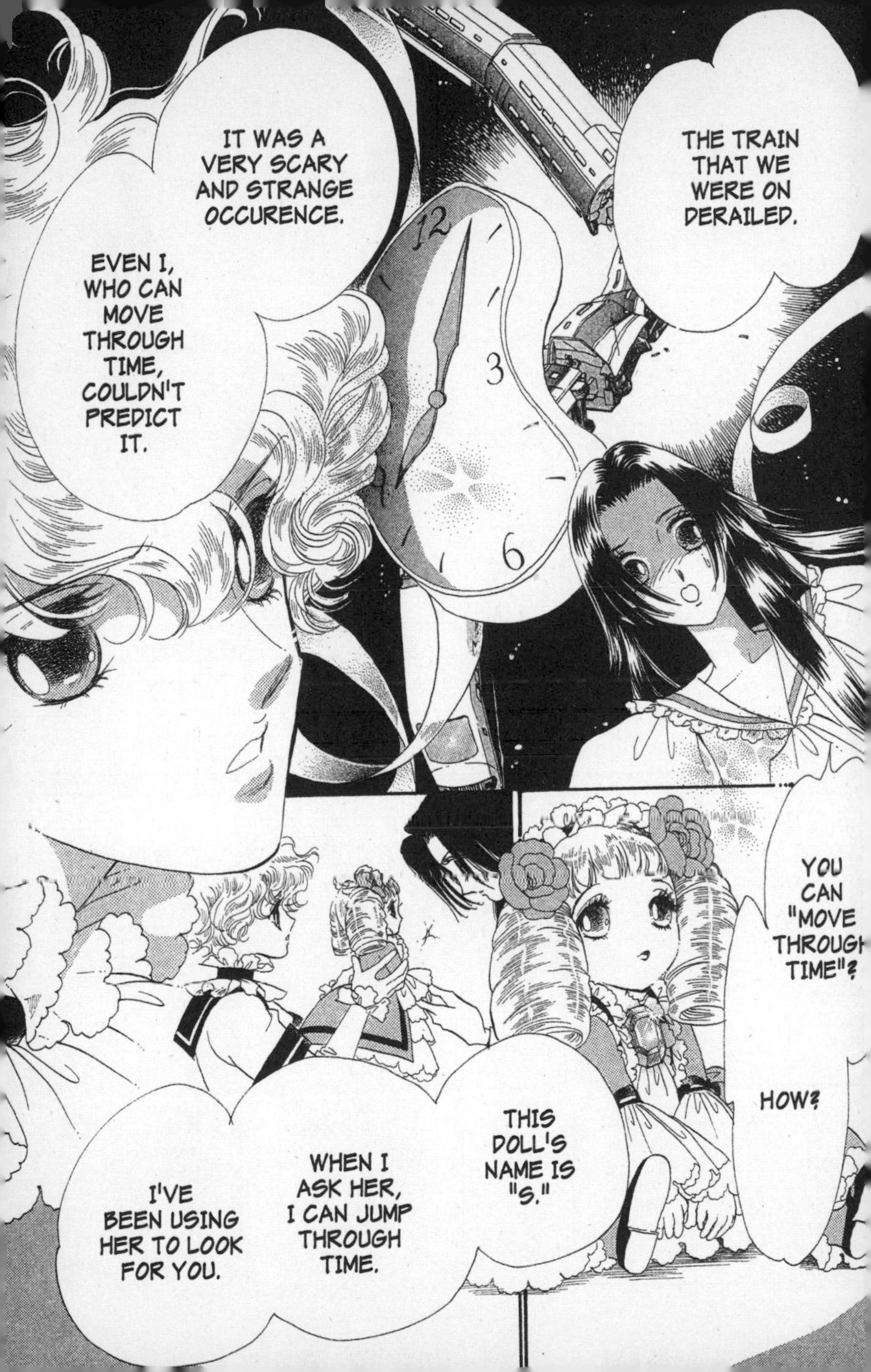
THE TRAIN THAT WE WERE ON DERAILED.
IT WAS A VERY SCARY AND STRANGE OCCURENCE.
EVEN I, WHO CAN MOVE THROUGH TIME, COULDN'T PREDICT IT.
YOU CAN "MOVE THROUG TIME"?
HOW?
THIS DOLL'S NAME IS "S."
WHEN I ASK HER, I CAN JUMP THROUGH TIME.
I'VE BEEN USING HER TO LOOK FOR YOU.

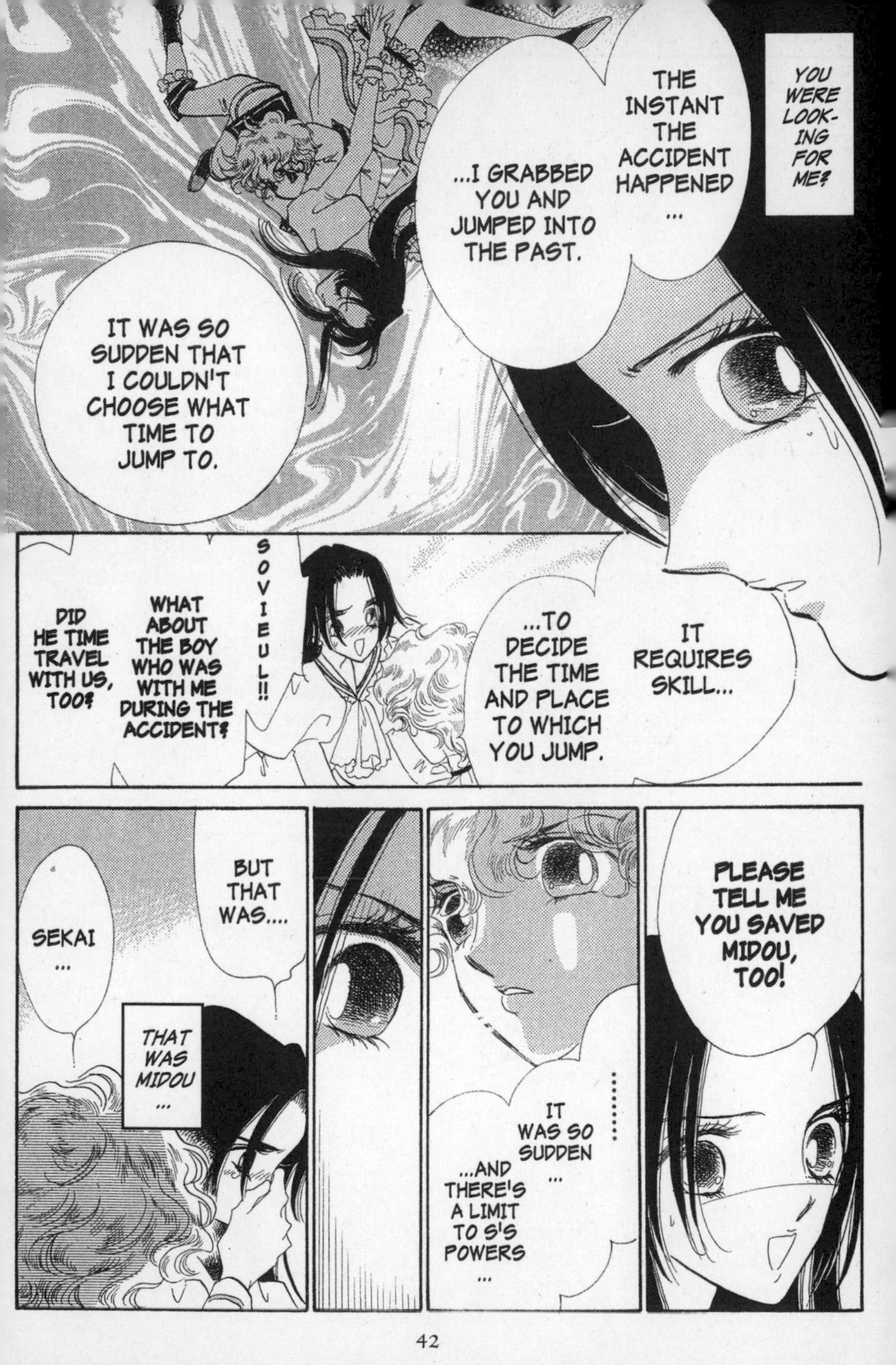
YOU WERE LOOK-ING FOR ME?
THE INSTANT THE ACCIDENT HAPPENED ...
...I GRABBED YOU AND JUMPED INTO THE PAST.
IT WAS SO SUDDEN THAT I COULDN'T CHOOSE WHAT TIME TO JUMP TO.
IT REQUIRES SKILL...
...TO DECIDE THE TIME AND PLACE TO WHICH YOU JUMP.
SOVIEUL!!
WHAT ABOUT THE BOY WHO WAS WITH ME DURING THE ACCIDENT?
DID HE TIME TRAVEL WITH US, TOO?
PLEASE TELL ME YOU SAVED MIDOU, TOO!
......
IT WAS SO SUDDEN ...
...AND THERE'S A LIMIT TO S'S POWERS ...
BUT THAT WAS....
SEKAI ...
THAT WAS MIDOU ...

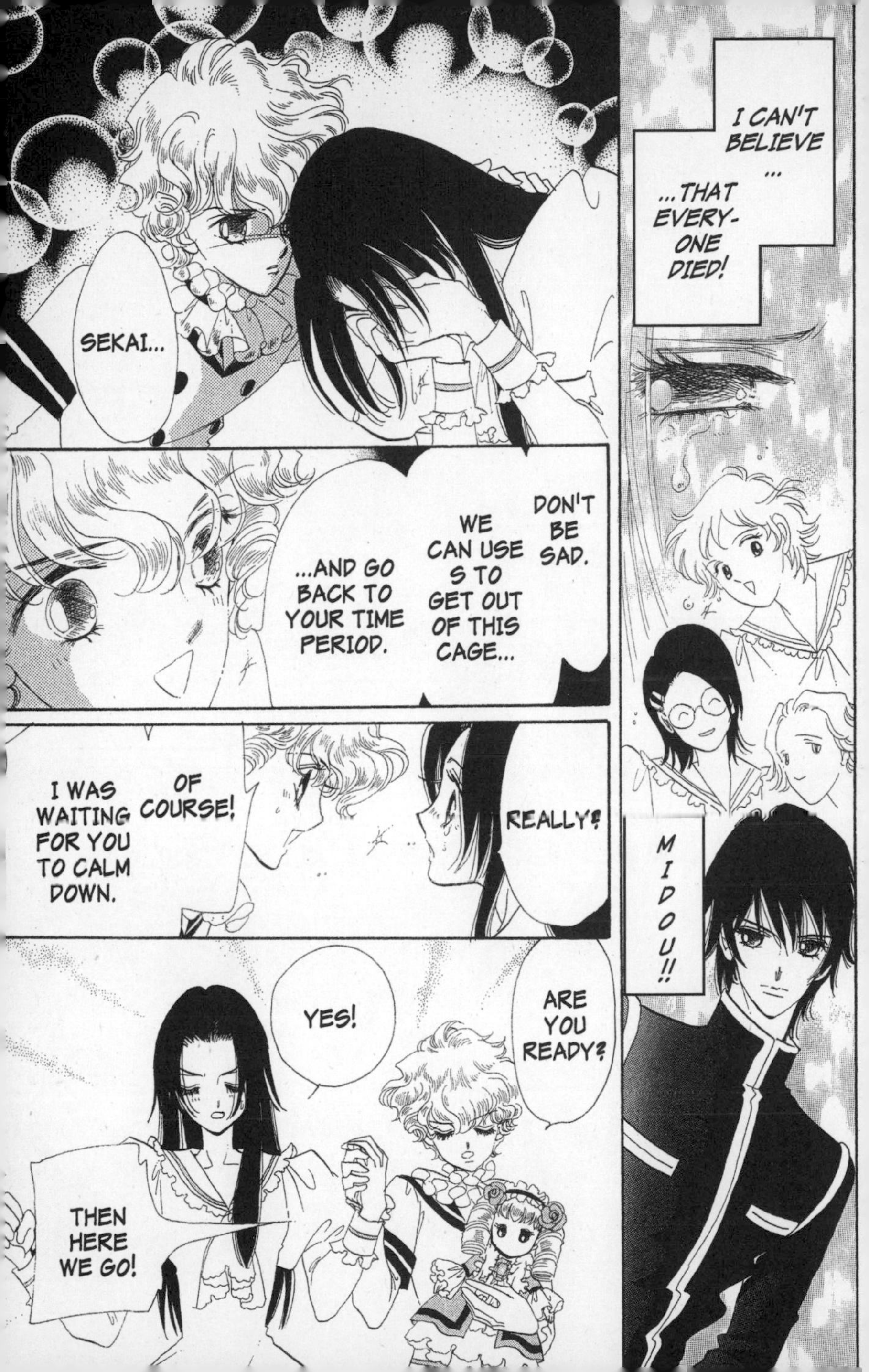
I CAN'T BELIEVE ...
...THAT EVERY-ONE DIED!
MIDOU!!
SEKAI...
DON'T BE SAD.
WE CAN USE S TO GET OUT OF THIS CAGE...
...AND GO BACK TO YOUR TIME PERIOD.
REALLY?
OF COURSE!
I WAS WAITING FOR YOU TO CALM DOWN.
ARE YOU READY?
YES!
THEN HERE WE GO!

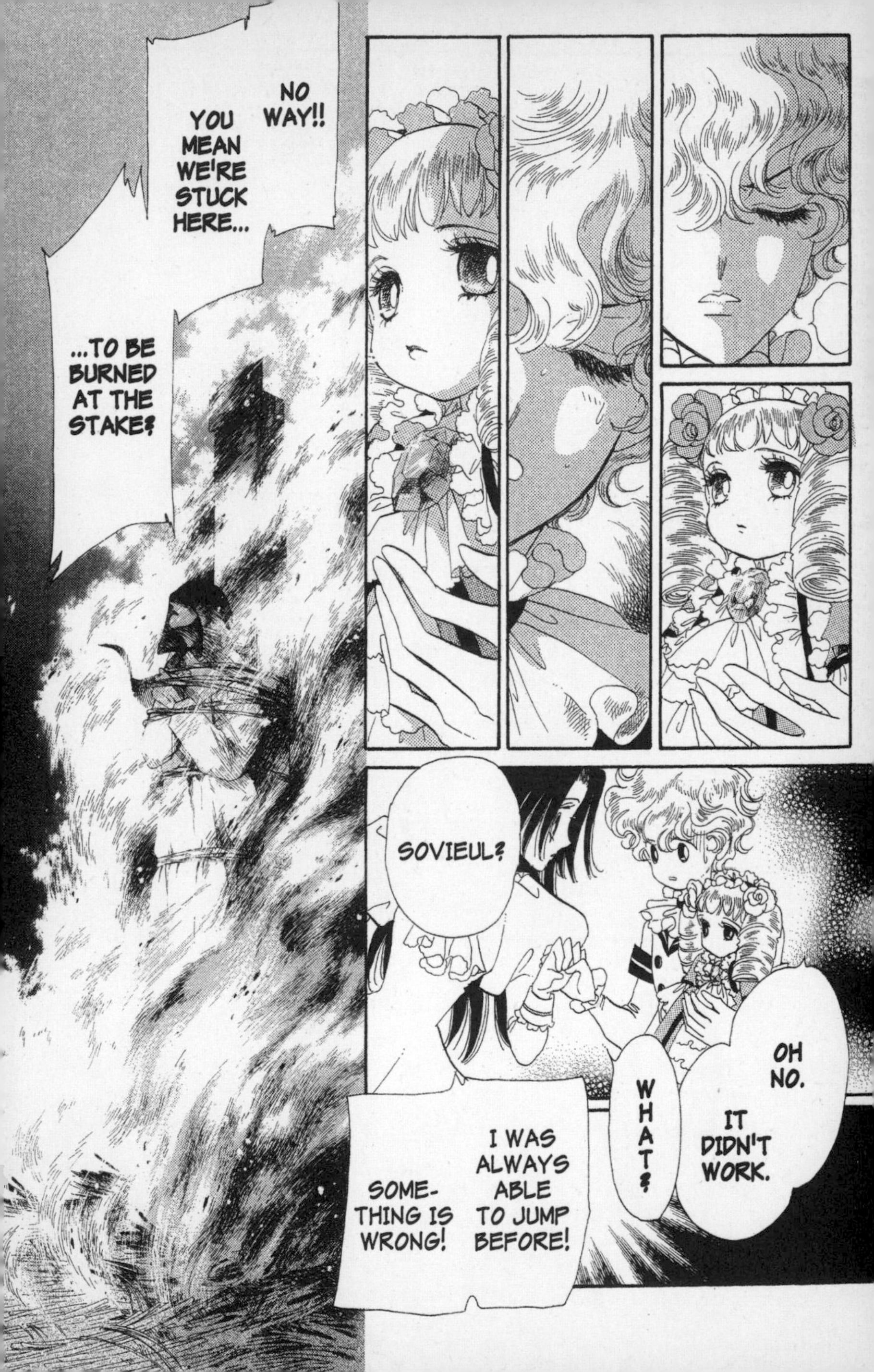
SOVIEUL?
OH NO. IT DIDN'T WORK.
WHAT?
I WAS ALWAYS ABLE TO JUMP BEFORE!
SOME-THING IS WRONG!
NO WAY!!
YOU MEAN WE'RE STUCK HERE...
...TO BE BURNED AT THE STAKE?

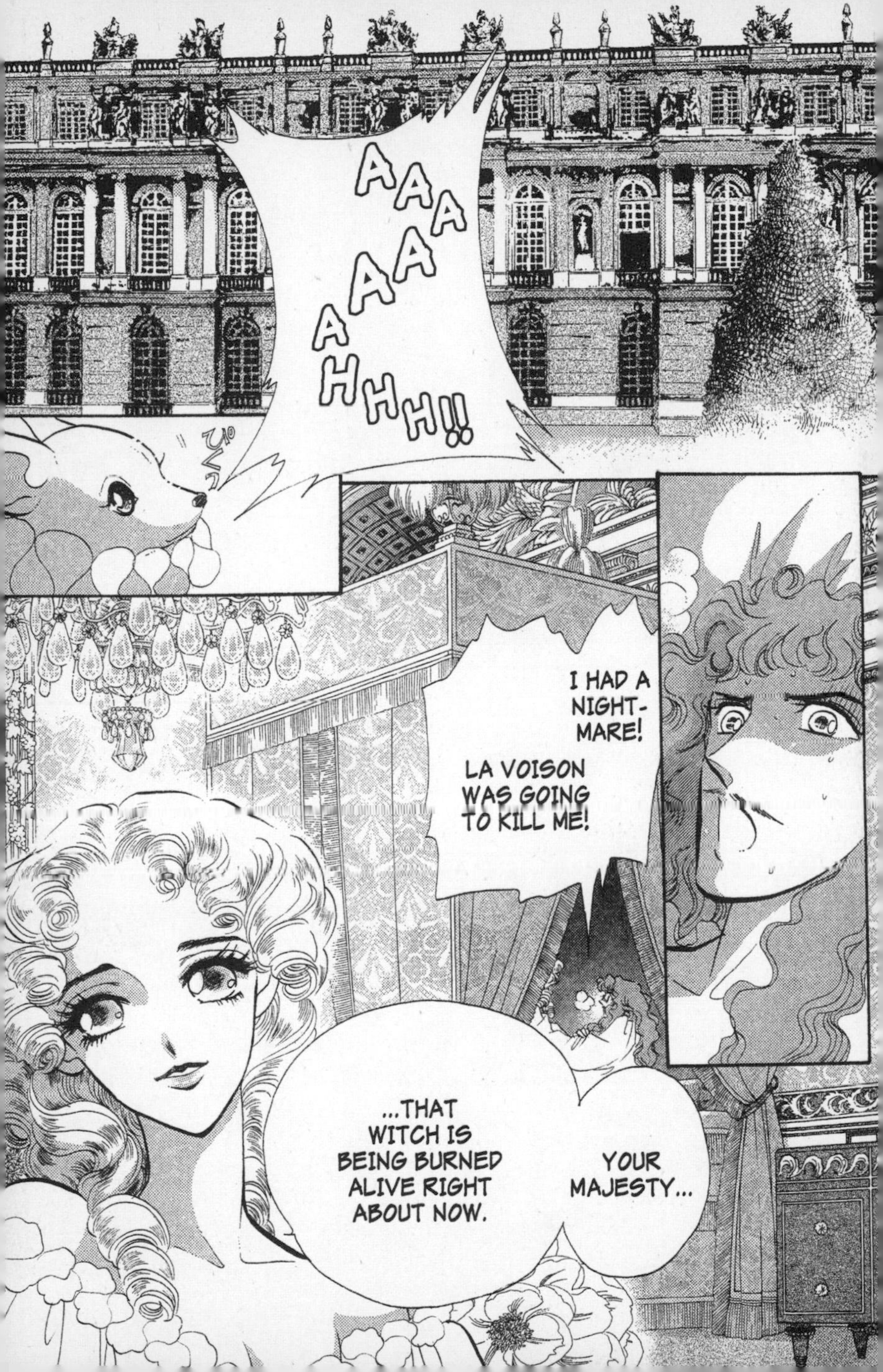
AAAAAAHHH!!
I HAD A NIGHTMARE!
LA VOISON WAS GOING TO KILL ME!
YOUR MAJESTY...
...THAT WITCH IS BEING BURNED ALIVE RIGHT ABOUT NOW.

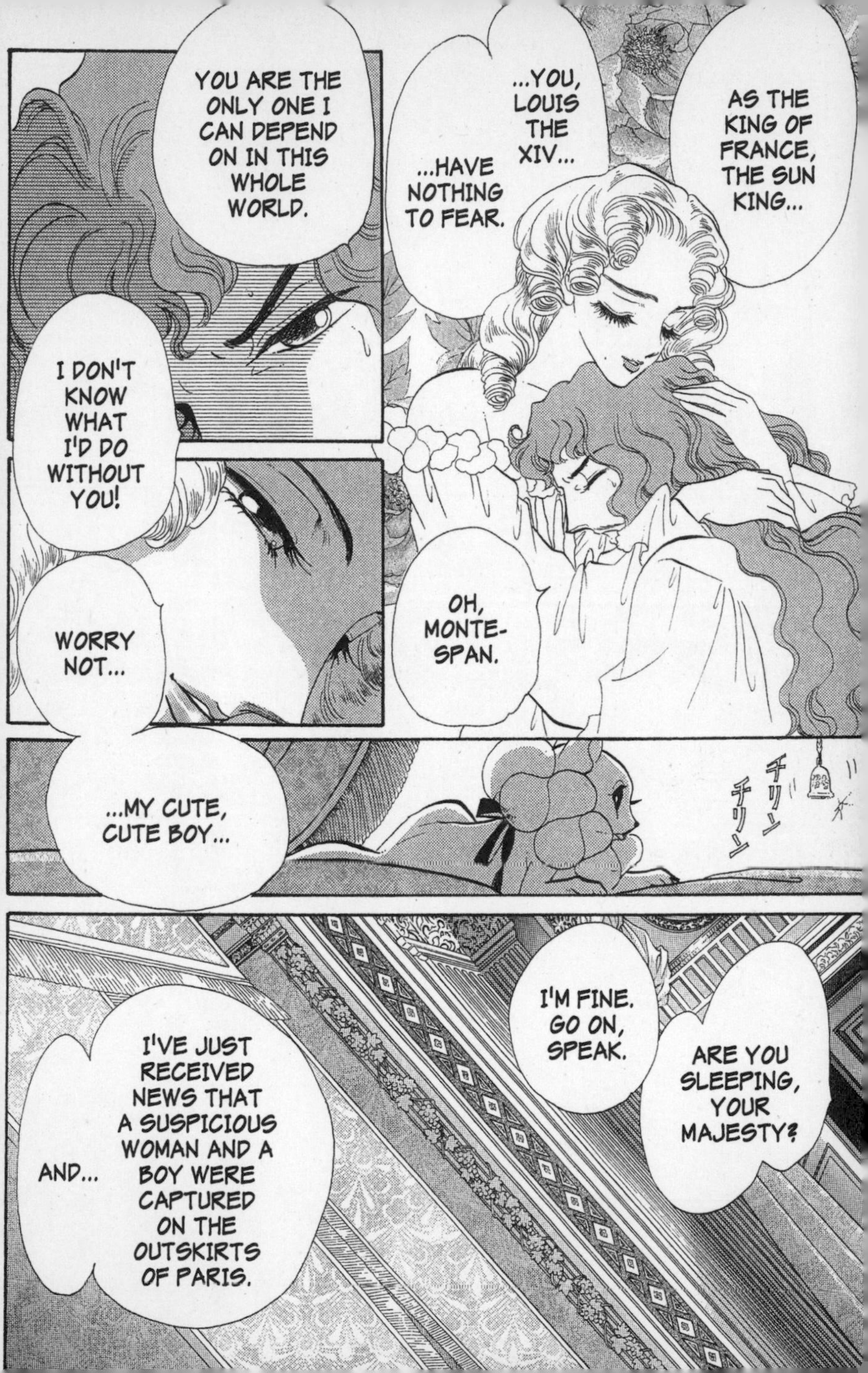
AS THE KING OF FRANCE, THE SUN KING...
...YOU, LOUIS THE XIV...
...HAVE NOTHING TO FEAR.
OH, MONTE-SPAN.
YOU ARE THE ONLY ONE I CAN DEPEND ON IN THIS WHOLE WORLD.
I DON'T KNOW WHAT I'D DO WITHOUT YOU!
WORRY NOT...
...MY CUTE, CUTE BOY...
チリン チリン
ARE YOU SLEEPING, YOUR MAJESTY?
I'M FINE. GO ON, SPEAK.
I'VE JUST RECEIVED NEWS THAT A SUSPICIOUS WOMAN AND A BOY WERE CAPTURED ON THE OUTSKIRTS OF PARIS.
AND...

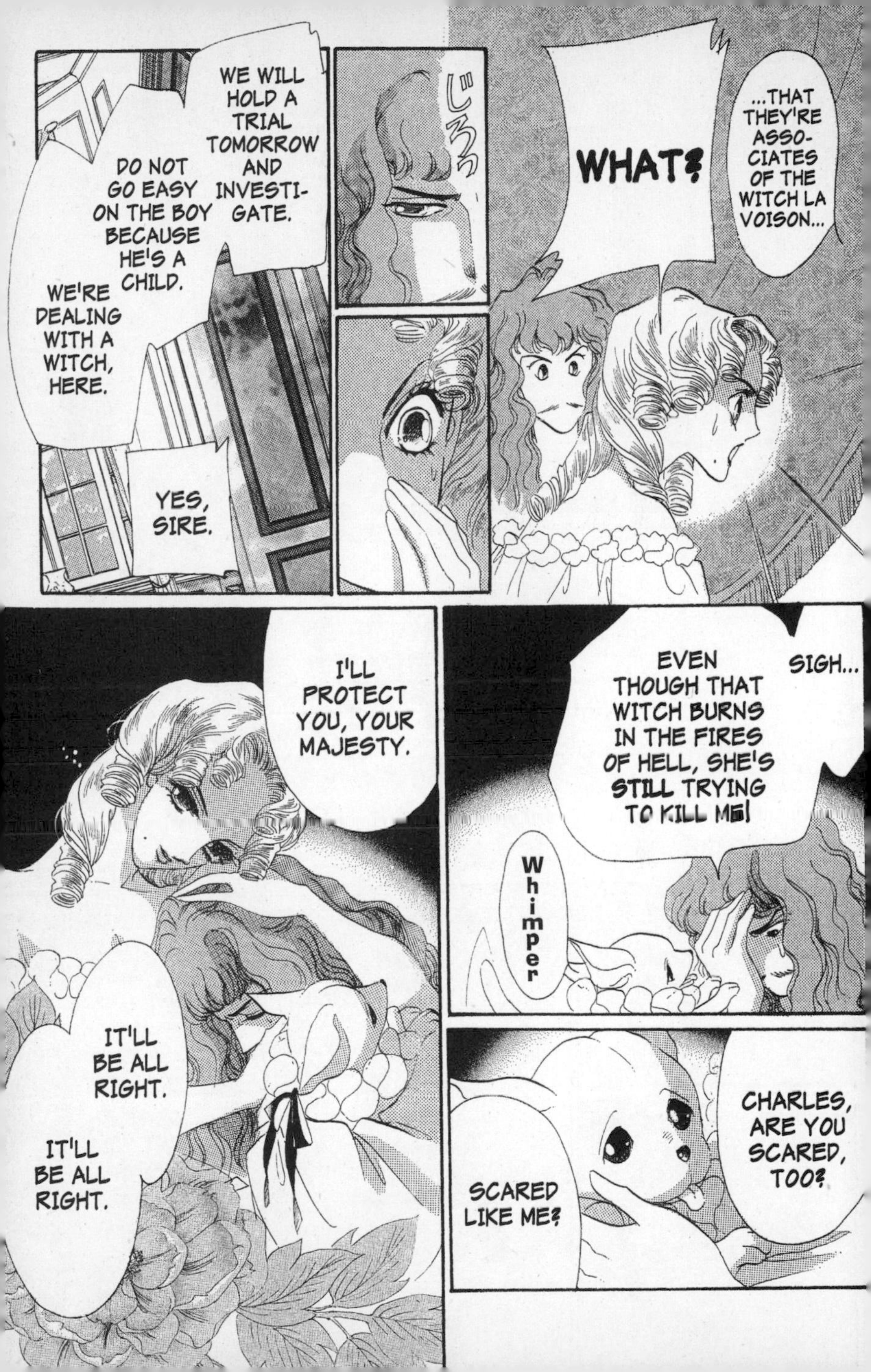
...THAT THEY'RE ASSO-CIATES OF THE WITCH LA VOISON...
WHAT?
じろっ
WE WILL HOLD A TRIAL TOMORROW AND INVESTI-GATE.
DO NOT GO EASY ON THE BOY BECAUSE HE'S A CHILD.
WE'RE DEALING WITH A WITCH, HERE.
YES, SIRE.
SIGH...
EVEN THOUGH THAT WITCH BURNS IN THE FIRES OF HELL, SHE'S STILL TRYING TO KILL ME!
Whimper
CHARLES, ARE YOU SCARED, TOO?
SCARED LIKE ME?
I'LL PROTECT YOU, YOUR MAJESTY.
IT'LL BE ALL RIGHT.
IT'LL BE ALL RIGHT.

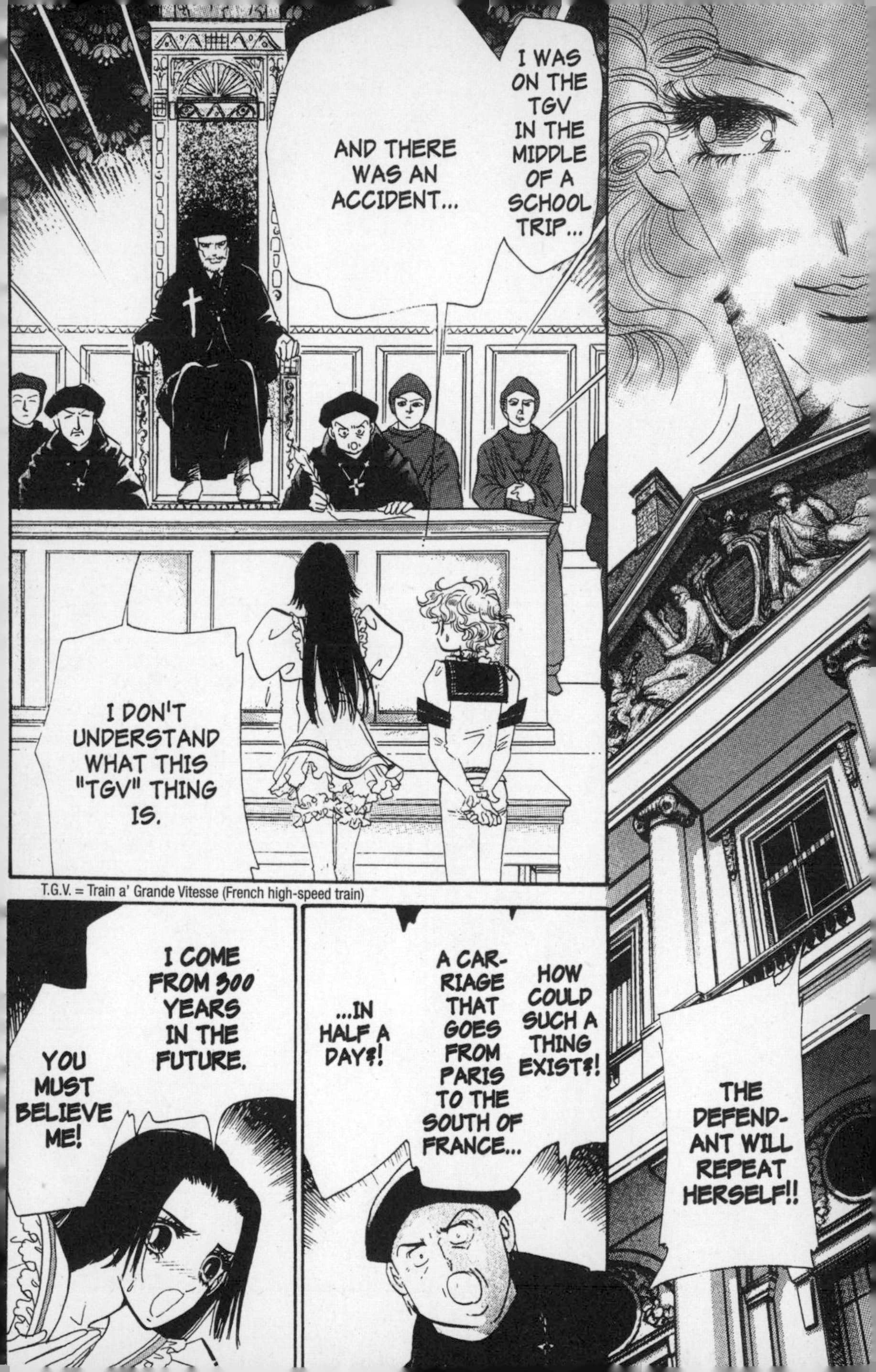
THE DEFENDANT WILL REPEAT HERSELF!!
I WAS ON THE TGV IN THE MIDDLE OF A SCHOOL TRIP...
AND THERE WAS AN ACCIDENT...
I DON'T UNDERSTAND WHAT THIS "TGV" THING IS.
HOW COULD SUCH A THING EXIST?!
A CARRIAGE THAT GOES FROM PARIS TO THE SOUTH OF FRANCE...
...IN HALF A DAY?!
I COME FROM 300 YEARS IN THE FUTURE.
YOU MUST BELIEVE ME!

T.G.V. = Train a' Grande Vitesse (French high-speed train)

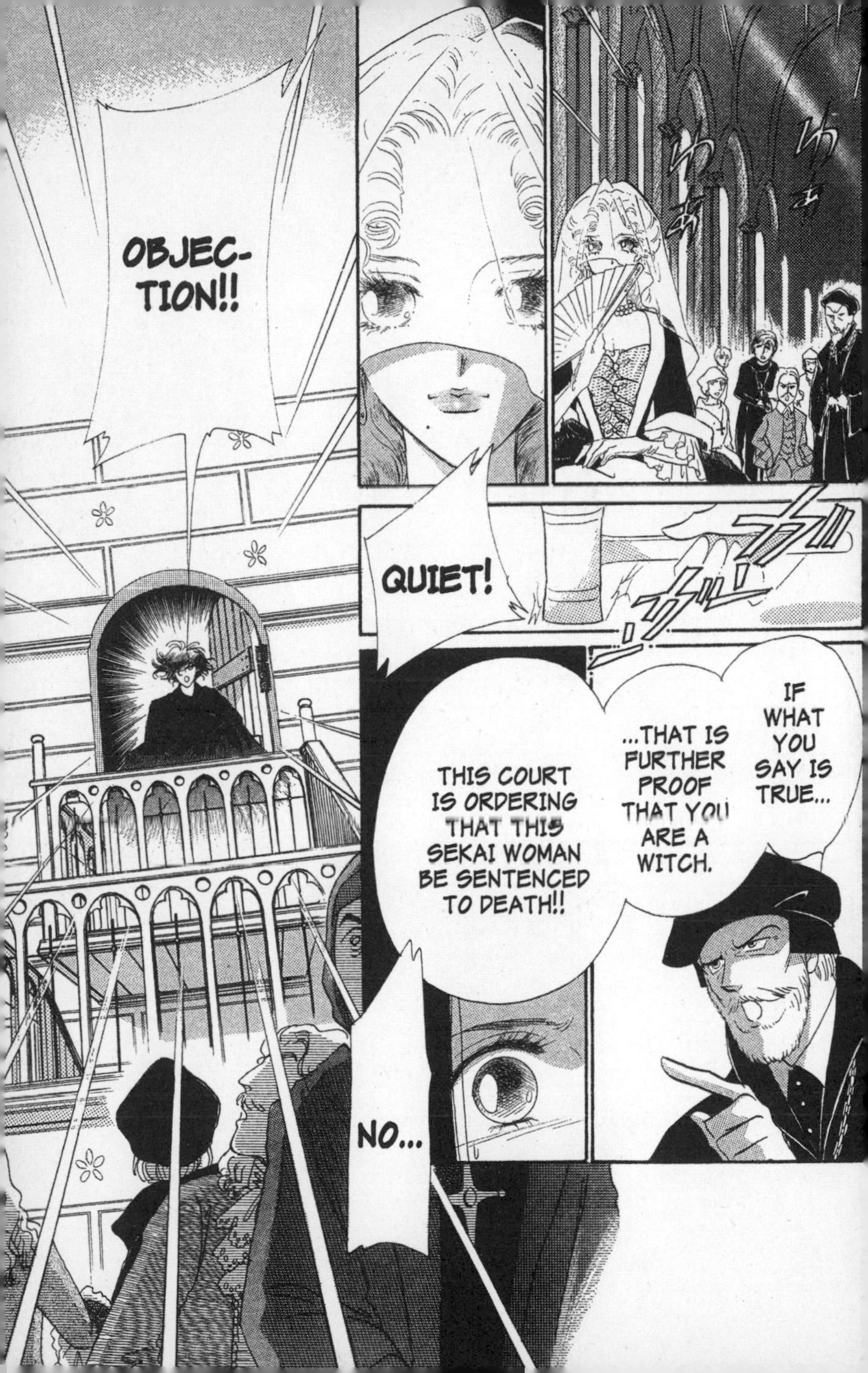
QUIET!
IF WHAT YOU SAY IS TRUE...
...THAT IS FURTHER PROOF THAT YOU ARE A WITCH.
THIS COURT IS ORDERING THAT THIS SEKAI WOMAN BE SENTENCED TO DEATH!!
NO...
OBJECTION!!

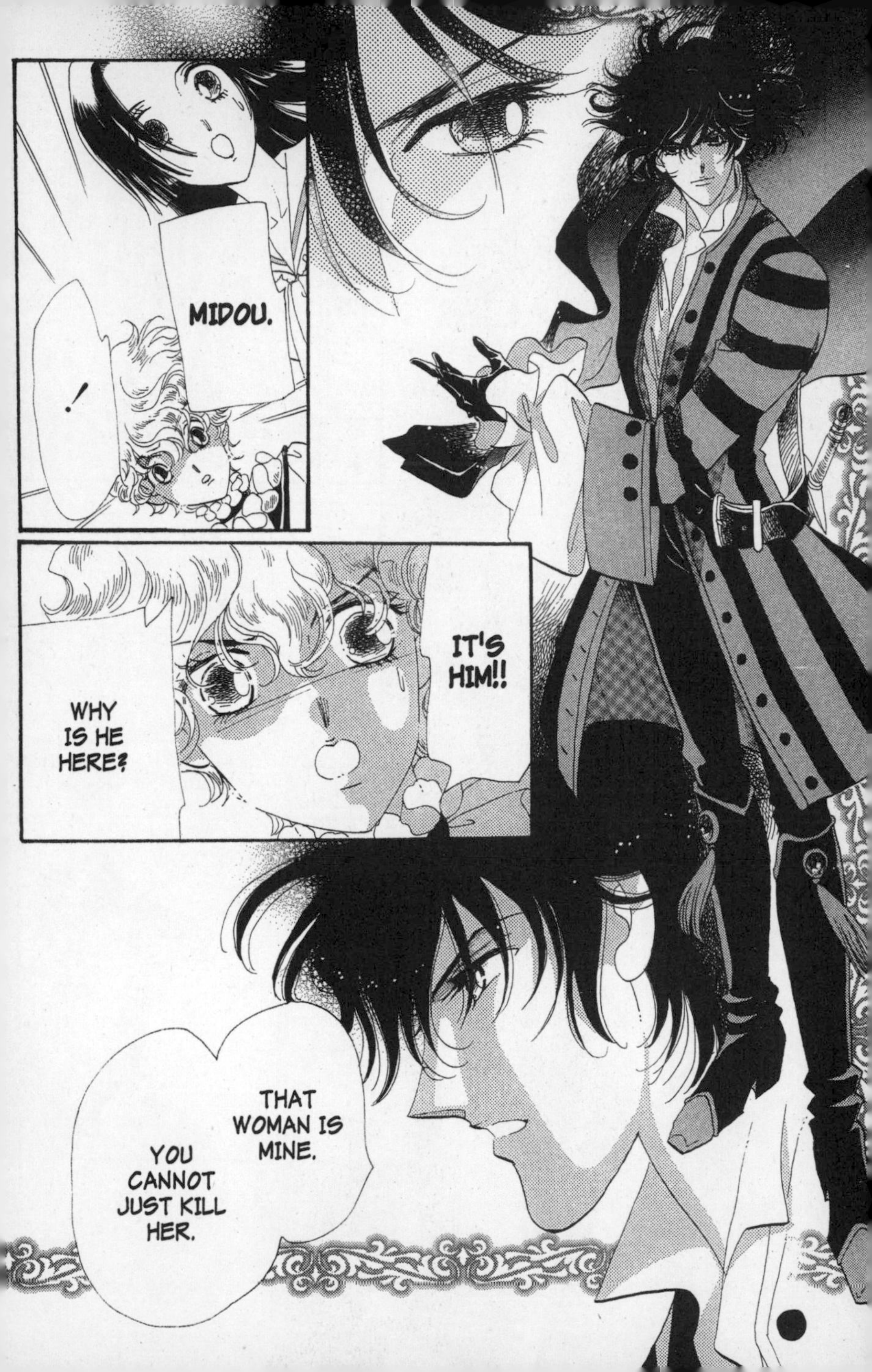
MIDOU.
!
IT'S HIM!!
WHY IS HE HERE?
THAT WOMAN IS MINE.
YOU CANNOT JUST KILL HER.

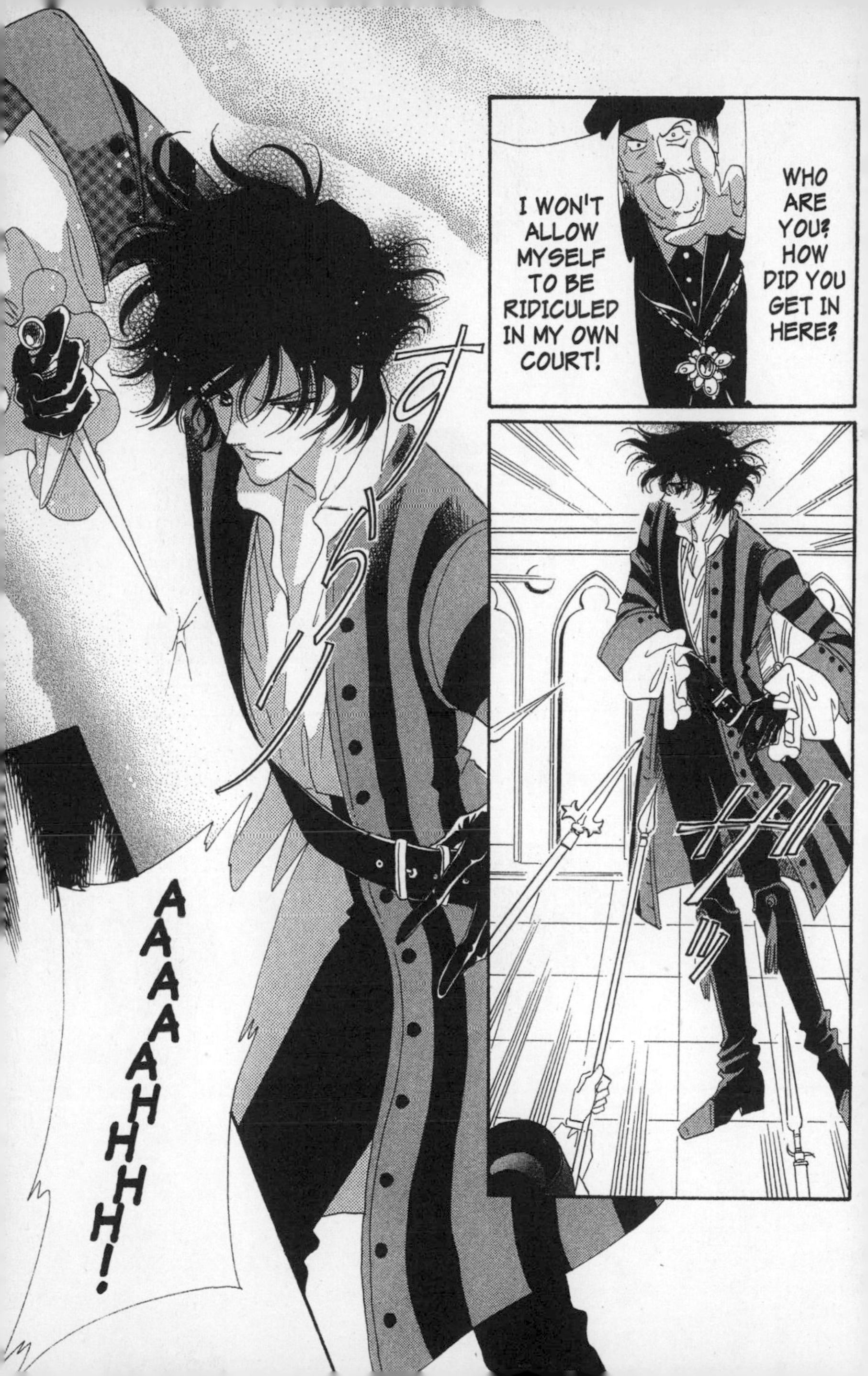
WHO ARE YOU? HOW DID YOU GET IN HERE?
I WON'T ALLOW MYSELF TO BE RIDICULED IN MY OWN COURT!
AAAAAHHHH!

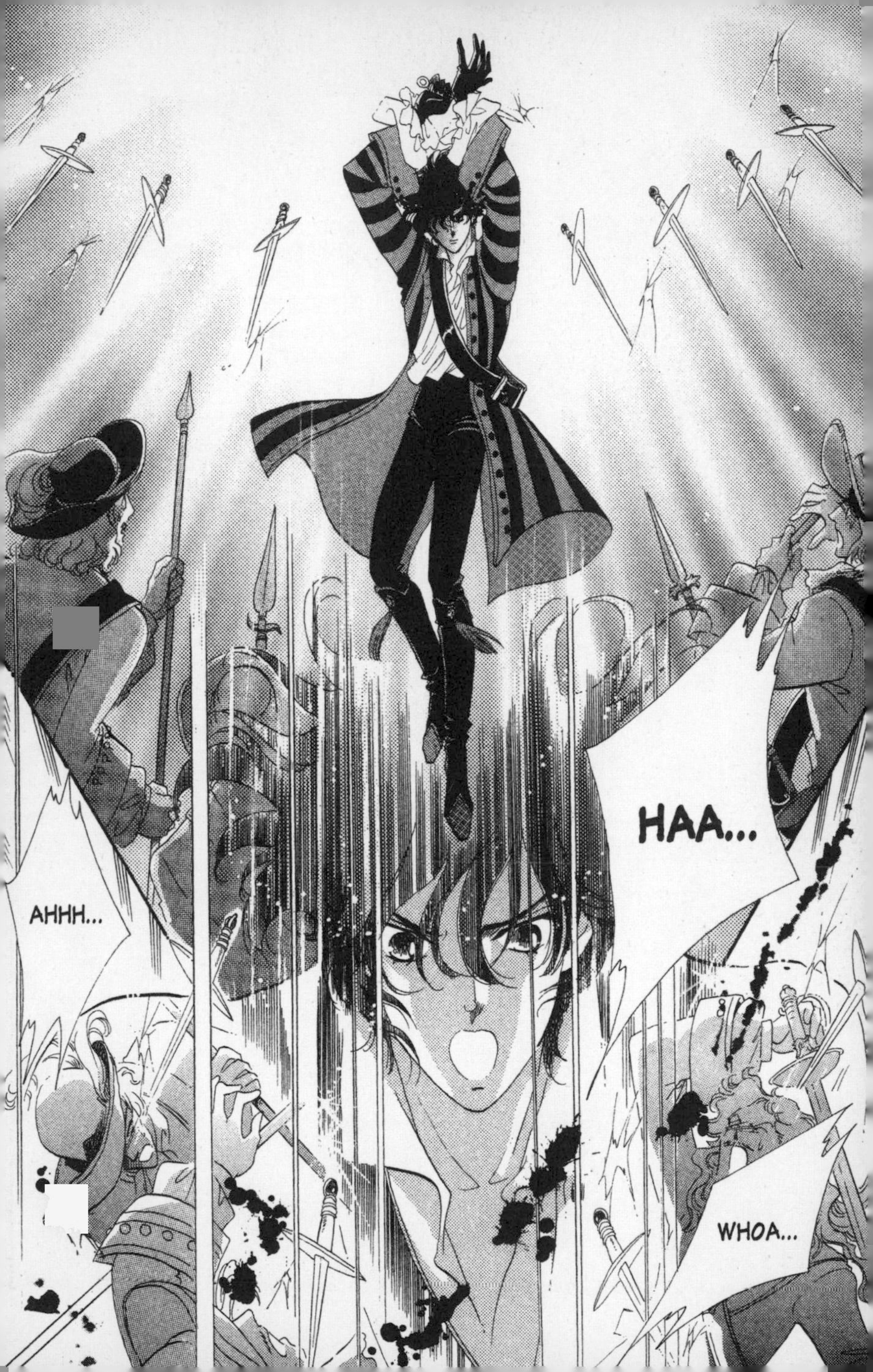
HAA...
AHHH...
WHOA...

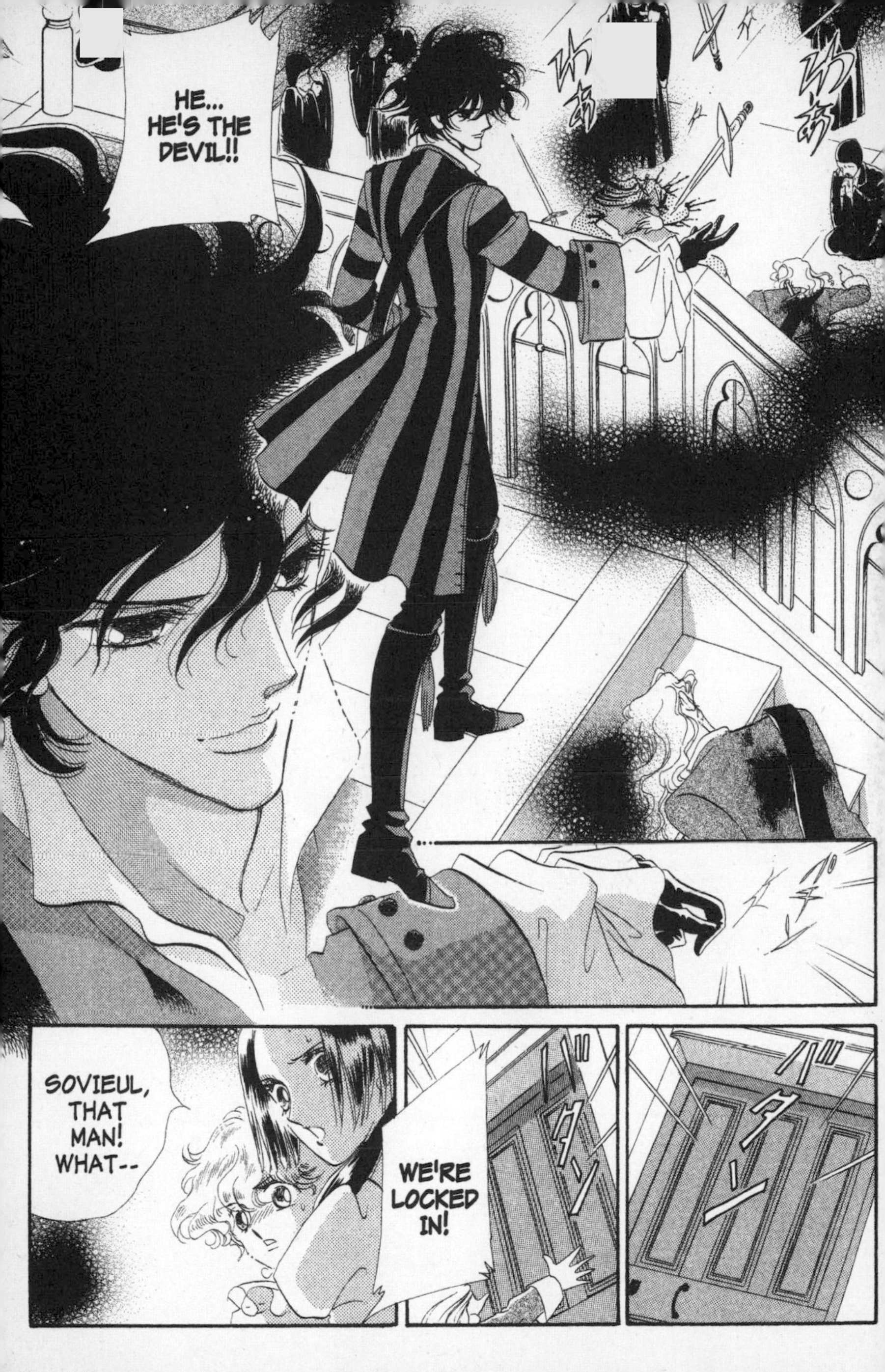
HE... HE'S THE DEVIL!!
WE'RE LOCKED IN!
SOVIEUL, THAT MAN! WHAT--

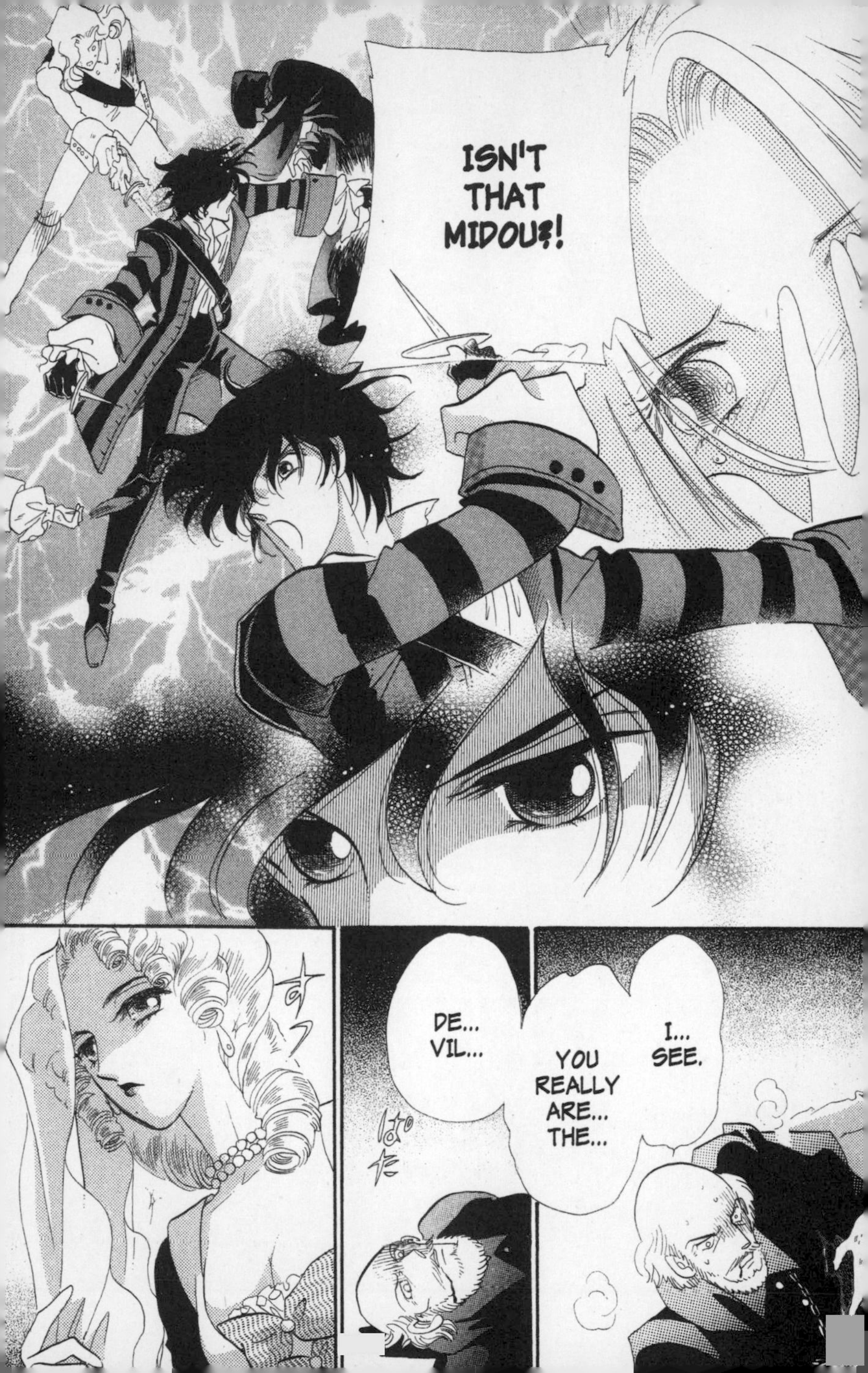
ISN'T THAT MIDOU?!
I... SEE.
YOU REALLY ARE... THE...
DE... VIL...
ぱた
すっ

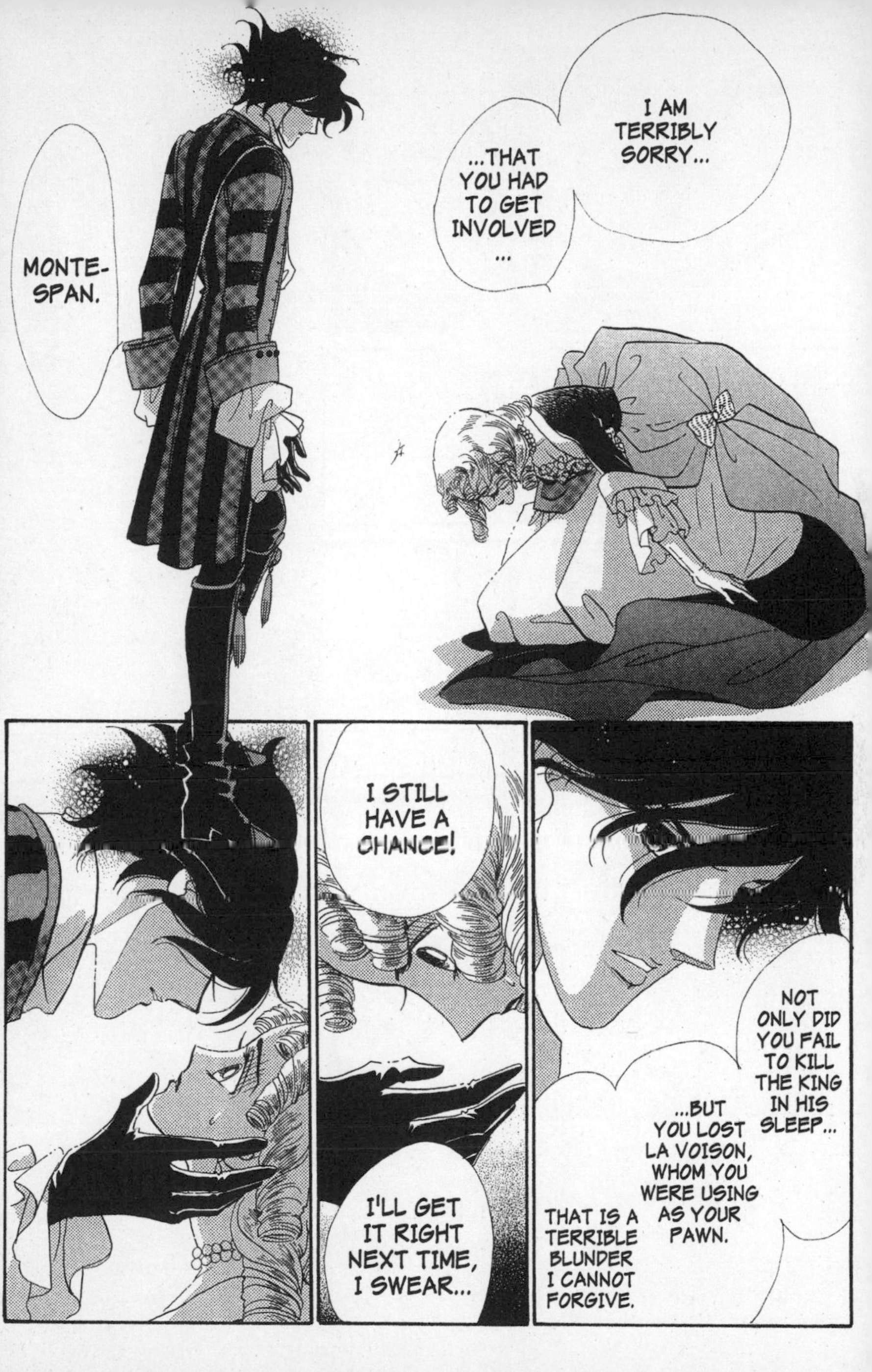
I AM TERRIBLY SORRY...
...THAT YOU HAD TO GET INVOLVED ...
MONTE-SPAN.
NOT ONLY DID YOU FAIL TO KILL THE KING IN HIS SLEEP...
...BUT YOU LOST LA VOISON, WHOM YOU WERE USING AS YOUR PAWN.
THAT IS A TERRIBLE BLUNDER I CANNOT FORGIVE.
I STILL HAVE A CHANCE!
I'LL GET IT RIGHT NEXT TIME, I SWEAR...

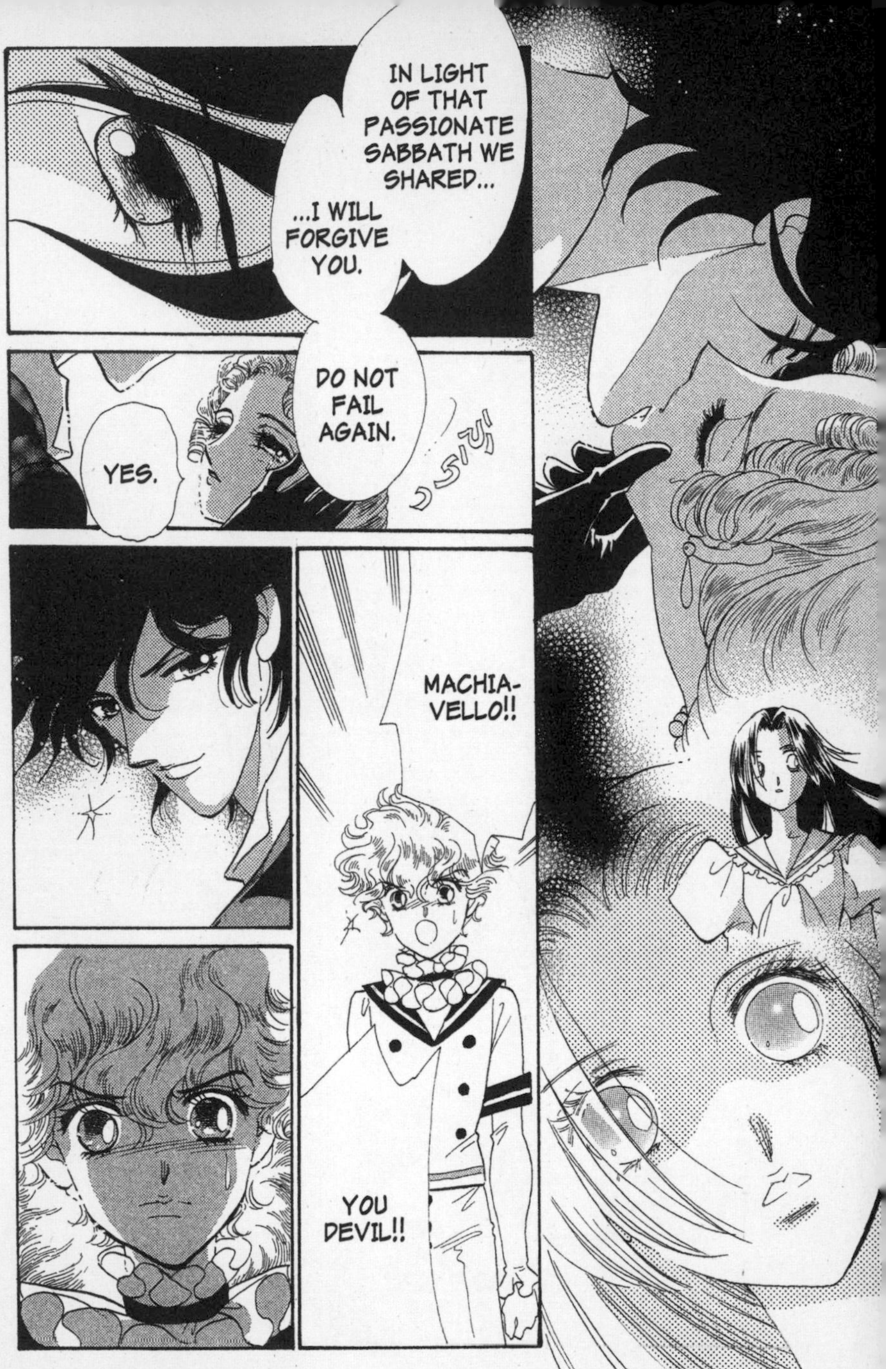
IN LIGHT OF THAT PASSIONATE SABBATH WE SHARED...
...I WILL FORGIVE YOU.
DO NOT FAIL AGAIN.
YES.
MACHIA-VELLO!!
YOU DEVIL!!

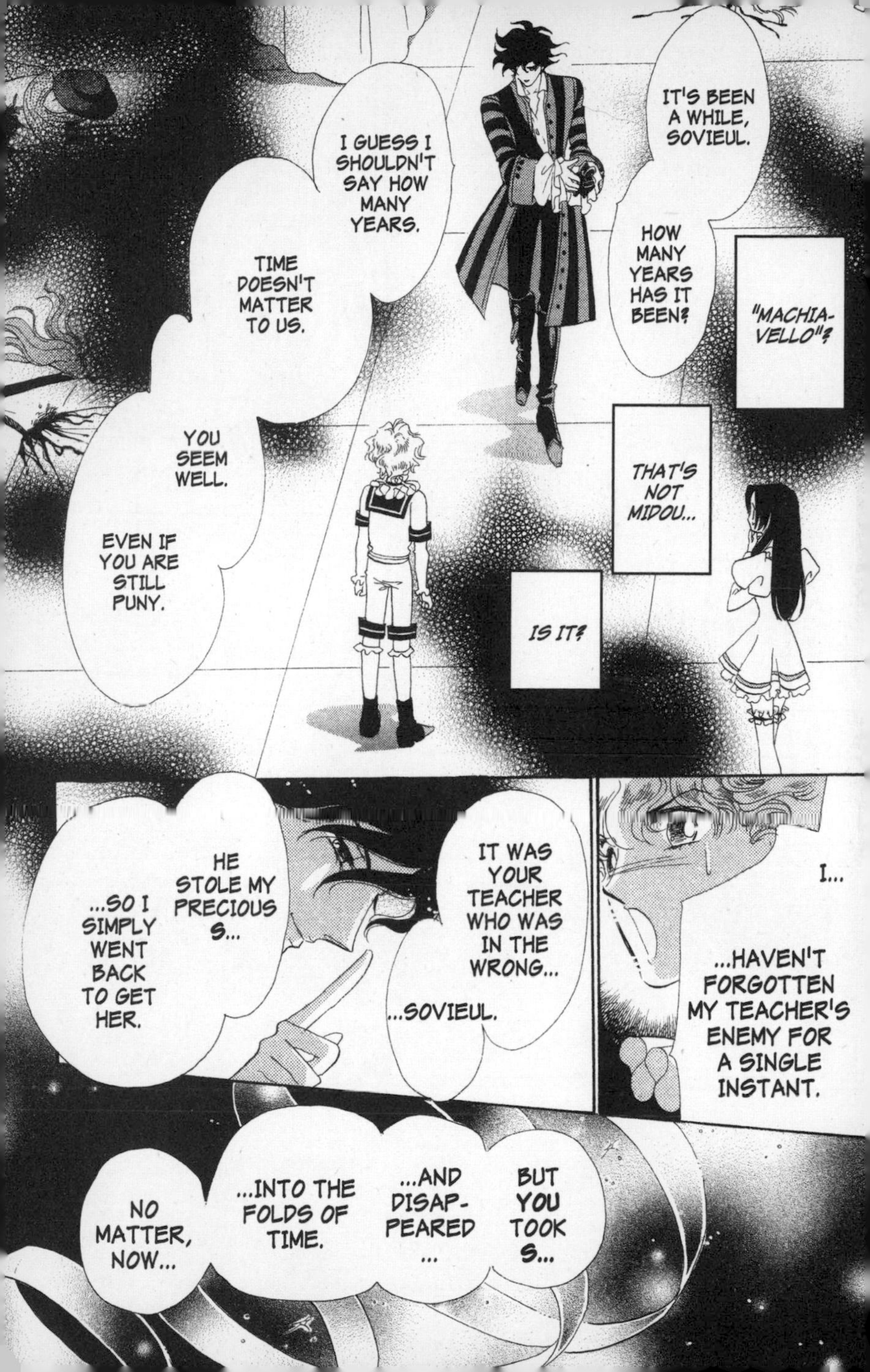
IT'S BEEN A WHILE, SOVIEUL.
HOW MANY YEARS HAS IT BEEN?
I GUESS I SHOULDN'T SAY HOW MANY YEARS.
TIME DOESN'T MATTER TO US.
YOU SEEM WELL.
EVEN IF YOU ARE STILL PUNY.
"MACHIA-VELLO"?
THAT'S NOT MIDOU...
IS IT?
I...
...HAVEN'T FORGOTTEN MY TEACHER'S ENEMY FOR A SINGLE INSTANT.
IT WAS YOUR TEACHER WHO WAS IN THE WRONG...
...SOVIEUL.
HE STOLE MY PRECIOUS S...
...SO I SIMPLY WENT BACK TO GET HER.
BUT YOU TOOK S...
...AND DISAP-PEARED ...
...INTO THE FOLDS OF TIME.
NO MATTER, NOW...

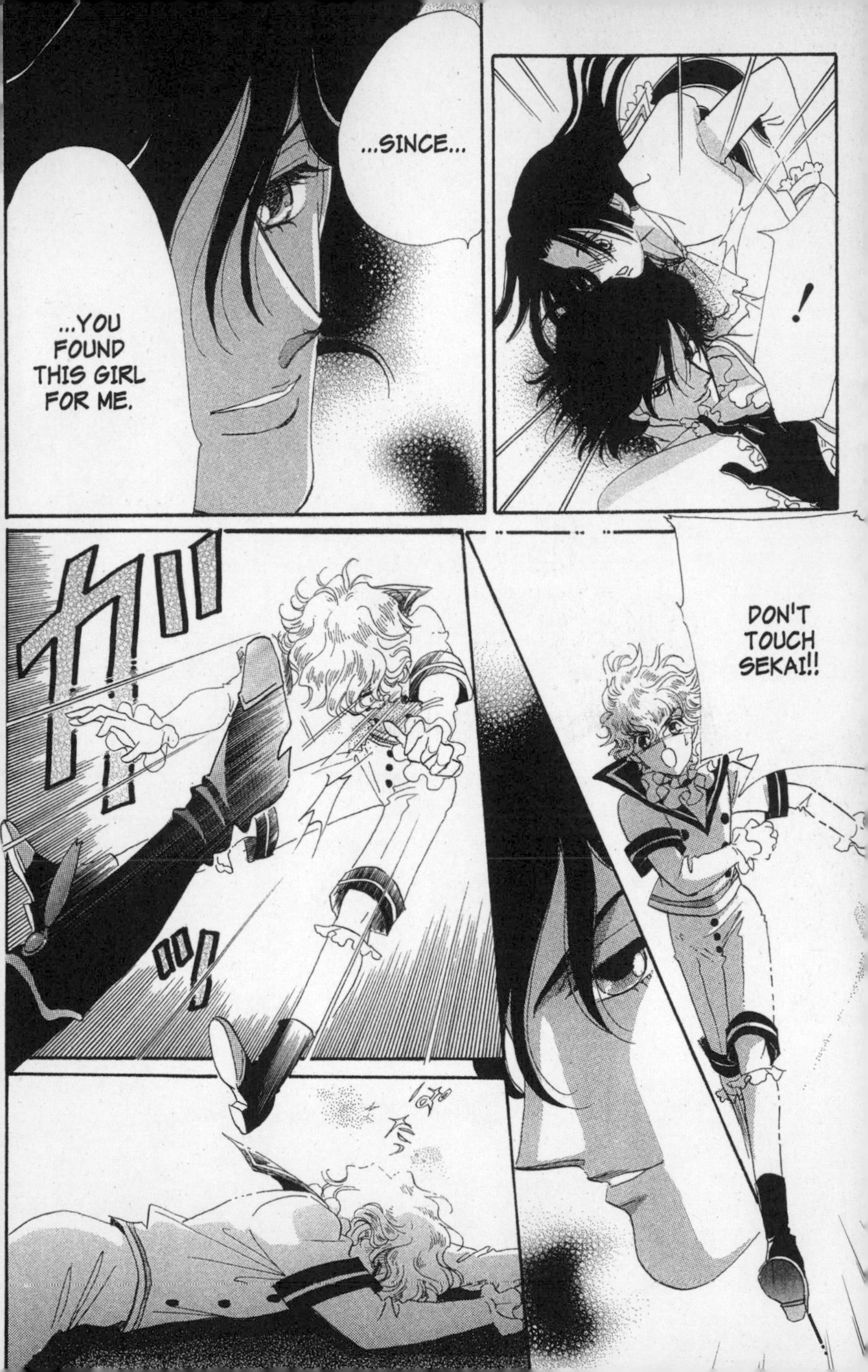
!
...SINCE...
...YOU FOUND THIS GIRL FOR ME.
DON'T TOUCH SEKAI!!

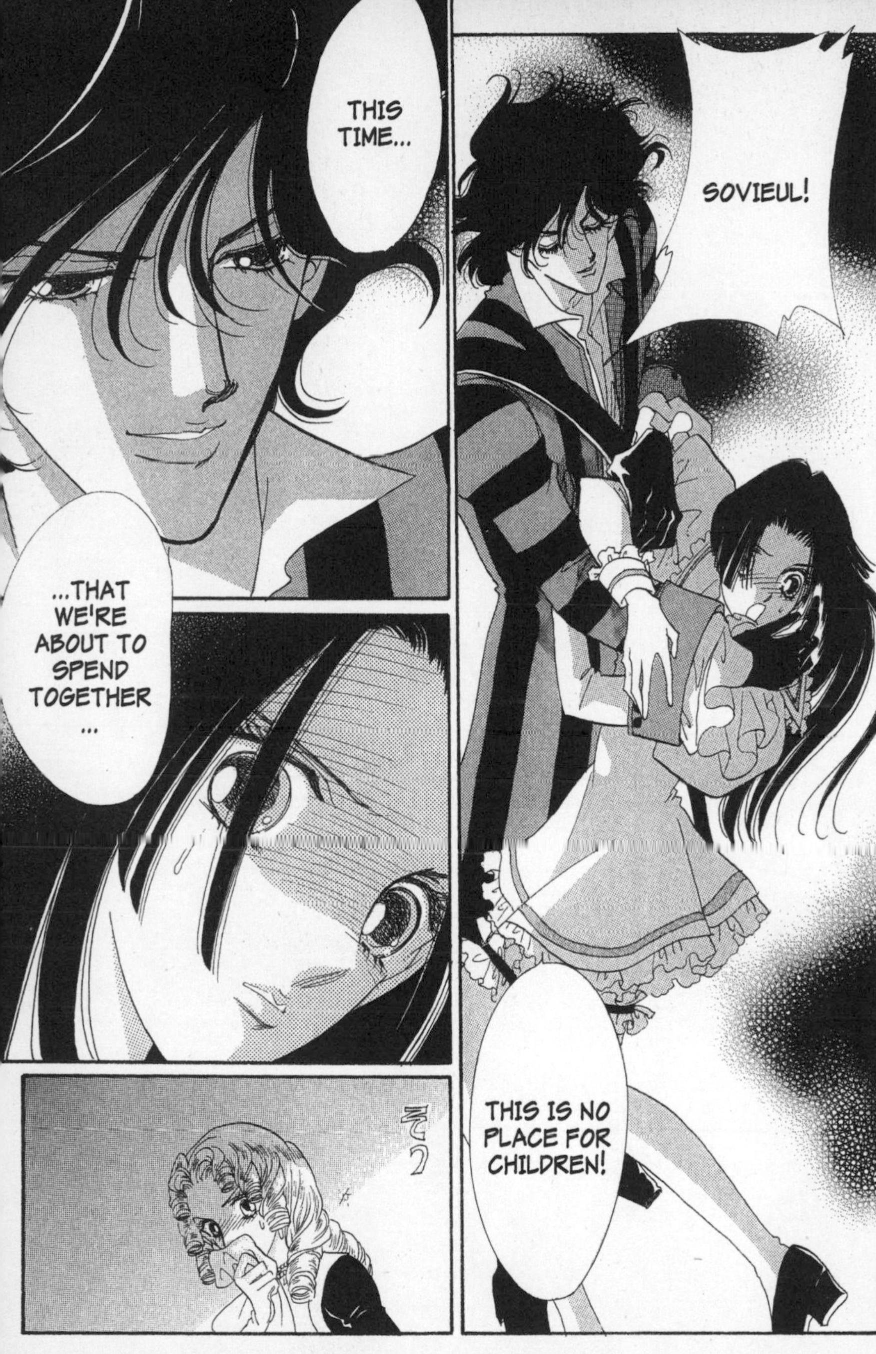
SOVIEUL!
THIS IS NO PLACE FOR CHILDREN!
THIS TIME...
...THAT WE'RE ABOUT TO SPEND TOGETHER ...

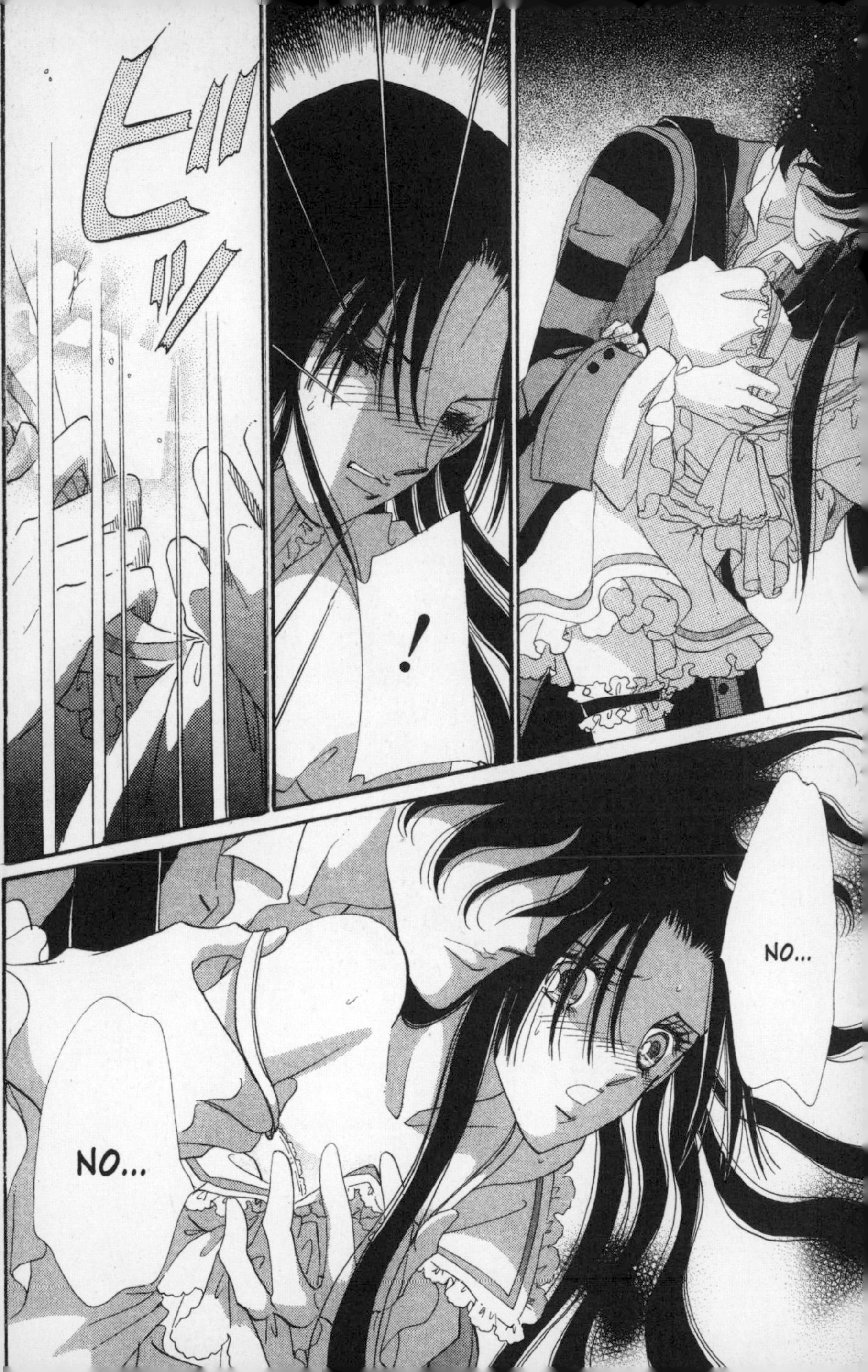
!
ビッ
NO...
NO...

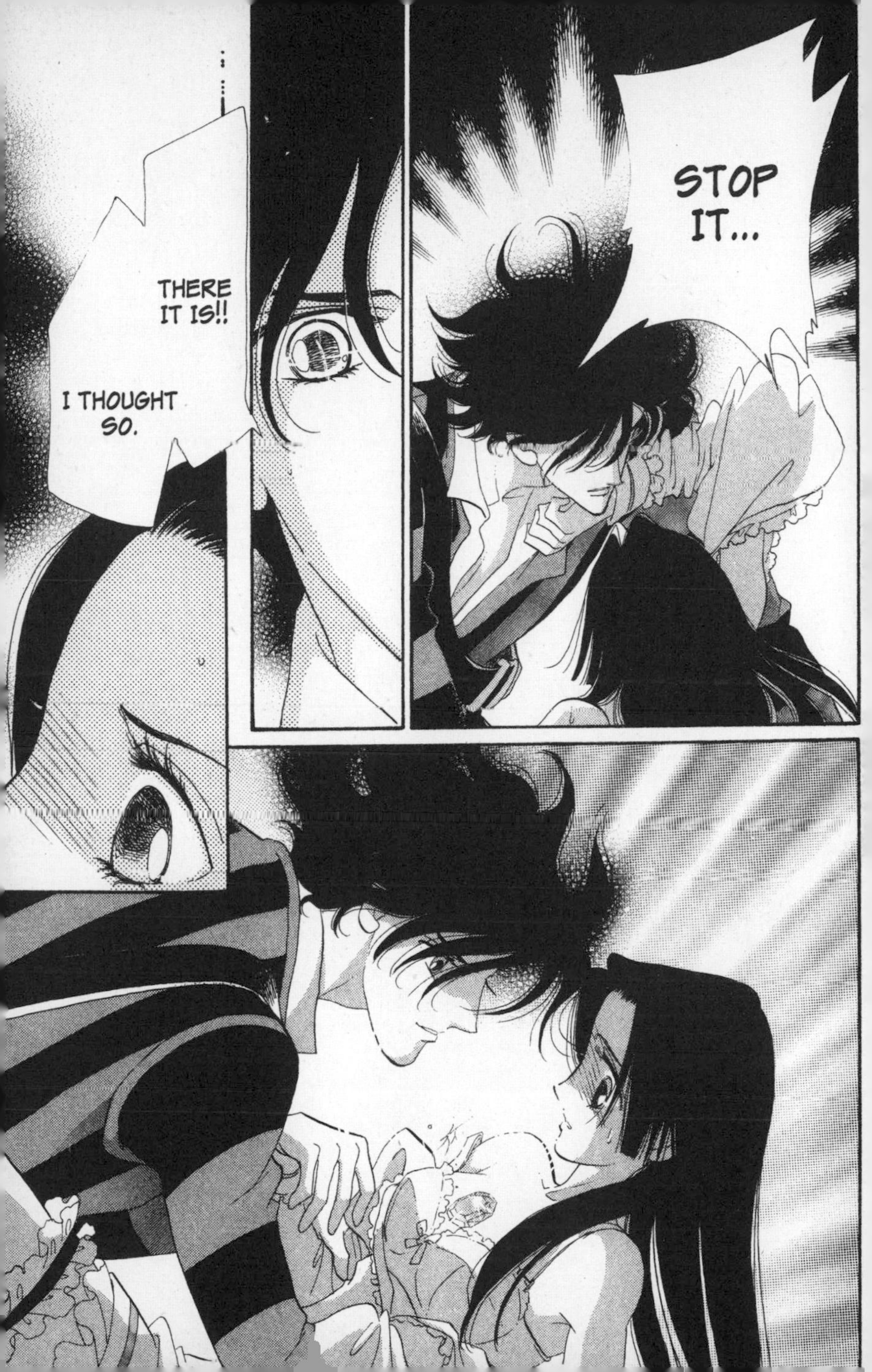
STOP IT...
THERE IT IS!!
I THOUGHT SO.

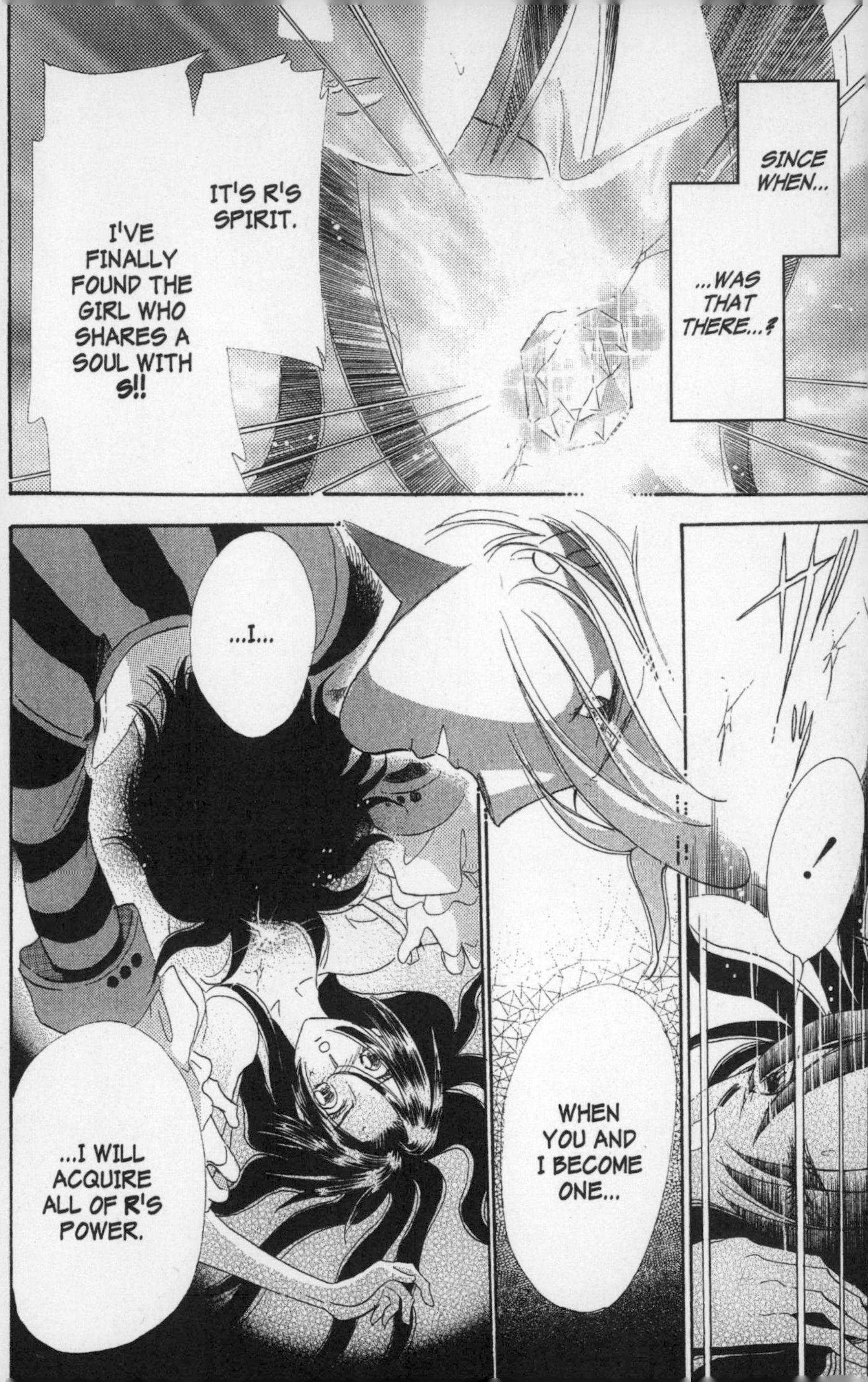
SINCE WHEN...
...WAS THAT THERE...?
IT'S R'S SPIRIT.
I'VE FINALLY FOUND THE GIRL WHO SHARES A SOUL WITH S!!
!
...I...
WHEN YOU AND I BECOME ONE...
...I WILL ACQUIRE ALL OF R'S POWER.

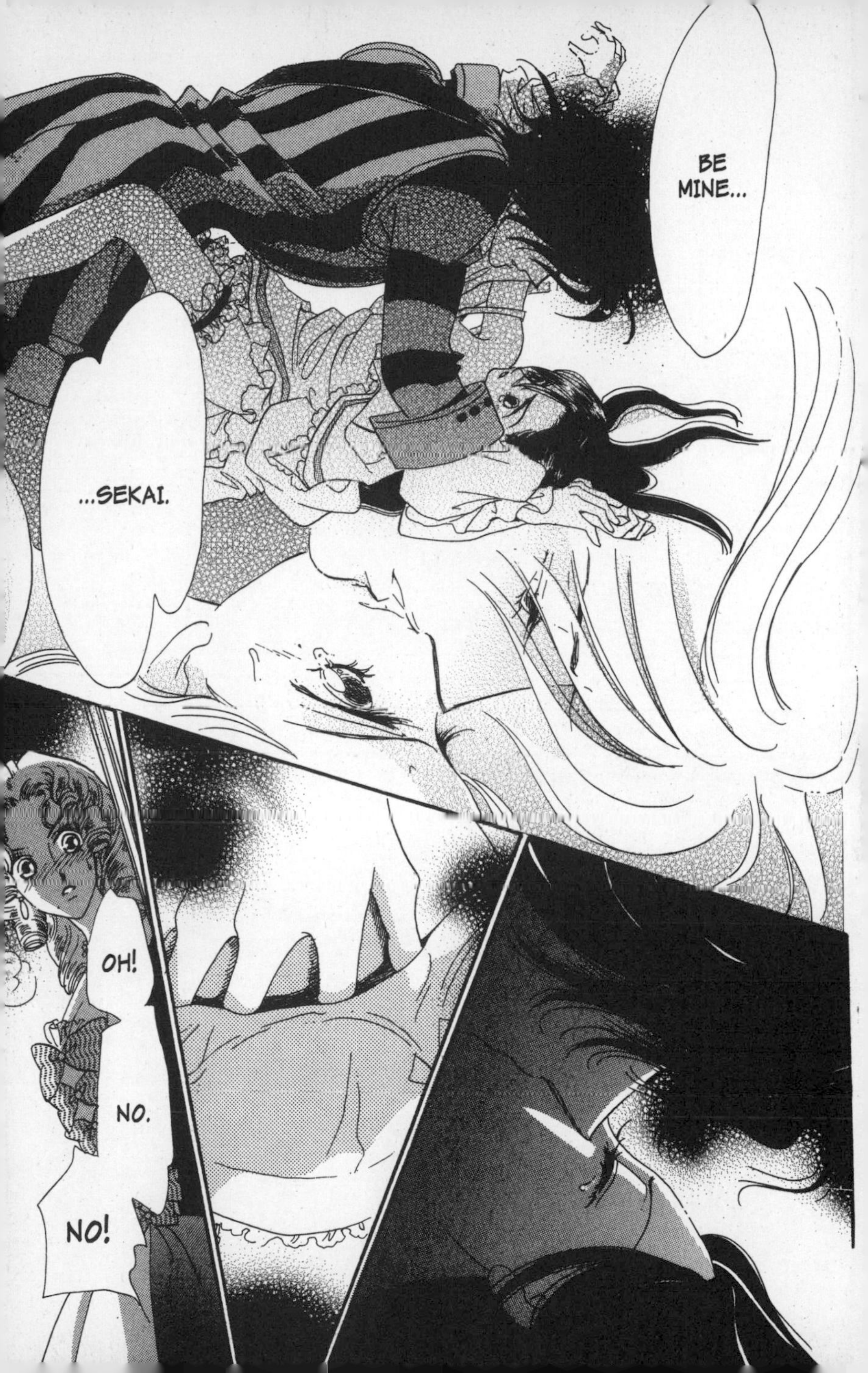
BE MINE...
...SEKAI.
OH!
NO.
NO!

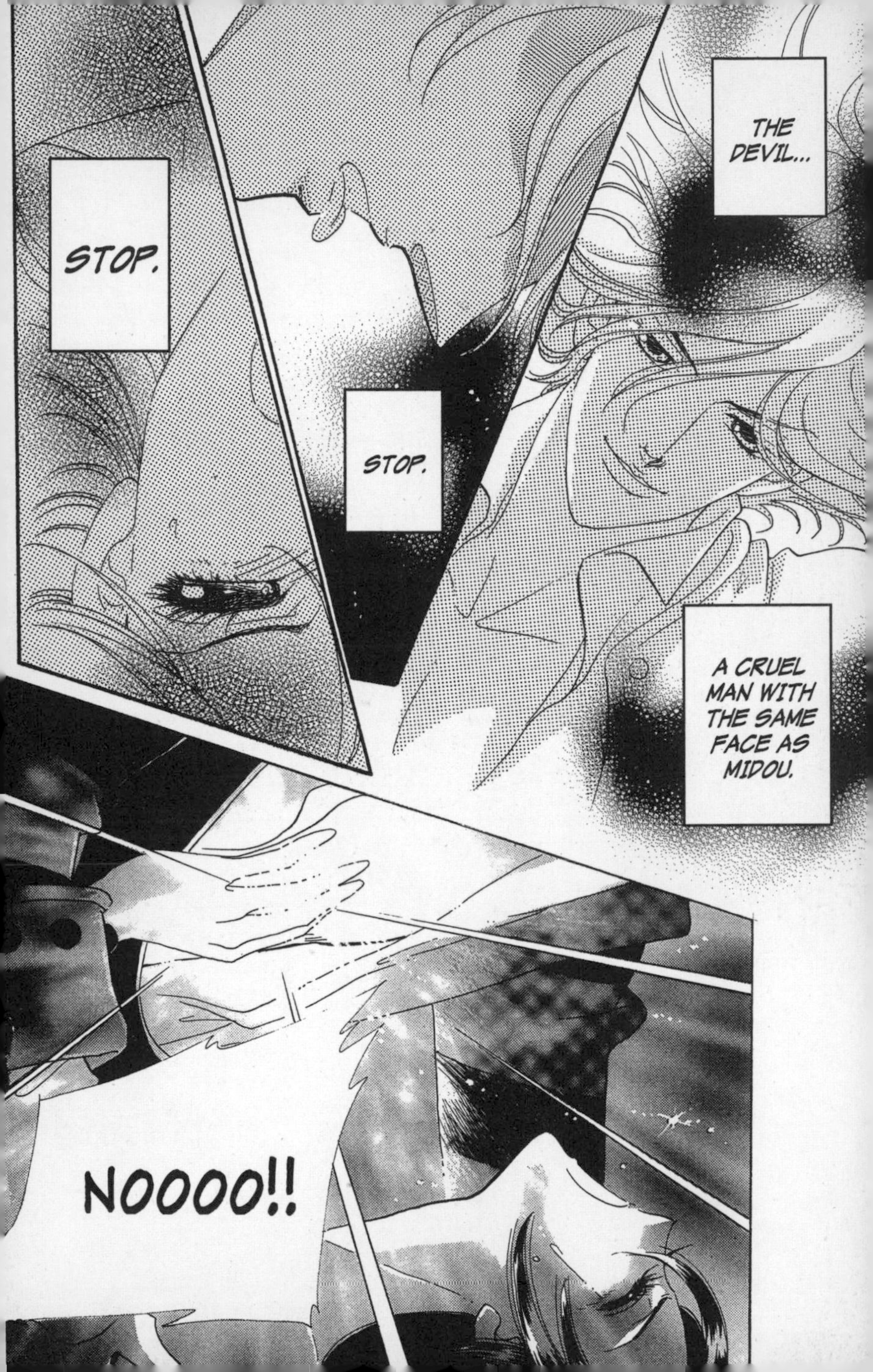
THE DEVIL...
A CRUEL MAN WITH THE SAME FACE AS MIDOU.
STOP.
STOP.
NOOOO!!

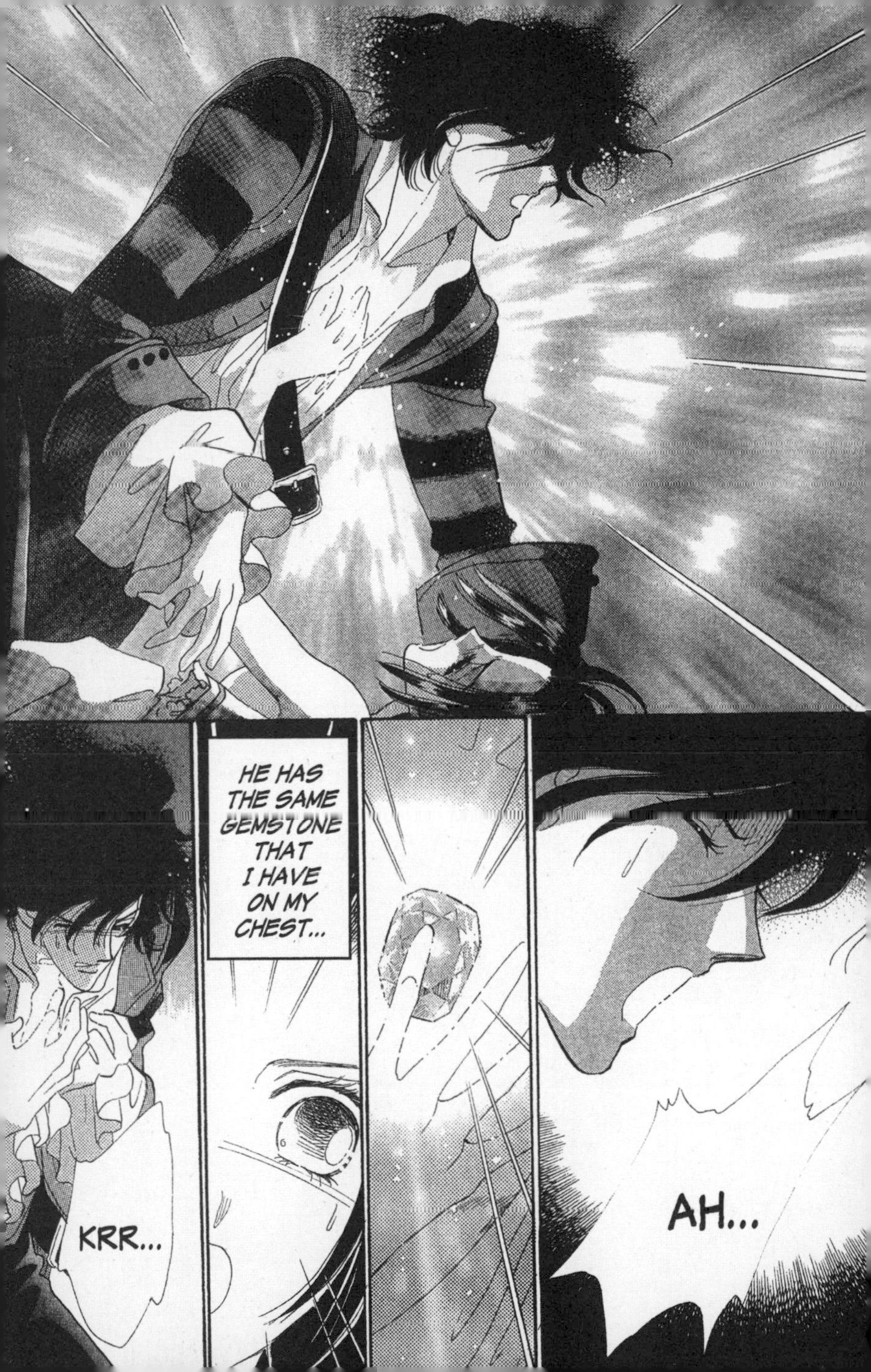
AH...
HE HAS THE SAME GEMSTONE THAT I HAVE ON MY CHEST...
KRR...

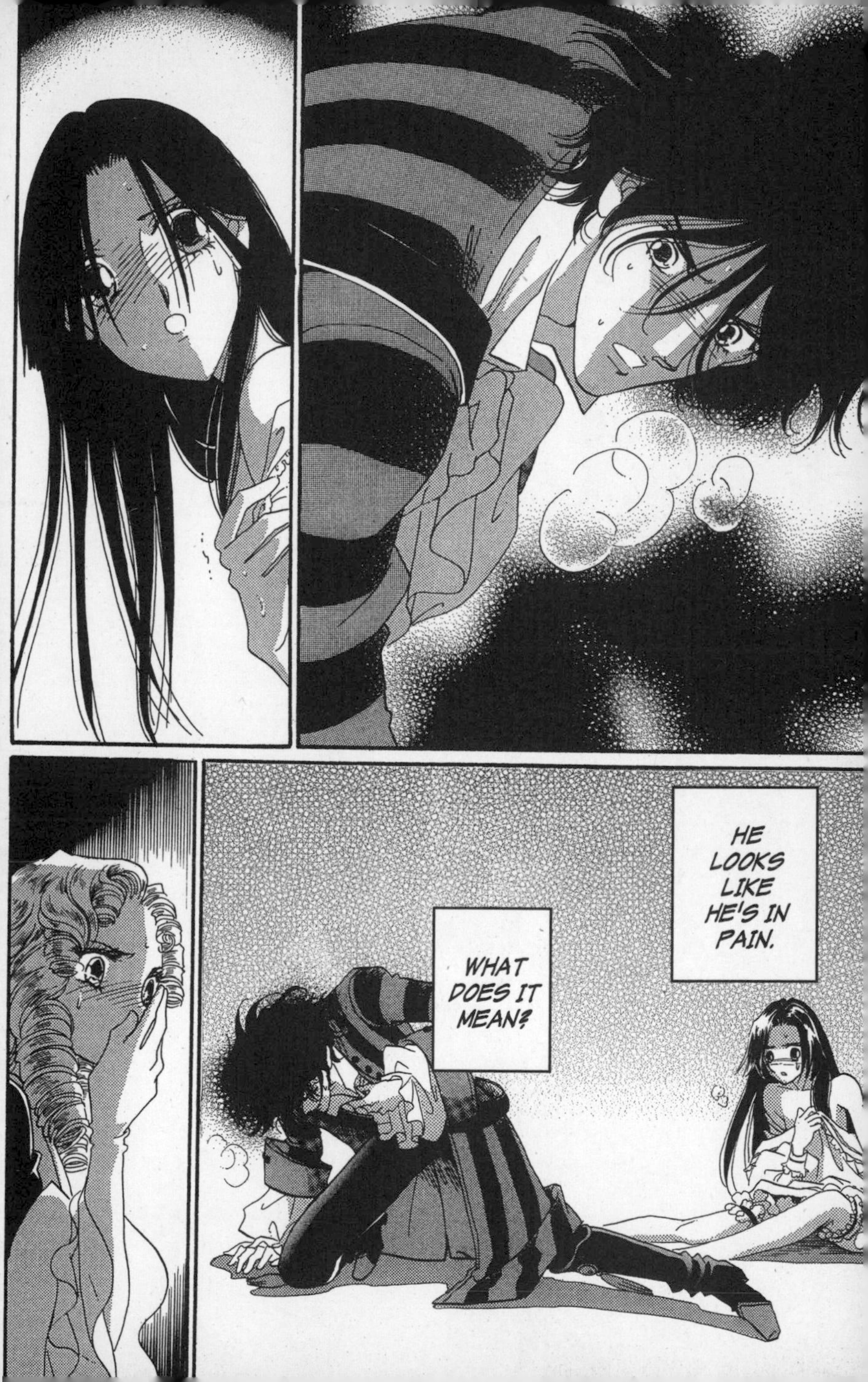
HE LOOKS LIKE HE'S IN PAIN.
WHAT DOES IT MEAN?

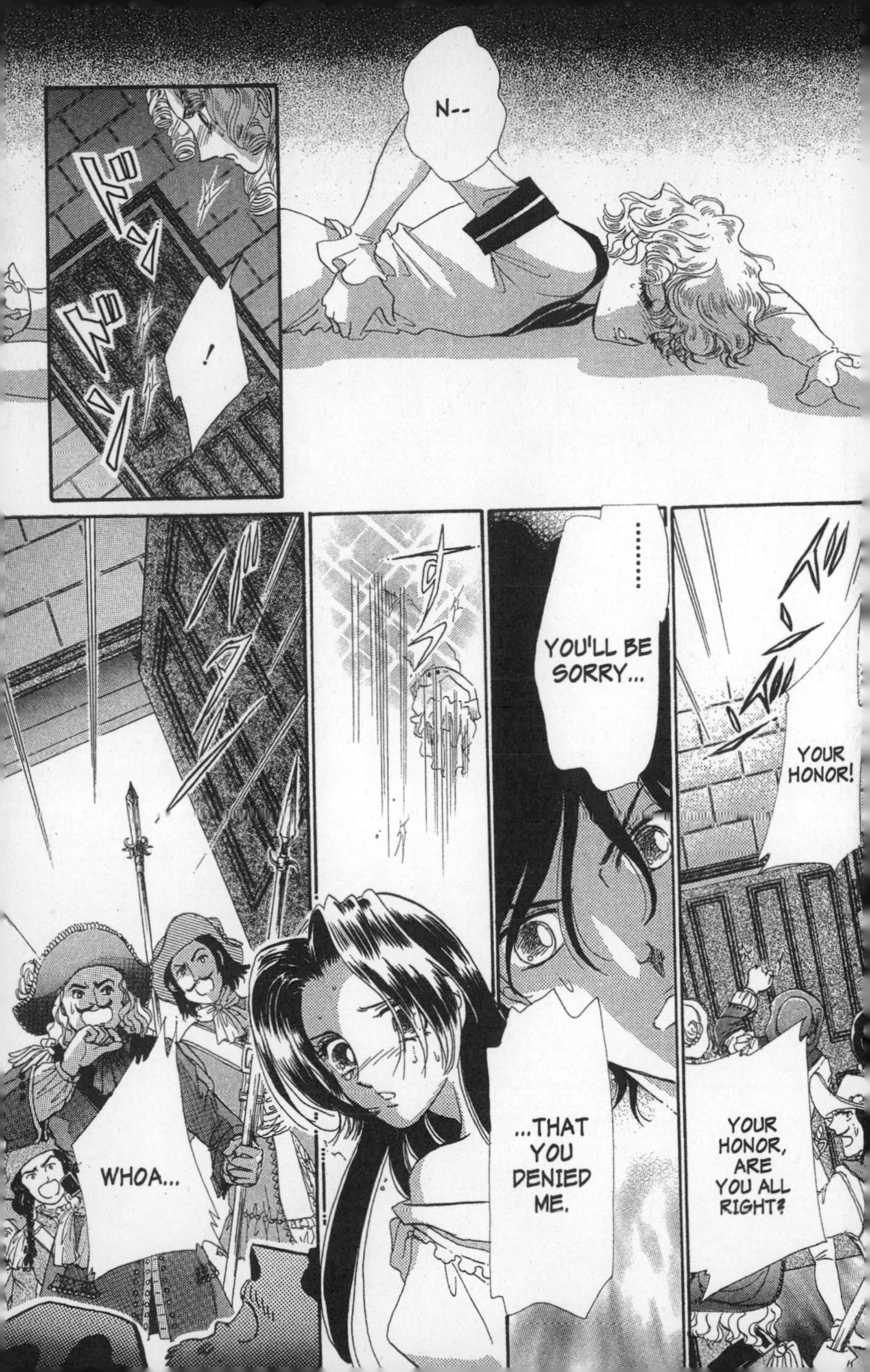
N--
!
YOUR HONOR!
YOUR HONOR, ARE YOU ALL RIGHT?
......
YOU'LL BE SORRY...
...THAT YOU DENIED ME.
WHOA...

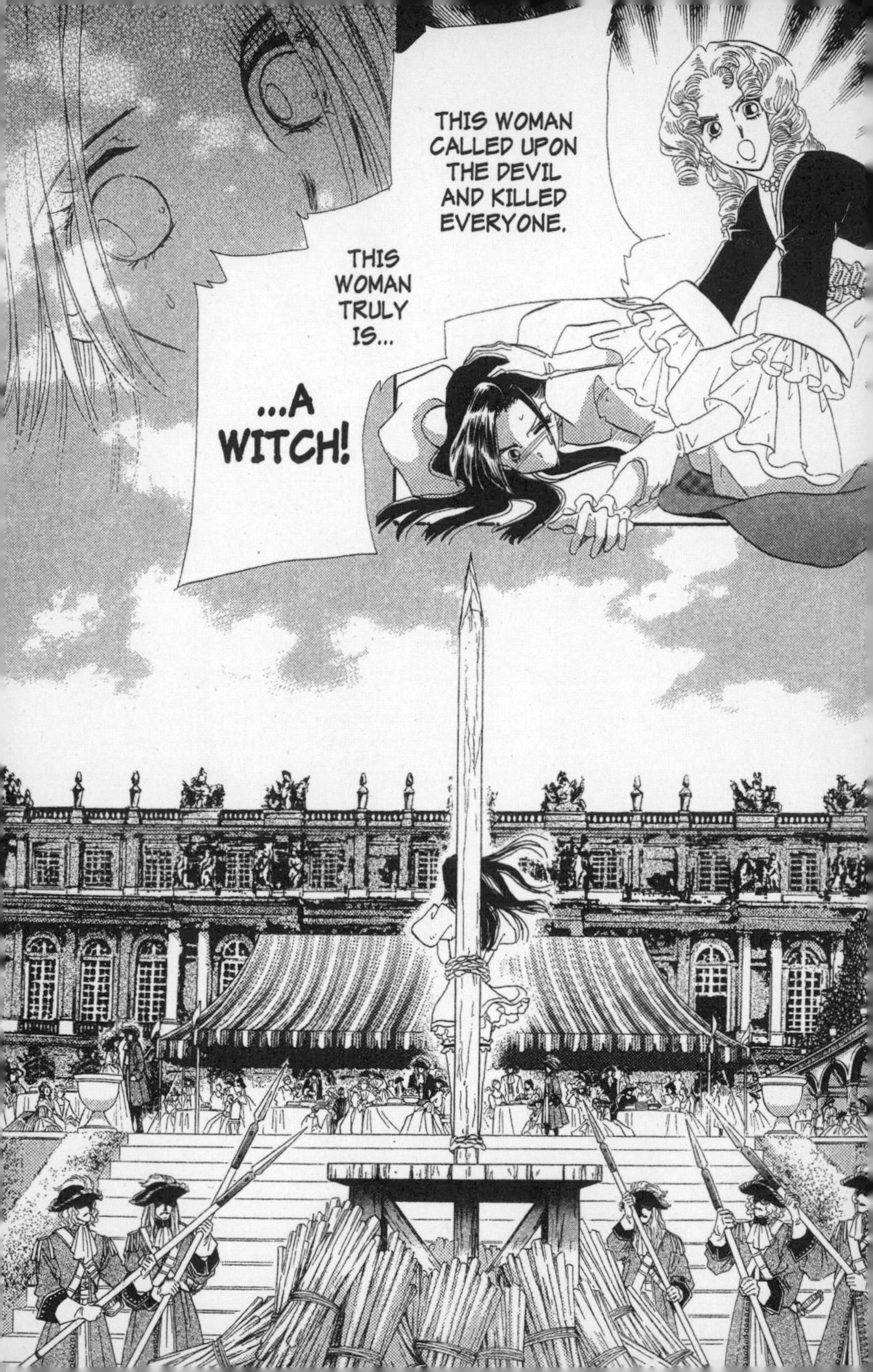
THIS WOMAN CALLED UPON THE DEVIL AND KILLED EVERYONE.
THIS WOMAN TRULY IS...
...A WITCH!

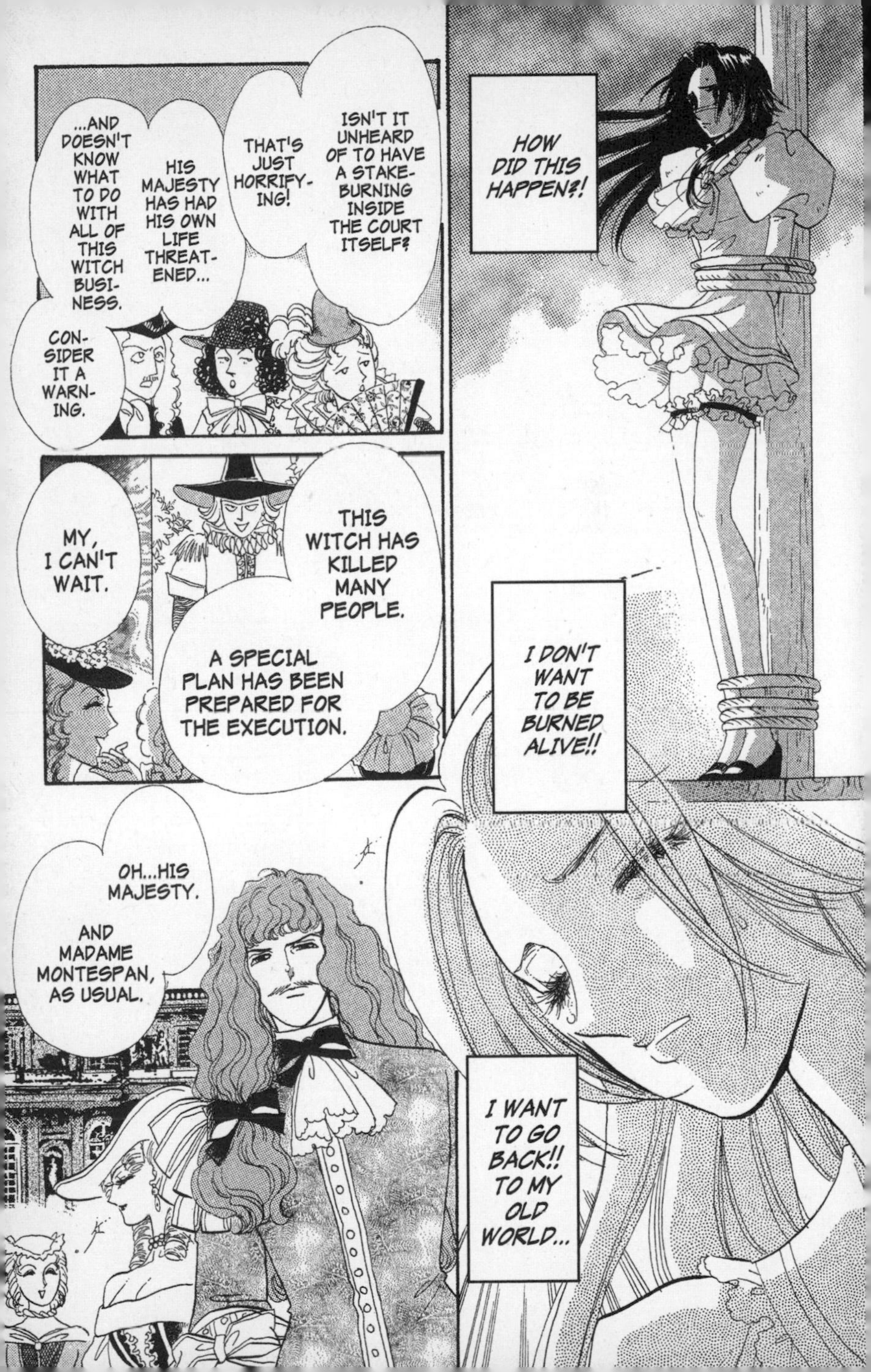
HOW DID THIS HAPPEN?!
I DON'T WANT TO BE BURNED ALIVE!!
I WANT TO GO BACK!! TO MY OLD WORLD...
ISN'T IT UNHEARD OF TO HAVE A STAKE-BURNING INSIDE THE COURT ITSELF?
THAT'S JUST HORRIFYING!
HIS MAJESTY HAS HAD HIS OWN LIFE THREATENED...
...AND DOESN'T KNOW WHAT TO DO WITH ALL OF THIS WITCH BUSINESS.
CONSIDER IT A WARNING.
THIS WITCH HAS KILLED MANY PEOPLE.
A SPECIAL PLAN HAS BEEN PREPARED FOR THE EXECUTION.
MY, I CAN'T WAIT.
OH...HIS MAJESTY.
AND MADAME MONTESPAN, AS USUAL.

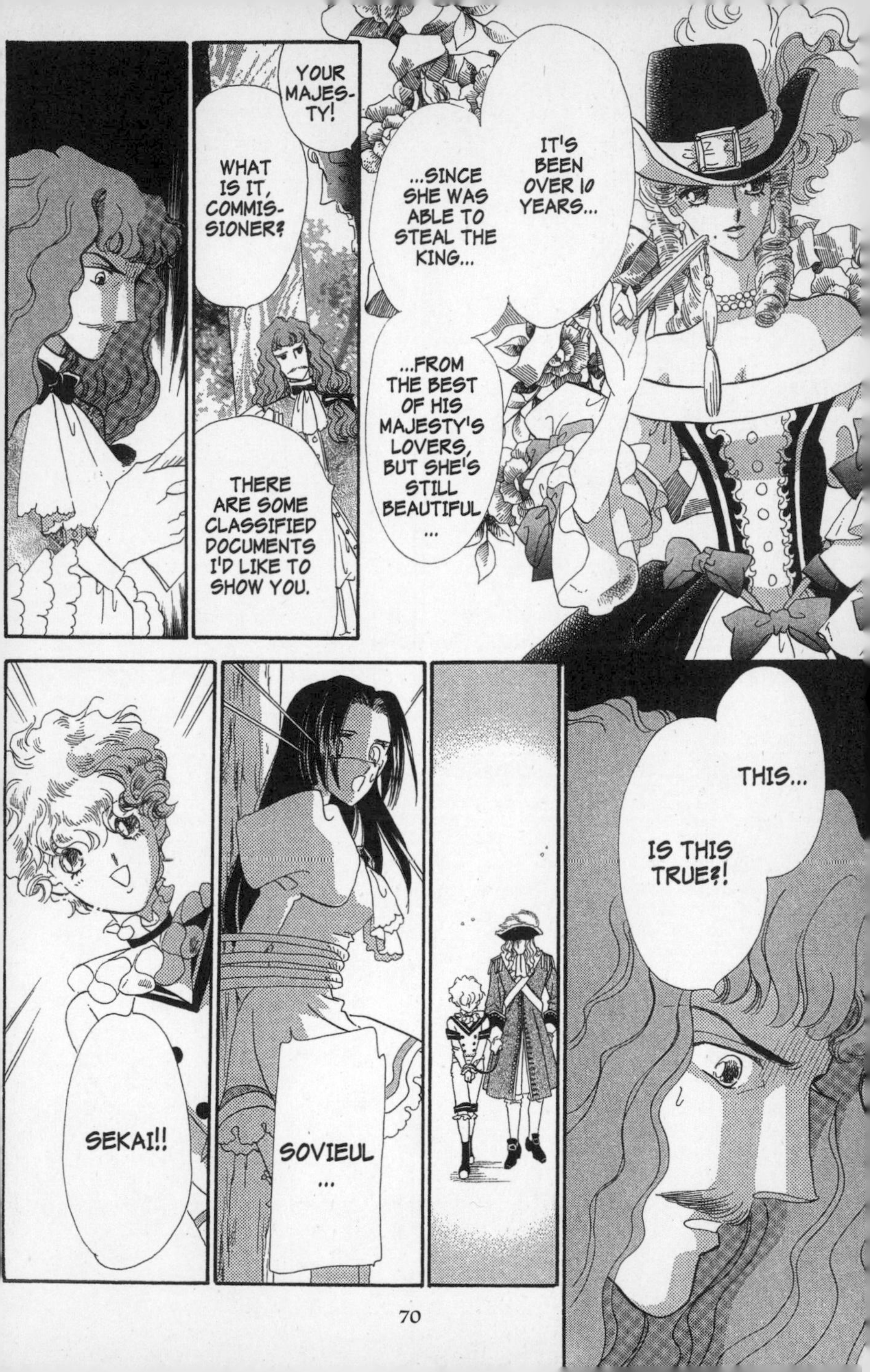
IT'S BEEN OVER 10 YEARS...
...SINCE SHE WAS ABLE TO STEAL THE KING...
...FROM THE BEST OF HIS MAJESTY'S LOVERS, BUT SHE'S STILL BEAUTIFUL ...
YOUR MAJESTY!
WHAT IS IT, COMMISSIONER?
THERE ARE SOME CLASSIFIED DOCUMENTS I'D LIKE TO SHOW YOU.
THIS...
IS THIS TRUE?!
SOVIEUL ...
SEKAI!!

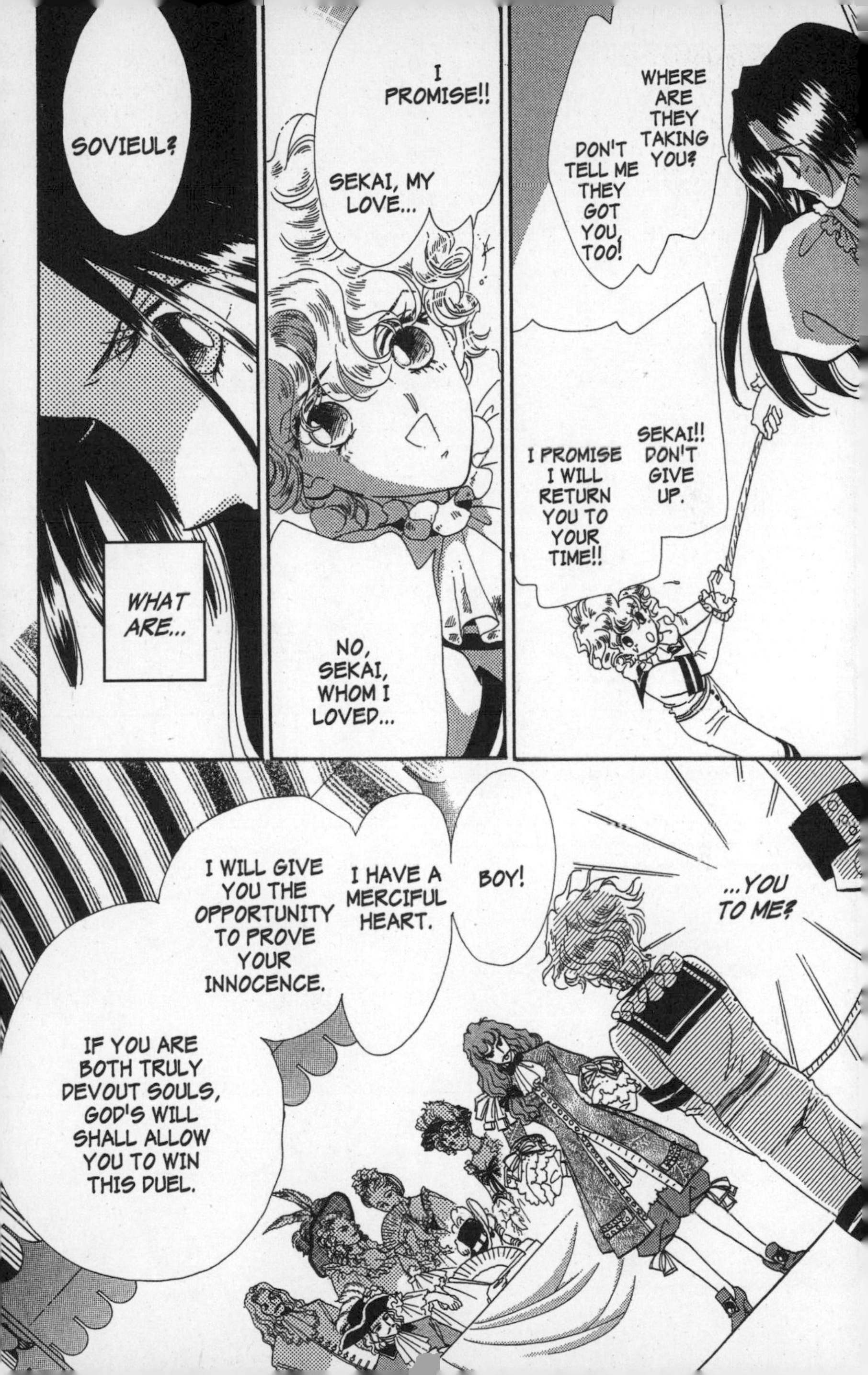
WHERE ARE THEY TAKING YOU?
DON'T TELL ME THEY GOT YOU, TOO!
SEKAI!! DON'T GIVE UP.
I PROMISE I WILL RETURN YOU TO YOUR TIME!!
I PROMISE!!
SEKAI, MY LOVE...
NO, SEKAI, WHOM I LOVED...
SOVIEUL?
WHAT ARE...
...YOU TO ME?
BOY!
I HAVE A MERCIFUL HEART.
I WILL GIVE YOU THE OPPORTUNITY TO PROVE YOUR INNOCENCE.
IF YOU ARE BOTH TRULY DEVOUT SOULS, GOD'S WILL SHALL ALLOW YOU TO WIN THIS DUEL.

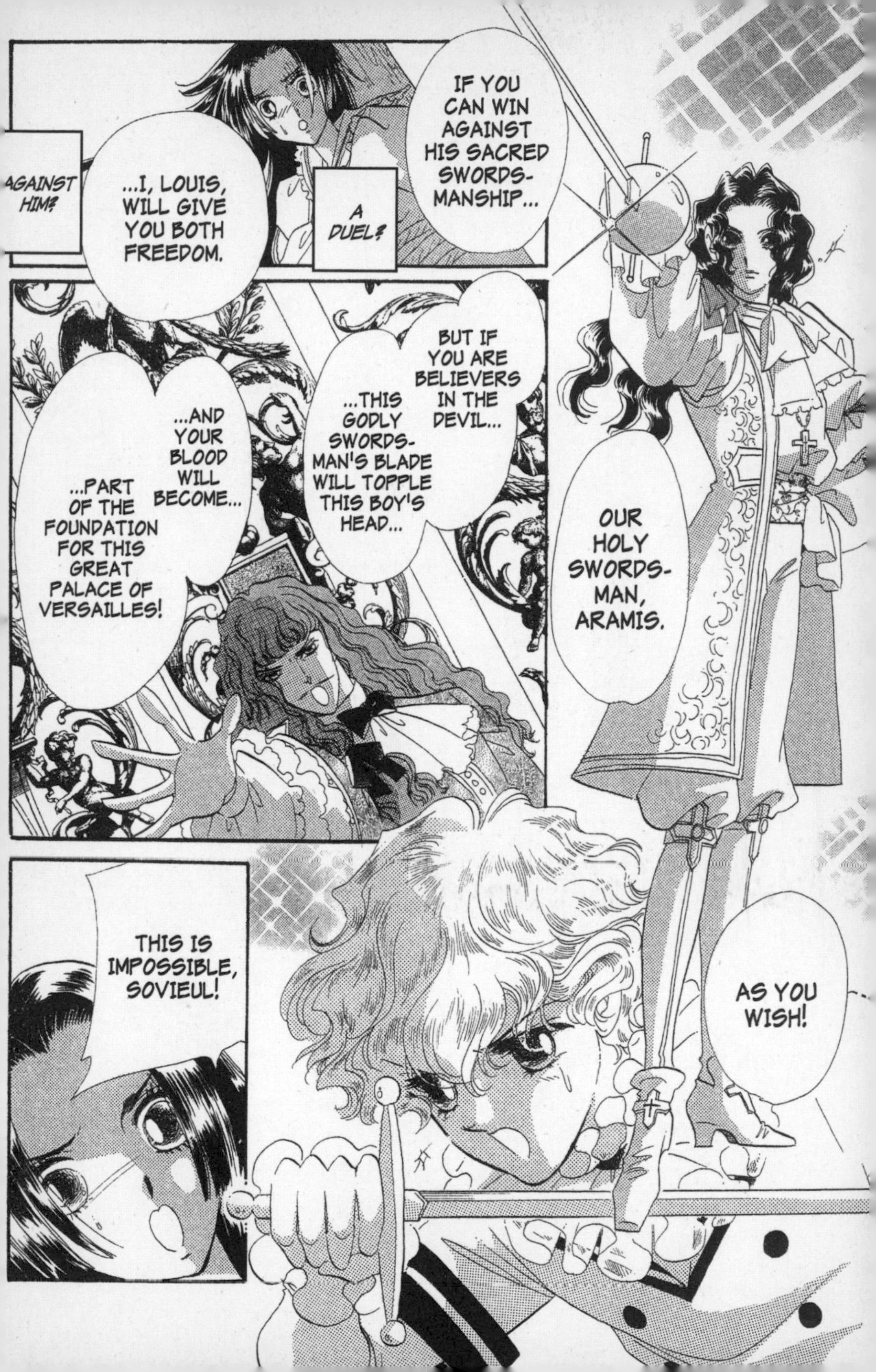
IF YOU CAN WIN AGAINST HIS SACRED SWORDS-MANSHIP...
A DUEL?
...I, LOUIS, WILL GIVE YOU BOTH FREEDOM.
AGAINST HIM?
OUR HOLY SWORDS-MAN, ARAMIS.
BUT IF YOU ARE BELIEVERS IN THE DEVIL...
...THIS GODLY SWORDS-MAN'S BLADE WILL TOPPLE THIS BOY'S HEAD...
...AND YOUR BLOOD WILL BECOME...
...PART OF THE FOUNDATION FOR THIS GREAT PALACE OF VERSAILLES!
AS YOU WISH!
THIS IS IMPOSSIBLE, SOVIEUL!

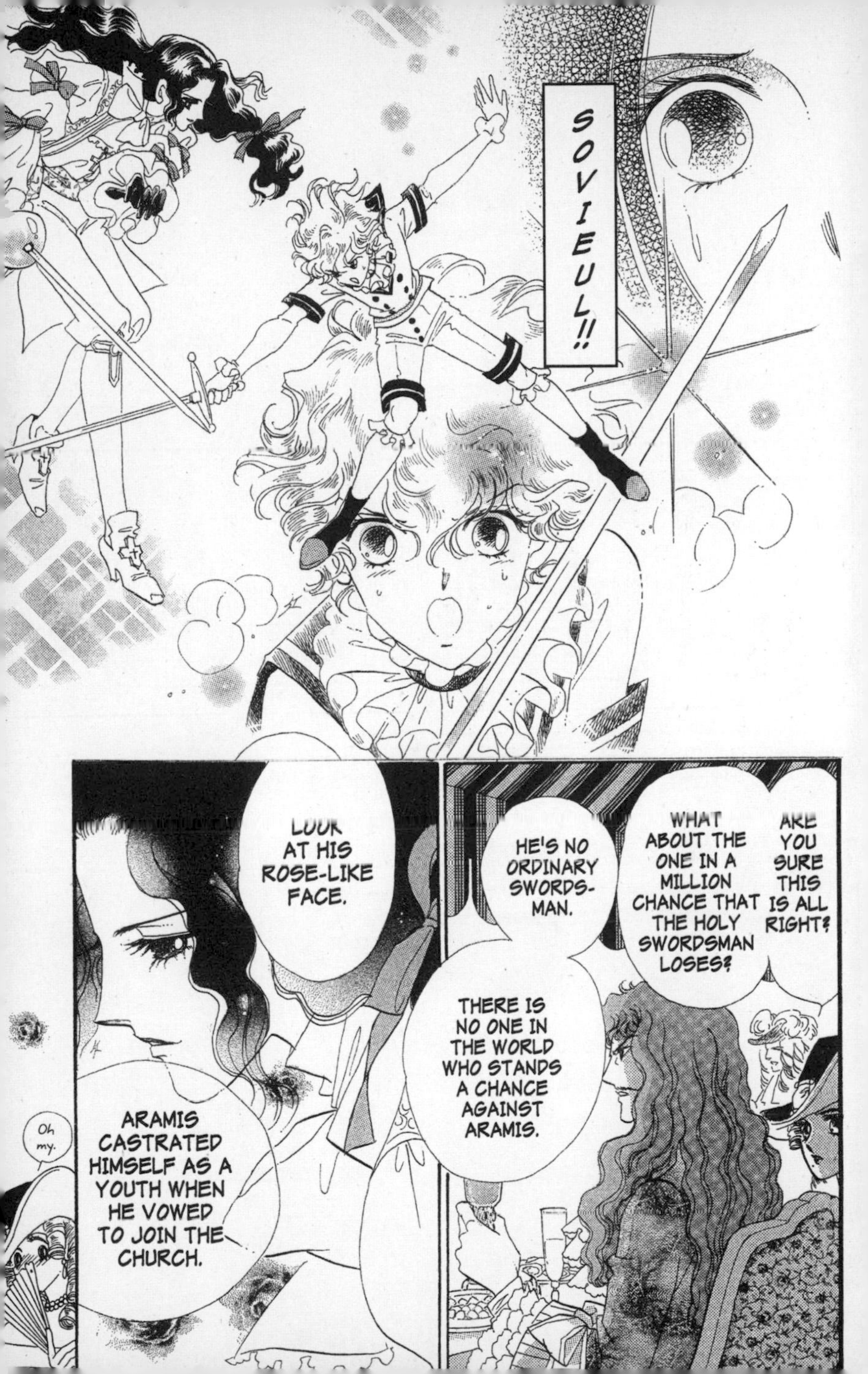
SOVIEUL!!
ARE YOU SURE THIS IS ALL RIGHT?
WHAT ABOUT THE ONE IN A MILLION CHANCE THAT THE HOLY SWORDSMAN LOSES?
HE'S NO ORDINARY SWORDS-MAN.
THERE IS NO ONE IN THE WORLD WHO STANDS A CHANCE AGAINST ARAMIS.
LOOK AT HIS ROSE-LIKE FACE.
ARAMIS CASTRATED HIMSELF AS A YOUTH WHEN HE VOWED TO JOIN THE CHURCH.
Oh my.

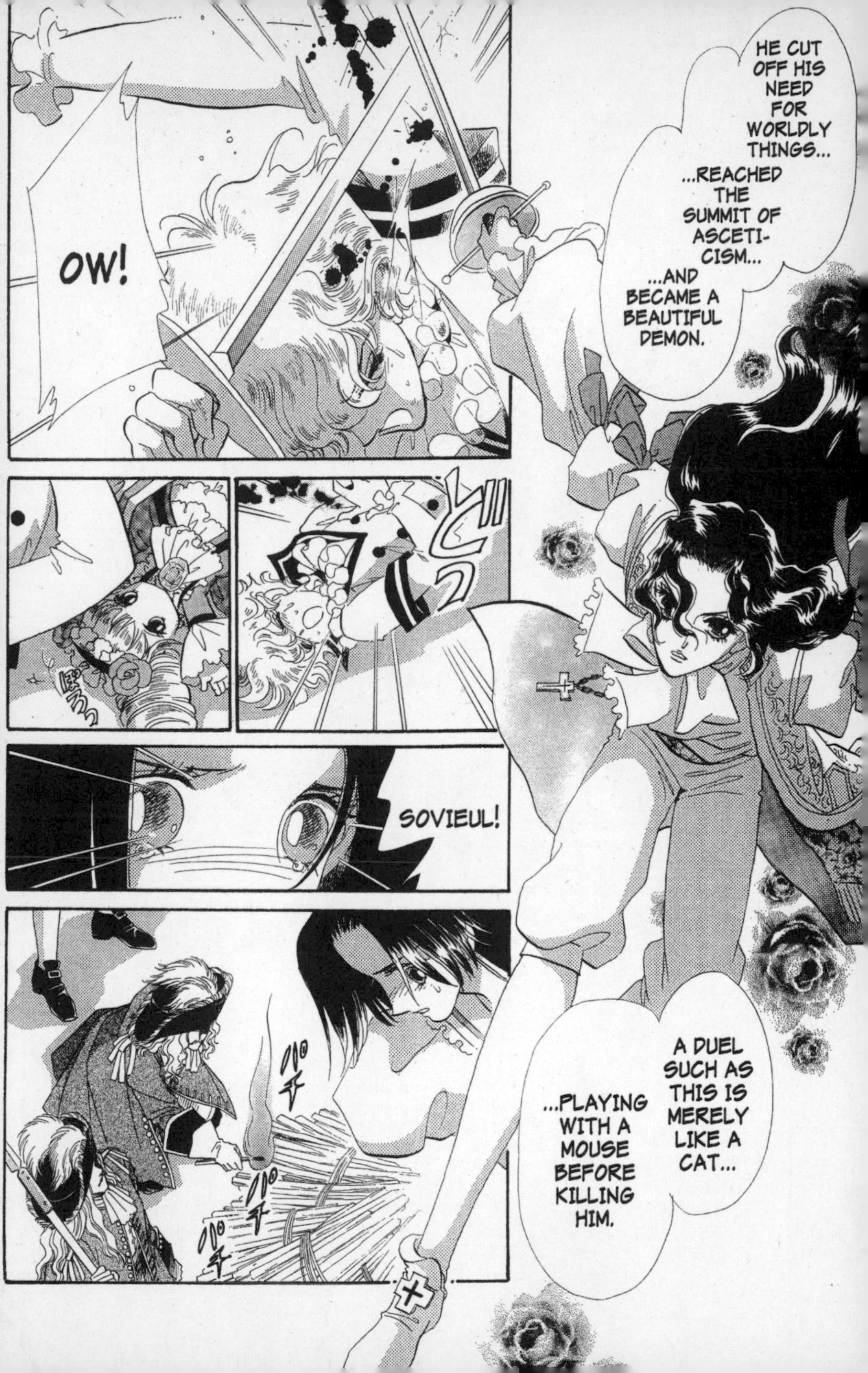
HE CUT OFF HIS NEED FOR WORLDLY THINGS...
...REACHED THE SUMMIT OF ASCETI-CISM...
...AND BECAME A BEAUTIFUL DEMON.
OW!
SOVIEUL!
A DUEL SUCH AS THIS IS MERELY LIKE A CAT...
...PLAYING WITH A MOUSE BEFORE KILLING HIM.

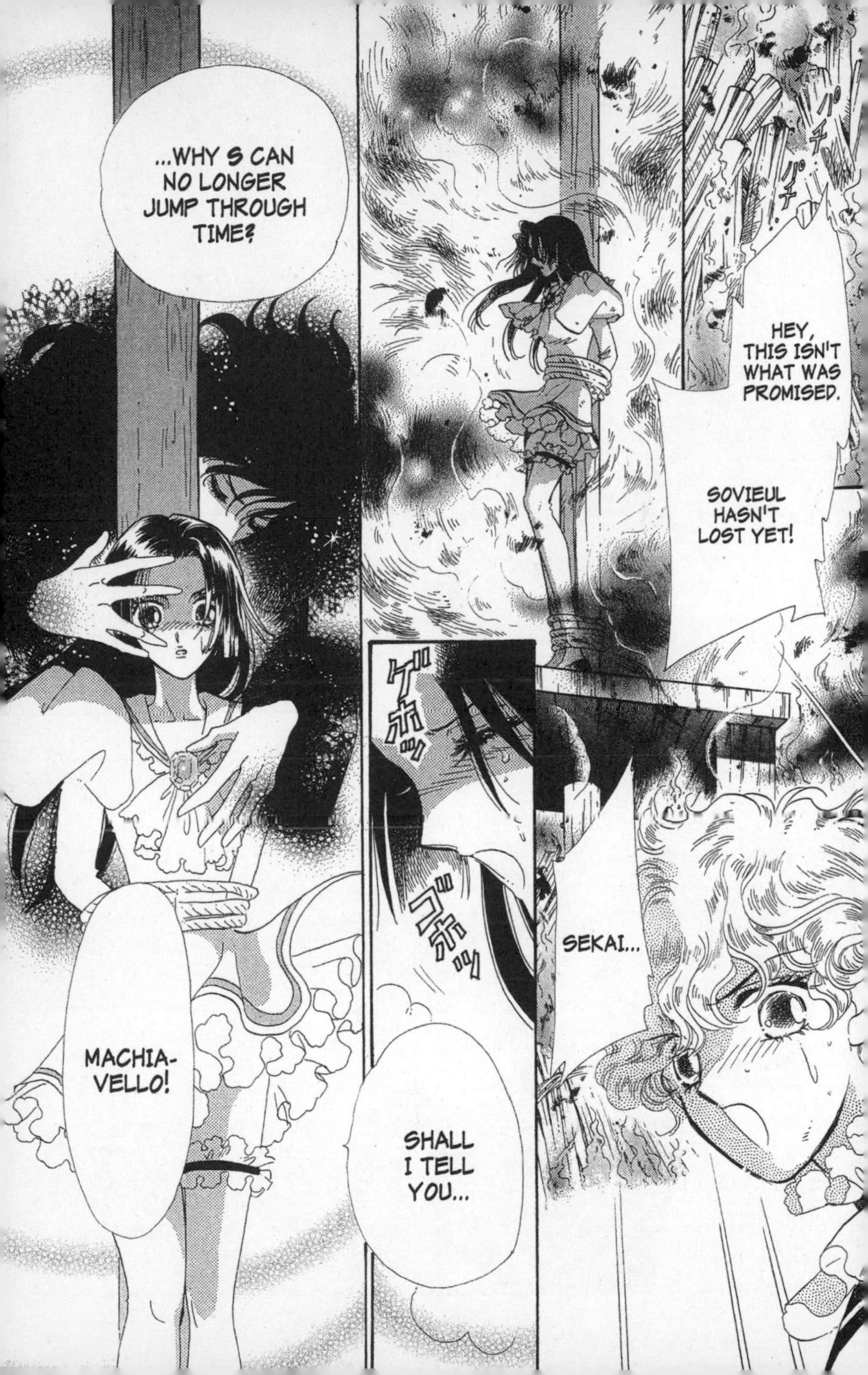
パチ
パチ
HEY, THIS ISN'T WHAT WAS PROMISED.
SOVIEUL HASN'T LOST YET!
SEKAI...
ゲホッ
ゴホッ
SHALL I TELL YOU...
...WHY S CAN NO LONGER JUMP THROUGH TIME?
MACHIA-VELLO!

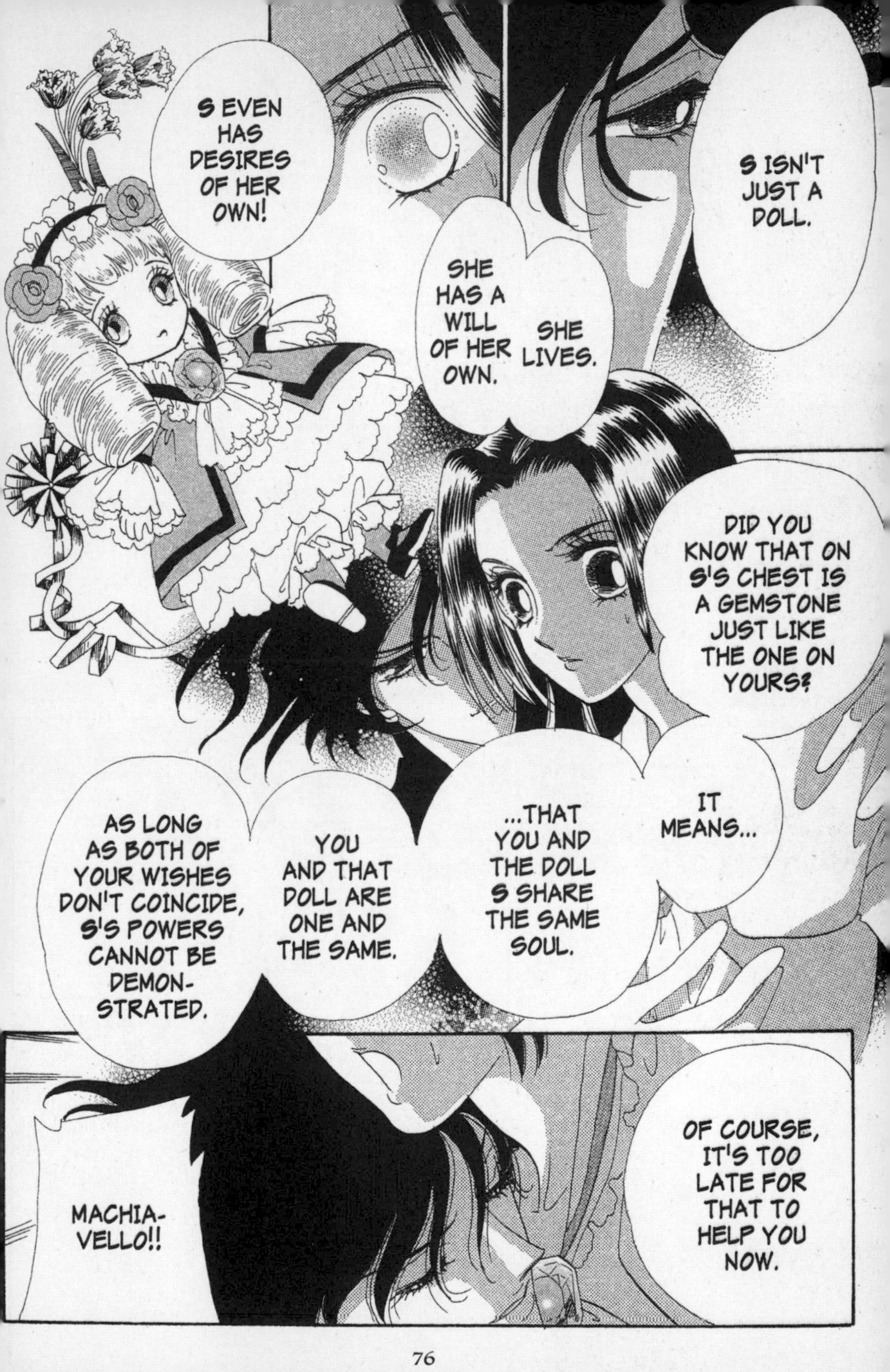
S ISN'T JUST A DOLL.
SHE HAS A WILL OF HER OWN.
SHE LIVES.
S EVEN HAS DESIRES OF HER OWN!
DID YOU KNOW THAT ON S'S CHEST IS A GEMSTONE JUST LIKE THE ONE ON YOURS?
IT MEANS...
...THAT YOU AND THE DOLL S SHARE THE SAME SOUL.
YOU AND THAT DOLL ARE ONE AND THE SAME.
AS LONG AS BOTH OF YOUR WISHES DON'T COINCIDE, S'S POWERS CANNOT BE DEMON-STRATED.
OF COURSE, IT'S TOO LATE FOR THAT TO HELP YOU NOW.
MACHIA-VELLO!!

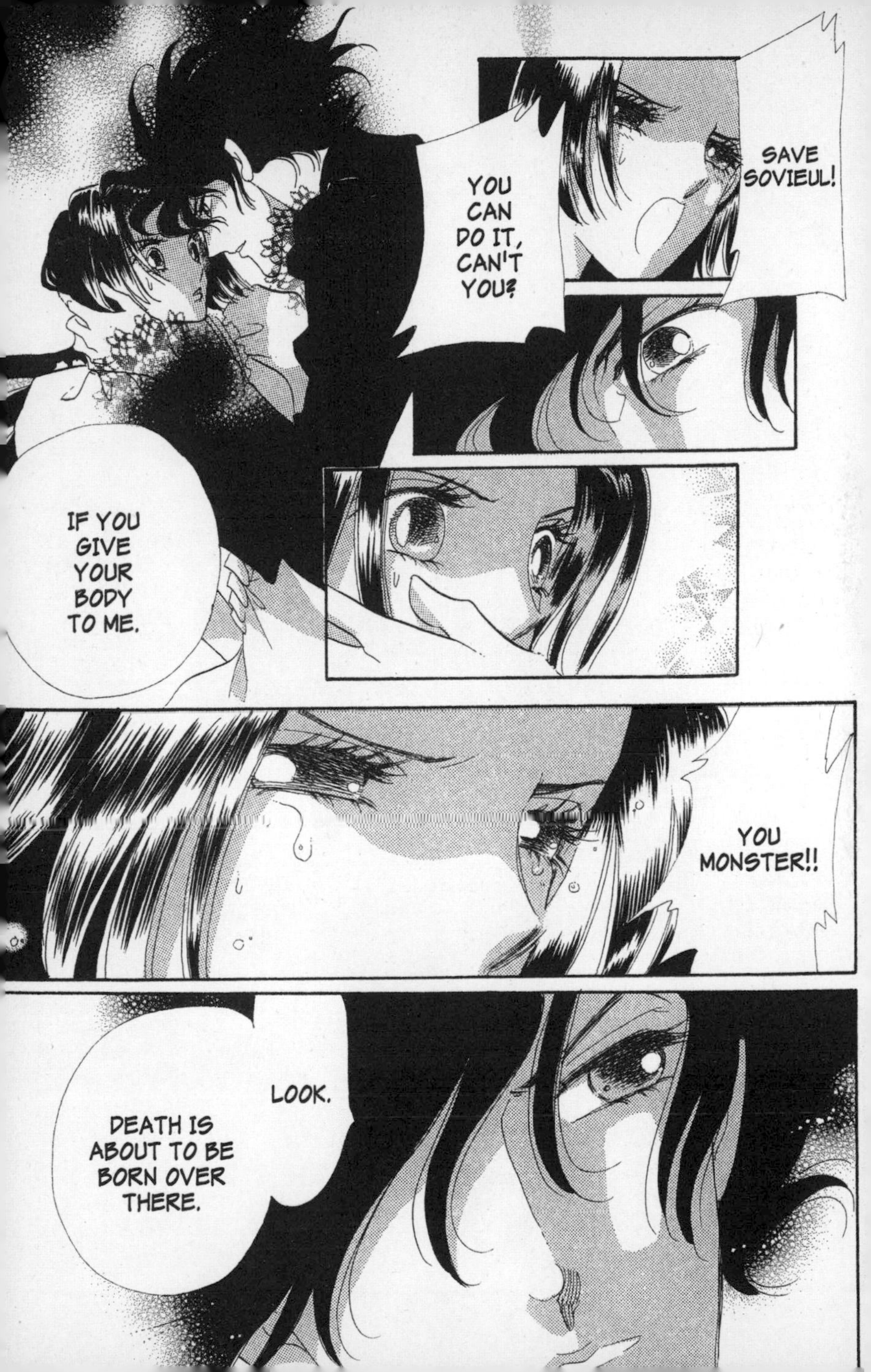
SAVE SOVIEUL!
YOU CAN DO IT, CAN'T YOU?
IF YOU GIVE YOUR BODY TO ME.
YOU MONSTER!!
LOOK.
DEATH IS ABOUT TO BE BORN OVER THERE.

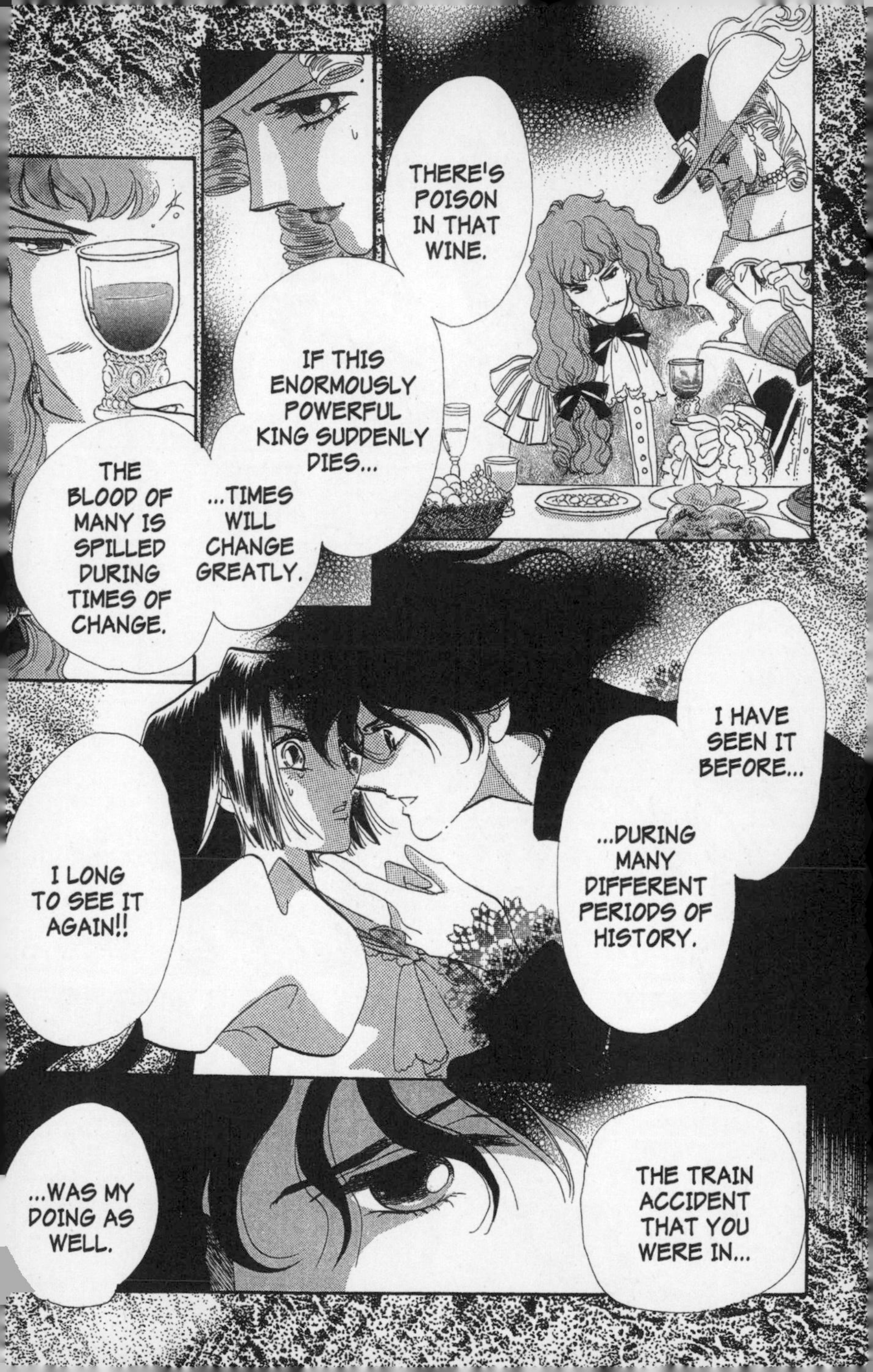
THERE'S POISON IN THAT WINE.
IF THIS ENORMOUSLY POWERFUL KING SUDDENLY DIES...
...TIMES WILL CHANGE GREATLY.
THE BLOOD OF MANY IS SPILLED DURING TIMES OF CHANGE.
I HAVE SEEN IT BEFORE...
...DURING MANY DIFFERENT PERIODS OF HISTORY.
I LONG TO SEE IT AGAIN!!
THE TRAIN ACCIDENT THAT YOU WERE IN...
...WAS MY DOING AS WELL.

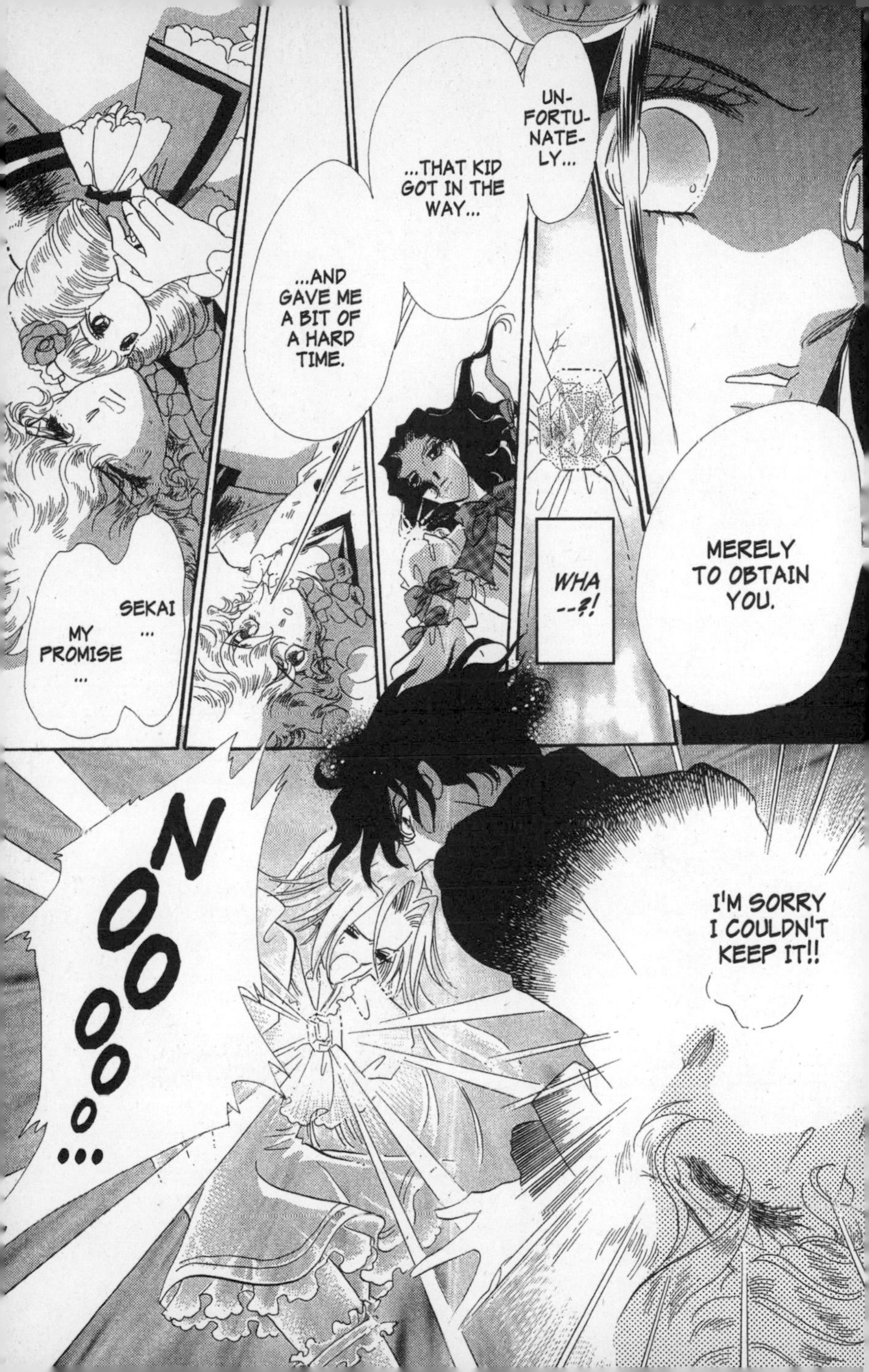
MERELY TO OBTAIN YOU.
UN-FORTU-NATE-LY...
...THAT KID GOT IN THE WAY...
...AND GAVE ME A BIT OF A HARD TIME.
WHA--?!
SEKAI...
MY PROMISE...
I'M SORRY I COULDN'T KEEP IT!!
NOOOOO...

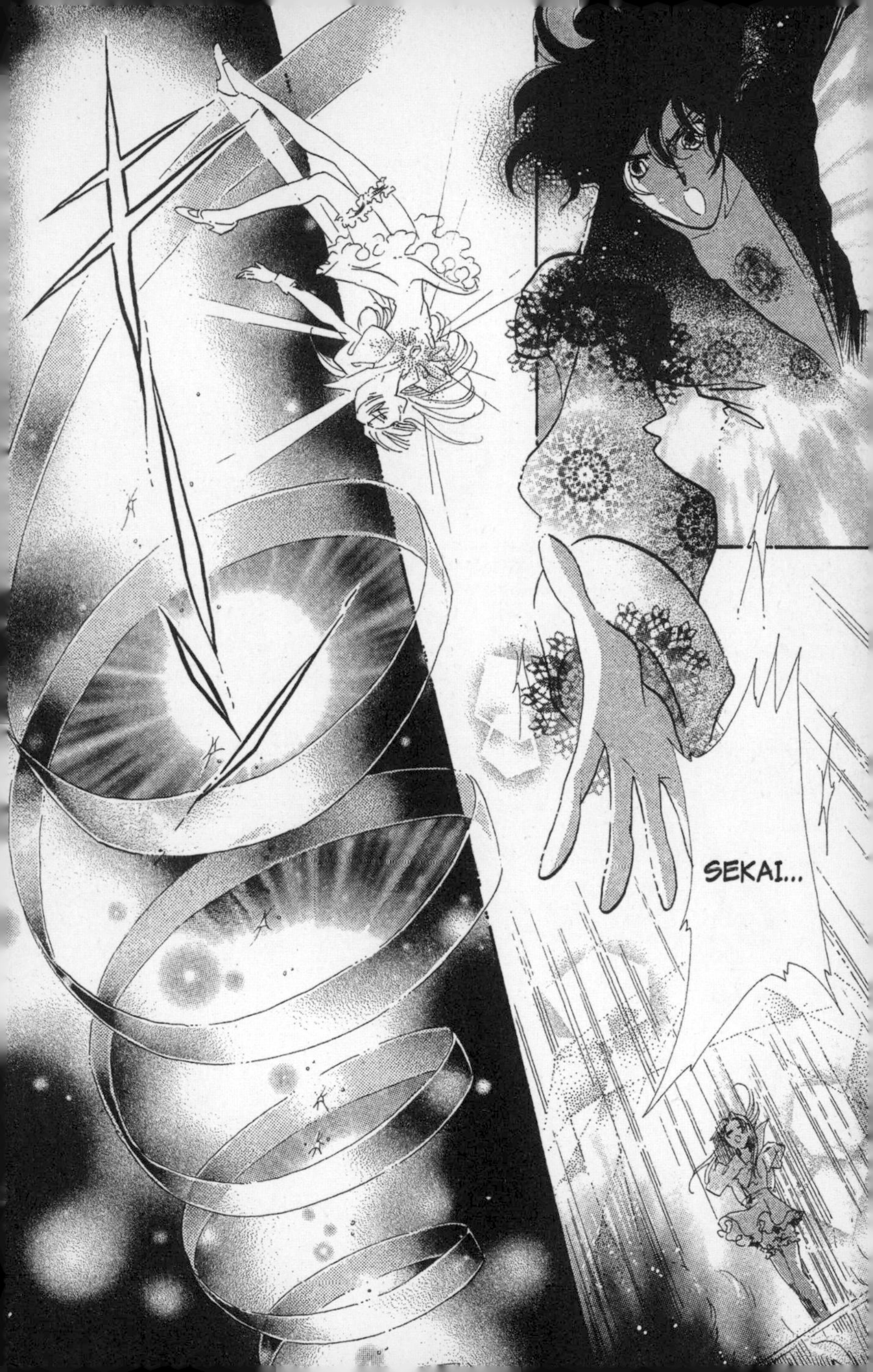
SEKAI...

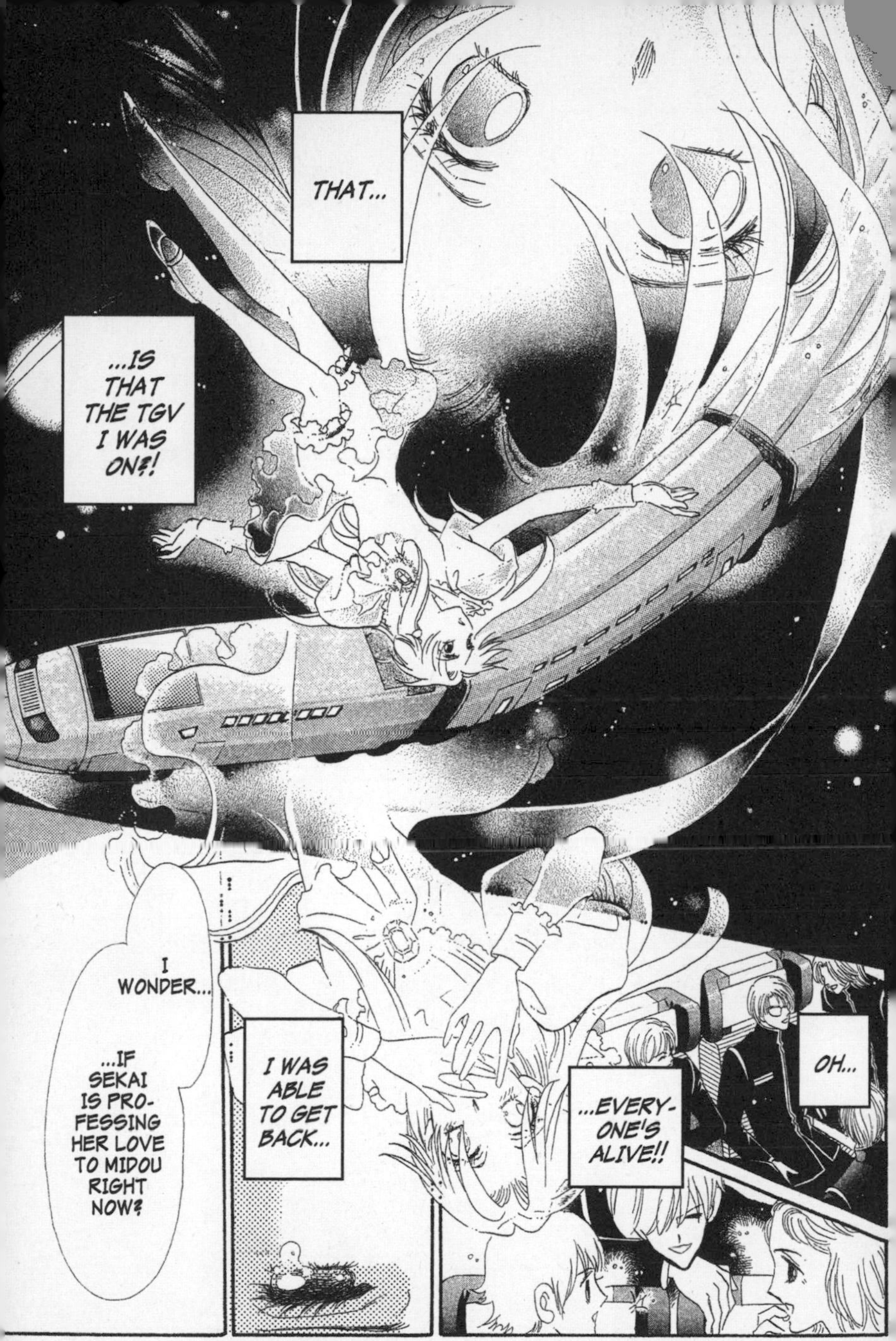
THAT...
...IS THAT THE TGV I WAS ON?!
OH...
...EVERYONE'S ALIVE!!
I WAS ABLE TO GET BACK...
I WONDER...
...IF SEKAI IS PROFESSING HER LOVE TO MIDOU RIGHT NOW?

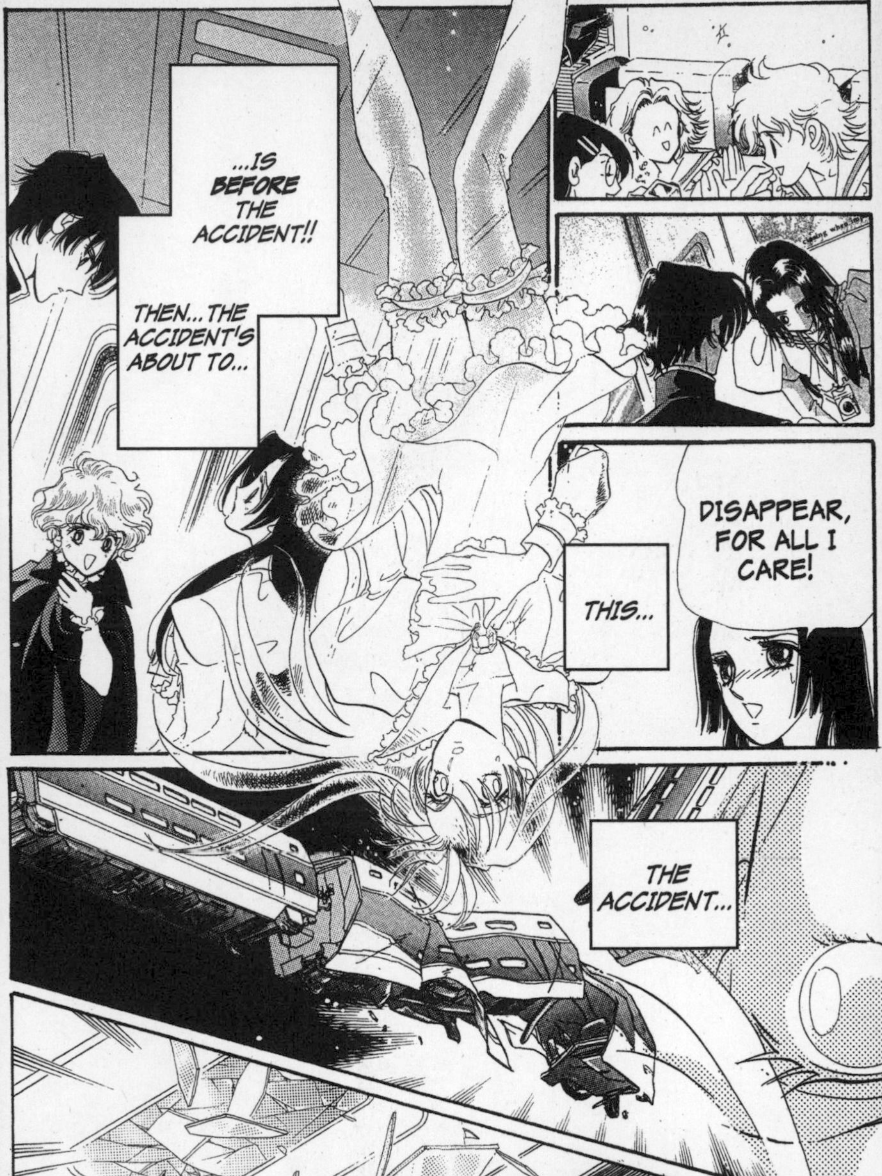
DISAPPEAR, FOR ALL I CARE!
THIS...
...IS BEFORE THE ACCIDENT!!
THEN...THE ACCIDENT'S ABOUT TO...
THE ACCIDENT...

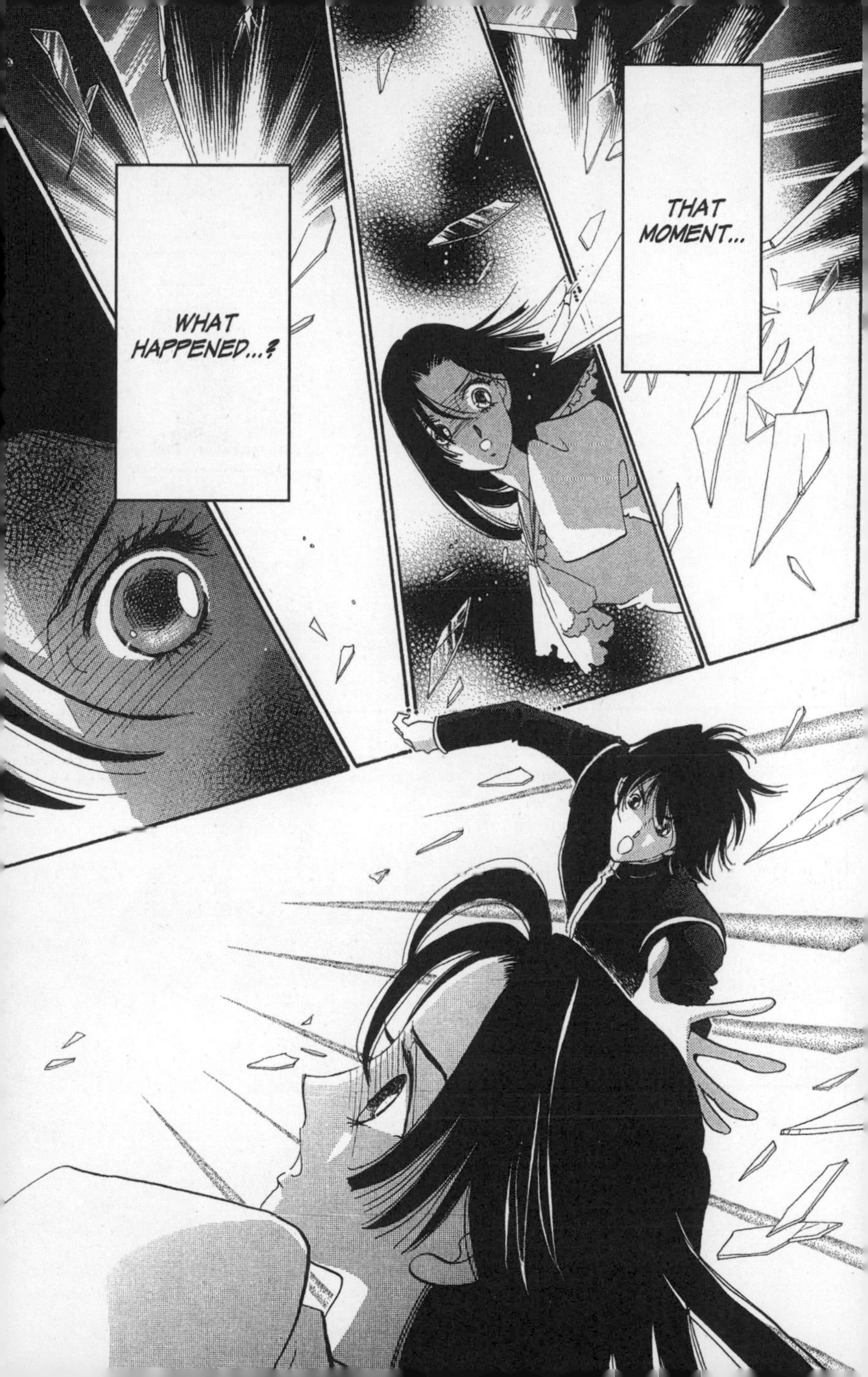
THAT MOMENT...
WHAT HAPPENED...?

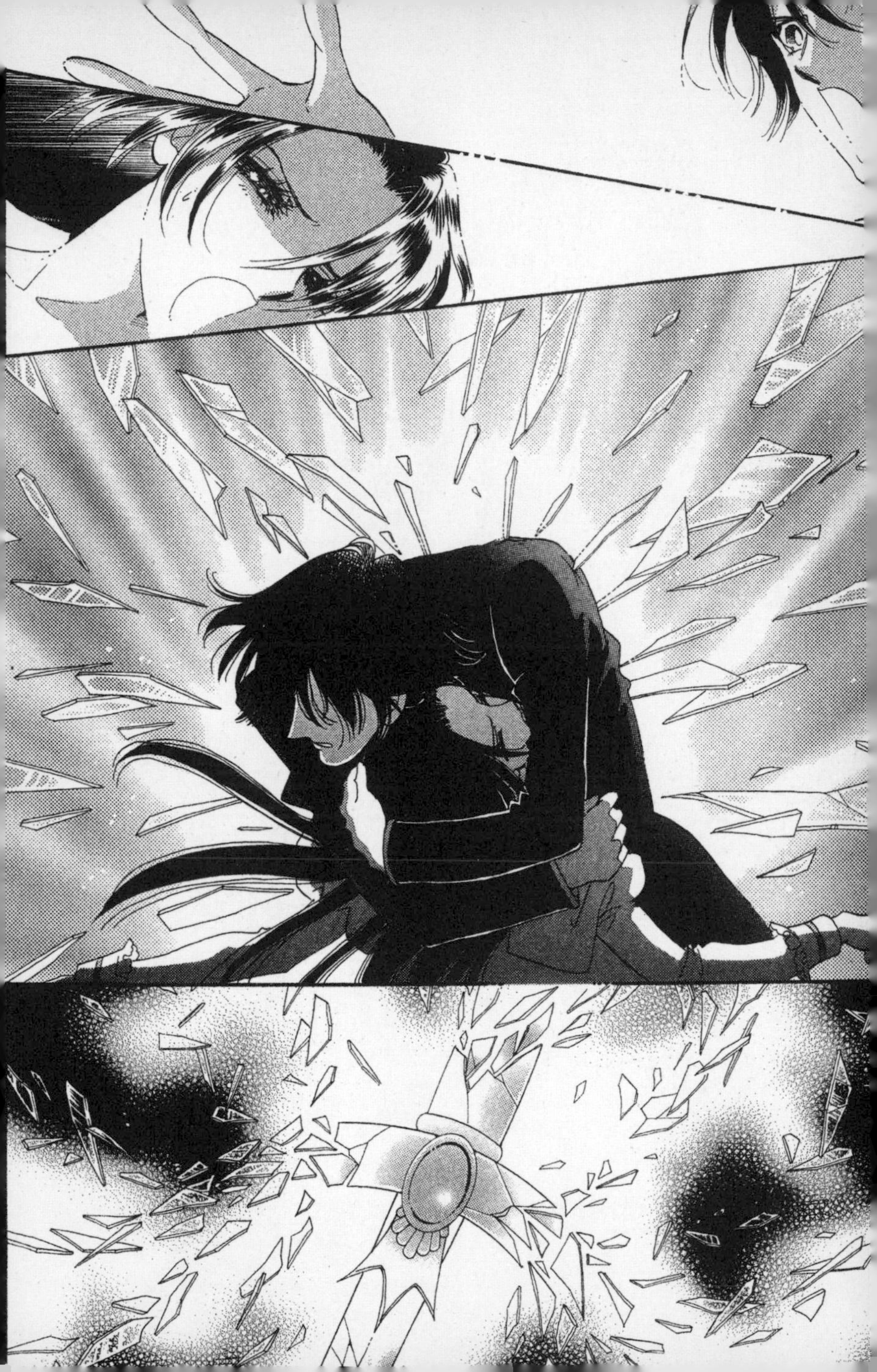

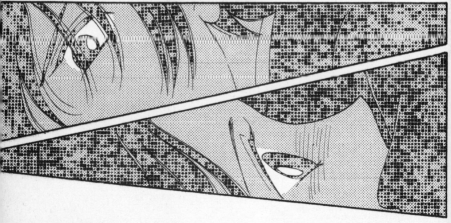

DISAPPEAR, FOR
ALL I CARE!

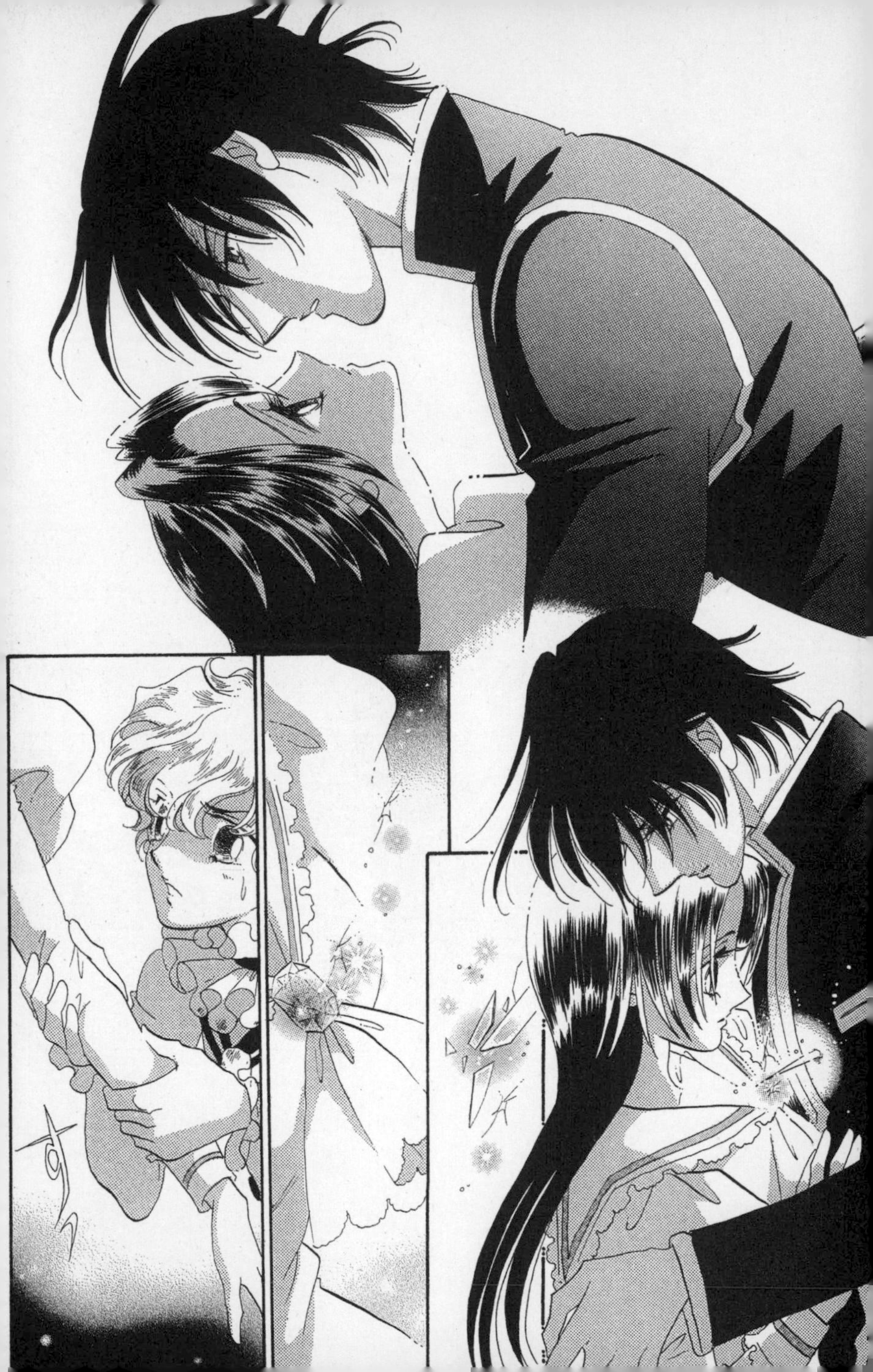

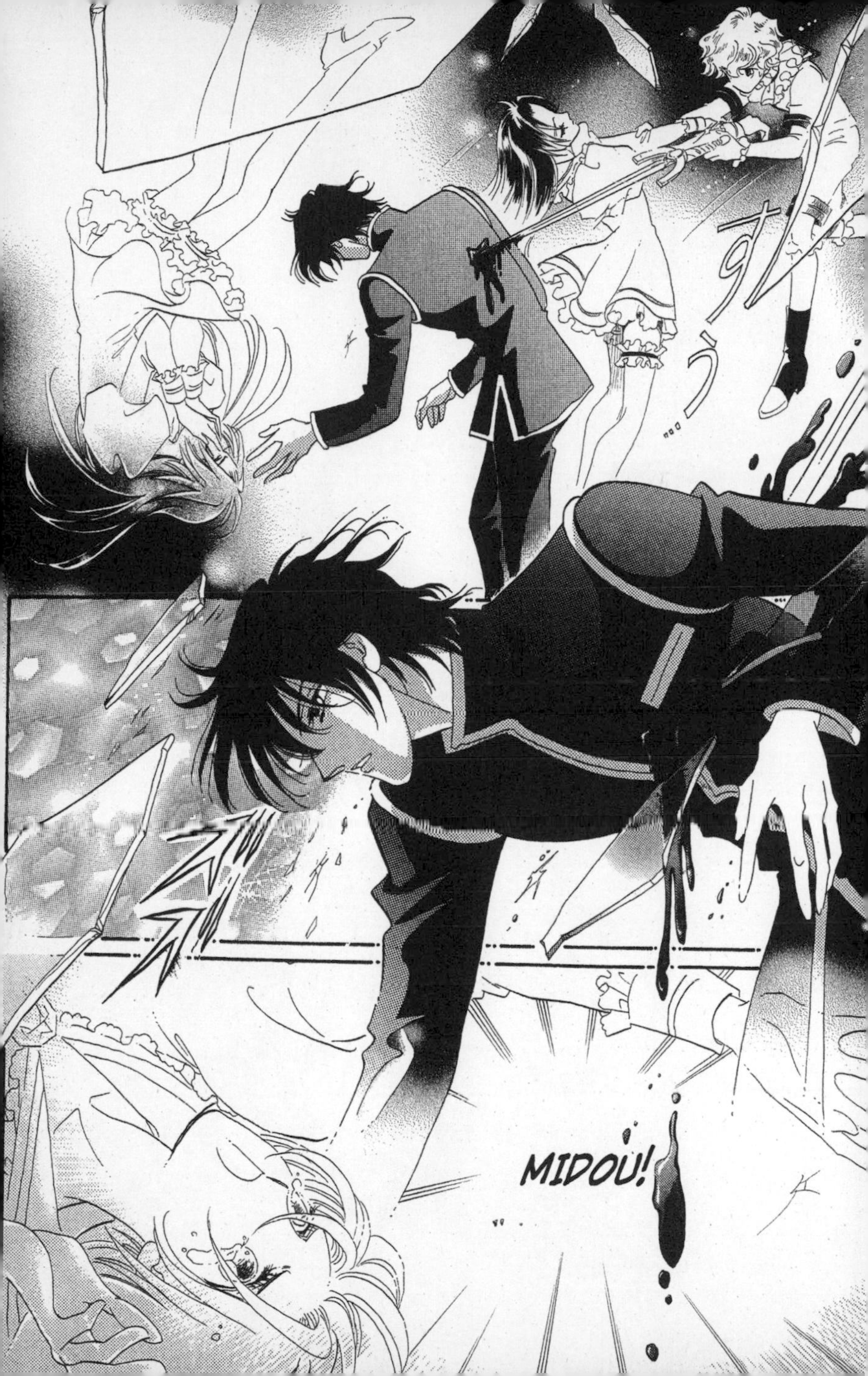
すう
MIDOU!

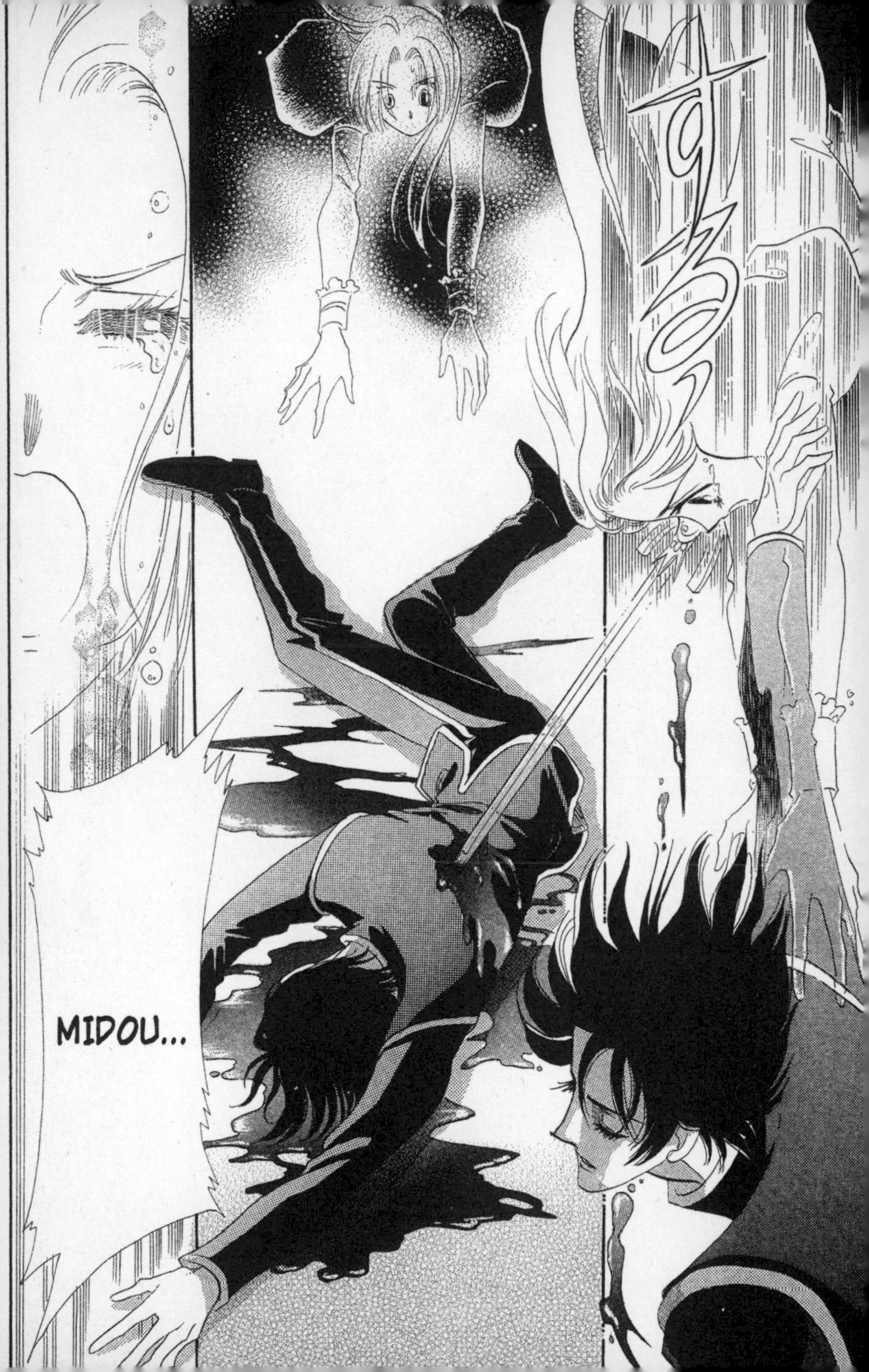
MIDOU...

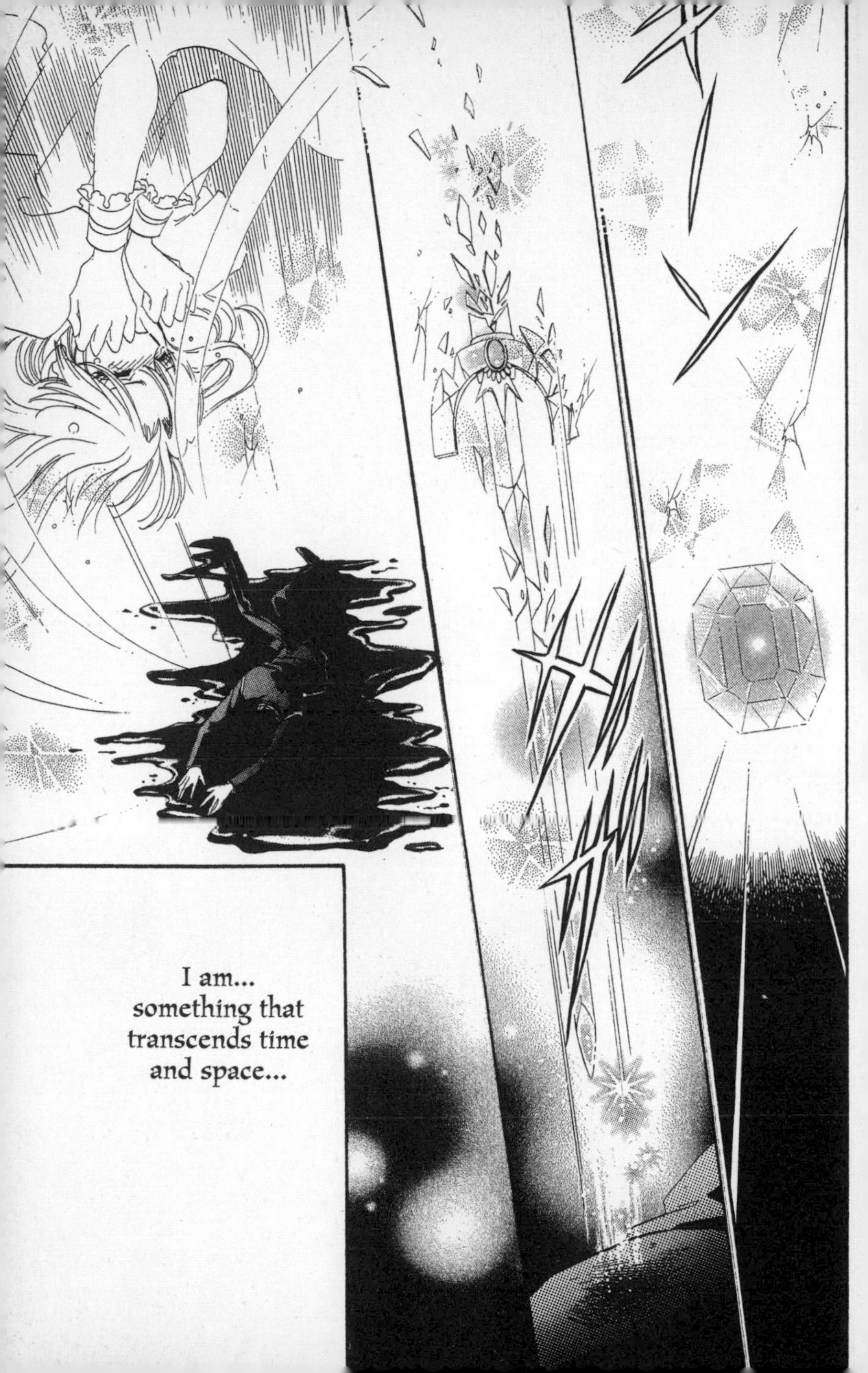
I am... something that transcends time and space...

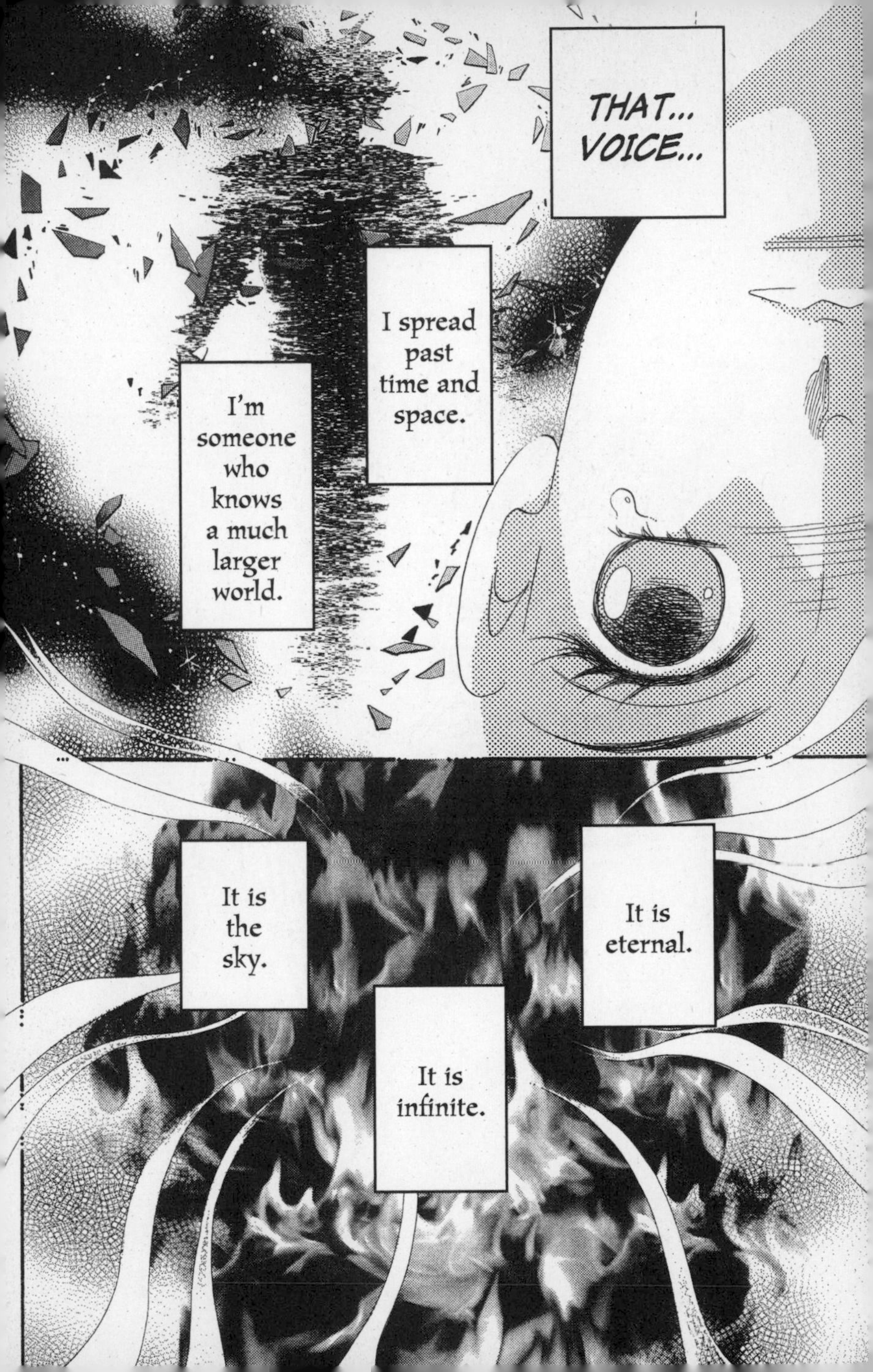
THAT... VOICE...
I spread past time and space.
I'm someone who knows a much larger world.
It is eternal.
It is the sky.
It is infinite.

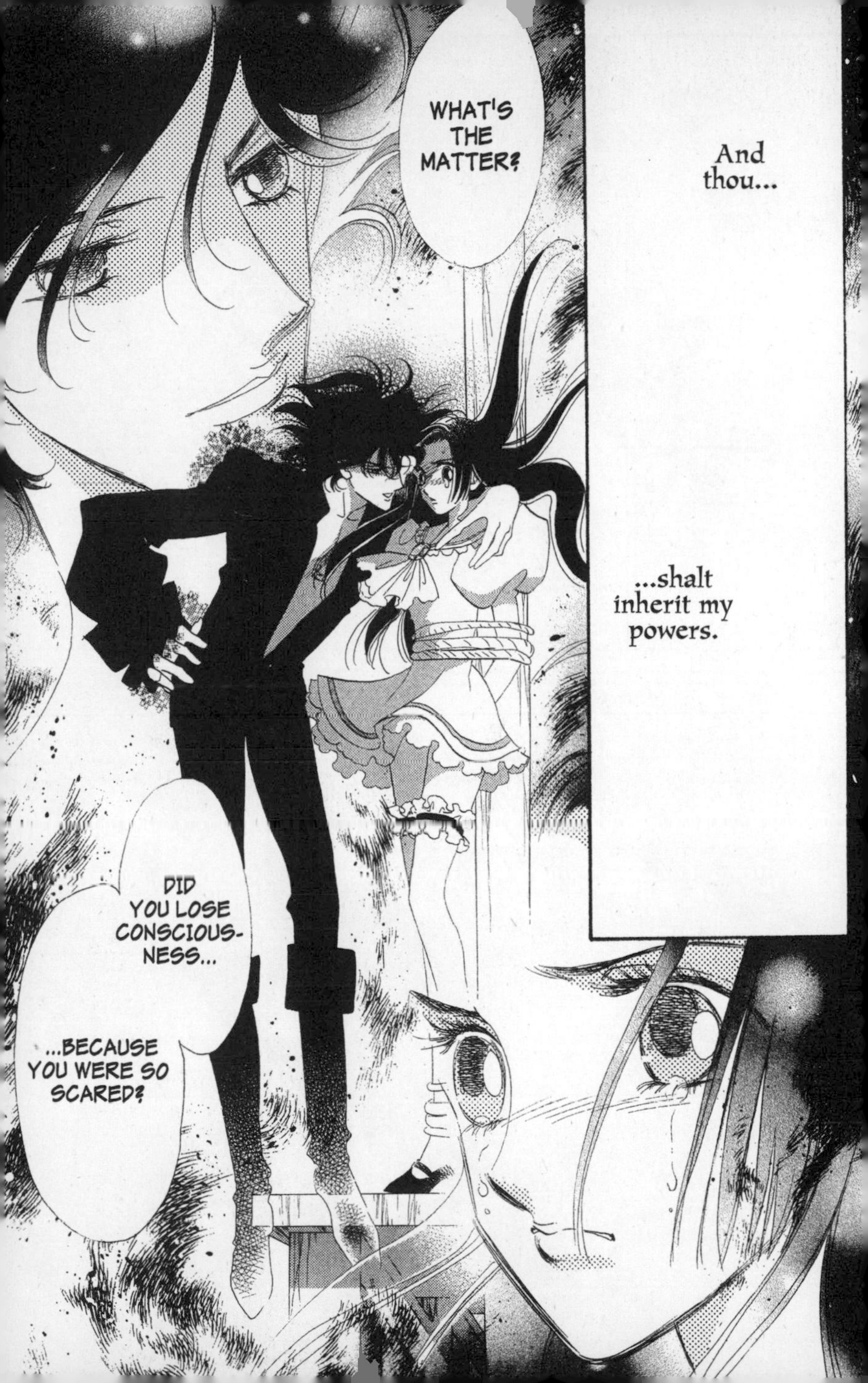
And thou...
...shalt inherit my powers.
WHAT'S THE MATTER?
DID YOU LOSE CONSCIOUS-NESS...
...BECAUSE YOU WERE SO SCARED?

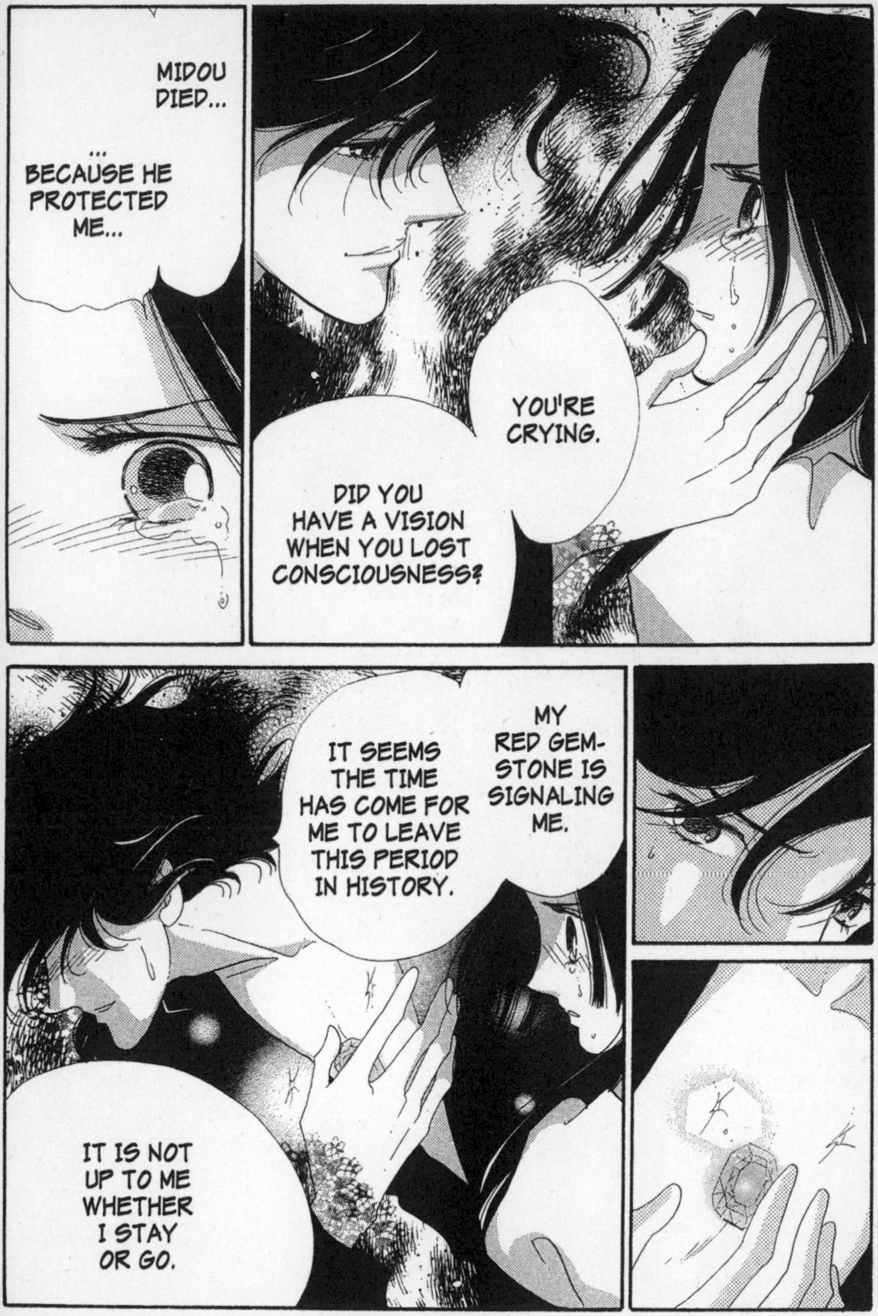
YOU'RE CRYING.
DID YOU HAVE A VISION WHEN YOU LOST CONSCIOUSNESS?
MIDOU DIED...
... BECAUSE HE PROTECTED ME...
MY RED GEM-STONE IS SIGNALING ME.
IT SEEMS THE TIME HAS COME FOR ME TO LEAVE THIS PERIOD IN HISTORY.
IT IS NOT UP TO ME WHETHER I STAY OR GO.

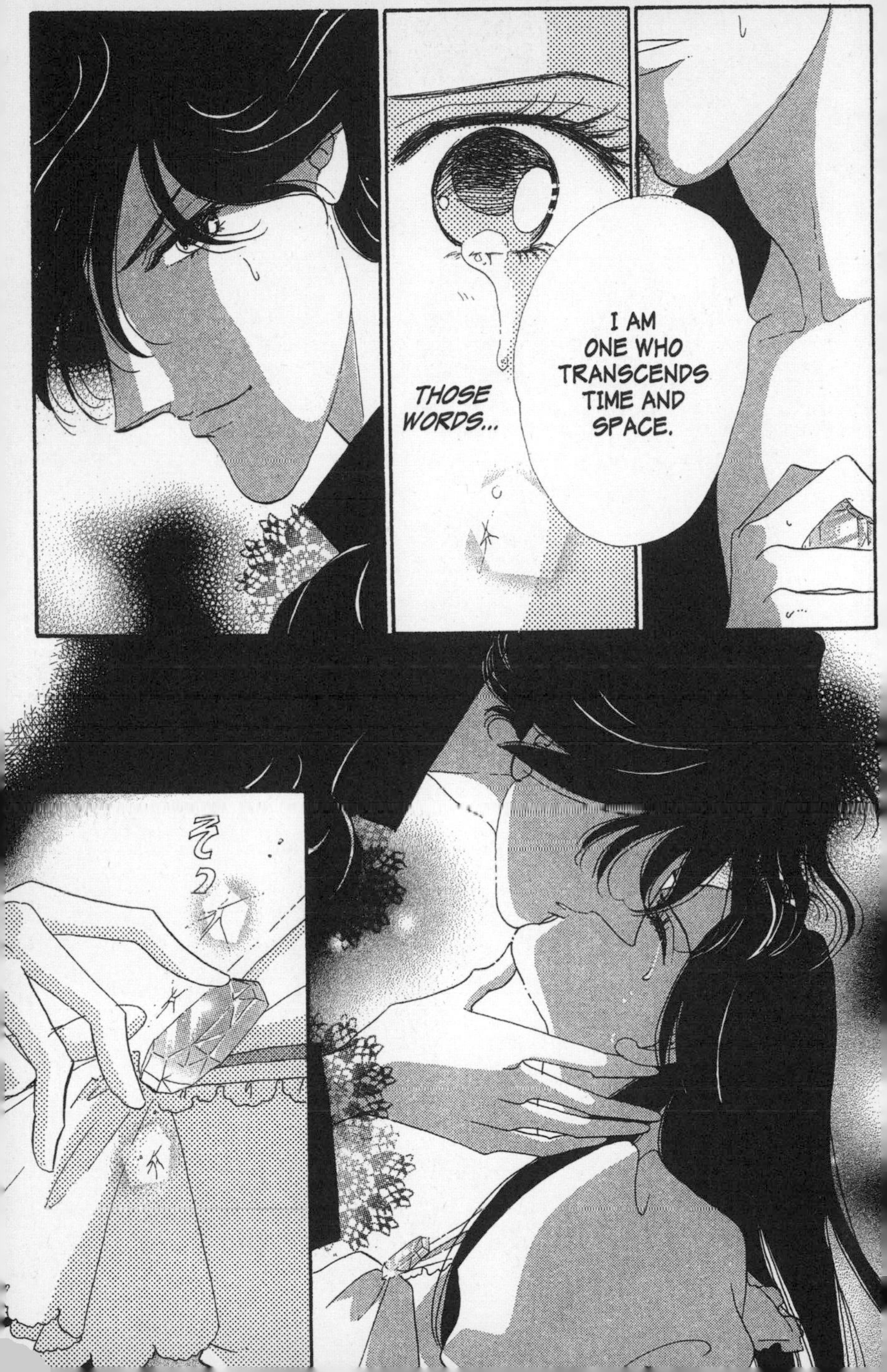
I AM ONE WHO TRANSCENDS TIME AND SPACE.
THOSE WORDS...
そっ

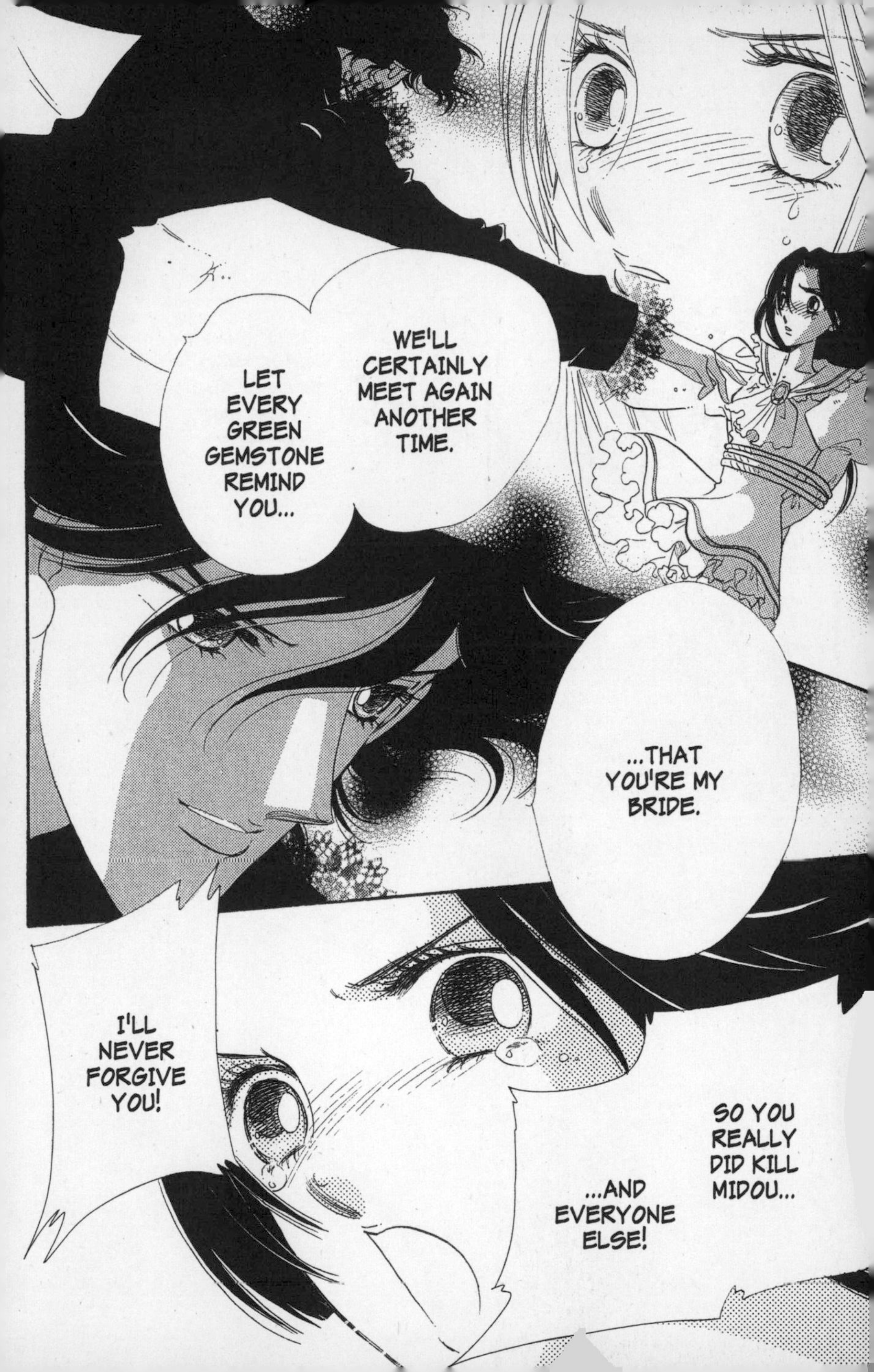
WE'LL CERTAINLY MEET AGAIN ANOTHER TIME.
LET EVERY GREEN GEMSTONE REMIND YOU...
...THAT YOU'RE MY BRIDE.
SO YOU REALLY DID KILL MIDOU...
...AND EVERYONE ELSE!
I'LL NEVER FORGIVE YOU!

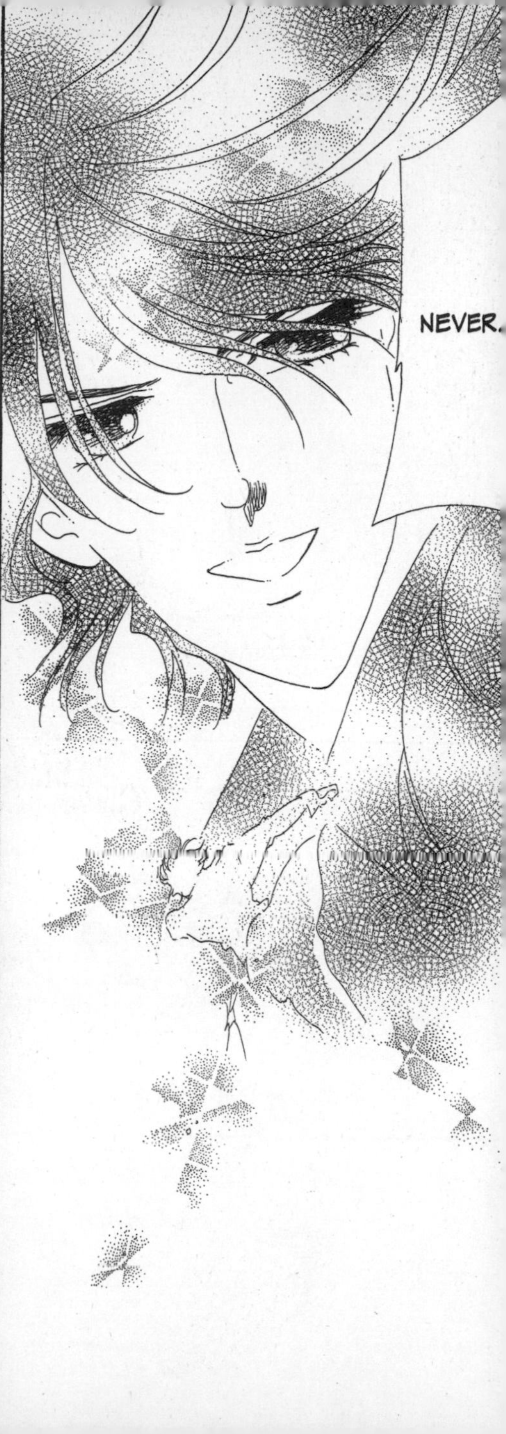
NEVER.
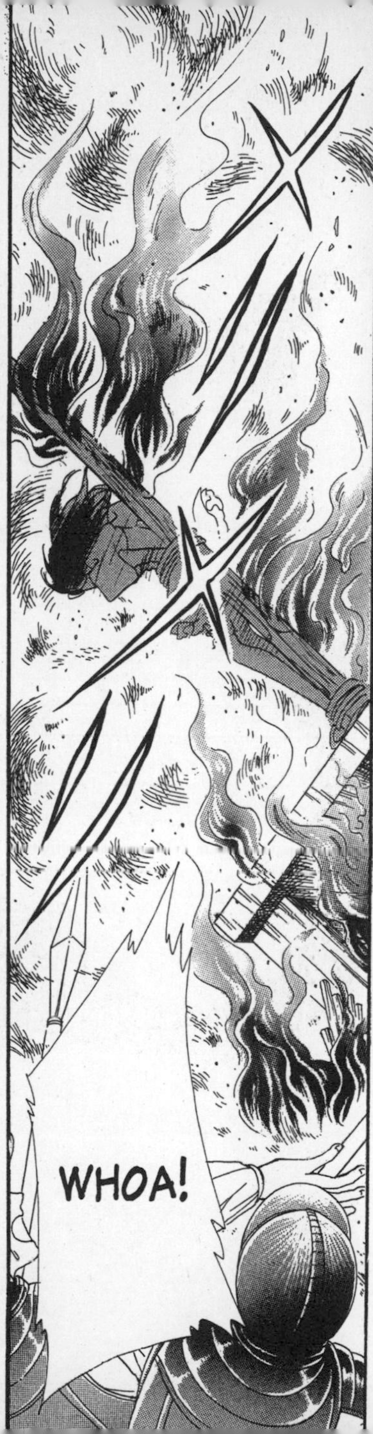
WHOA!

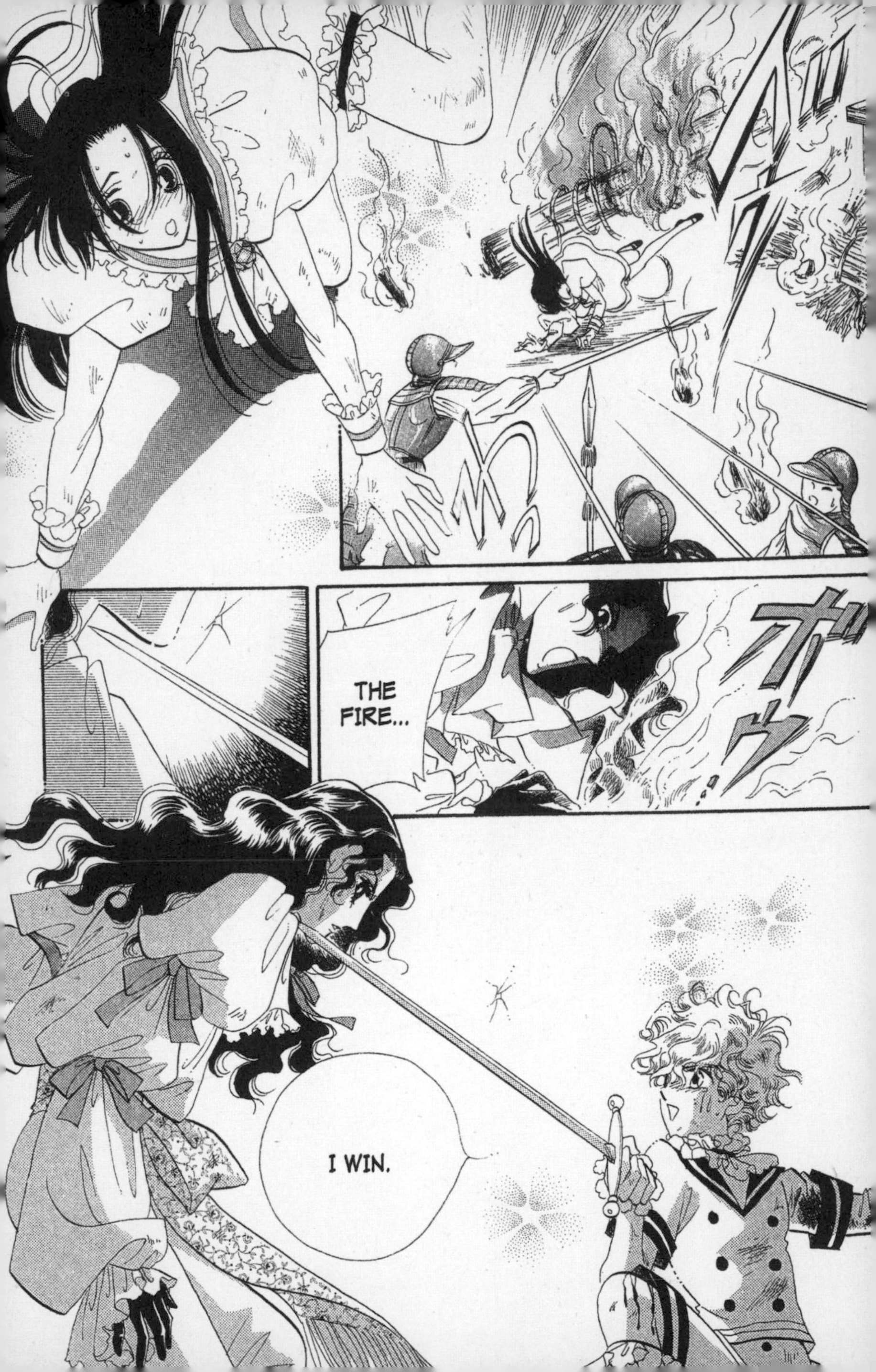
THE FIRE...
I WIN.

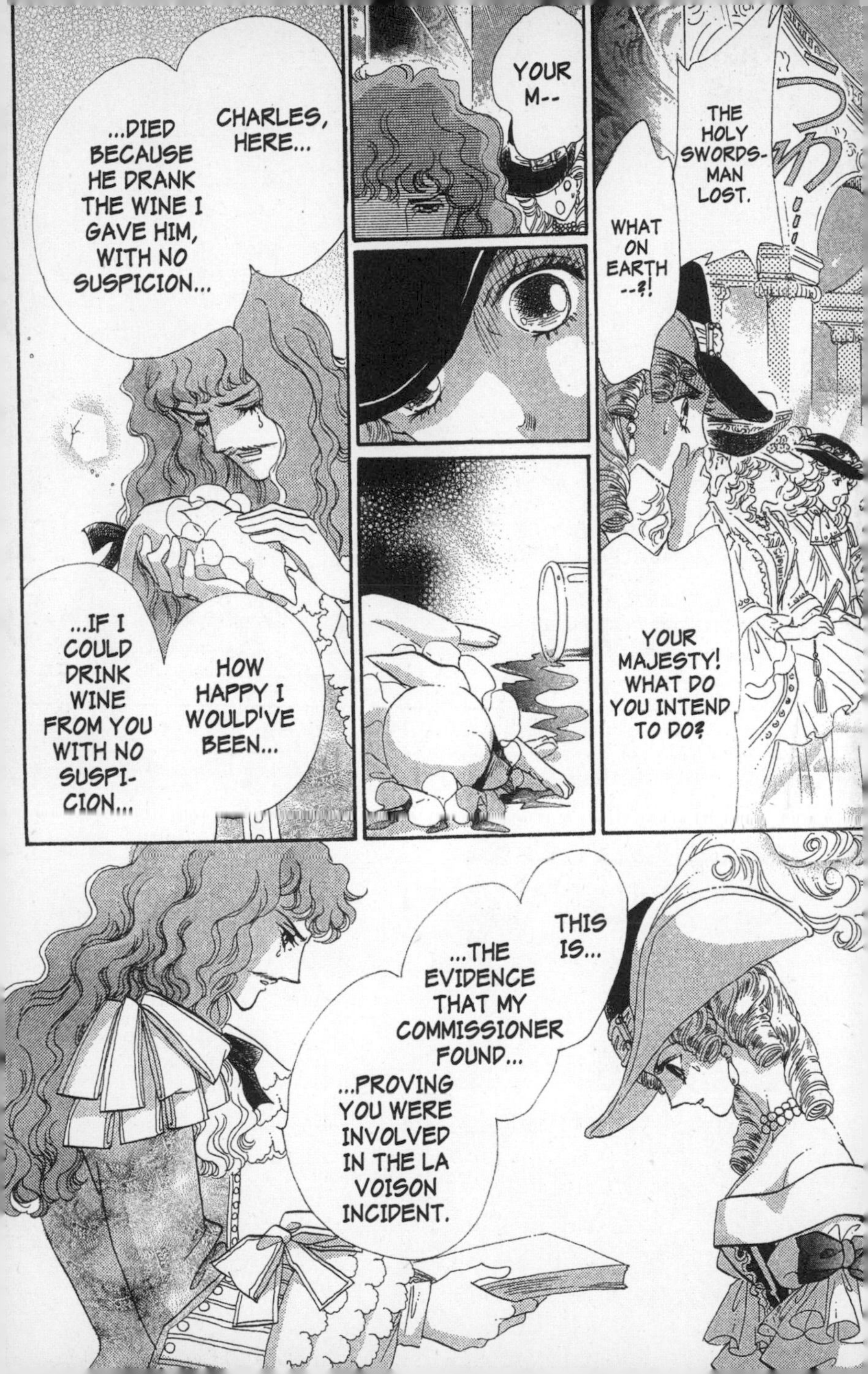
THE HOLY SWORDS-MAN LOST.
WHAT ON EARTH --?!
YOUR MAJESTY! WHAT DO YOU INTEND TO DO?
YOUR M--
CHARLES, HERE...
...DIED BECAUSE HE DRANK THE WINE I GAVE HIM, WITH NO SUSPICION...
...IF I COULD DRINK WINE FROM YOU WITH NO SUSPI-CION...
HOW HAPPY I WOULD'VE BEEN...
THIS IS...
...THE EVIDENCE THAT MY COMMISSIONER FOUND...
...PROVING YOU WERE INVOLVED IN THE LA VOISON INCIDENT.

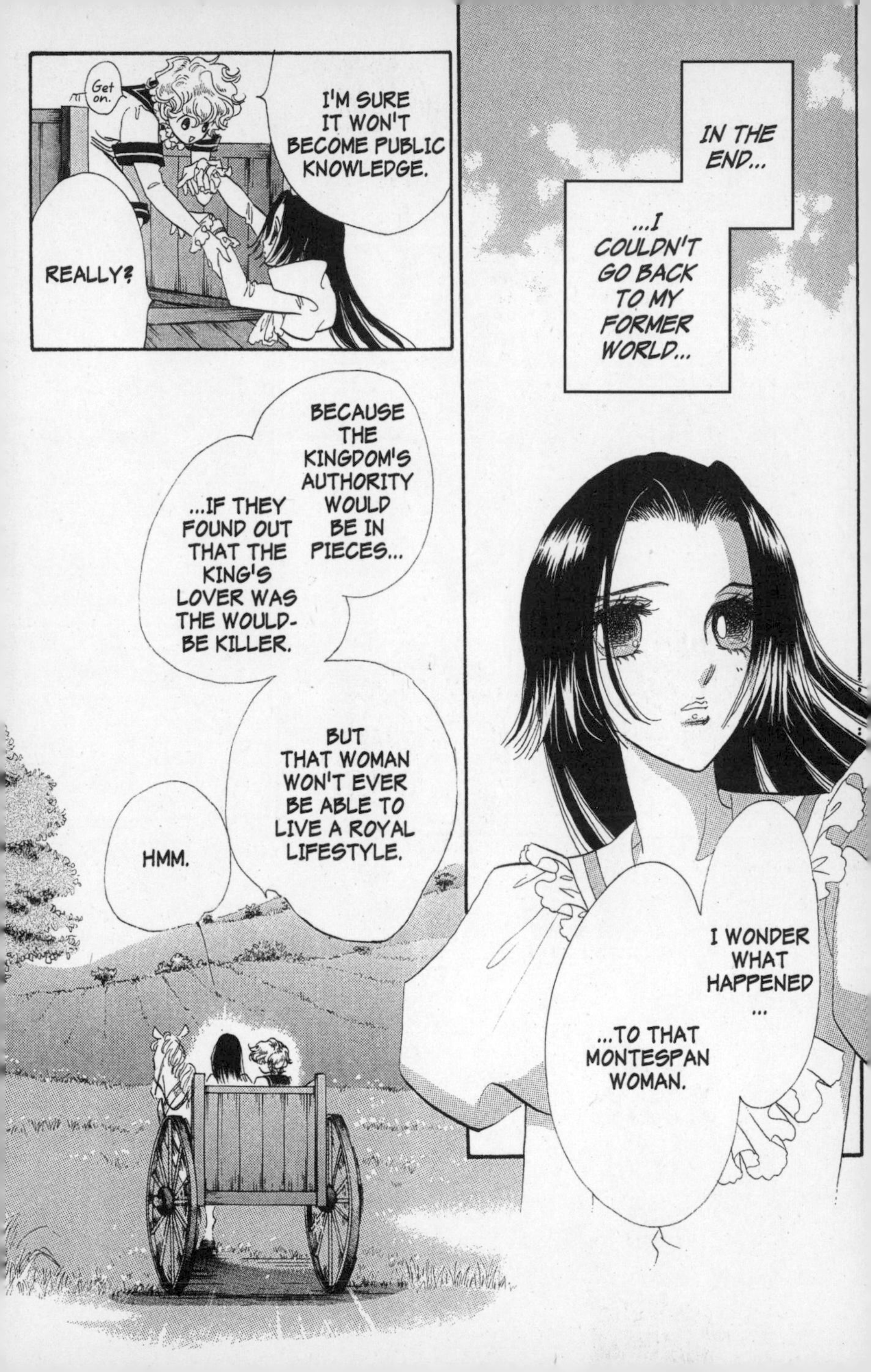
IN THE END...
...I COULDN'T GO BACK TO MY FORMER WORLD...
I WONDER WHAT HAPPENED ...
...TO THAT MONTESPAN WOMAN.
I'M SURE IT WON'T BECOME PUBLIC KNOWLEDGE.
Get on.
REALLY?
BECAUSE THE KINGDOM'S AUTHORITY WOULD BE IN PIECES...
...IF THEY FOUND OUT THAT THE KING'S LOVER WAS THE WOULD-BE KILLER.
BUT THAT WOMAN WON'T EVER BE ABLE TO LIVE A ROYAL LIFESTYLE.
HMM.

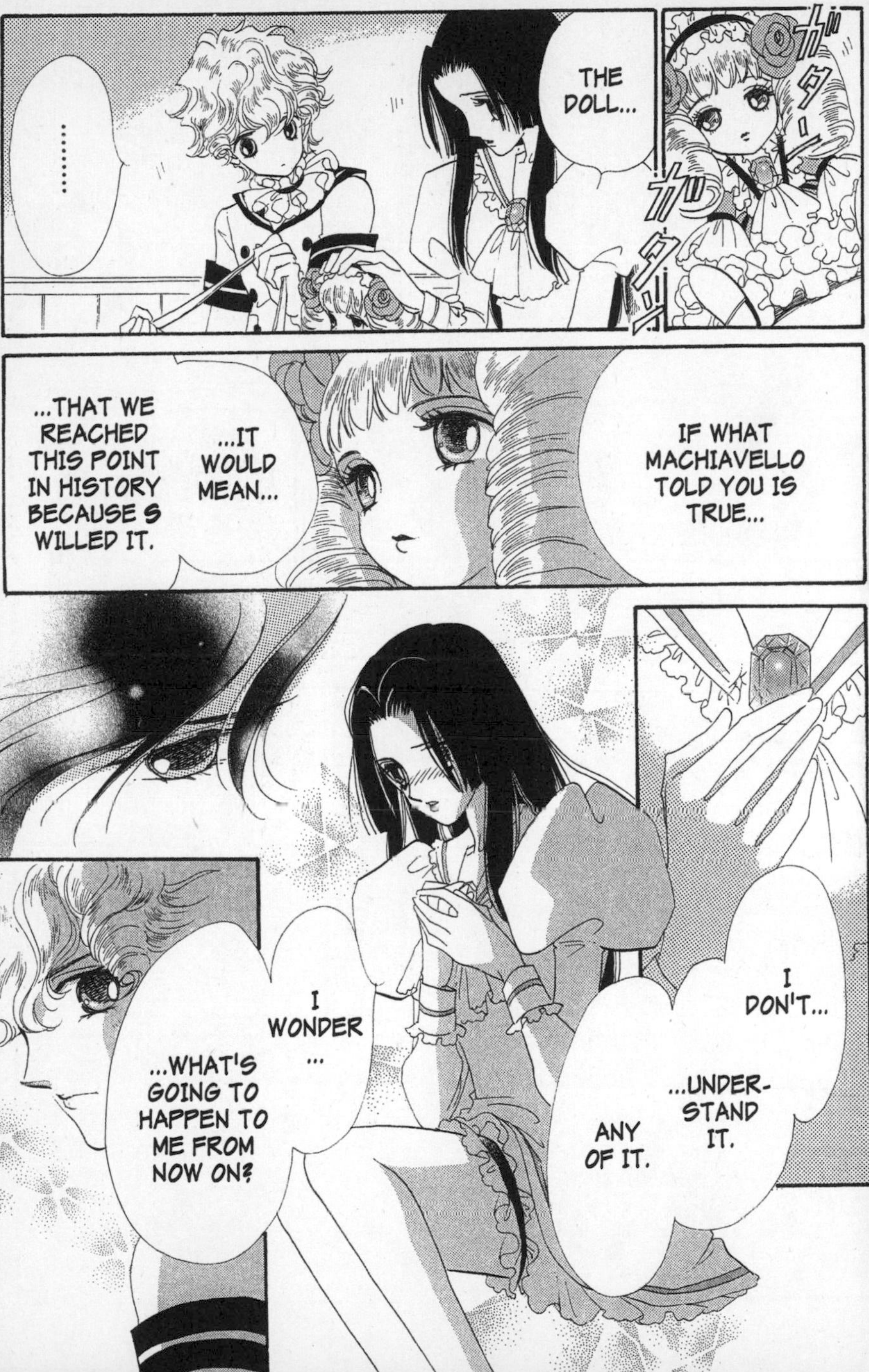
THE DOLL...
......
IF WHAT MACHIAVELLO TOLD YOU IS TRUE...
...IT WOULD MEAN...
...THAT WE REACHED THIS POINT IN HISTORY BECAUSE S WILLED IT.
I DON'T...
...UNDER-STAND IT.
ANY OF IT.
I WONDER ...
...WHAT'S GOING TO HAPPEN TO ME FROM NOW ON?

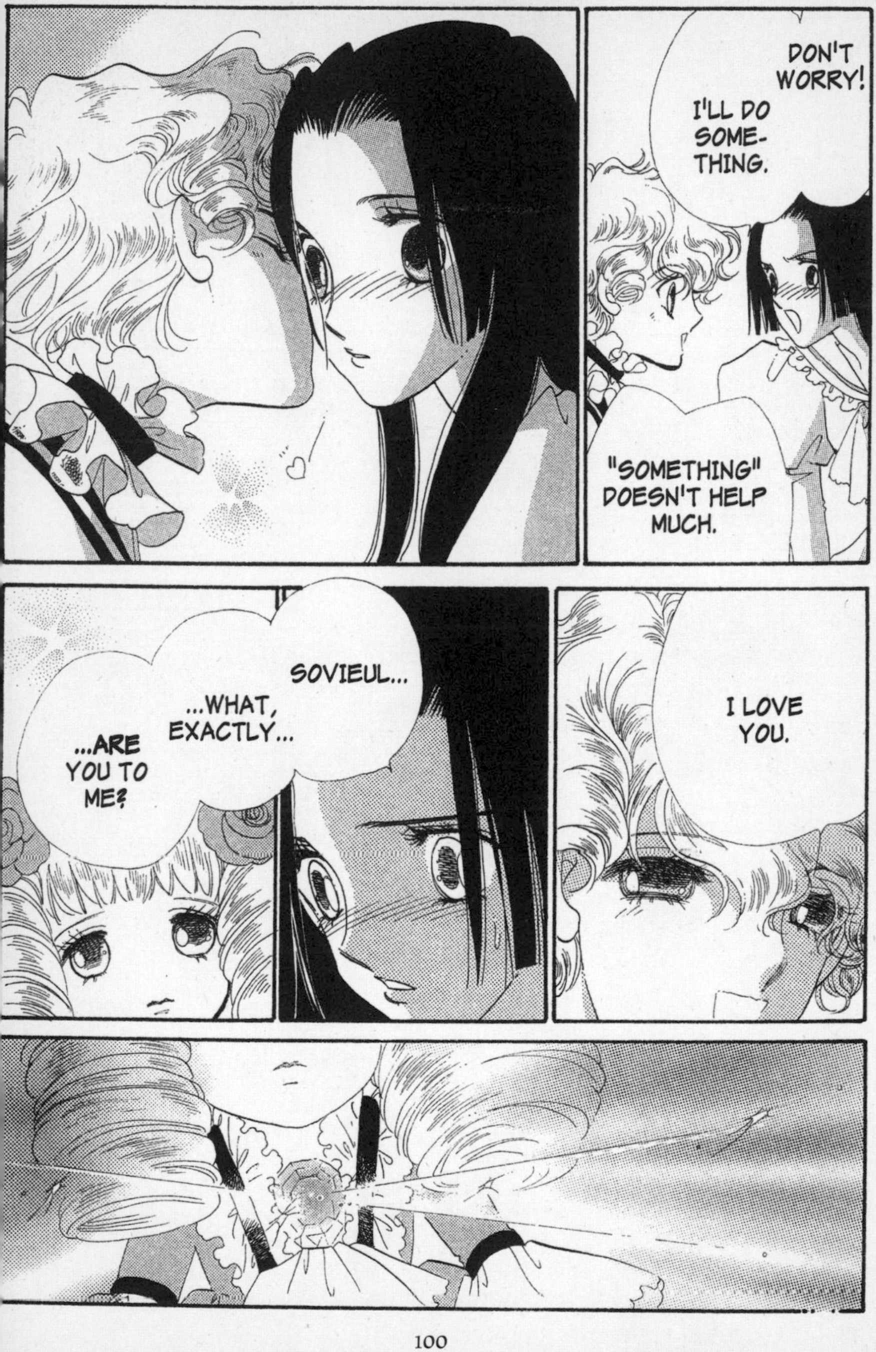
DON'T WORRY! I'LL DO SOMETHING.
"SOMETHING" DOESN'T HELP MUCH.
I LOVE YOU.
SOVIEUL... ...WHAT, EXACTLY... ...ARE YOU TO ME?

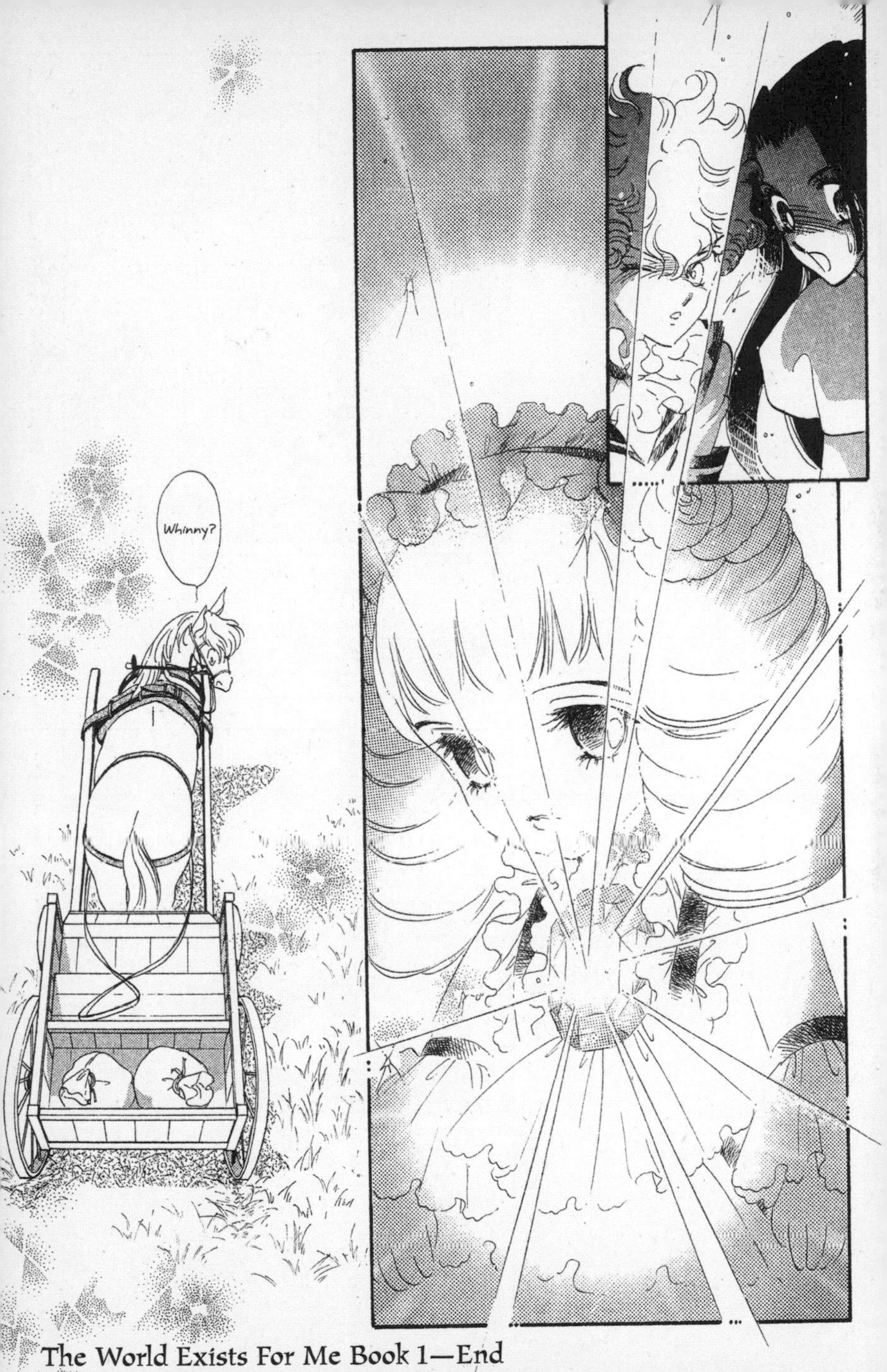
Whinny?

The World Exists For Me Book 1—End

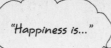

“Happiness is...”

Attn: The creator, Ikuhara, is now in America, in Los Angeles...

Ikuhara does nothing but swim at the pool every day in L.A.
Or so I hear.
ロス
ロス
はははは
He swims 50 meter dashes.
8:05am L.A. time
This is Saitou who does nothing but work all day in Tokyo.
Please ink it quickly.
Assistant
ルルル
Assistant
Hurry up with this, too.
Sorry, publisher.
I'm way over my deadline.
I forgot.
Sorry, I also forgot about that.
ルルルル
12:05am Tokyo time
This is the cat Chuchutaro who does nothing but sleep all day.
Everyone's happy! ♡
Really?
I haven't slept.
Really? Really?
It seems like it...

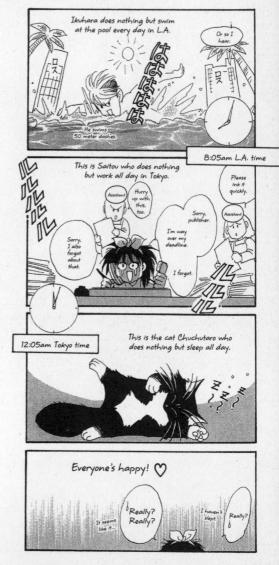

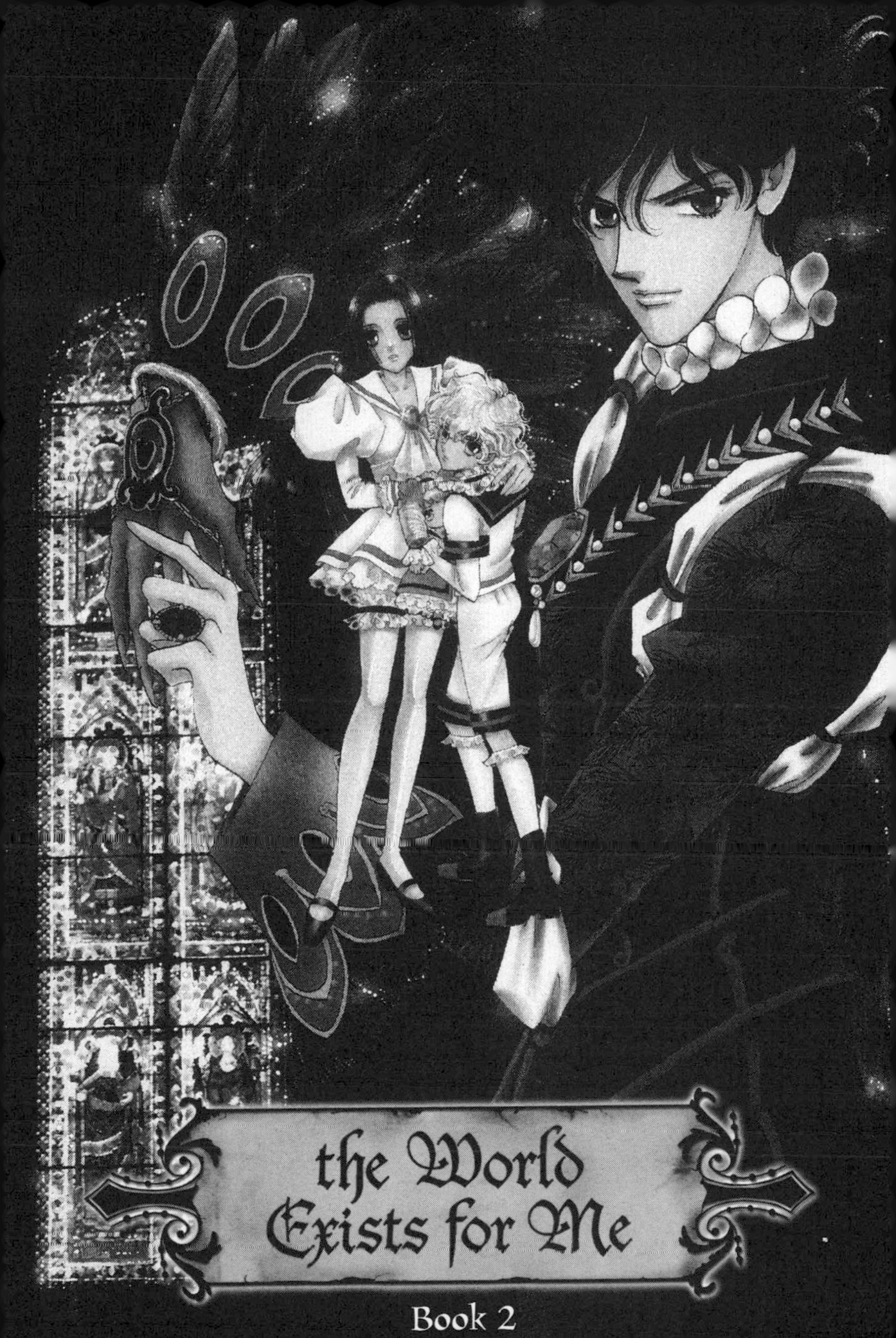
the World
Exists for Me

Book 2
Bluebeard's Castle

BE-PAPAS. Presents

"WORLD OF THE S&M"

MANGA BY CHIHO SAITOU STORY BY KUNIHIKO IKUHARA
And SEINOSUKE ITO
Associate costume designer:KIWA TAKADO
Distributed by KADOKAWASHOTEN

"The world exists for me"

APAS. Presents
RLD OF THE S&
MANGA BY CHIHO SAITOU STORY BY KUNIHI
And SEINOSUKE ITO
Associate costume designer:KIWA TAKAD
ributed by KADOKAWASHOTEN
"The world exists for m

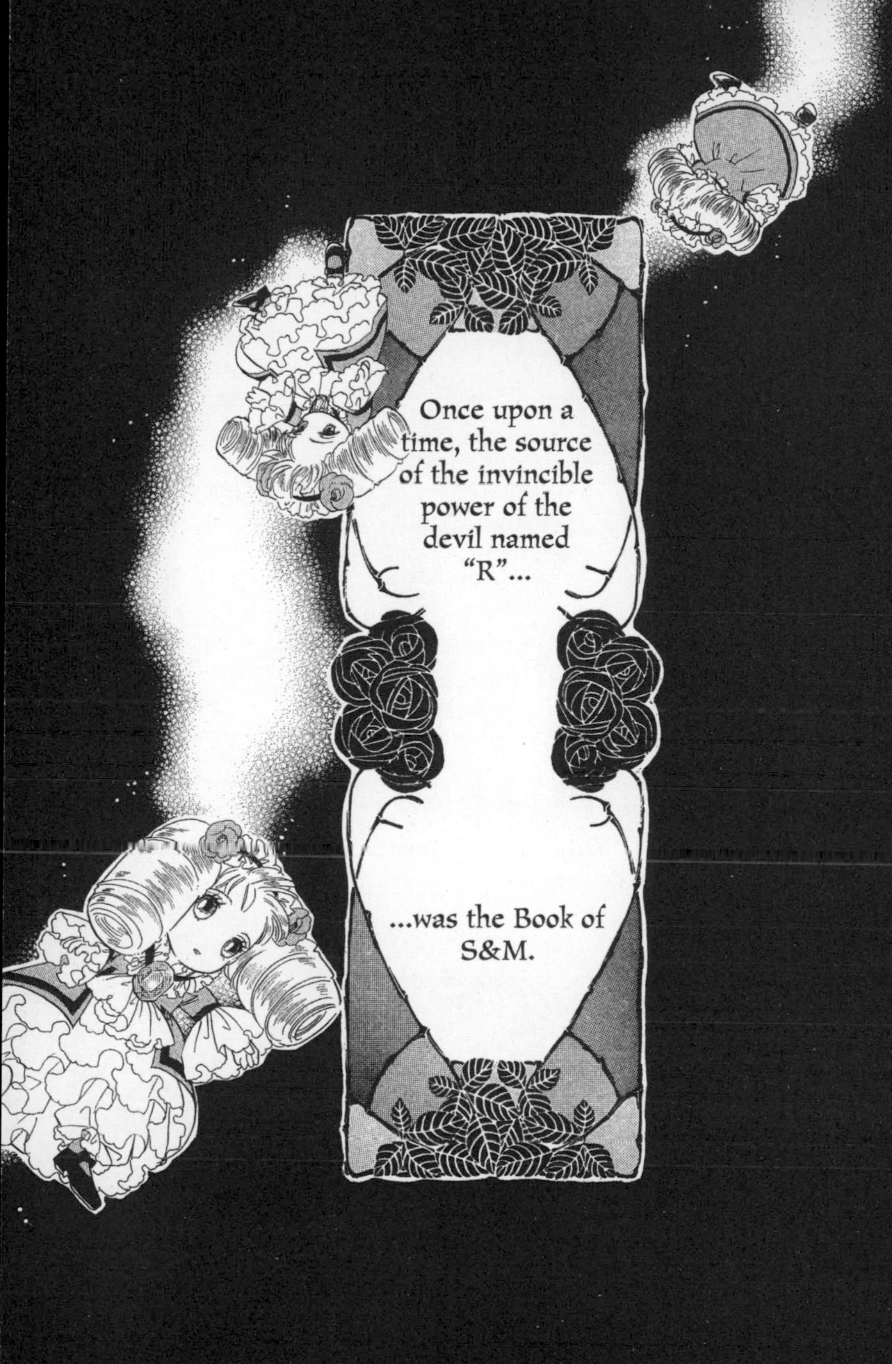
Once upon a time, the source of the invincible power of the devil named "R"...
...was the Book of S&M.

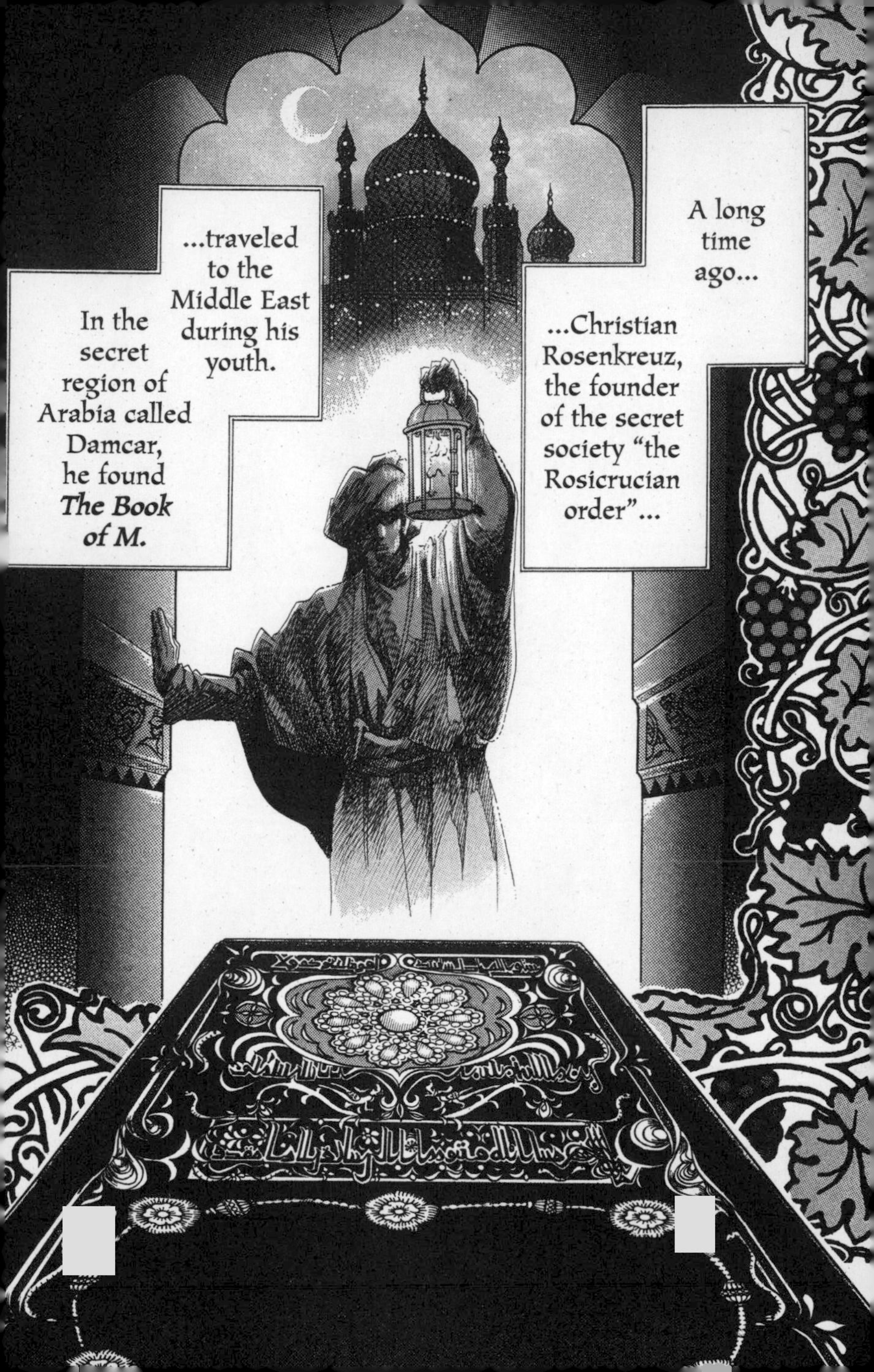
A long time ago...
...Christian Rosenkreuz, the founder of the secret society "the Rosicrucian order"...
...traveled to the Middle East during his youth.
In the secret region of Arabia called Damcar, he found *The Book of M.*

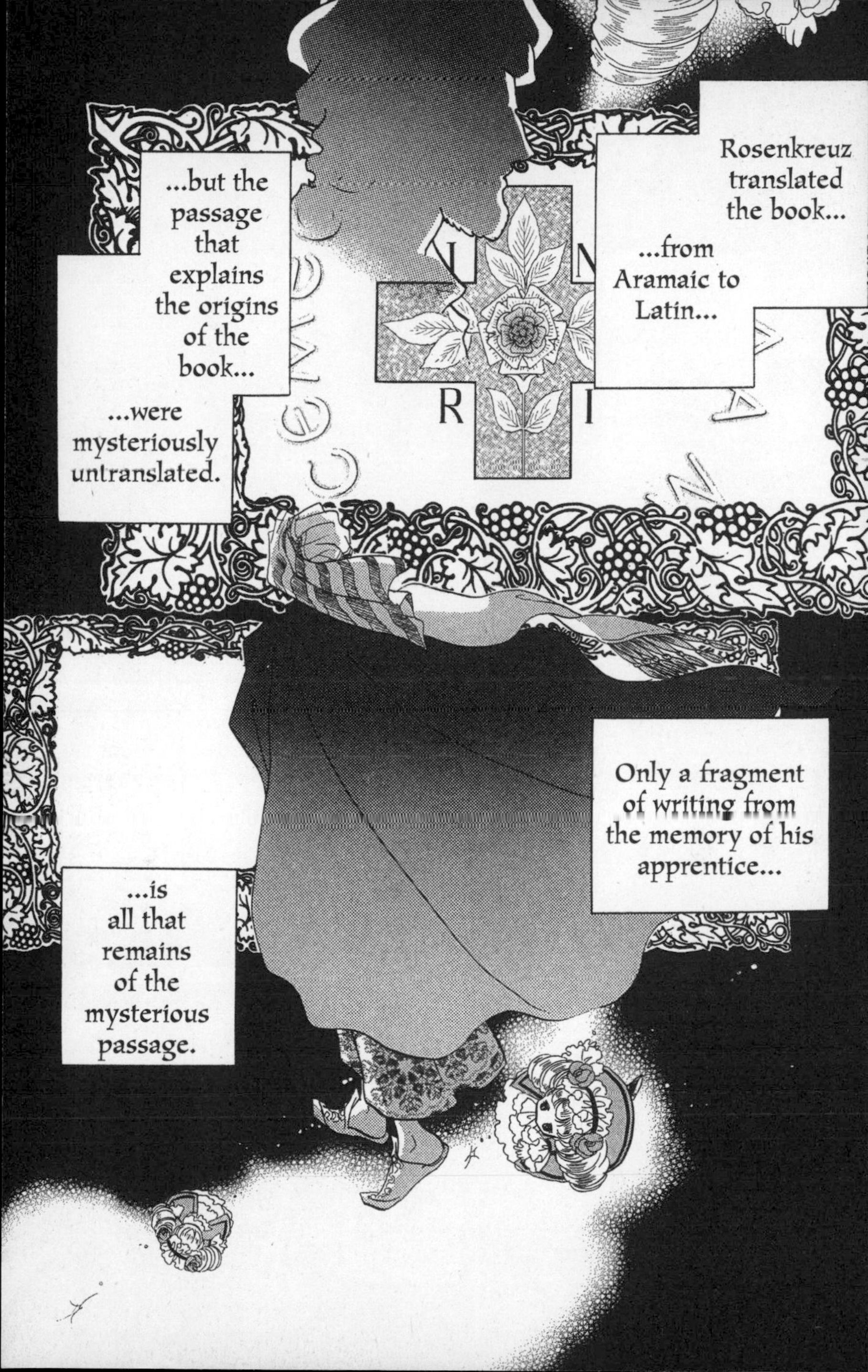
Rosenkreuz translated the book...
...from Aramaic to Latin...
...but the passage that explains the origins of the book...
...were mysteriously untranslated.
Only a fragment of writing from the memory of his apprentice...
...is all that remains of the mysterious passage.

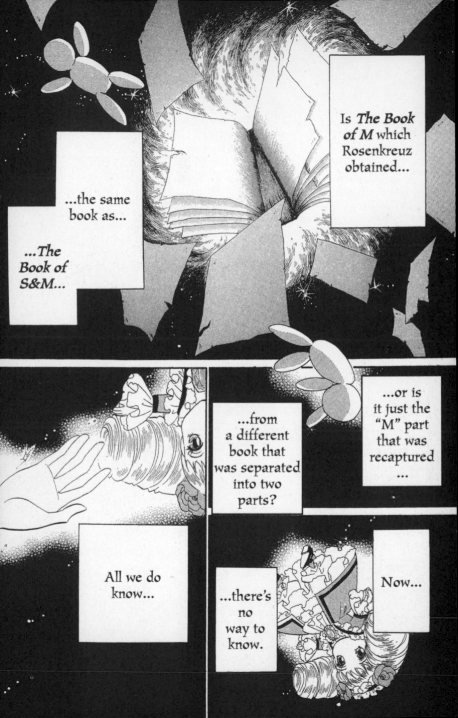

Is *The Book of M* which Rosenkreuz obtained...

...the same book as...

...*The Book of S&M*...

...or is it just the "M" part that was recaptured...

...from a different book that was separated into two parts?

All we do know...

...there's no way to know.

Now...

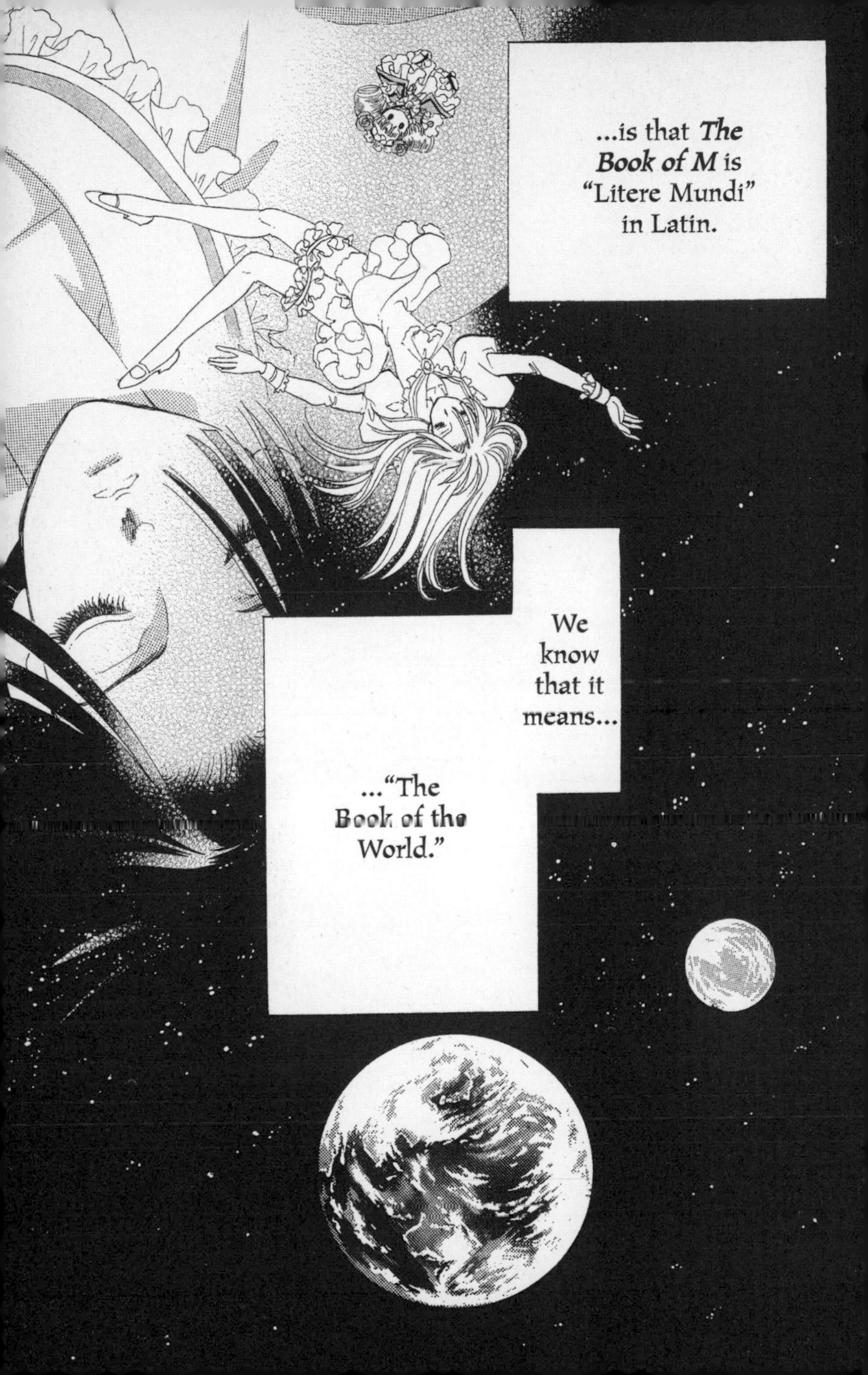
...is that *The Book of M* is "Litere Mundi" in Latin.
We know that it means...
..."The Book of the World."

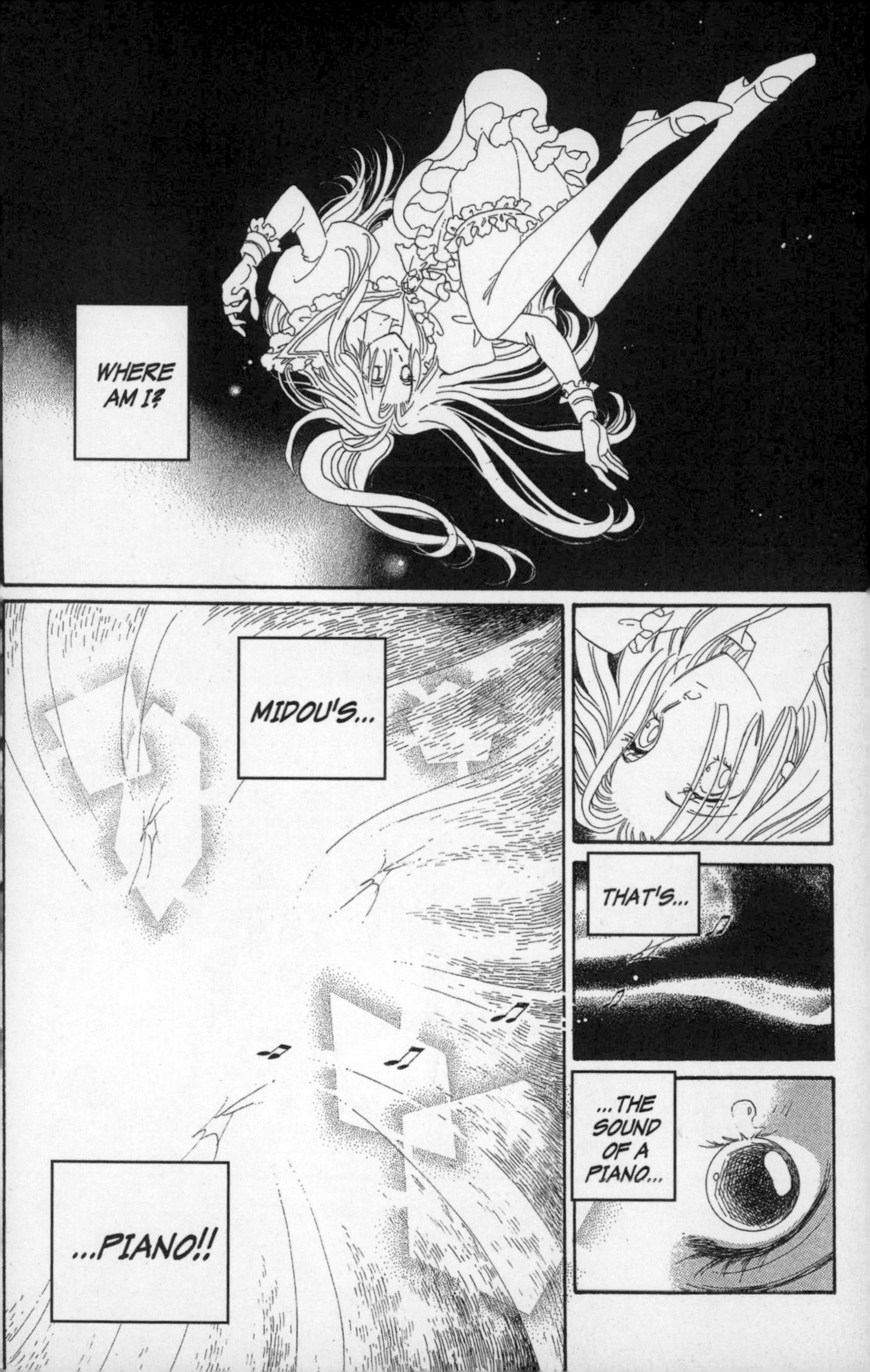
WHERE AM I?
THAT'S...
...THE SOUND OF A PIANO...
MIDOU'S...
...PIANO!!

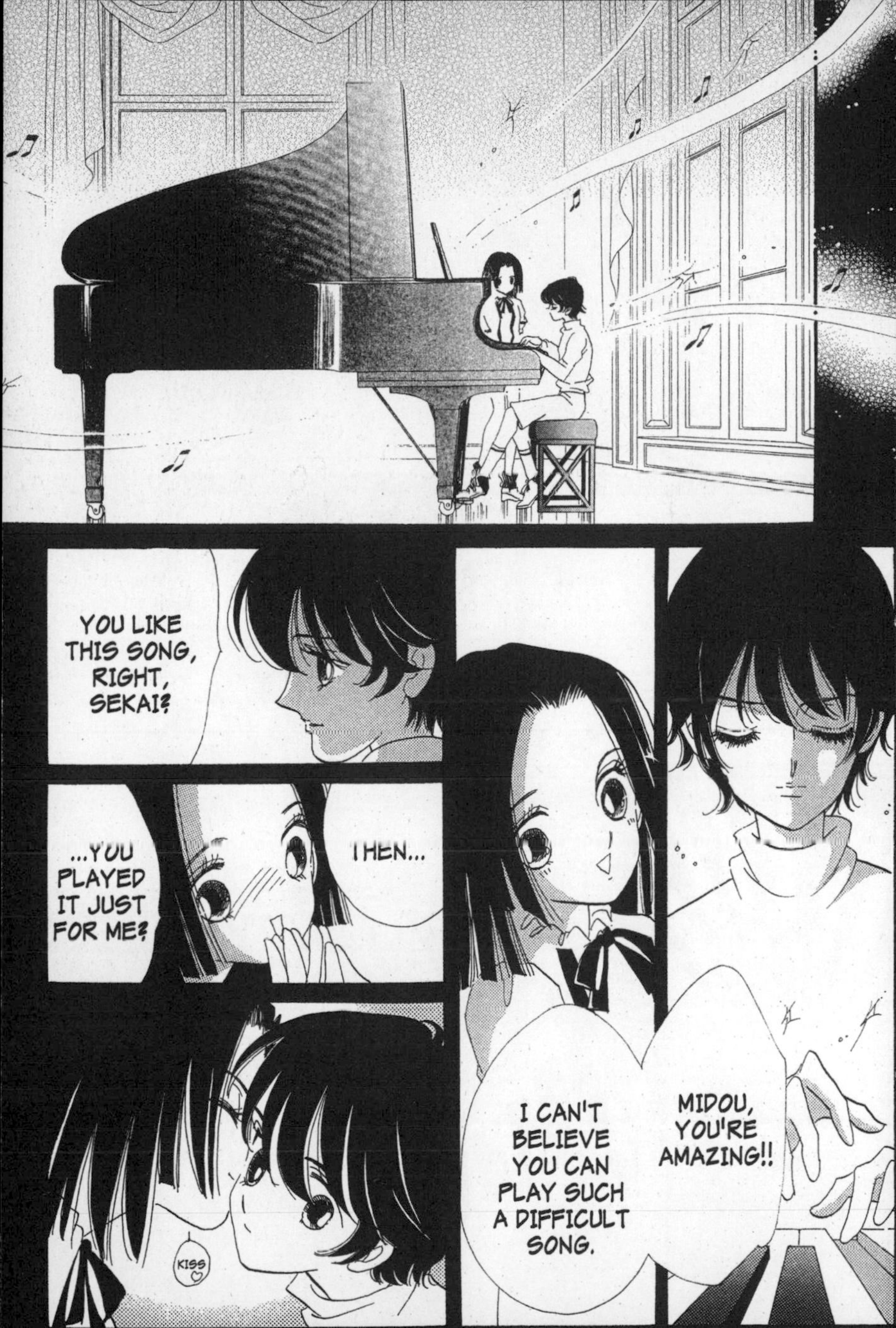
MIDOU, YOU'RE AMAZING!!
I CAN'T BELIEVE YOU CAN PLAY SUCH A DIFFICULT SONG.
YOU LIKE THIS SONG, RIGHT, SEKAI?
THEN...
...YOU PLAYED IT JUST FOR ME?
KISS

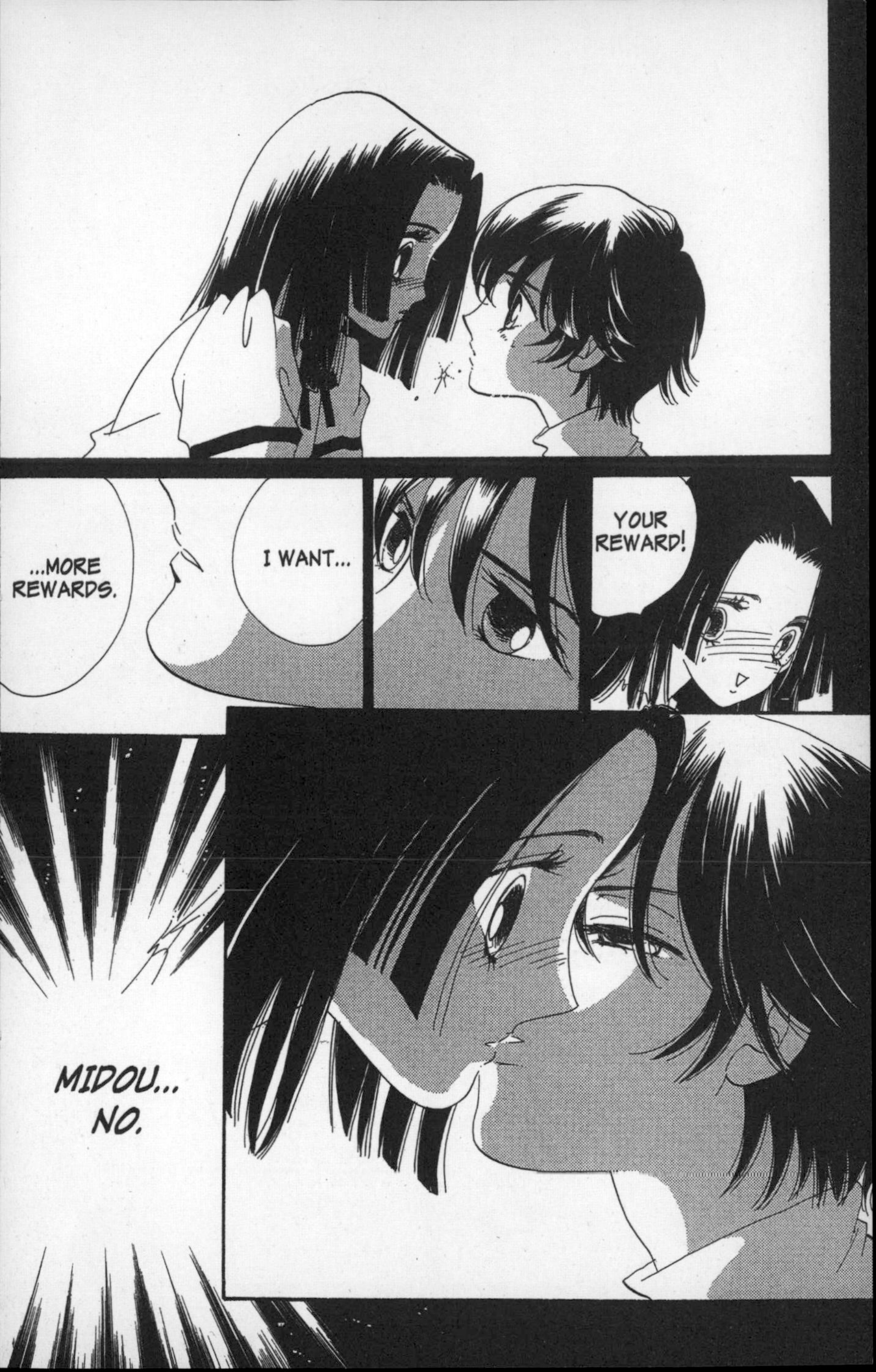
YOUR REWARD!
I WANT...
...MORE REWARDS.
MIDOU... NO.

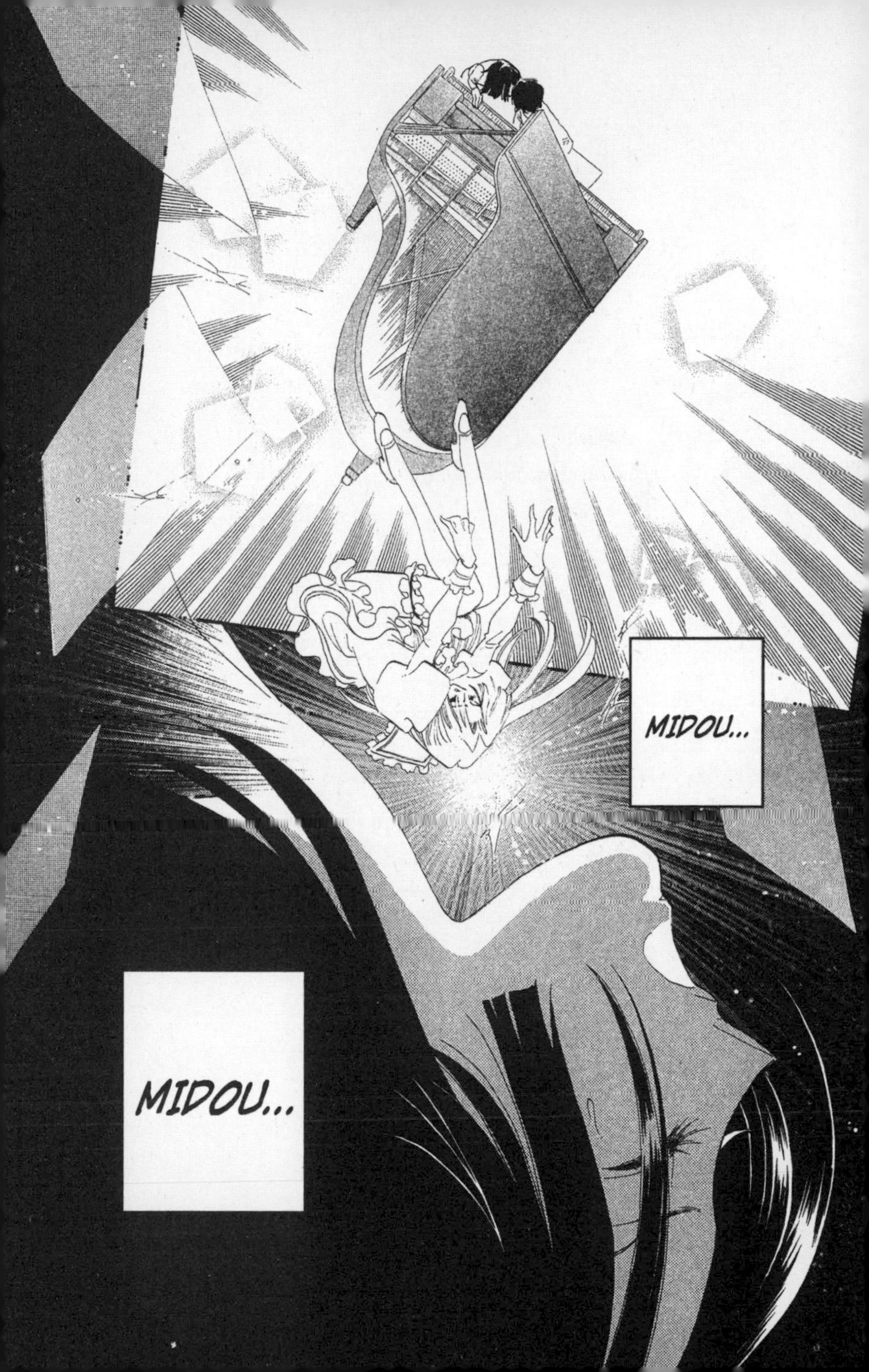
MIDOU...
MIDOU...

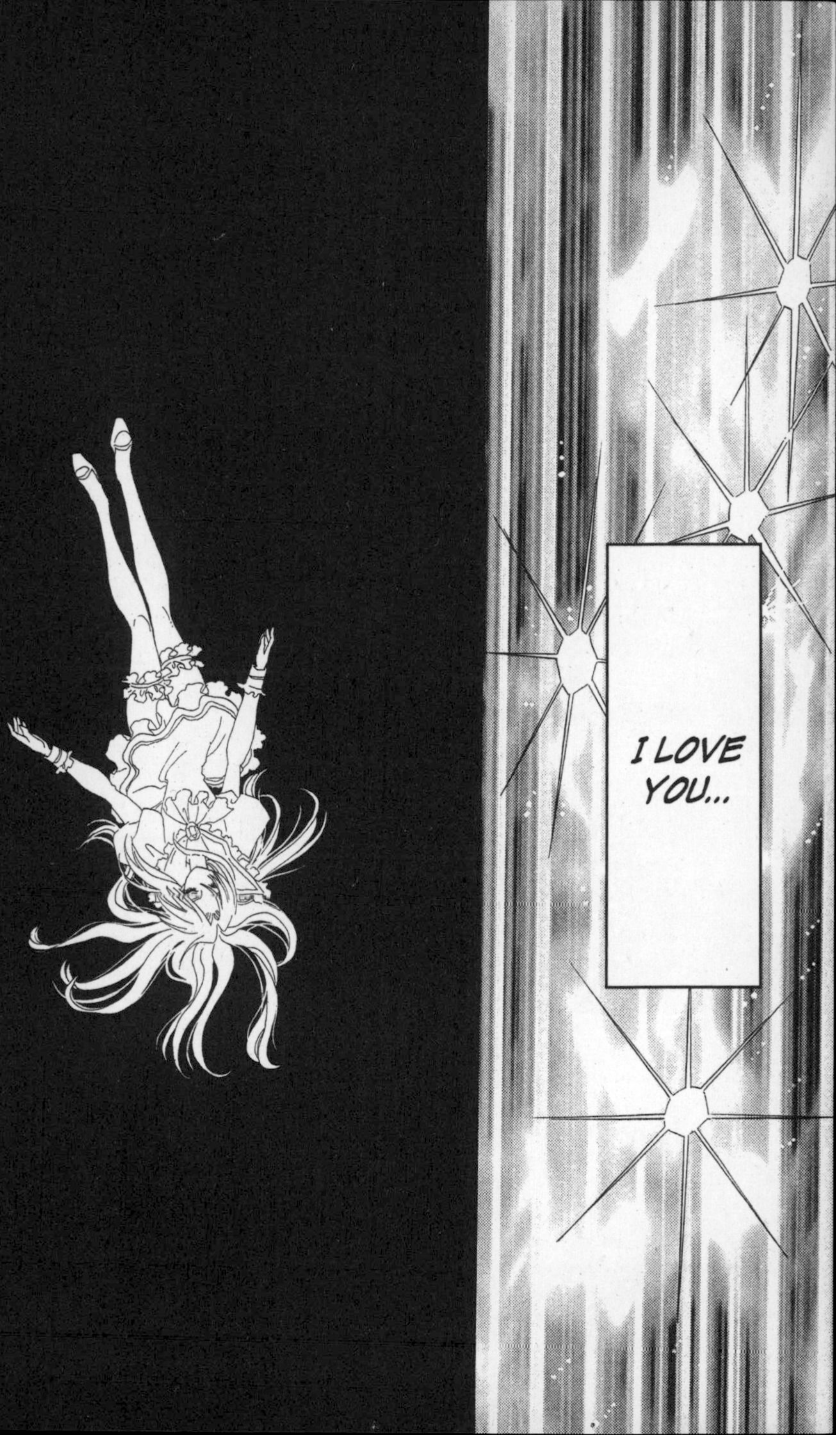
I LOVE YOU...

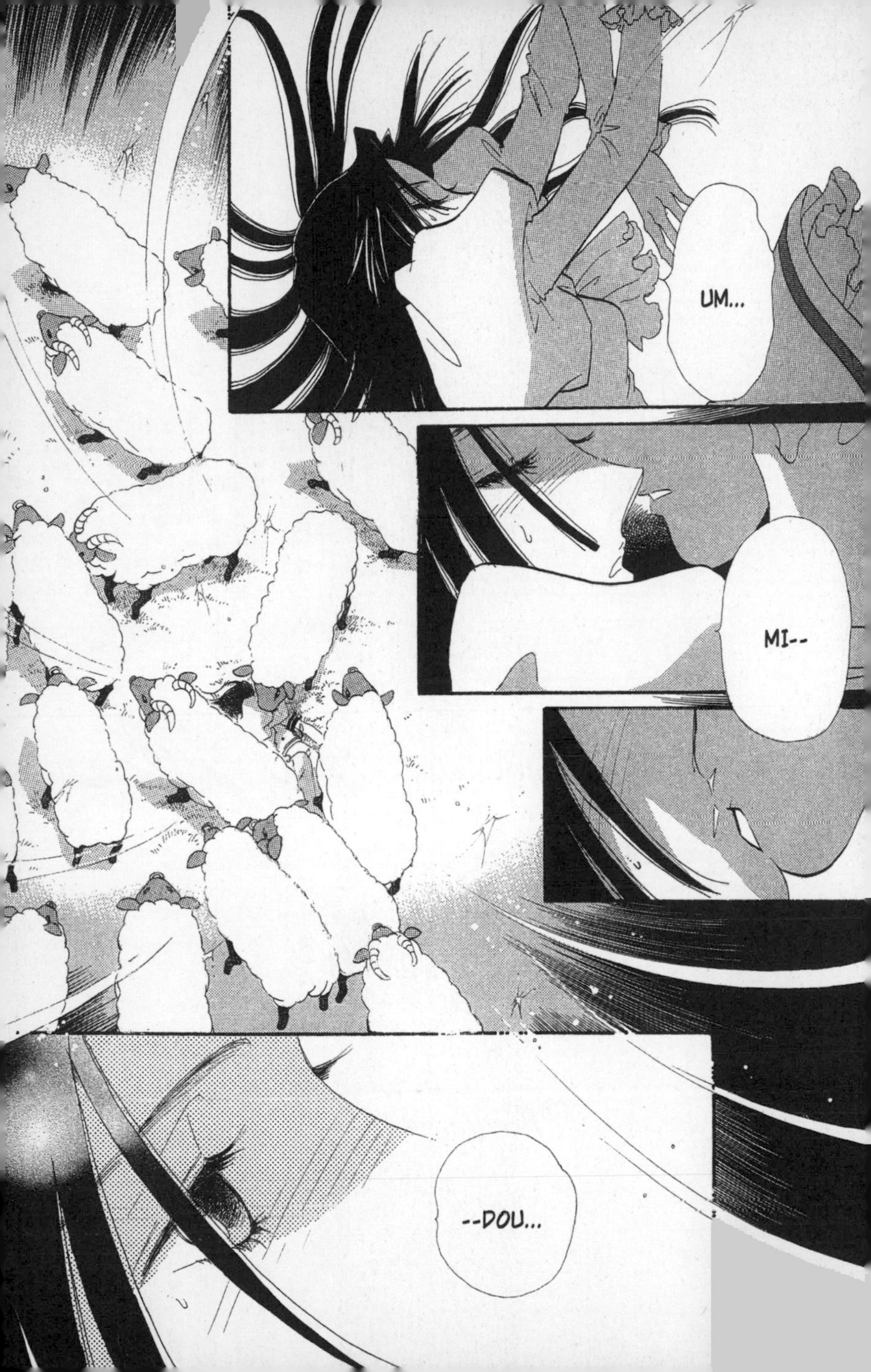
UM...
MI--
--DOU...

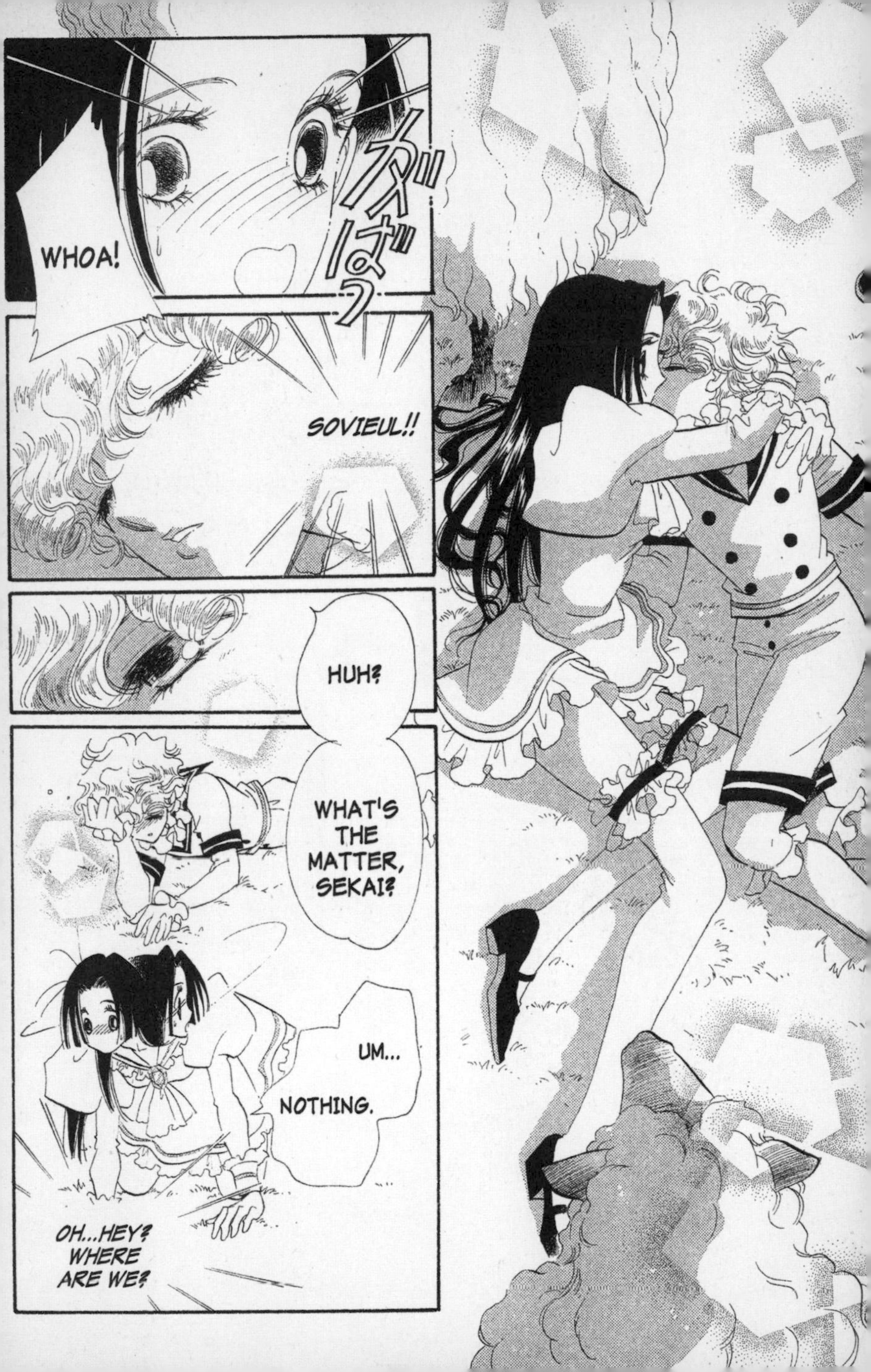
がばっ
WHOA!
SOVIEUL!!
HUH?
WHAT'S THE MATTER, SEKAI?
UM...
NOTHING.
OH...HEY? WHERE ARE WE?

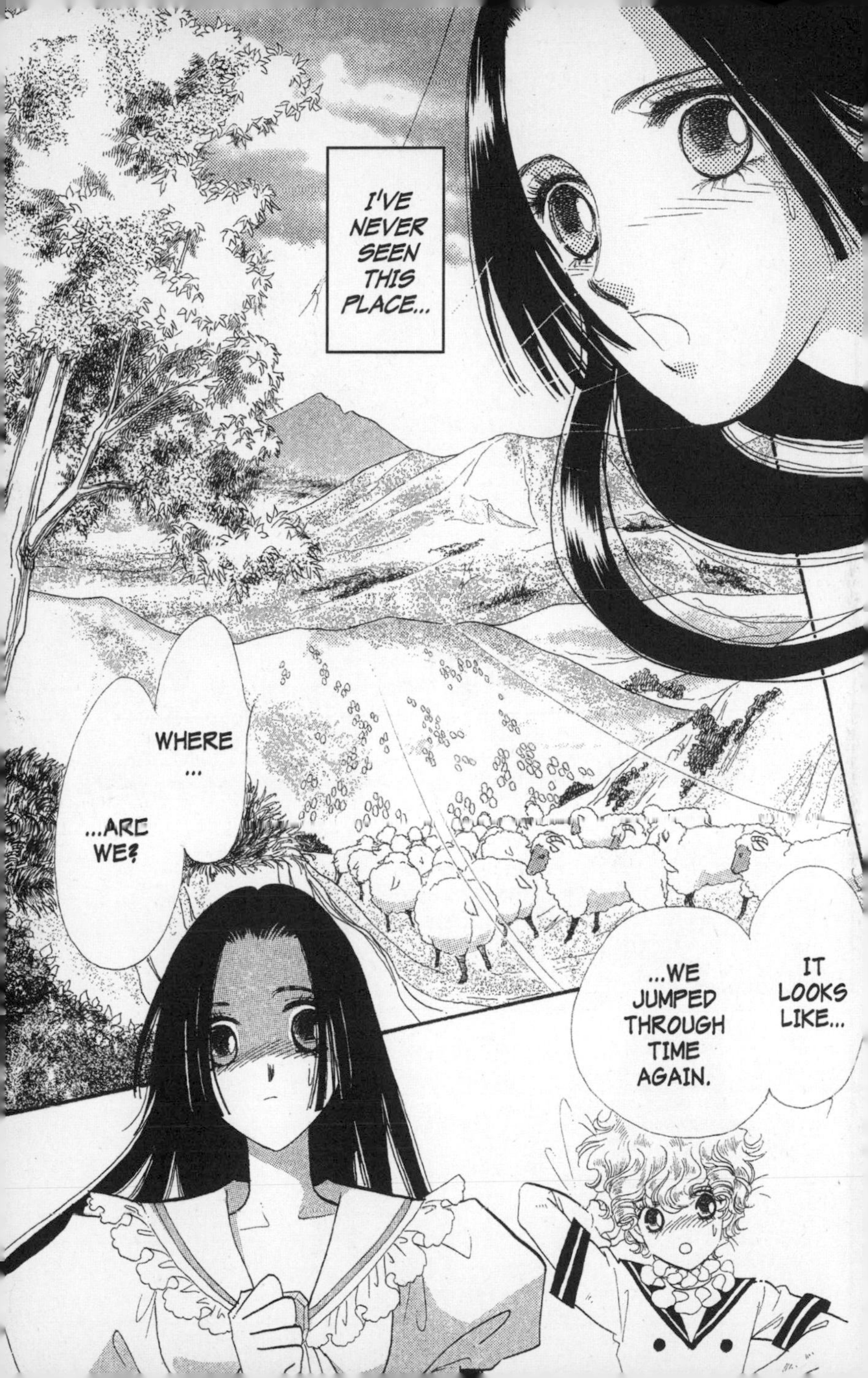
I'VE NEVER SEEN THIS PLACE...
IT LOOKS LIKE...
...WE JUMPED THROUGH TIME AGAIN.
WHERE ...
...ARE WE?

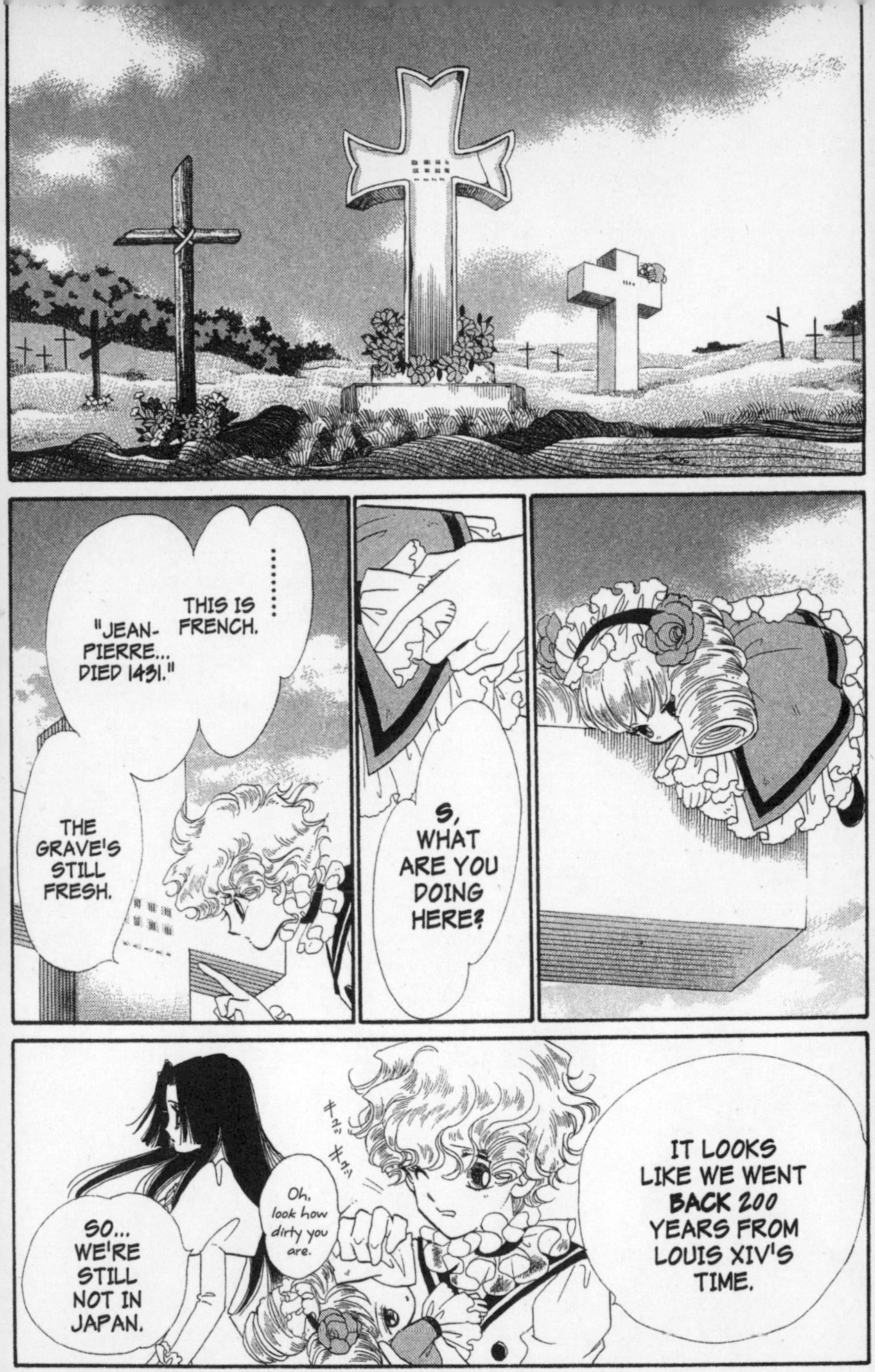
S, WHAT ARE YOU DOING HERE?
......
THIS IS FRENCH.
"JEAN-PIERRE... DIED 1431."
THE GRAVE'S STILL FRESH.
IT LOOKS LIKE WE WENT BACK 200 YEARS FROM LOUIS XIV'S TIME.
キュッ キュッ
Oh, look how dirty you are.
SO... WE'RE STILL NOT IN JAPAN.

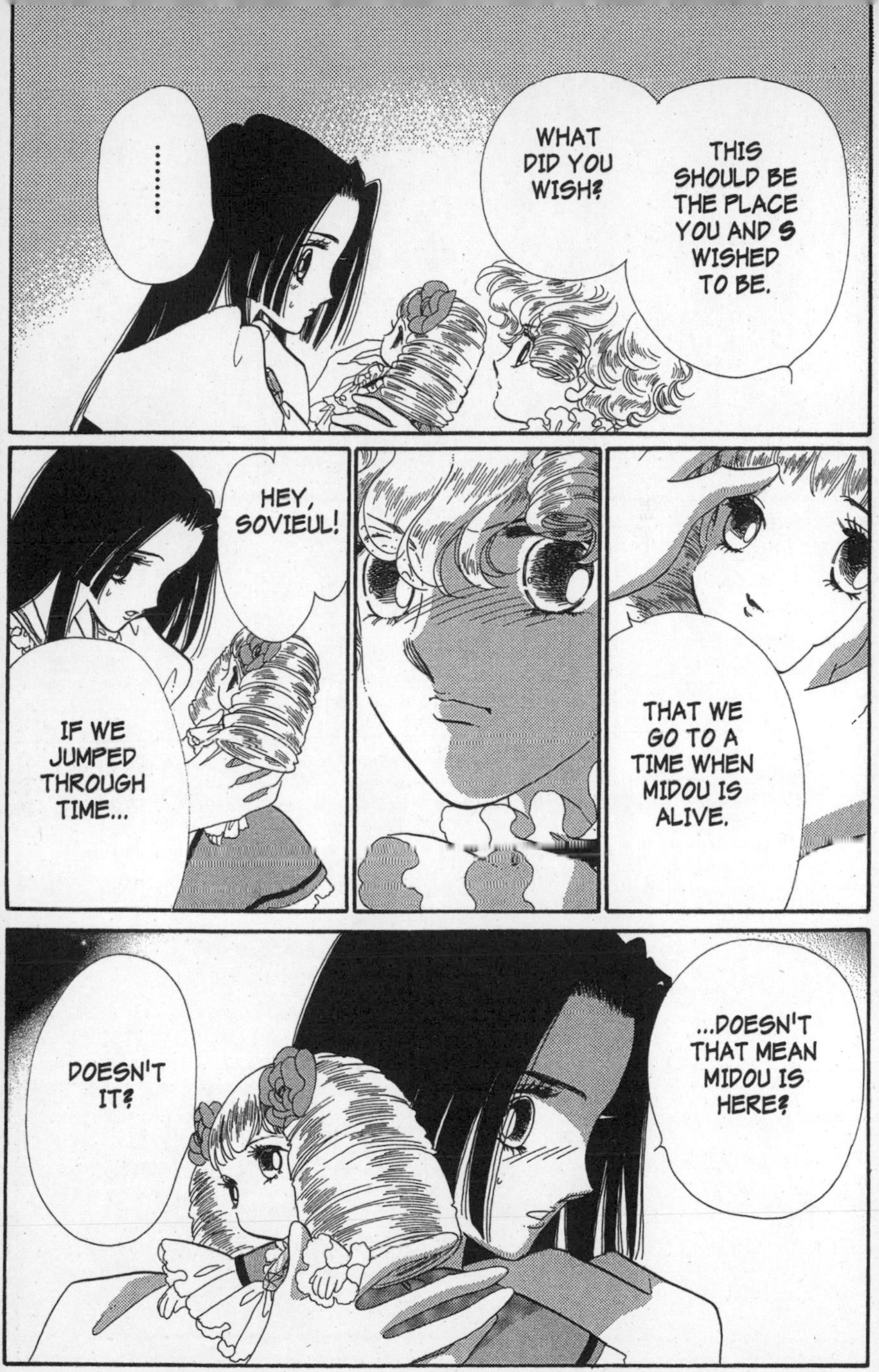
THIS SHOULD BE THE PLACE YOU AND S WISHED TO BE.
WHAT DID YOU WISH?
......
THAT WE GO TO A TIME WHEN MIDOU IS ALIVE.
HEY, SOVIEUL!
IF WE JUMPED THROUGH TIME...
...DOESN'T THAT MEAN MIDOU IS HERE?
DOESN'T IT?

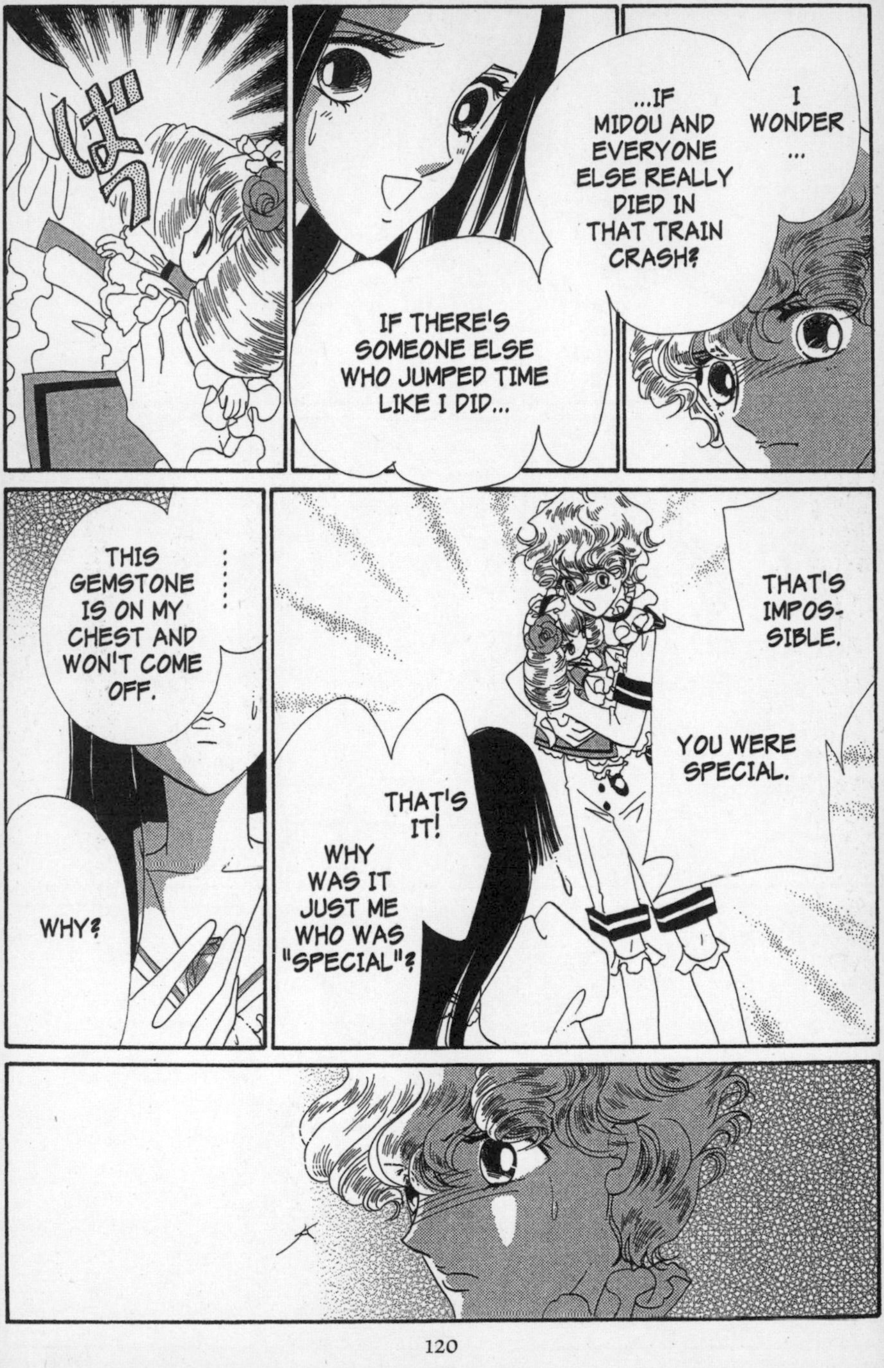
I WONDER ...
...IF MIDOU AND EVERYONE ELSE REALLY DIED IN THAT TRAIN CRASH?
IF THERE'S SOMEONE ELSE WHO JUMPED TIME LIKE I DID...
ぱっ
THAT'S IMPOSSIBLE.
YOU WERE SPECIAL.
THAT'S IT!
WHY WAS IT JUST ME WHO WAS "SPECIAL"?
......
THIS GEMSTONE IS ON MY CHEST AND WON'T COME OFF.
WHY?

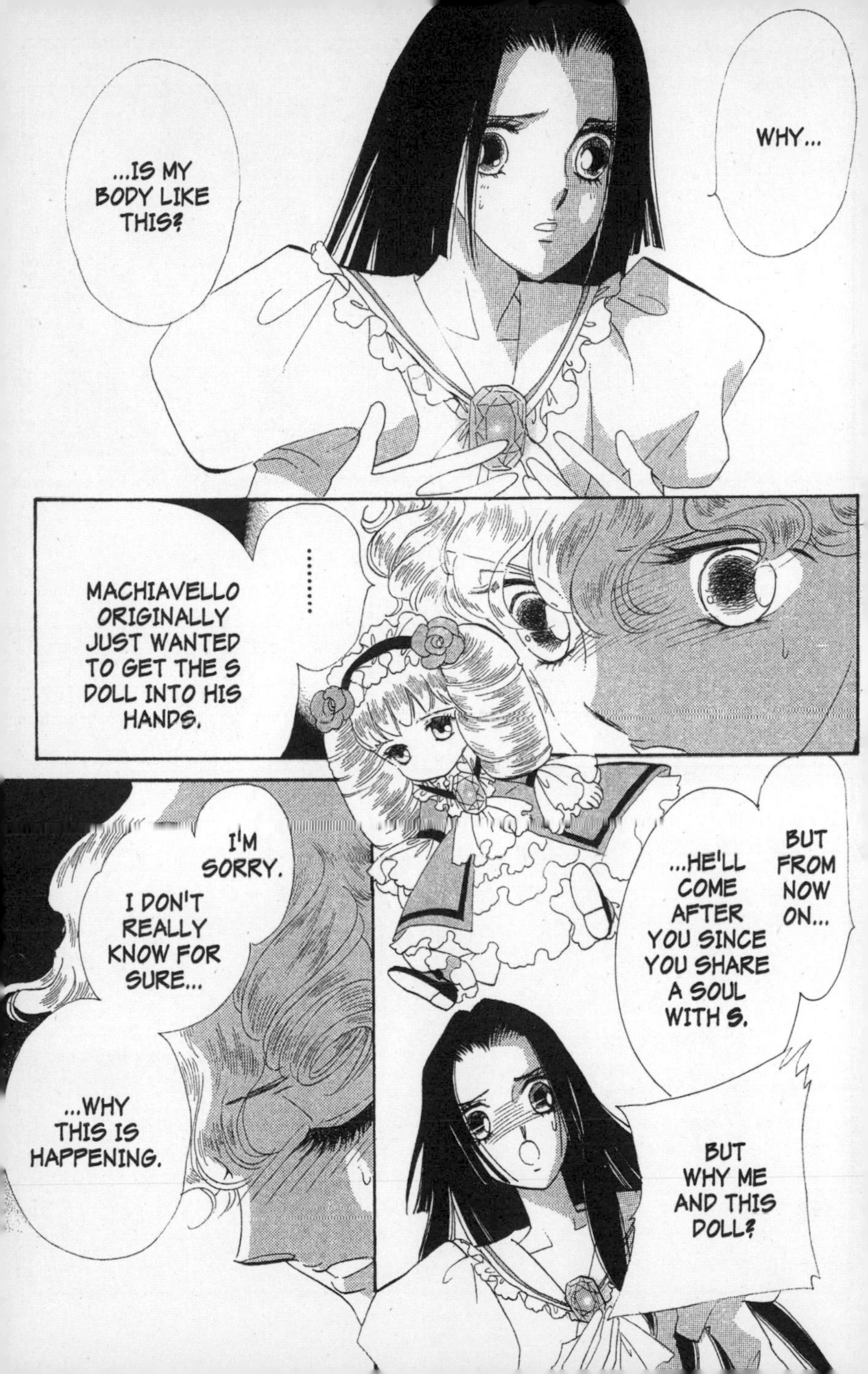
WHY...
...IS MY BODY LIKE THIS?
......
MACHIAVELLO ORIGINALLY JUST WANTED TO GET THE S DOLL INTO HIS HANDS.
BUT FROM NOW ON...
...HE'LL COME AFTER YOU SINCE YOU SHARE A SOUL WITH S.
BUT WHY ME AND THIS DOLL?
I'M SORRY.
I DON'T REALLY KNOW FOR SURE...
...WHY THIS IS HAPPENING.

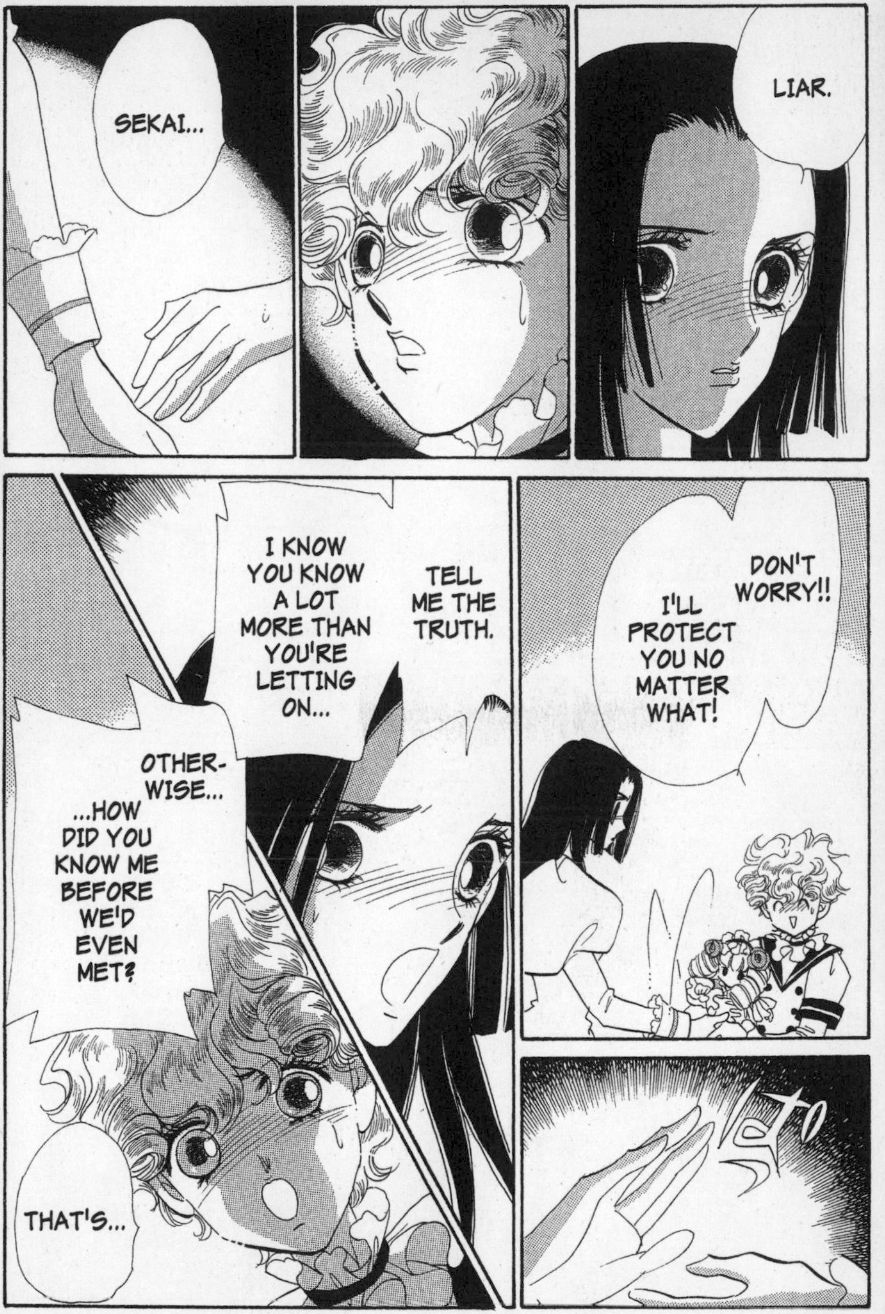
LIAR.
SEKAI...
DON'T WORRY!!
I'LL PROTECT YOU NO MATTER WHAT!
TELL ME THE TRUTH.
I KNOW YOU KNOW A LOT MORE THAN YOU'RE LETTING ON...
OTHER-WISE...
...HOW DID YOU KNOW ME BEFORE WE'D EVEN MET?
THAT'S...

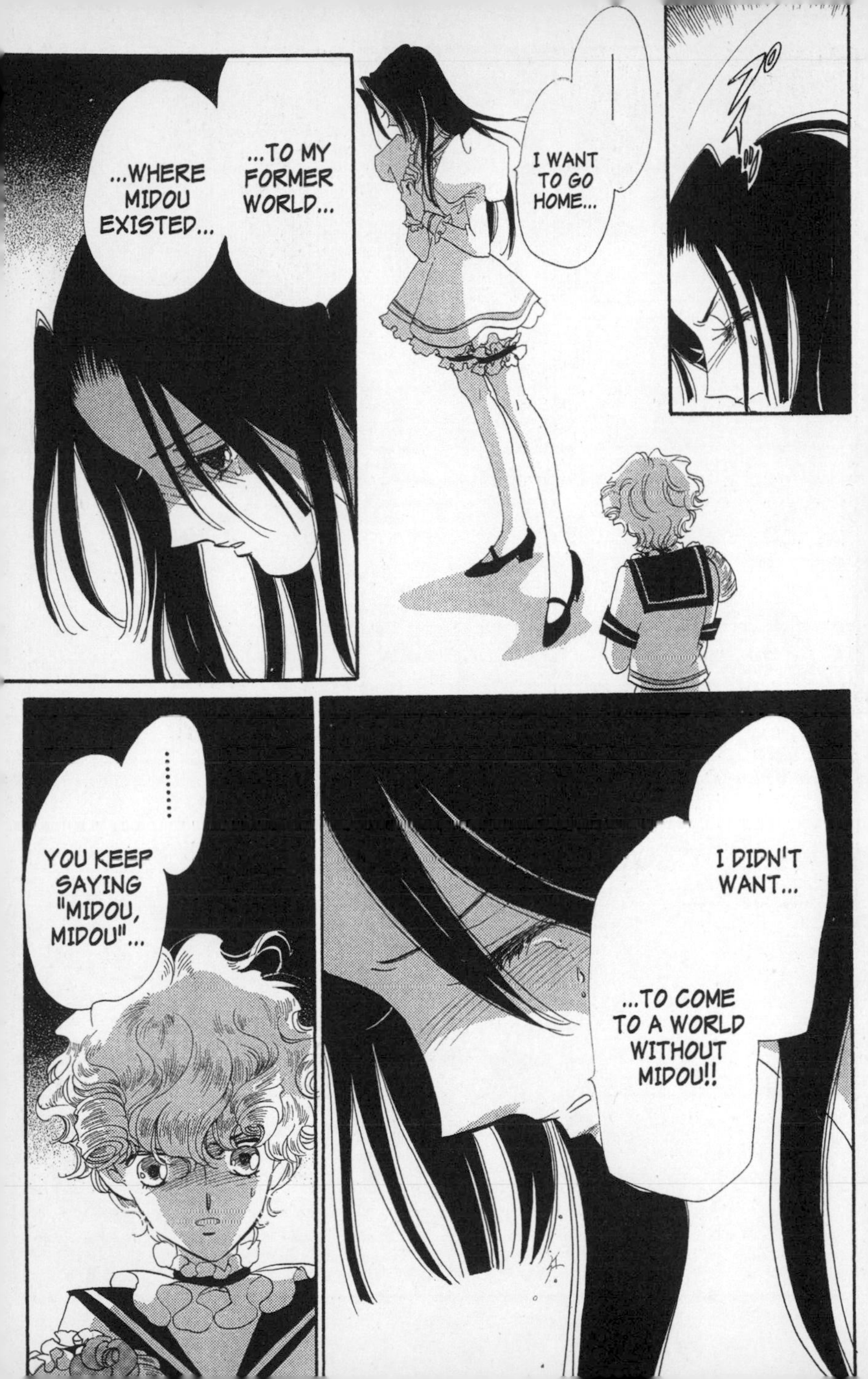
I WANT TO GO HOME...
...TO MY FORMER WORLD...
...WHERE MIDOU EXISTED...
I DIDN'T WANT...
...TO COME TO A WORLD WITHOUT MIDOU!!
......
YOU KEEP SAYING "MIDOU, MIDOU"...

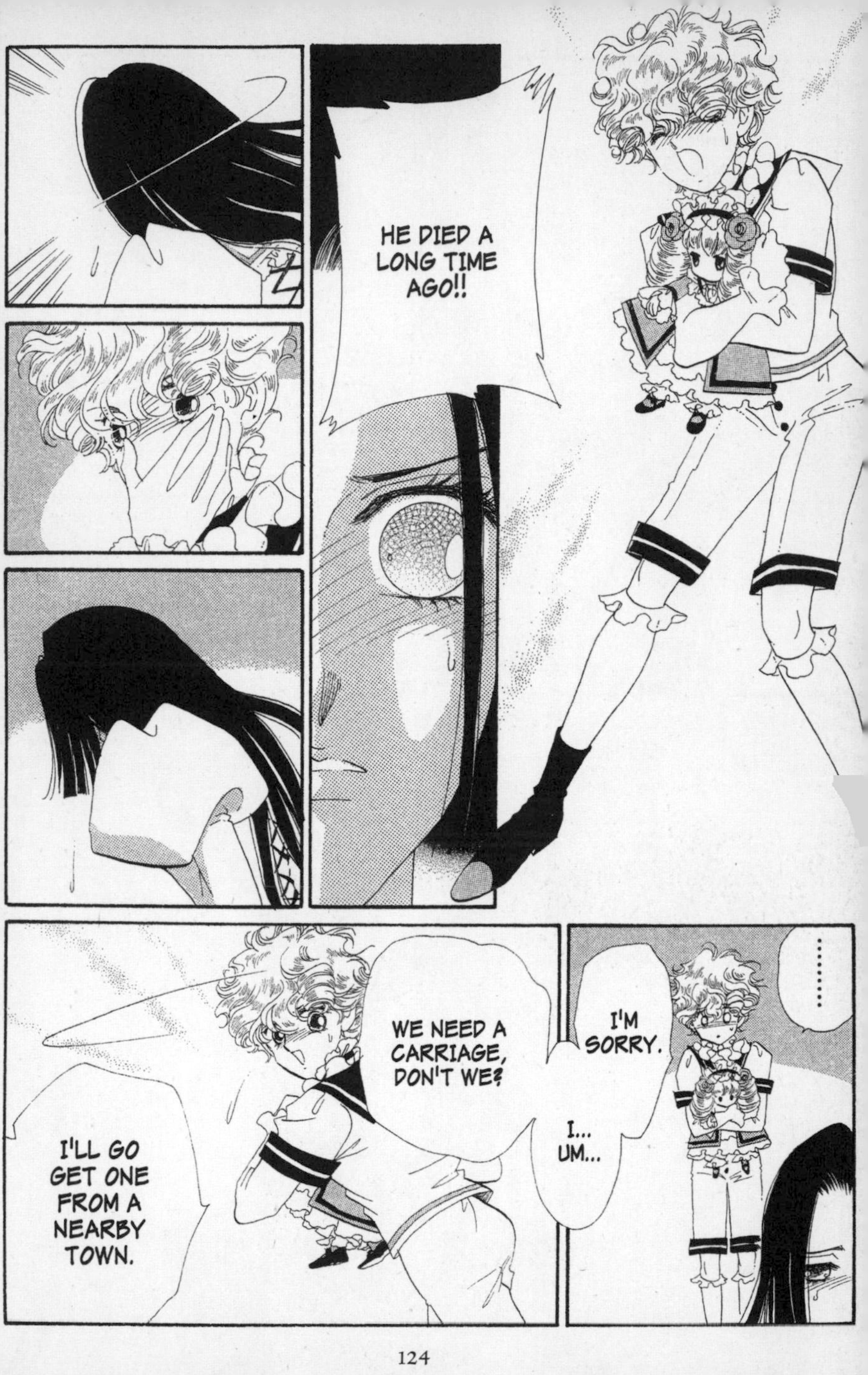
HE DIED A LONG TIME AGO!!
......
I'M SORRY.
I... UM...
WE NEED A CARRIAGE, DON'T WE?
I'LL GO GET ONE FROM A NEARBY TOWN.

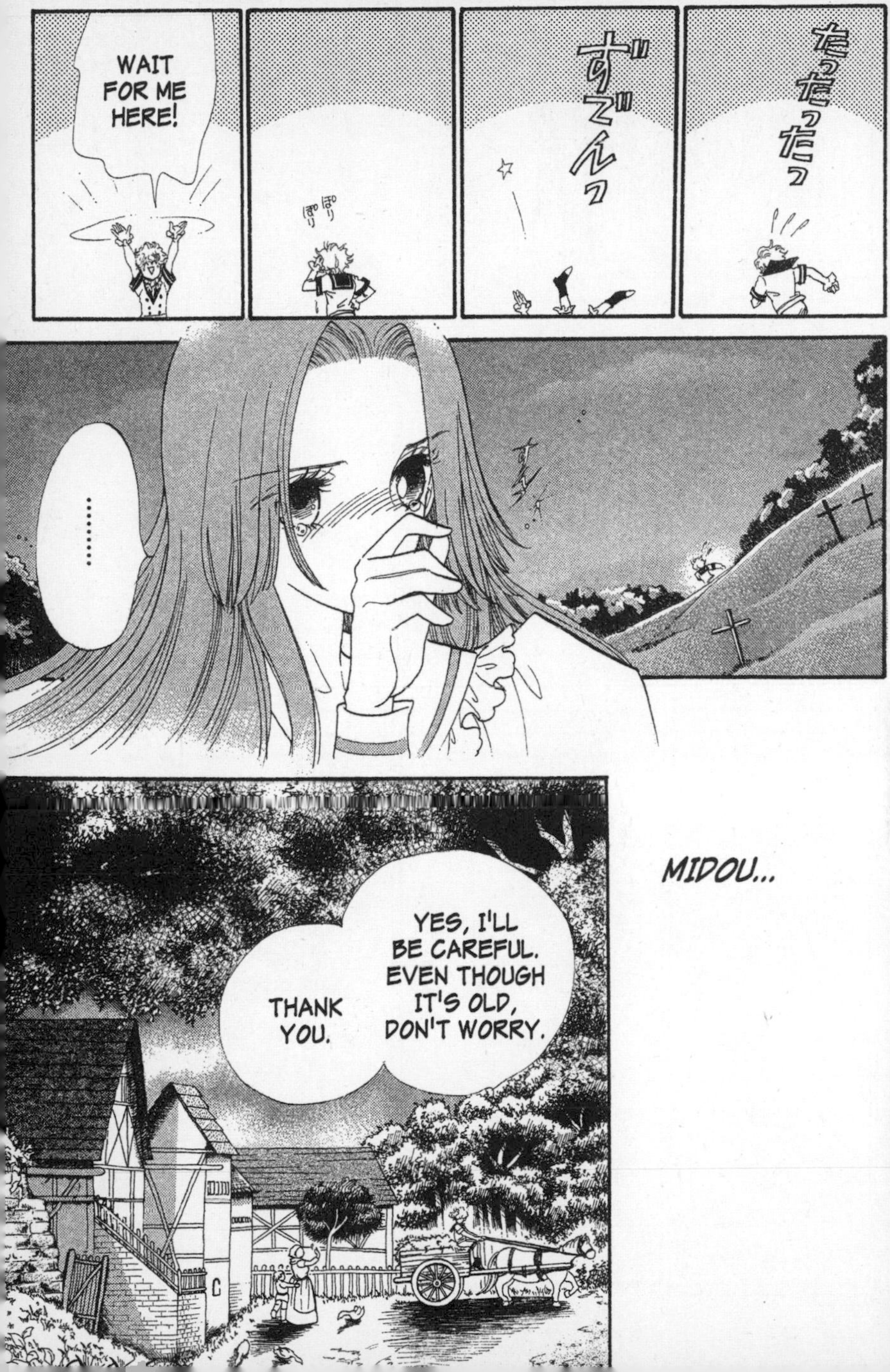
たったっ
ずでんっ
ぽりぽり
WAIT FOR ME HERE!
......
MIDOU...
YES, I'LL BE CAREFUL. EVEN THOUGH IT'S OLD, DON'T WORRY.
THANK YOU.

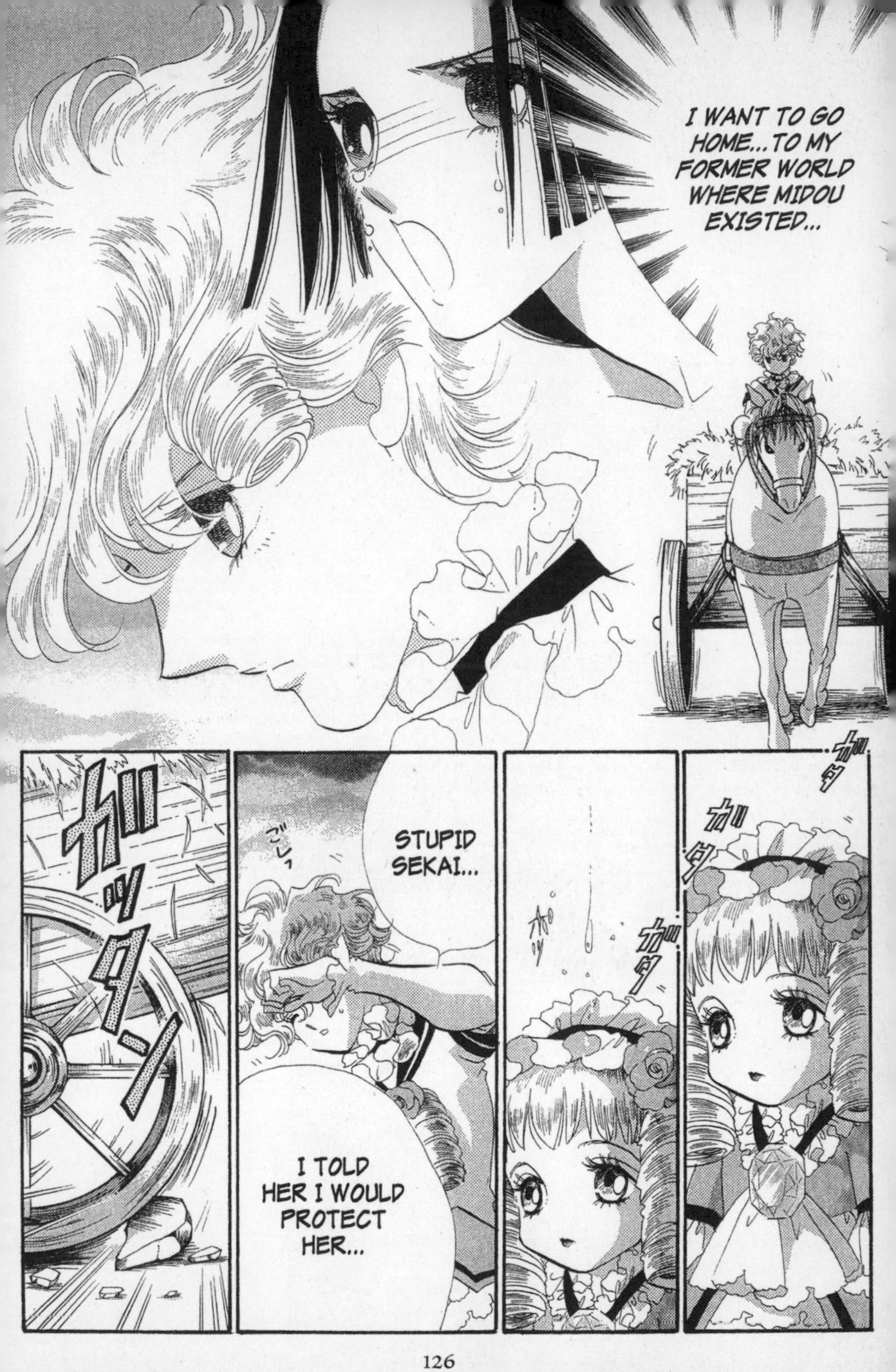
I WANT TO GO HOME...TO MY FORMER WORLD WHERE MIDOU EXISTED...
STUPID SEKAI...
I TOLD HER I WOULD PROTECT HER...

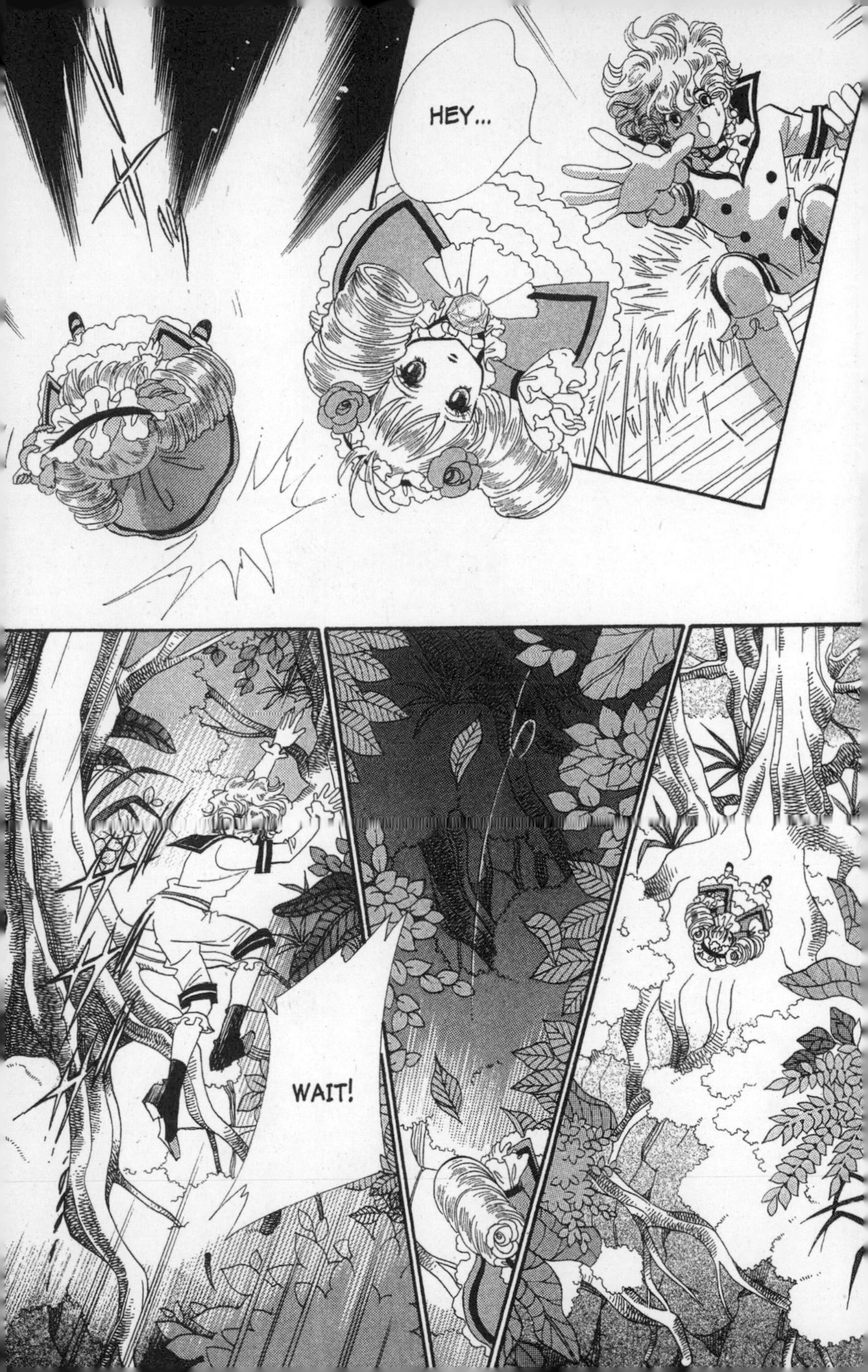
HEY...
WAIT!

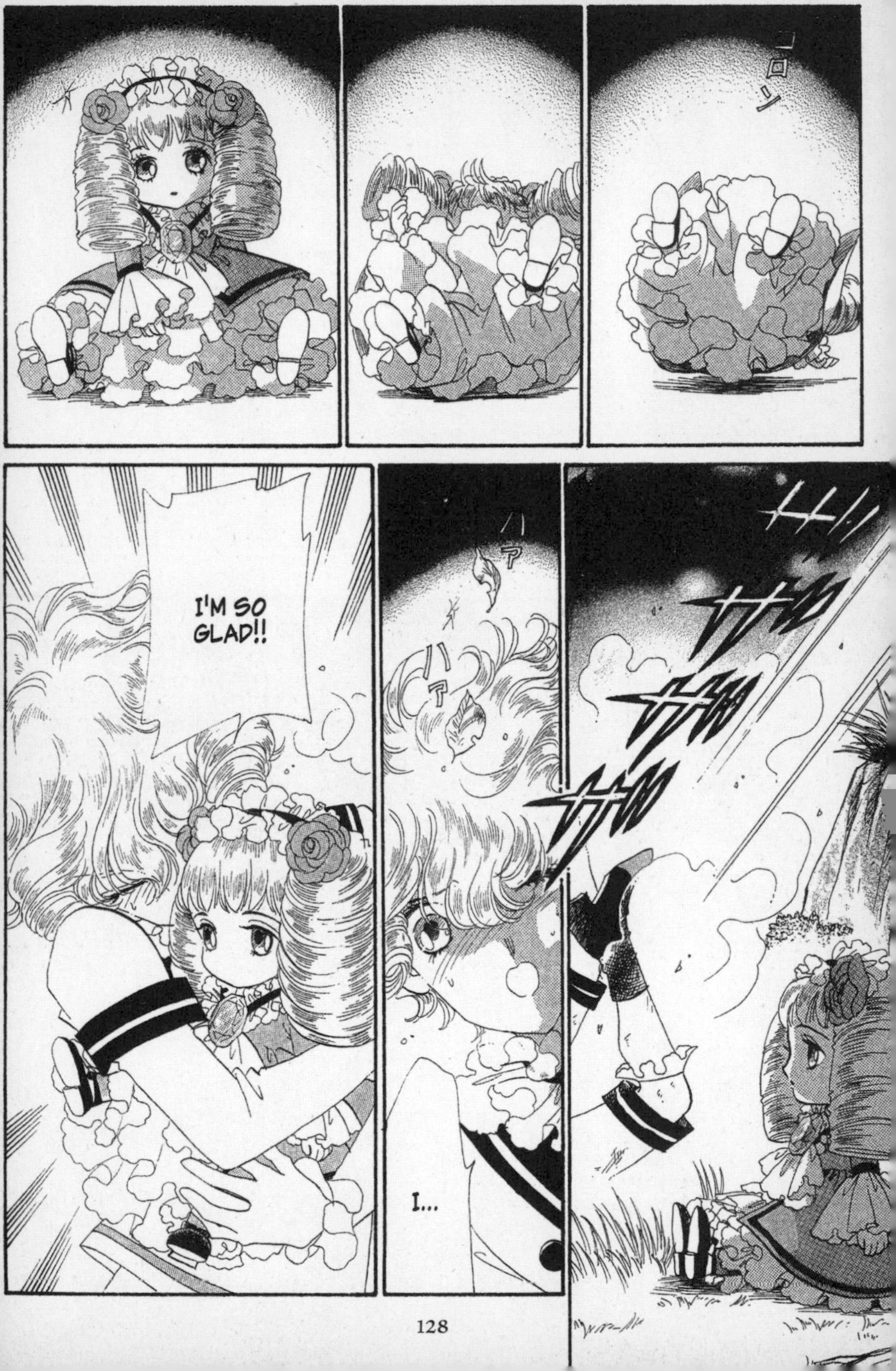
コロン
ハァ
ハァ
I...
I'M SO GLAD!!

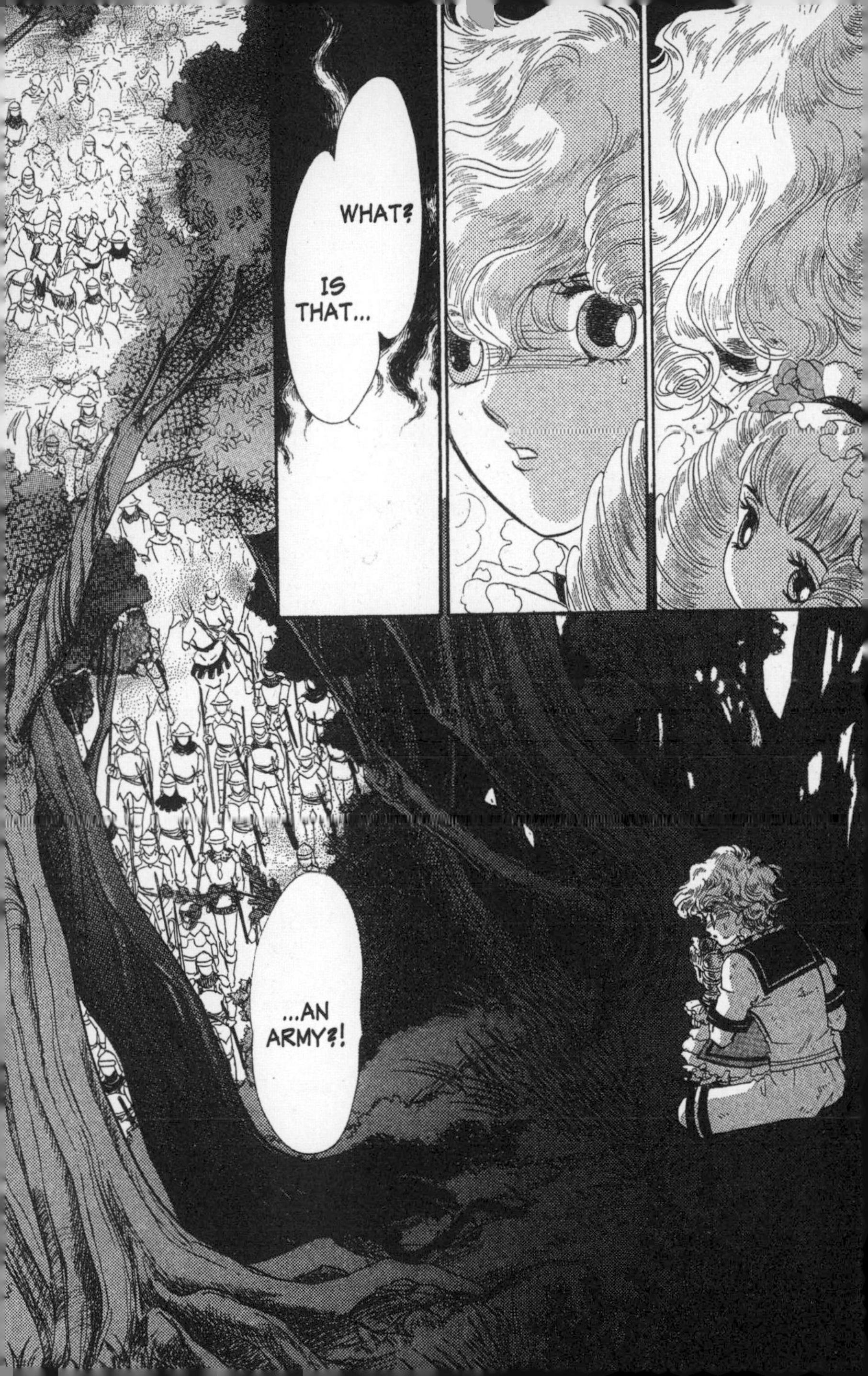
WHAT? IS THAT...
...AN ARMY?!

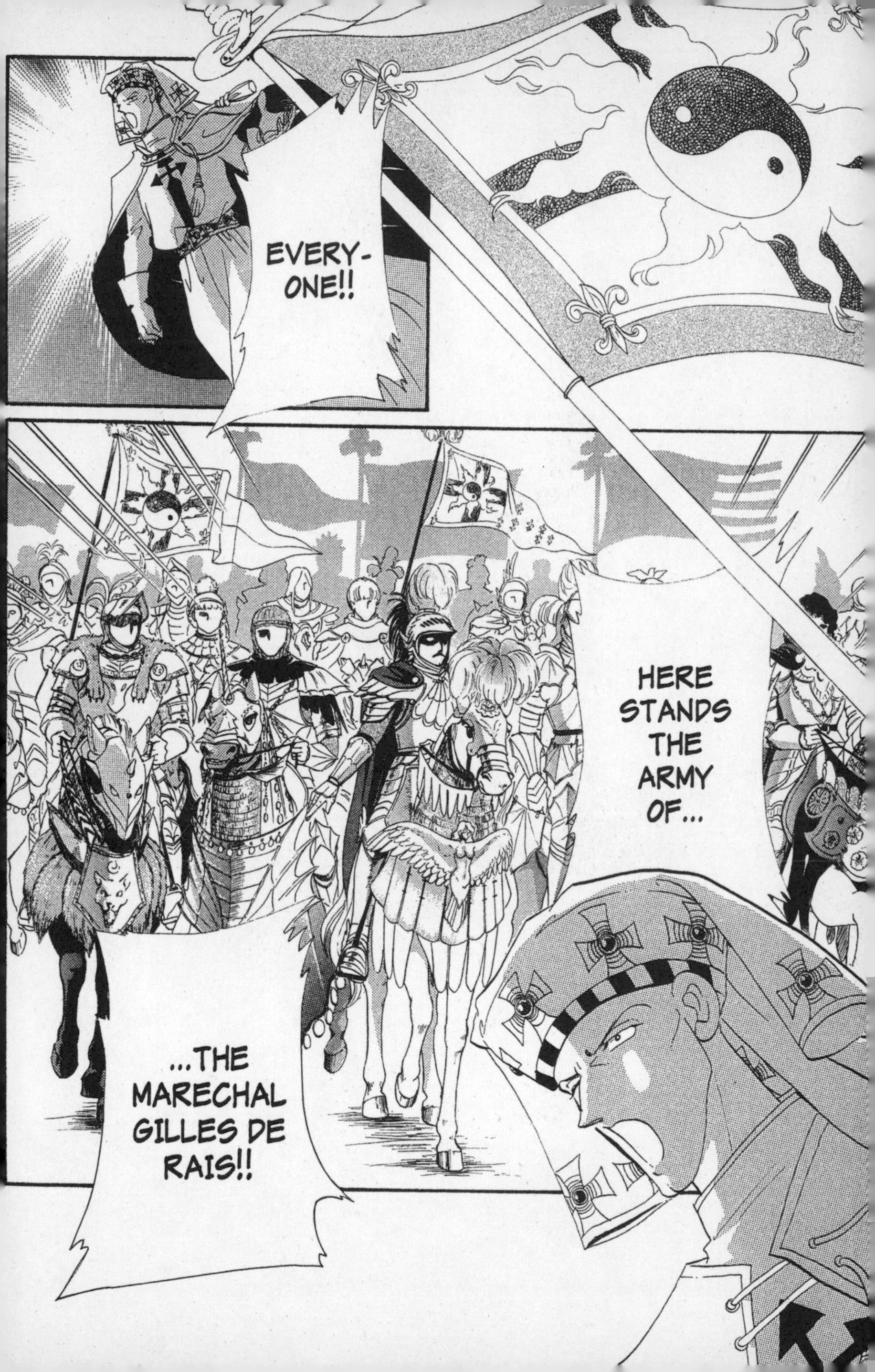
EVERY-ONE!!
HERE STANDS THE ARMY OF...
...THE MARECHAL GILLES DE RAIS!!

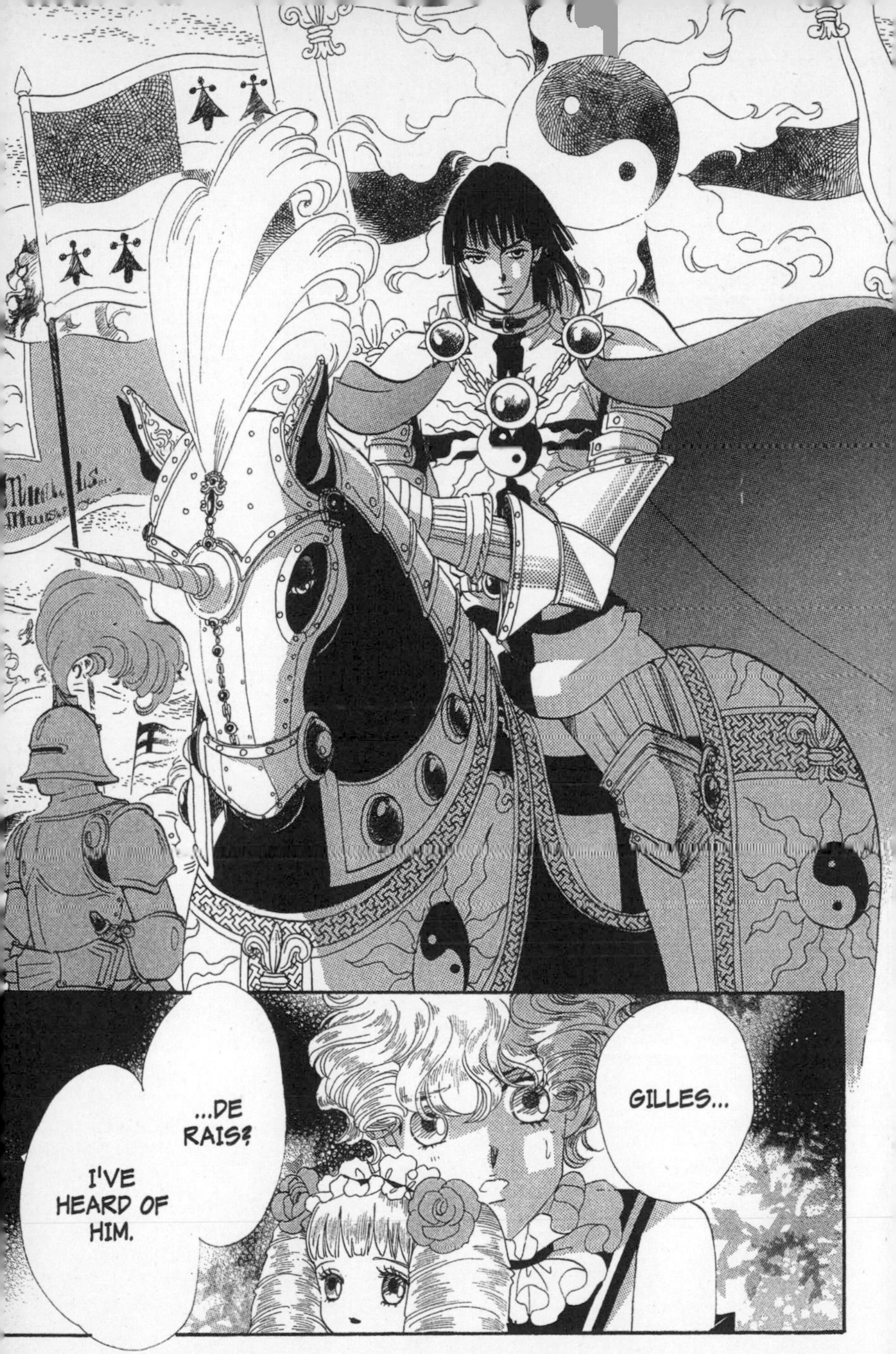
GILLES...
...DE RAIS?
I'VE HEARD OF HIM.

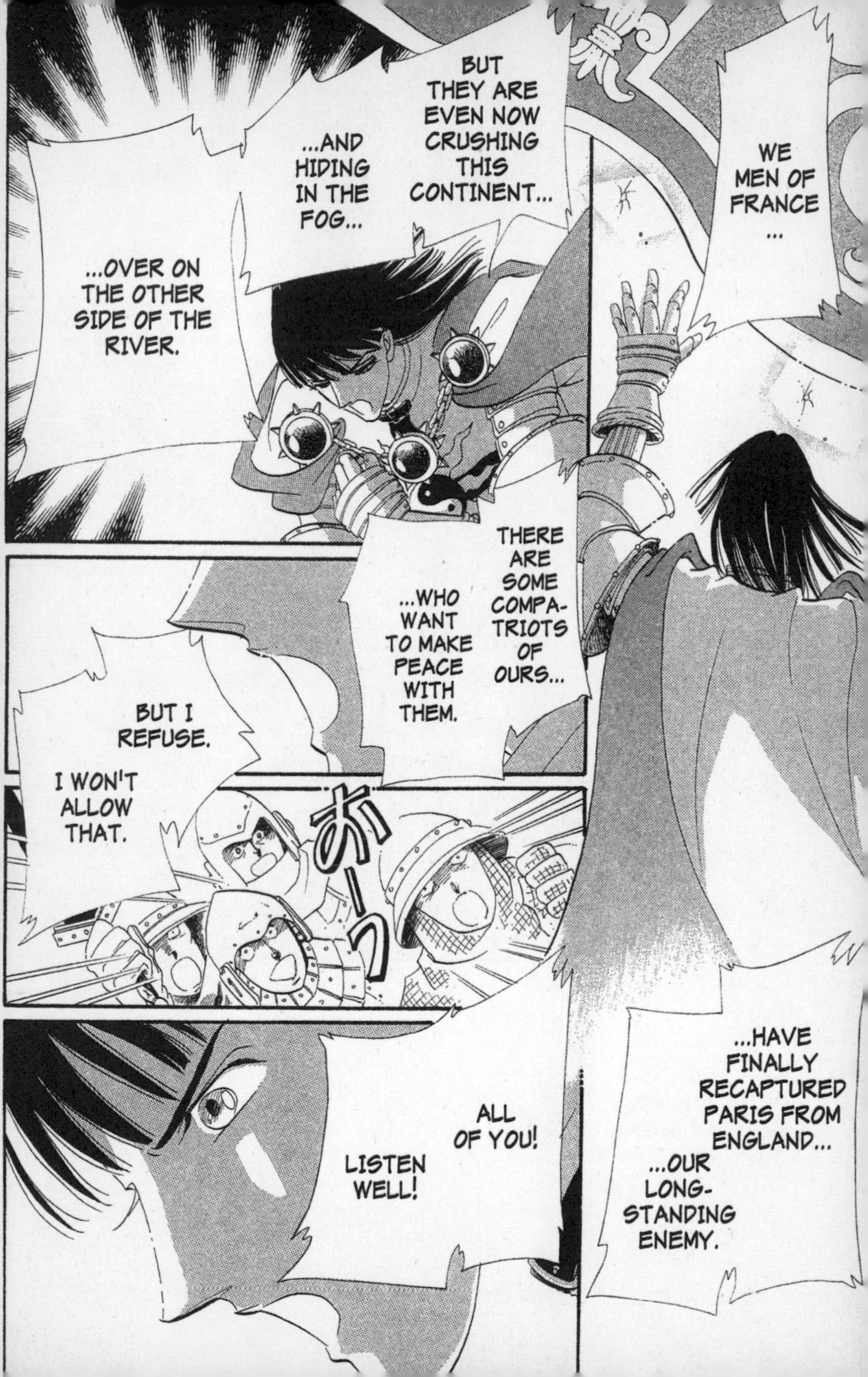
WE MEN OF FRANCE ...
...HAVE FINALLY RECAPTURED PARIS FROM ENGLAND...
...OUR LONG-STANDING ENEMY.
BUT THEY ARE EVEN NOW CRUSHING THIS CONTINENT...
...AND HIDING IN THE FOG...
...OVER ON THE OTHER SIDE OF THE RIVER.
THERE ARE SOME COMPA-TRIOTS OF OURS...
...WHO WANT TO MAKE PEACE WITH THEM.
BUT I REFUSE.
I WON'T ALLOW THAT.
あーっ
ALL OF YOU!
LISTEN WELL!

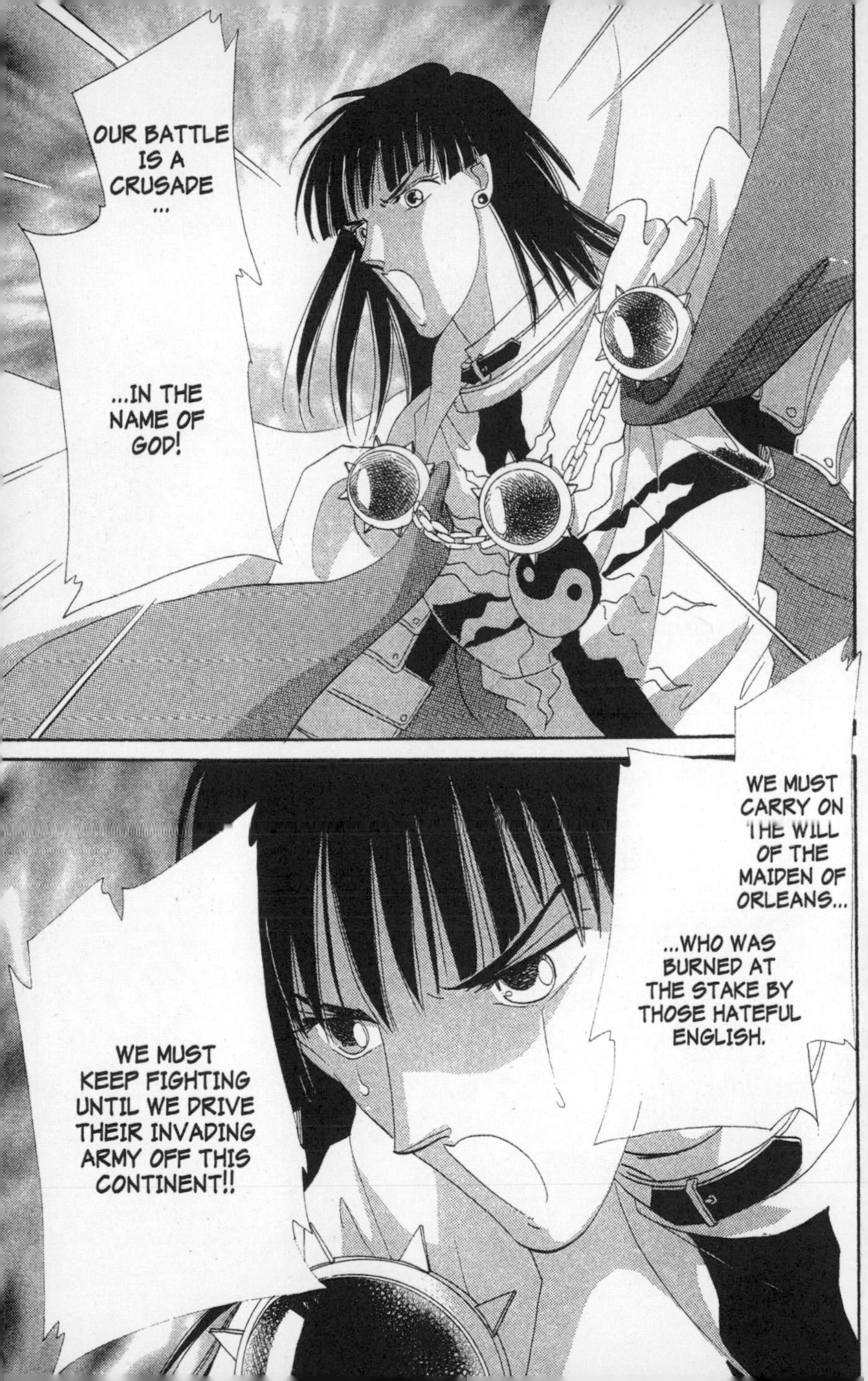
OUR BATTLE IS A CRUSADE ...
...IN THE NAME OF GOD!
WE MUST CARRY ON THE WILL OF THE MAIDEN OF ORLEANS...
...WHO WAS BURNED AT THE STAKE BY THOSE HATEFUL ENGLISH.
WE MUST KEEP FIGHTING UNTIL WE DRIVE THEIR INVADING ARMY OFF THIS CONTINENT!!

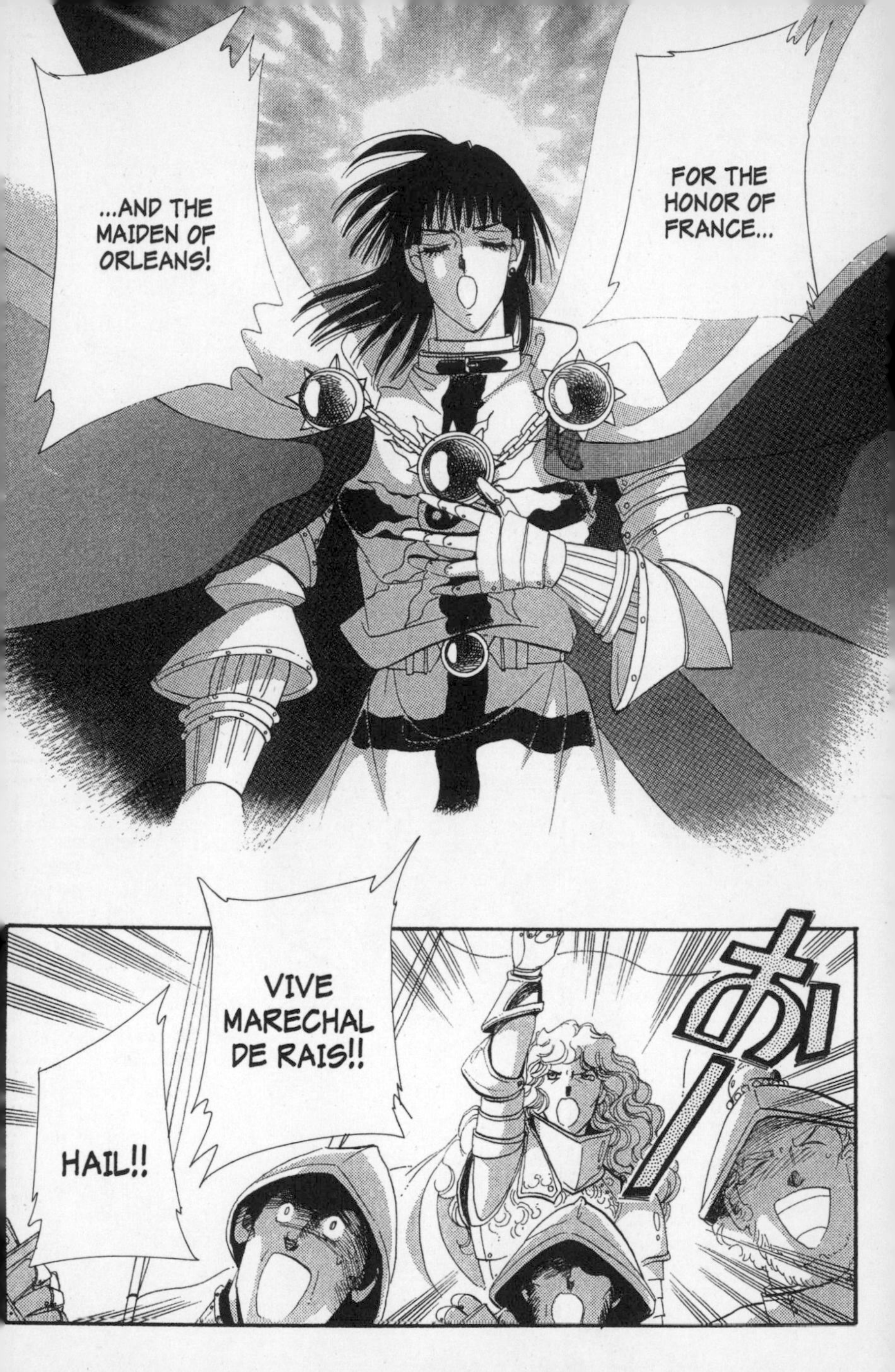
FOR THE HONOR OF FRANCE...
...AND THE MAIDEN OF ORLEANS!
VIVE MARECHAL DE RAIS!!
おー
HAIL!!

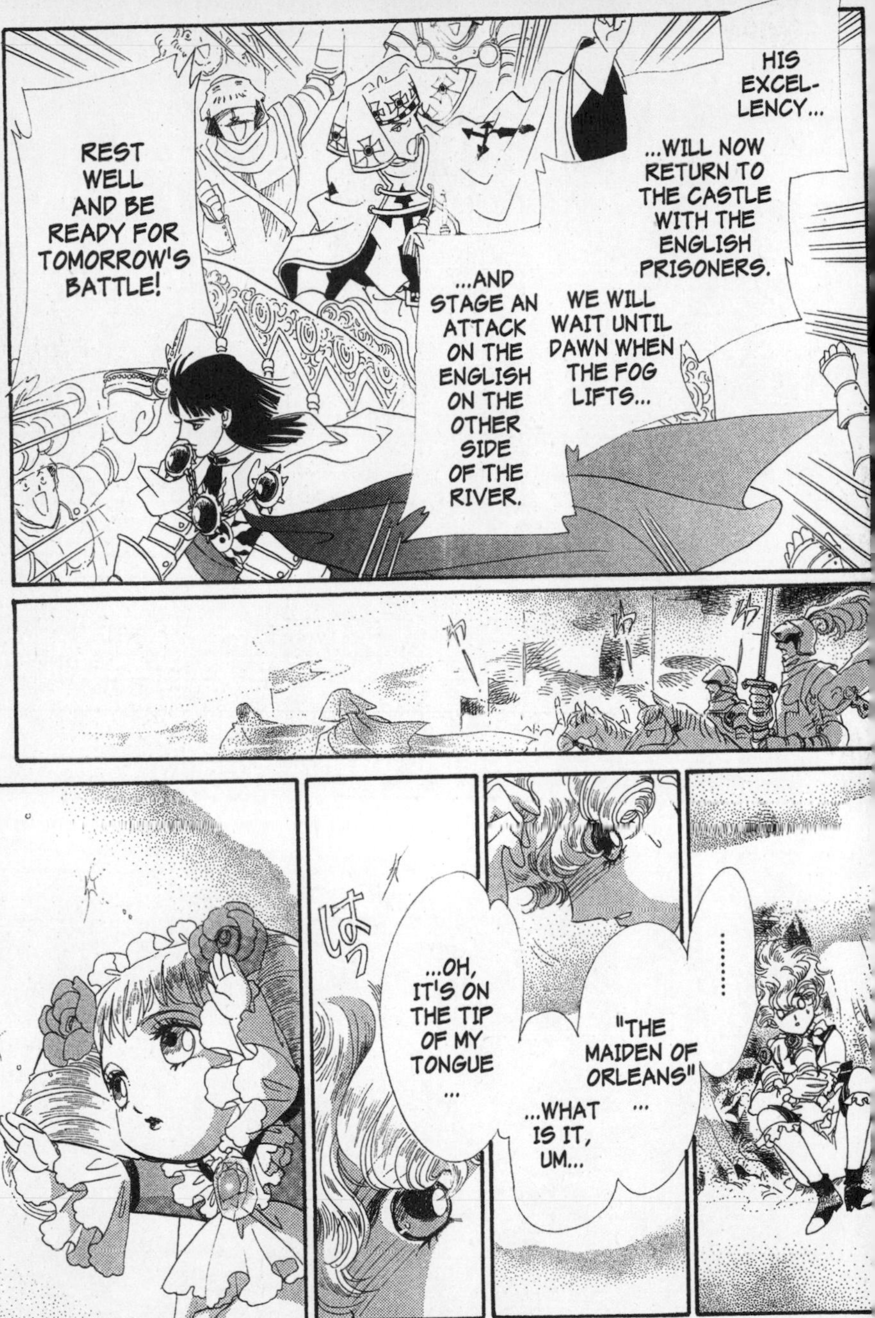
HIS EXCELLENCY...
...WILL NOW RETURN TO THE CASTLE WITH THE ENGLISH PRISONERS.
WE WILL WAIT UNTIL DAWN WHEN THE FOG LIFTS...
...AND STAGE AN ATTACK ON THE ENGLISH ON THE OTHER SIDE OF THE RIVER.
REST WELL AND BE READY FOR TOMORROW'S BATTLE!
......
"THE MAIDEN OF ORLEANS" ...
...WHAT IS IT, UM...
...OH, IT'S ON THE TIP OF MY TONGUE ...
はっ

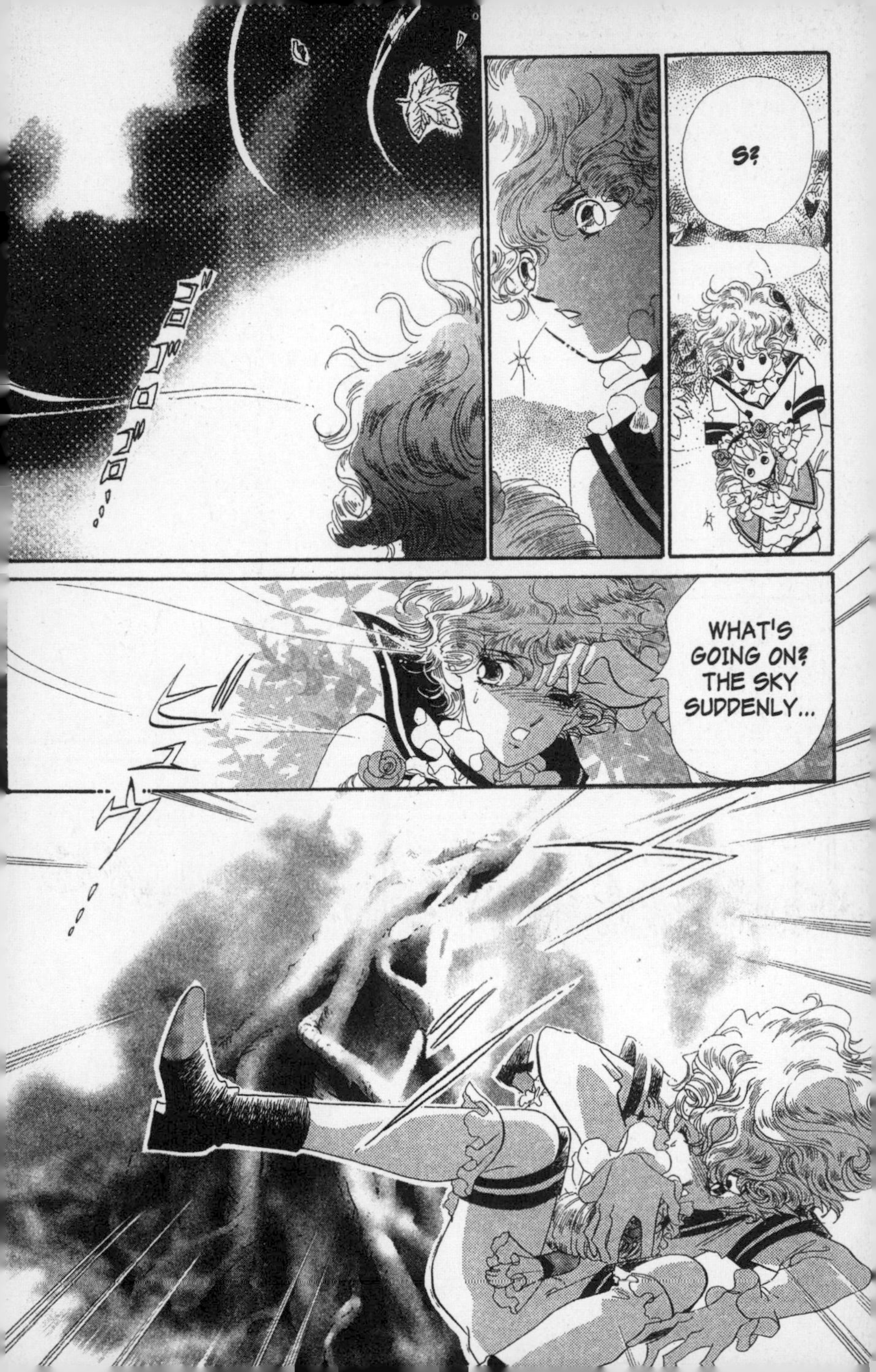
S?
WHAT'S GOING ON? THE SKY SUDDENLY...

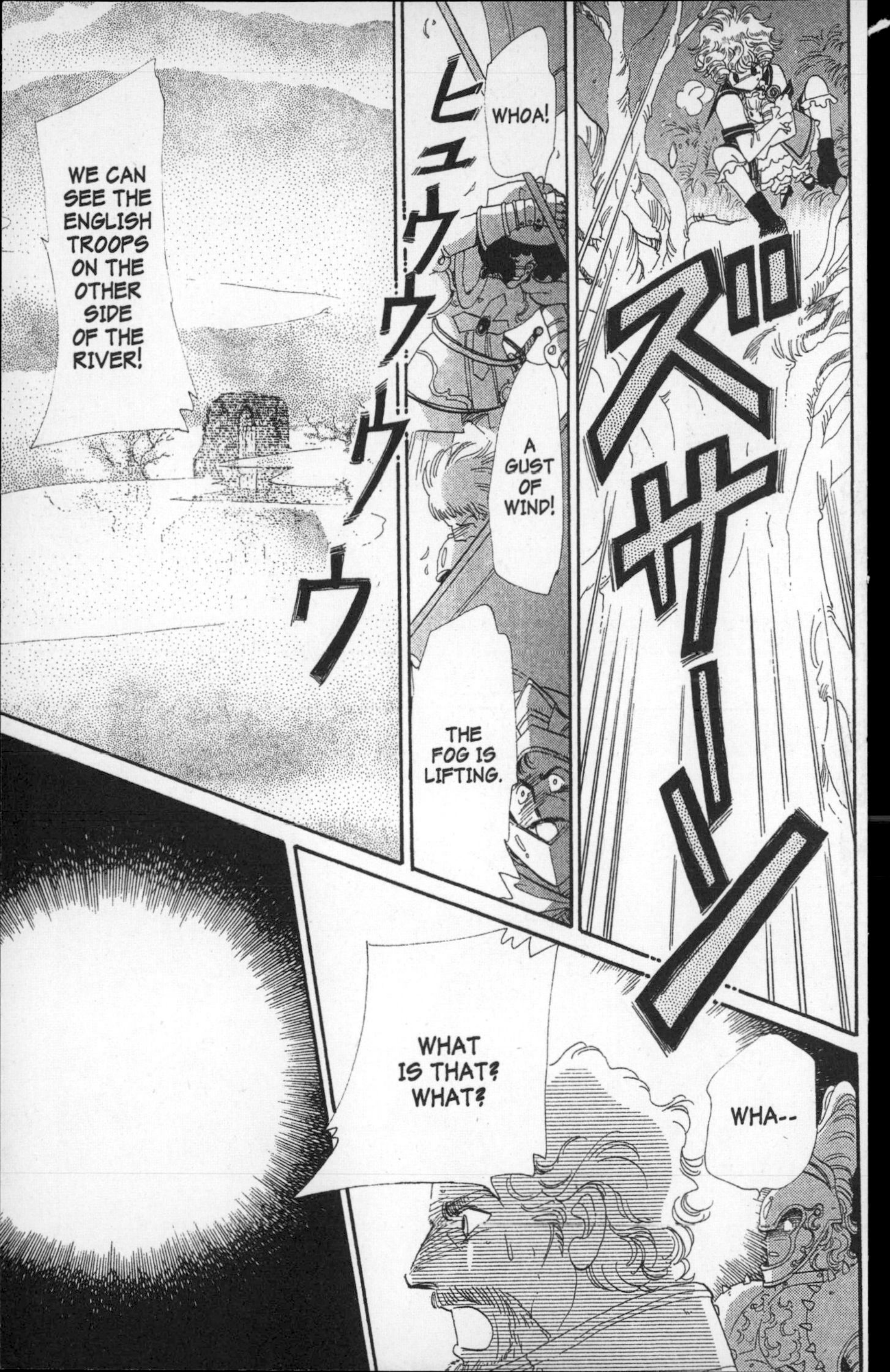

ズザーッ
WHOA!
A GUST OF WIND!
THE FOG IS LIFTING.
ヒュウウウウウ
WE CAN SEE THE ENGLISH TROOPS ON THE OTHER SIDE OF THE RIVER!
WHA--
WHAT IS THAT? WHAT?

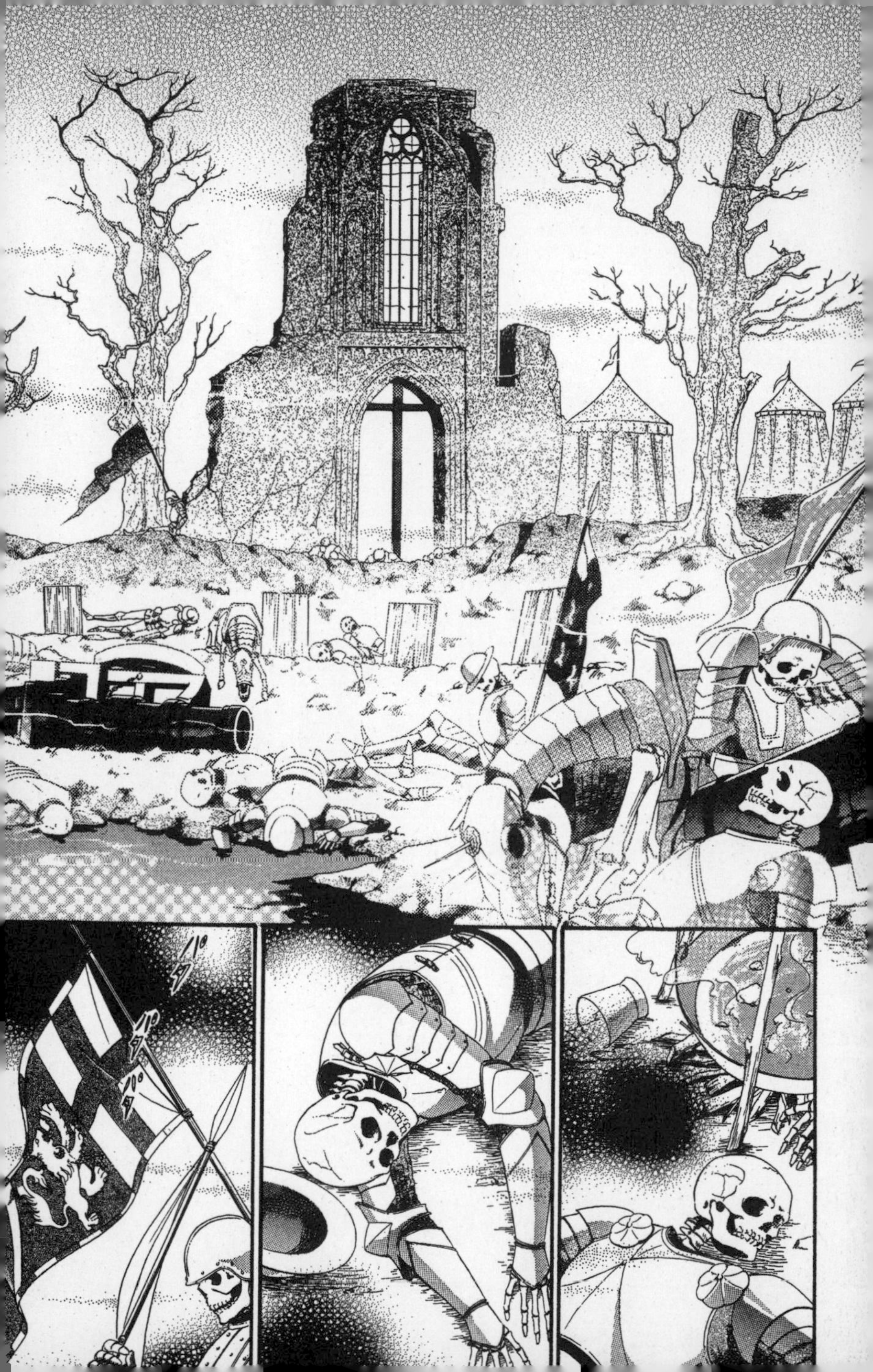
パタ
パタ
パタ

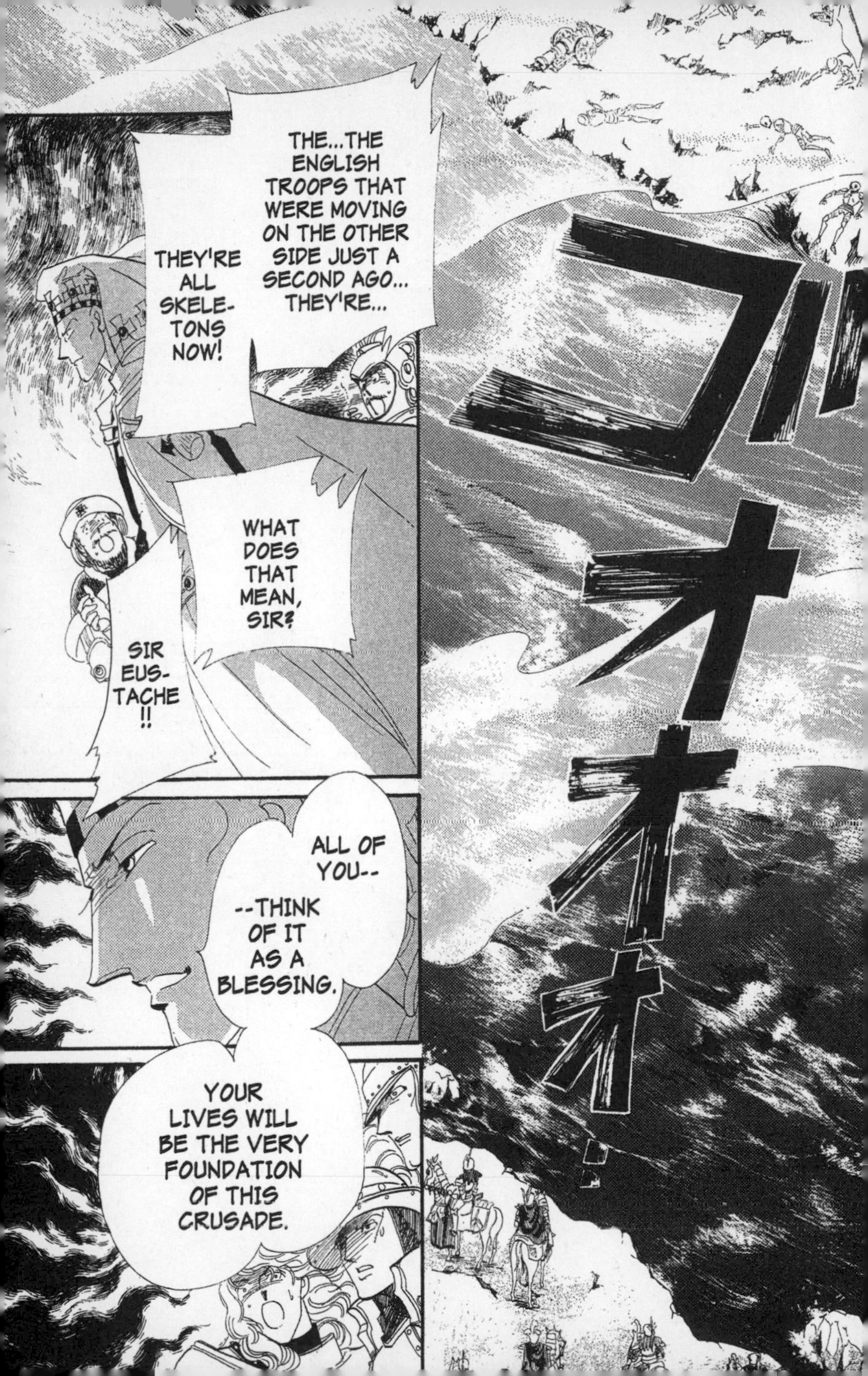
ゴオオオ
THE...THE ENGLISH TROOPS THAT WERE MOVING ON THE OTHER SIDE JUST A SECOND AGO... THEY'RE...
THEY'RE ALL SKELE-TONS NOW!
WHAT DOES THAT MEAN, SIR?
SIR EUS-TACHE!!
ALL OF YOU--
--THINK OF IT AS A BLESSING.
YOUR LIVES WILL BE THE VERY FOUNDATION OF THIS CRUSADE.

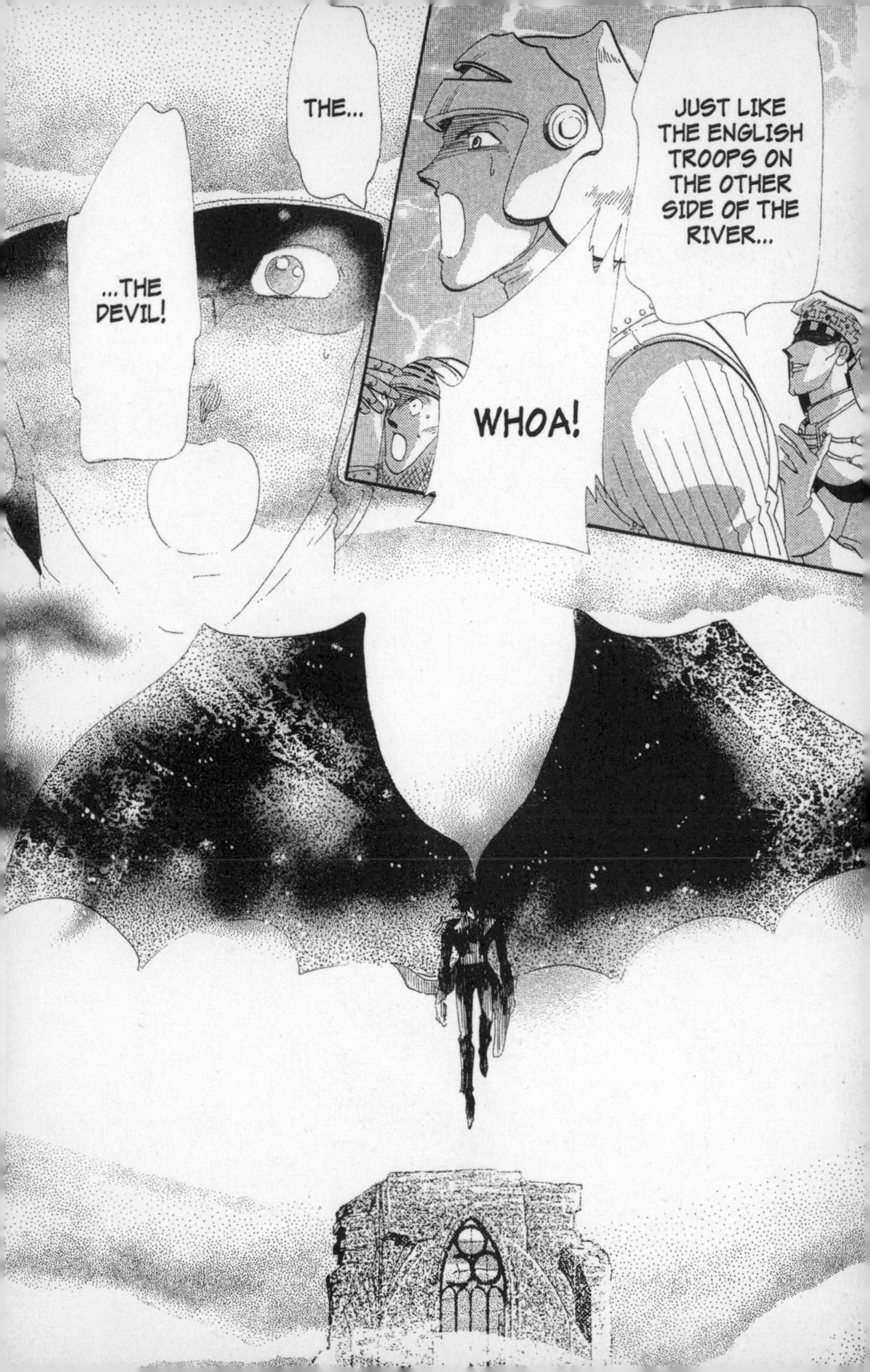
JUST LIKE THE ENGLISH TROOPS ON THE OTHER SIDE OF THE RIVER...
WHOA!
THE...
...THE DEVIL!

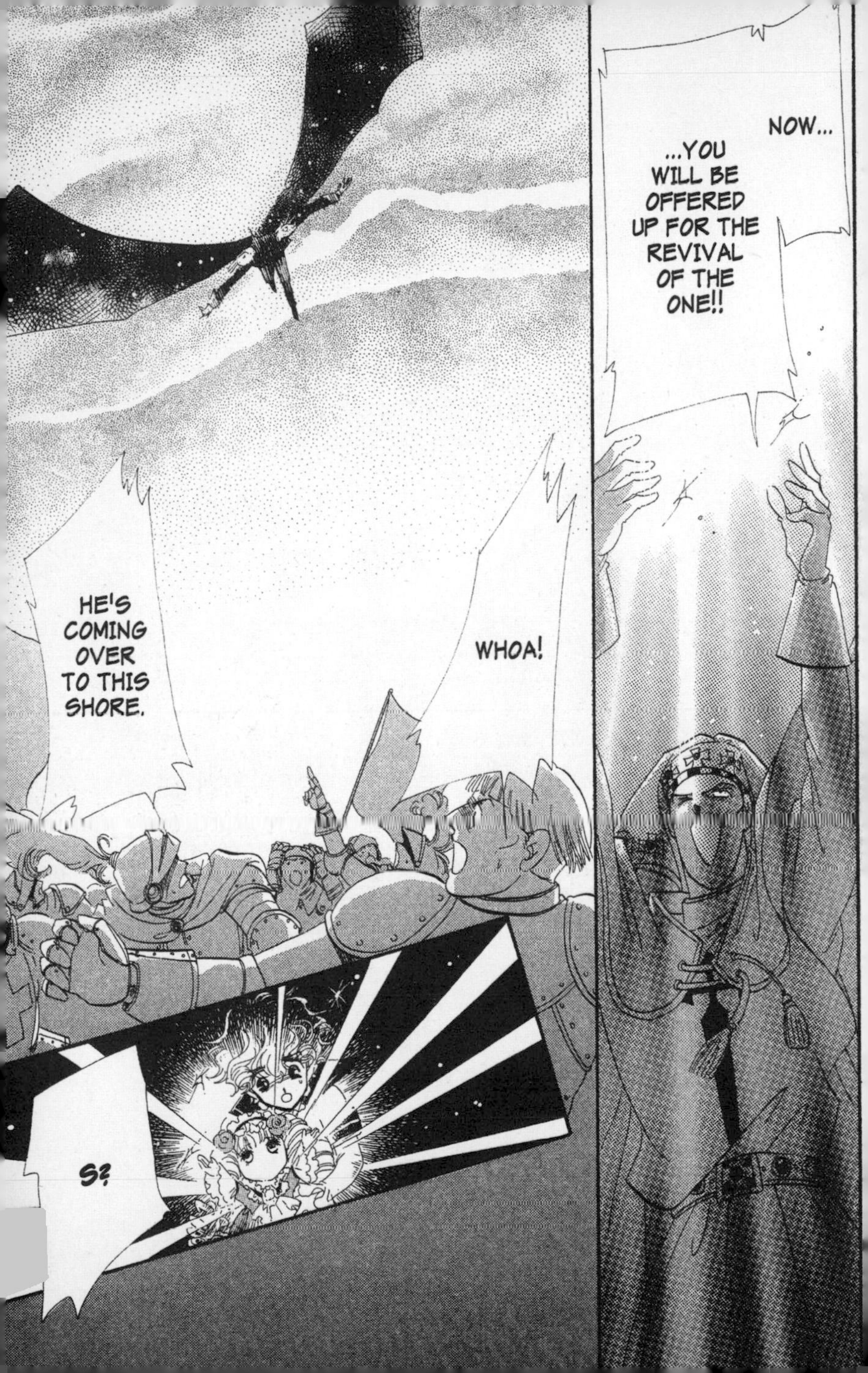
NOW...
...YOU WILL BE OFFERED UP FOR THE REVIVAL OF THE ONE!!
WHOA!
HE'S COMING OVER TO THIS SHORE.
S?

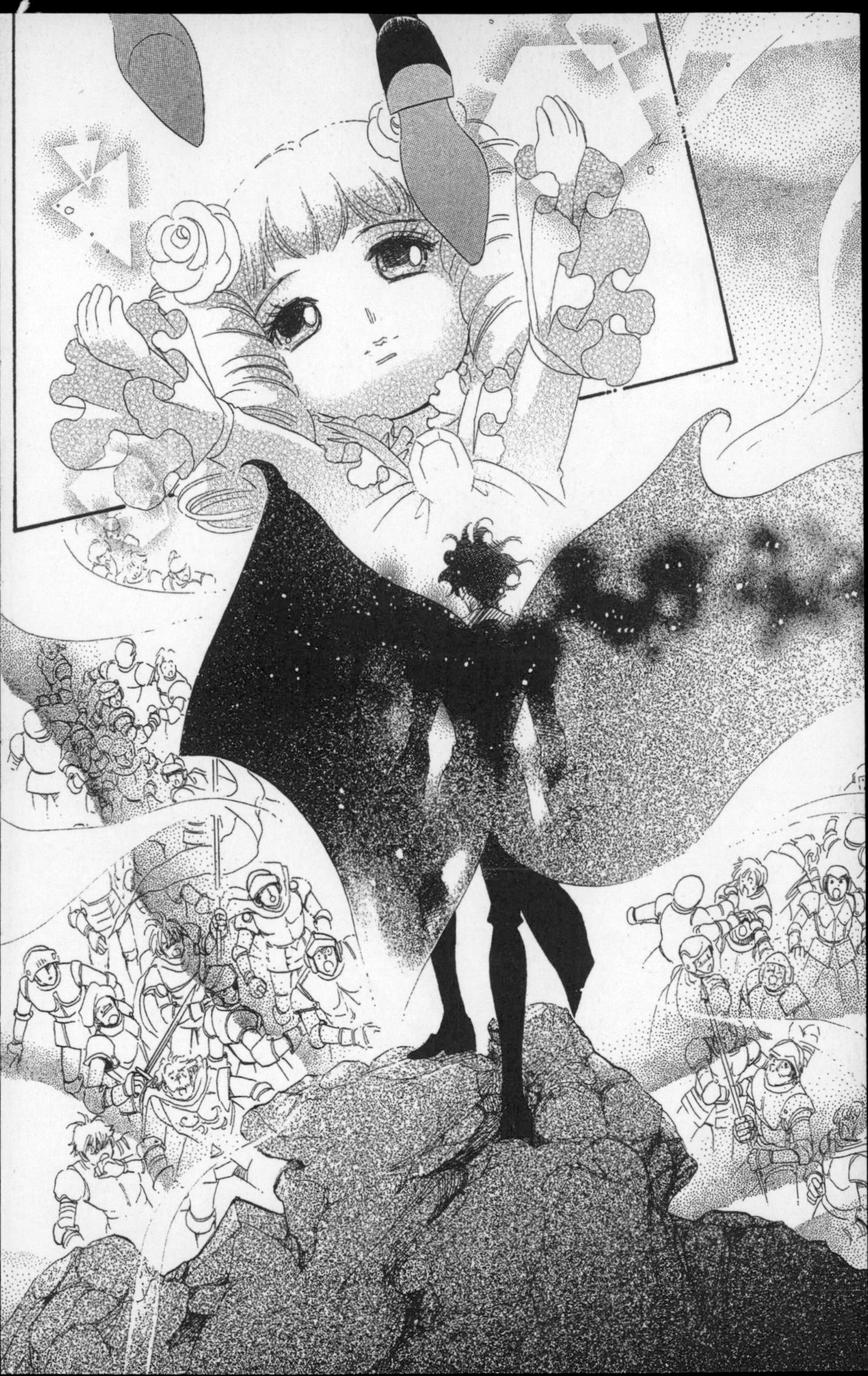

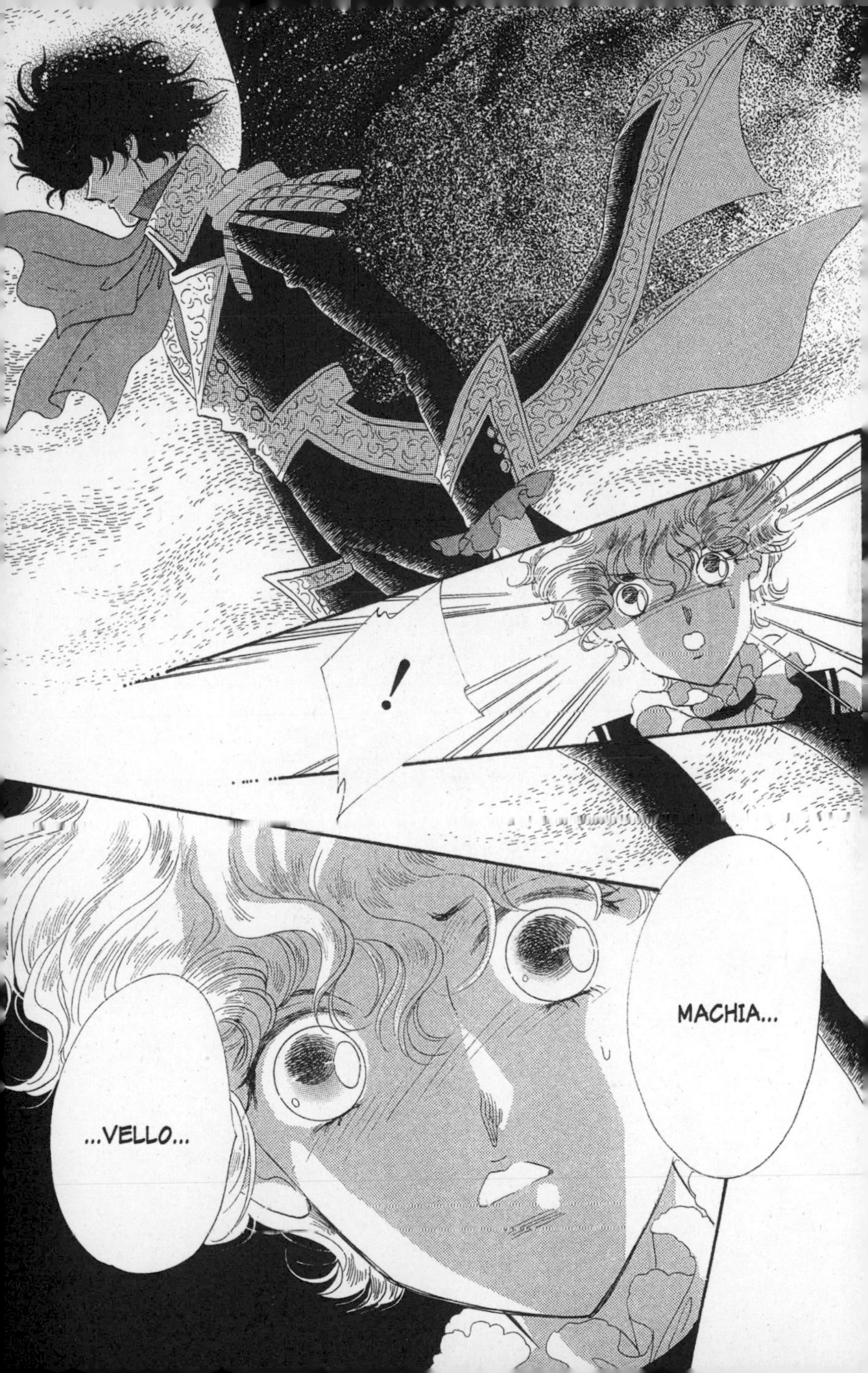
!
MACHIA...
...VELLO...

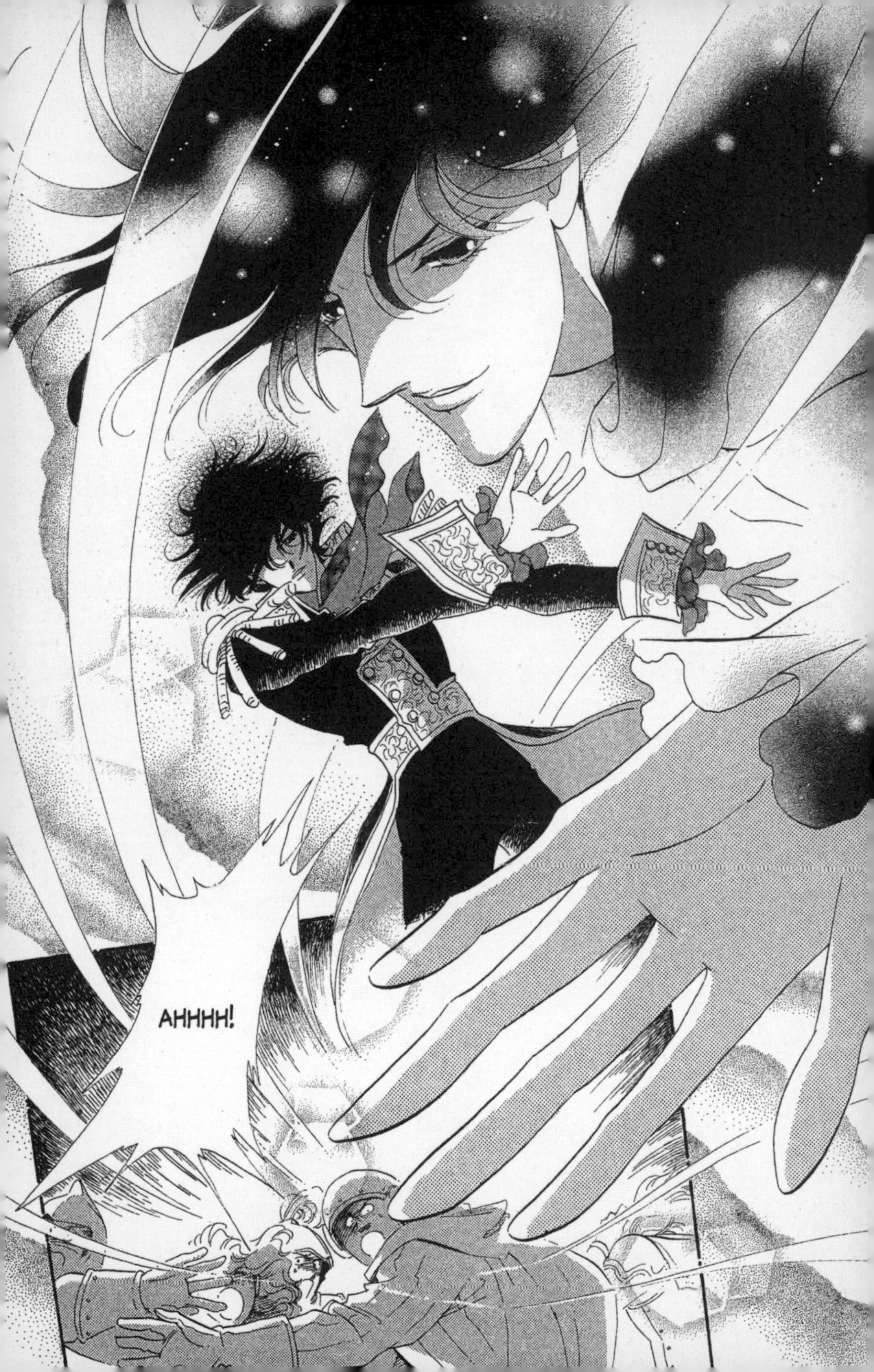
AHHHH!

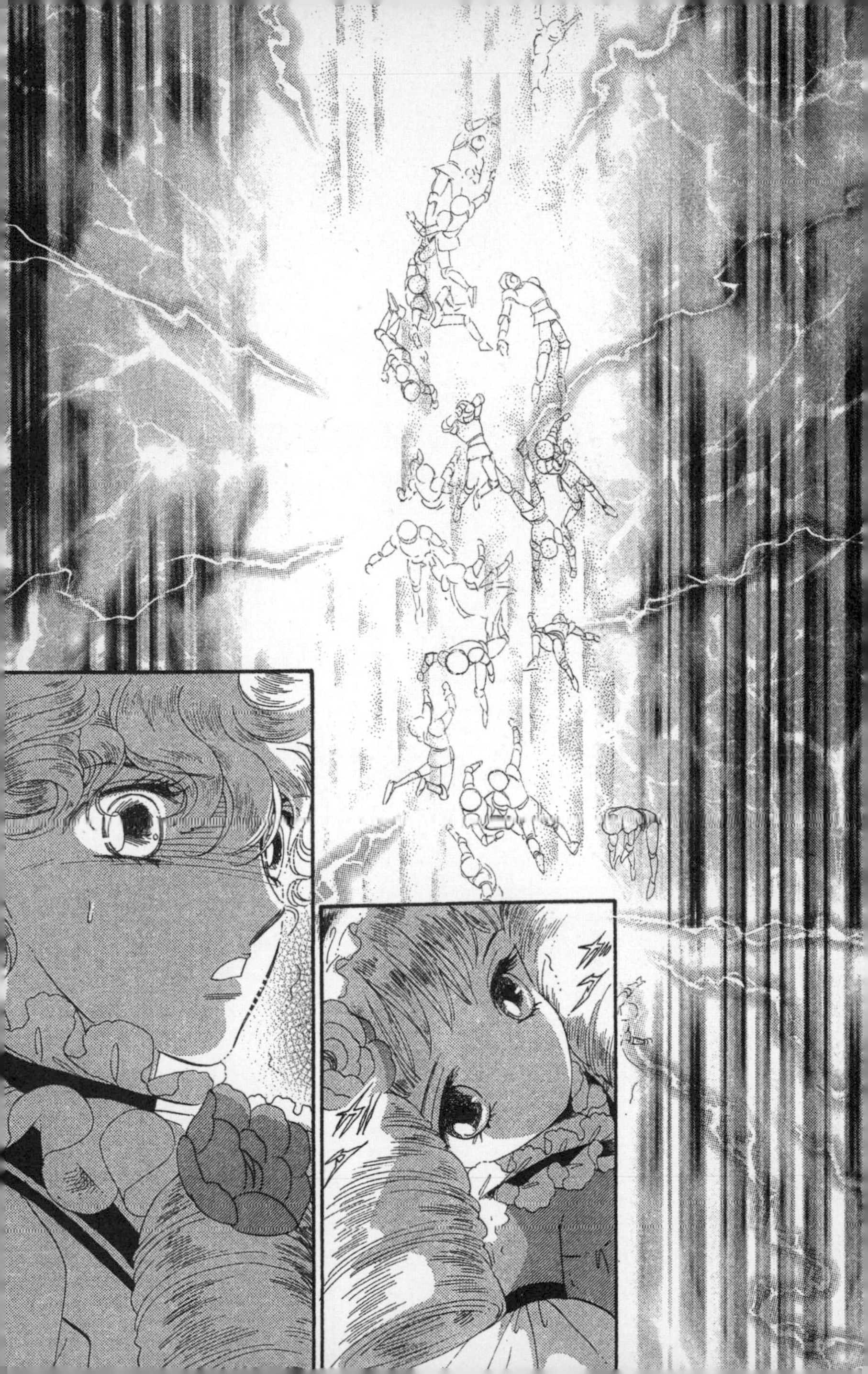

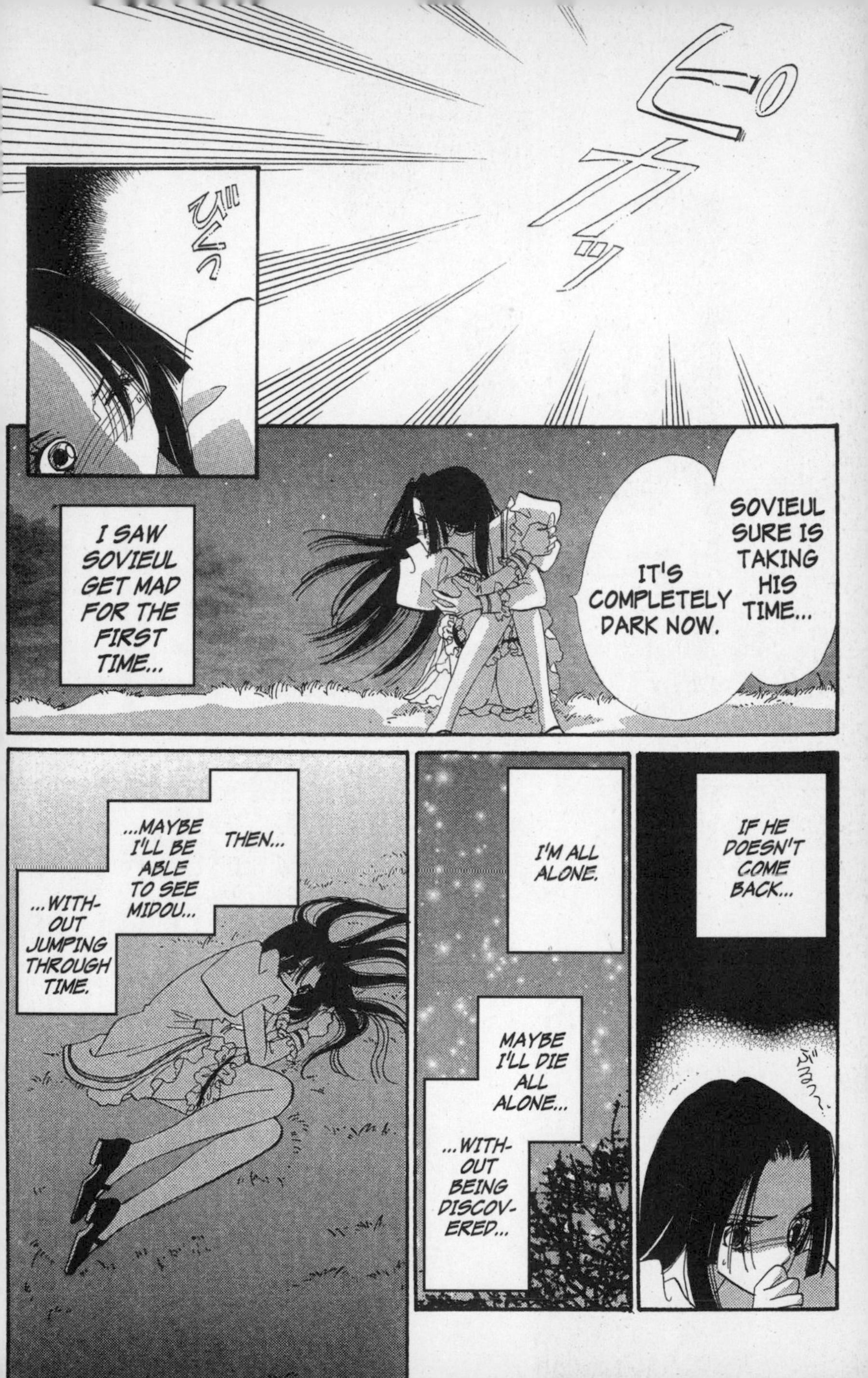
ピカッ
びくっ
SOVIEUL SURE IS TAKING HIS TIME...
IT'S COMPLETELY DARK NOW.
I SAW SOVIEUL GET MAD FOR THE FIRST TIME...
IF HE DOESN'T COME BACK...
I'M ALL ALONE.
MAYBE I'LL DIE ALL ALONE...
...WITH-OUT BEING DISCOV-ERED...
THEN...
...MAYBE I'LL BE ABLE TO SEE MIDOU...
...WITH-OUT JUMPING THROUGH TIME.

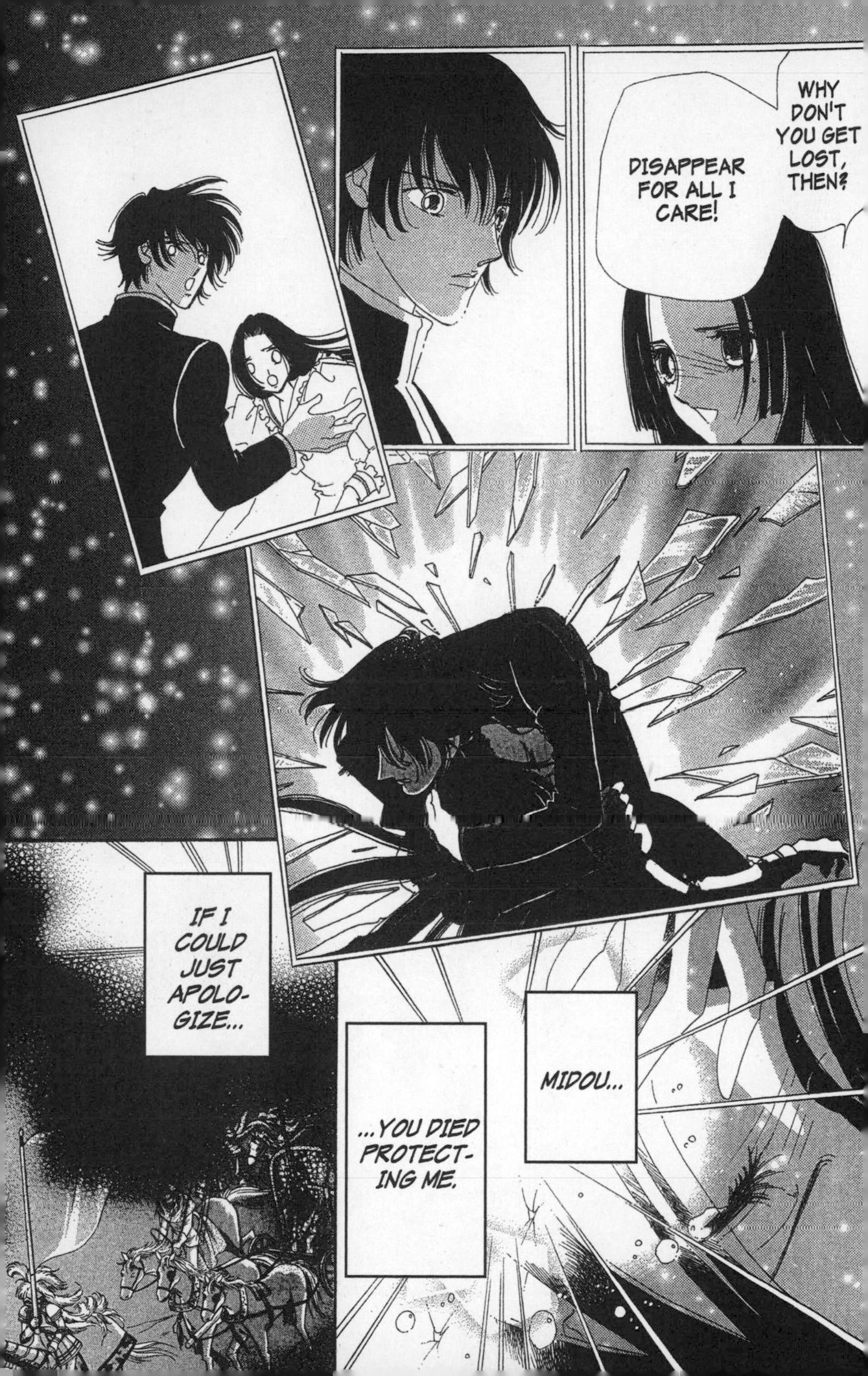
WHY DON'T YOU GET LOST, THEN?
DISAPPEAR FOR ALL I CARE!
MIDOU...
...YOU DIED PROTECT-ING ME.
IF I COULD JUST APOLO-GIZE...

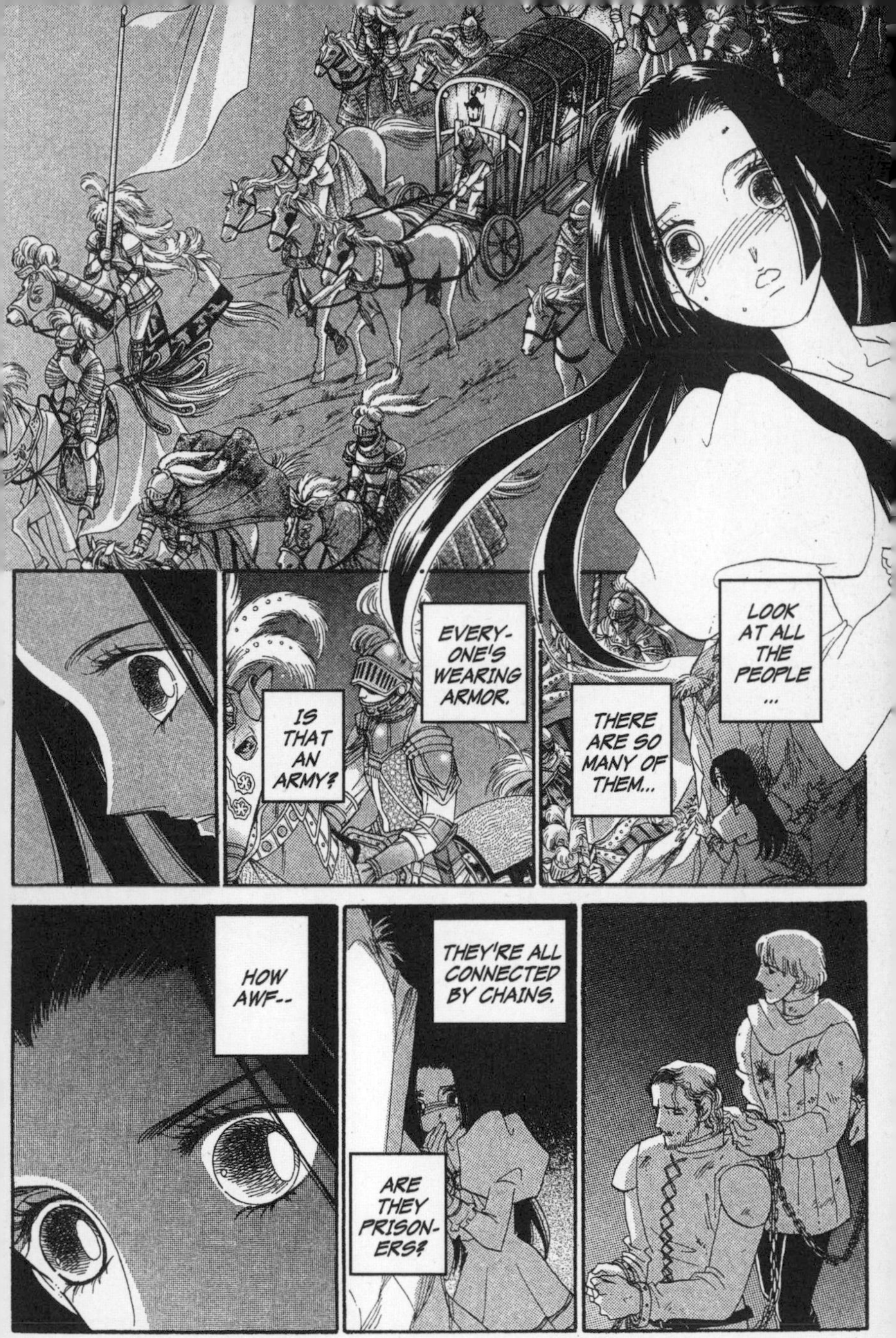
LOOK AT ALL THE PEOPLE ...
THERE ARE SO MANY OF THEM...
EVERY-ONE'S WEARING ARMOR.
IS THAT AN ARMY?
THEY'RE ALL CONNECTED BY CHAINS.
ARE THEY PRISON-ERS?
HOW AWF--

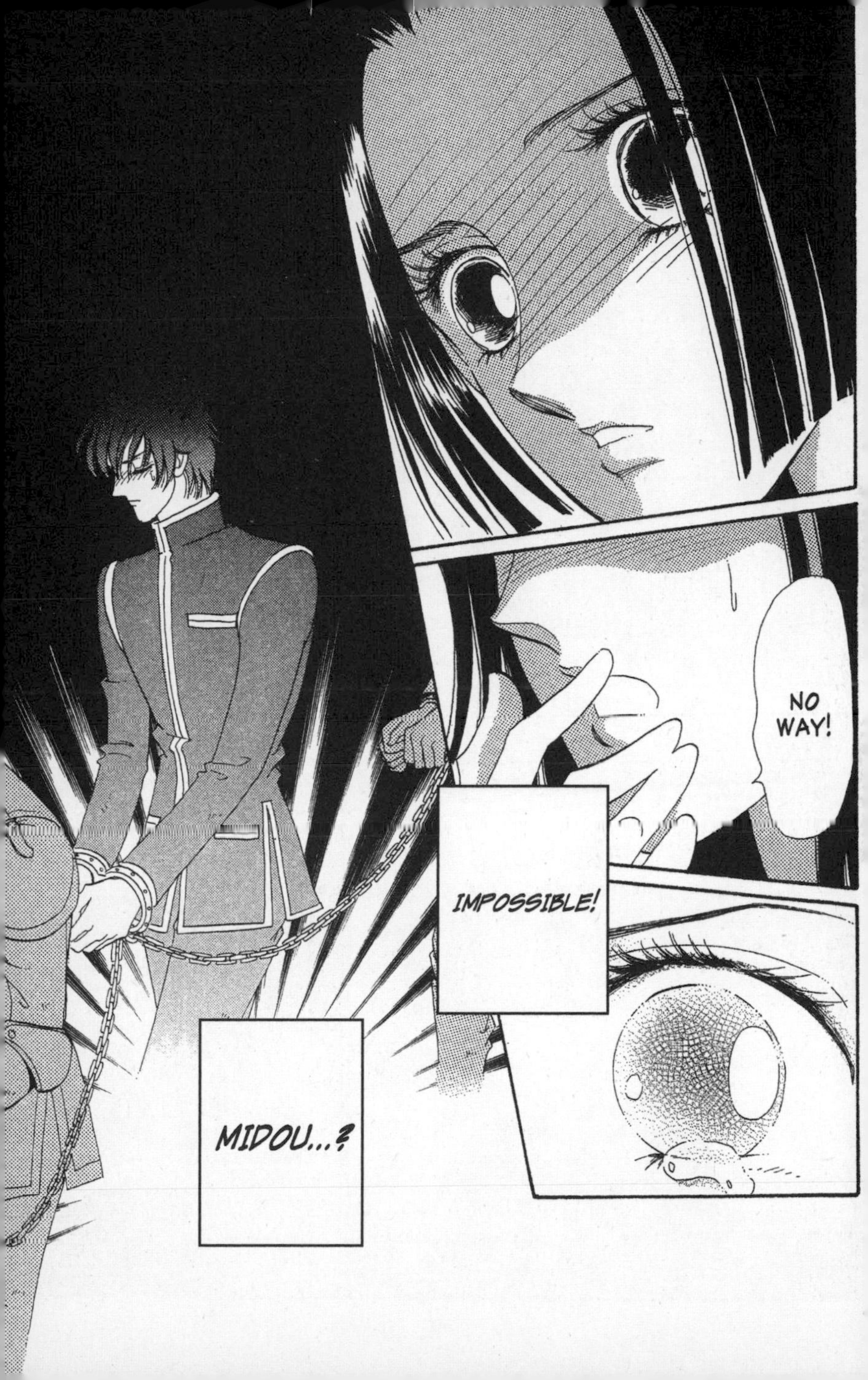
NO WAY!
IMPOSSIBLE!
MIDOU...?

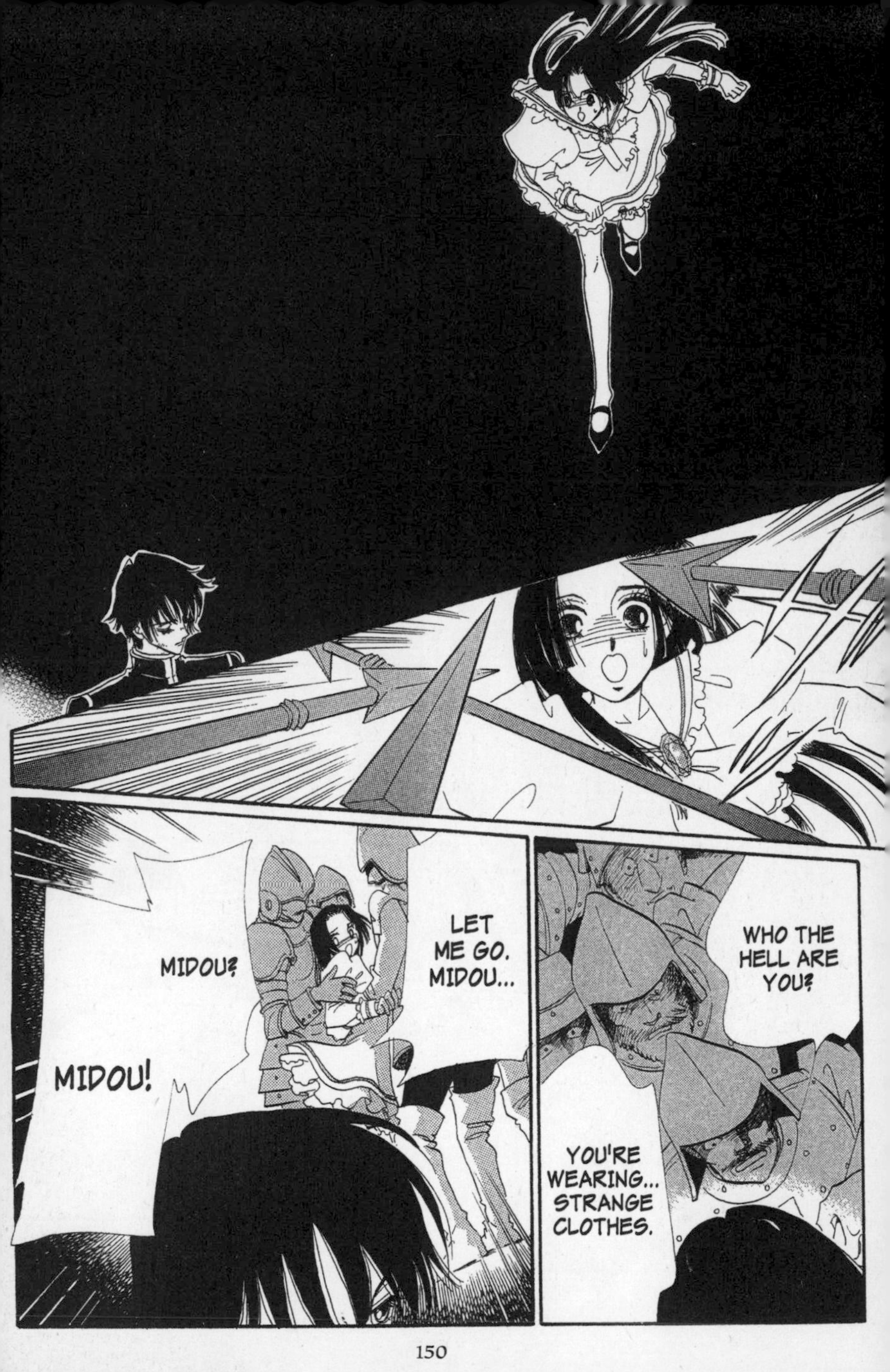
WHO THE HELL ARE YOU?
YOU'RE WEARING... STRANGE CLOTHES.
LET ME GO. MIDOU...
MIDOU?
MIDOU!

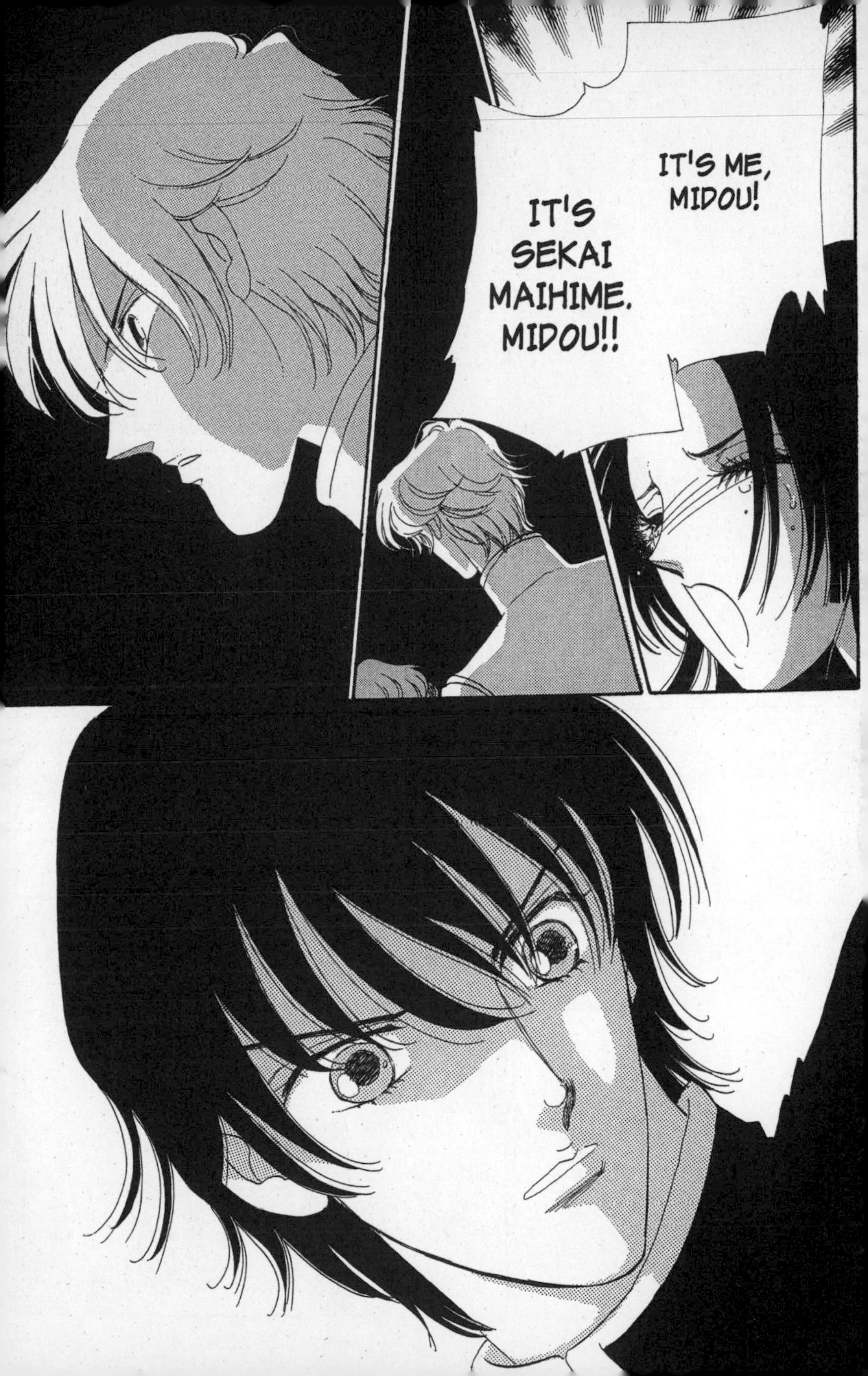
IT'S ME, MIDOU!
IT'S SEKAI MAIHIME. MIDOU!!

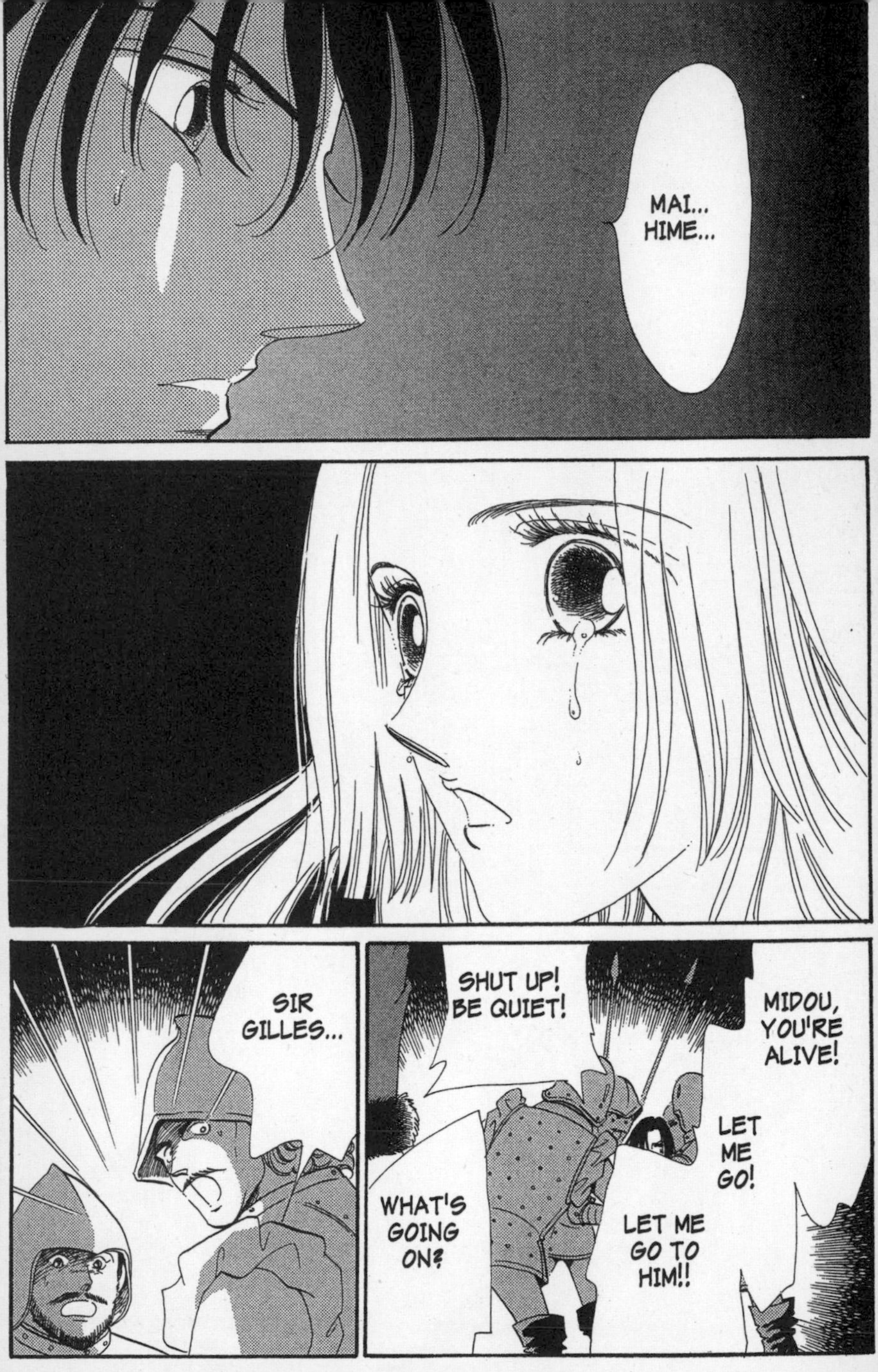
MAI... HIME...
MIDOU, YOU'RE ALIVE!
SHUT UP! BE QUIET!
LET ME GO!
LET ME GO TO HIM!!
WHAT'S GOING ON?
SIR GILLES...

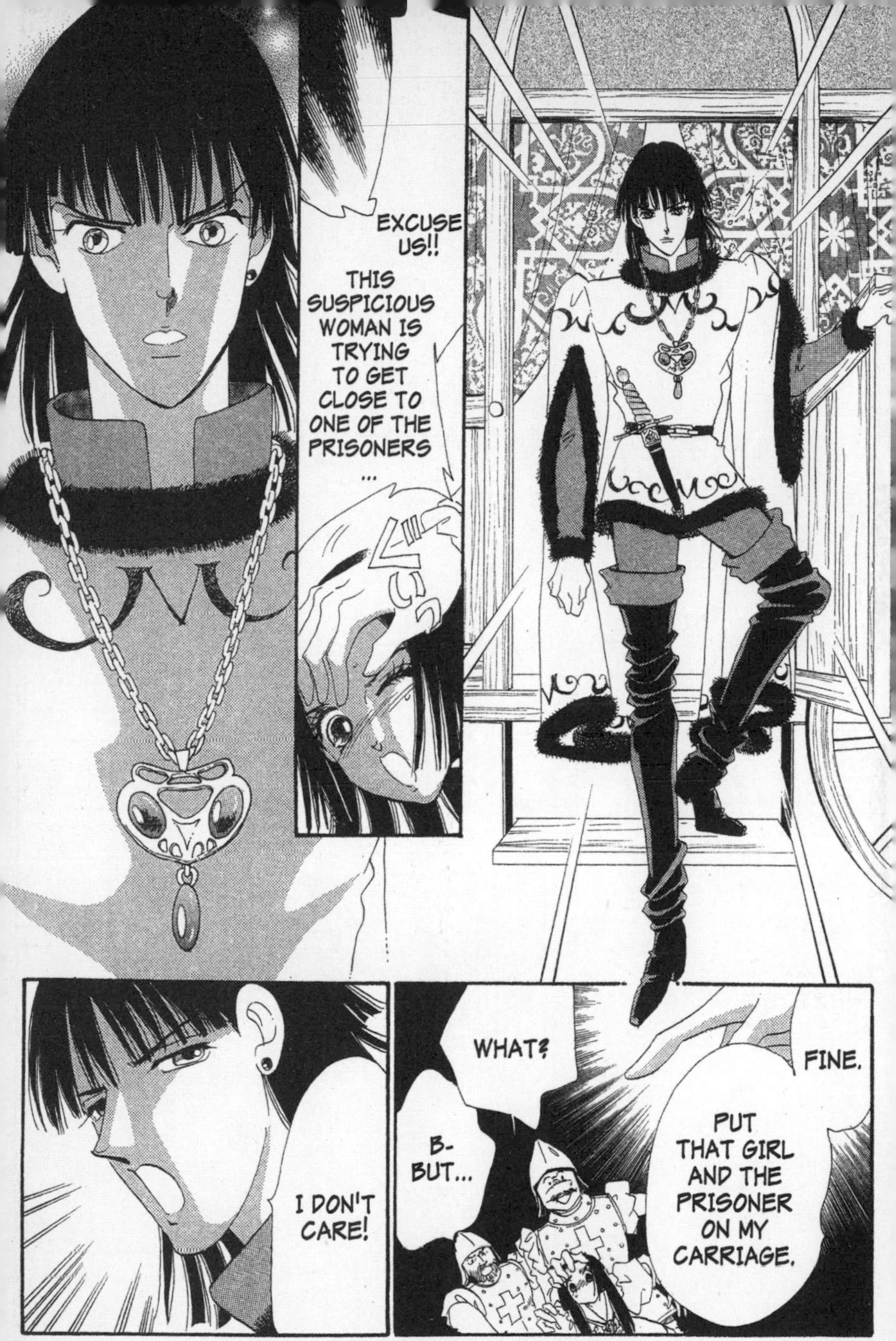
EXCUSE US!!
THIS SUSPICIOUS WOMAN IS TRYING TO GET CLOSE TO ONE OF THE PRISONERS ...
FINE.
PUT THAT GIRL AND THE PRISONER ON MY CARRIAGE.
WHAT?
B-BUT...
I DON'T CARE!

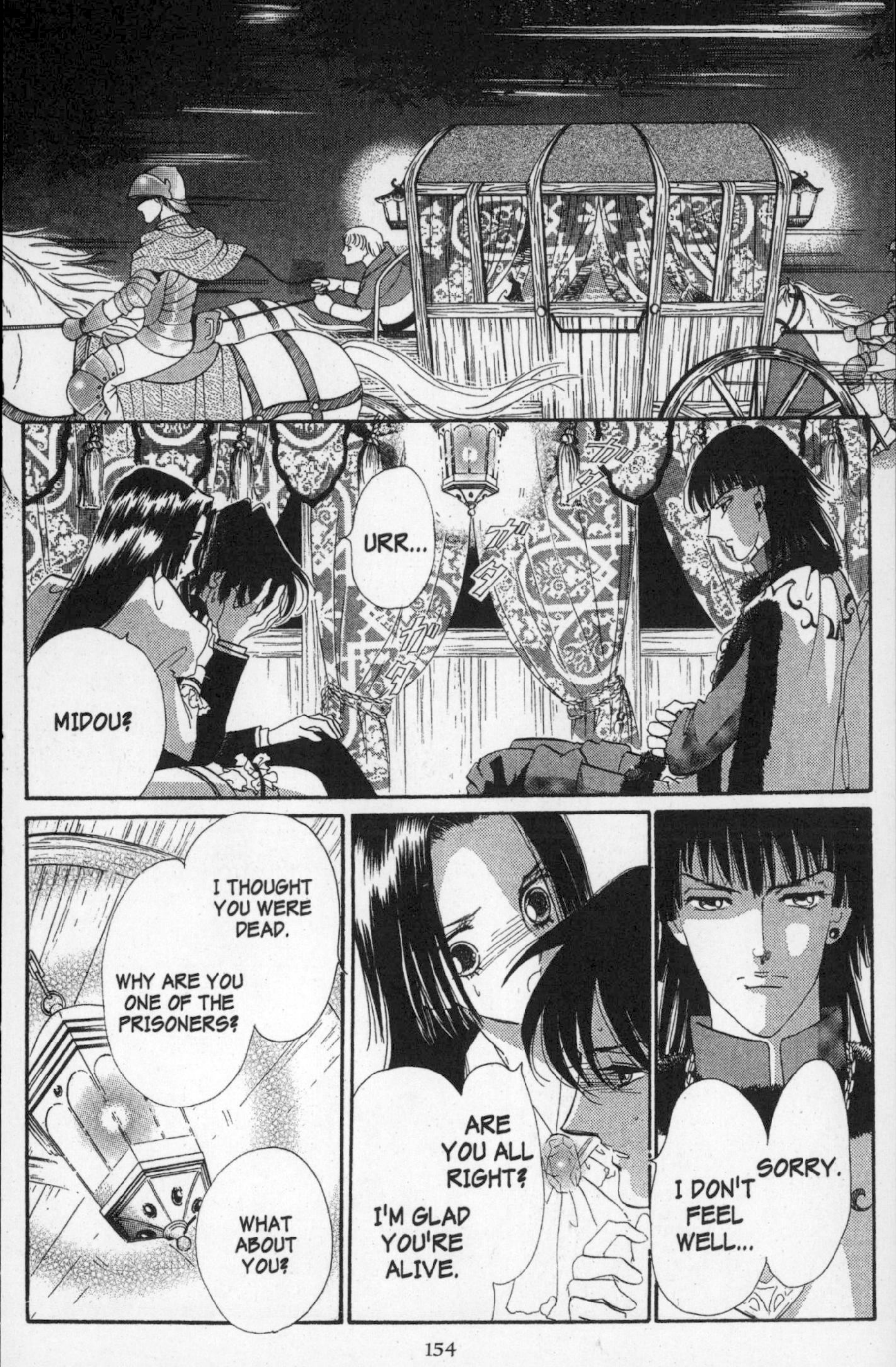
URR...
MIDOU?
SORRY.
I DON'T FEEL WELL...
ARE YOU ALL RIGHT?
I'M GLAD YOU'RE ALIVE.
I THOUGHT YOU WERE DEAD.
WHY ARE YOU ONE OF THE PRISONERS?
WHAT ABOUT YOU?

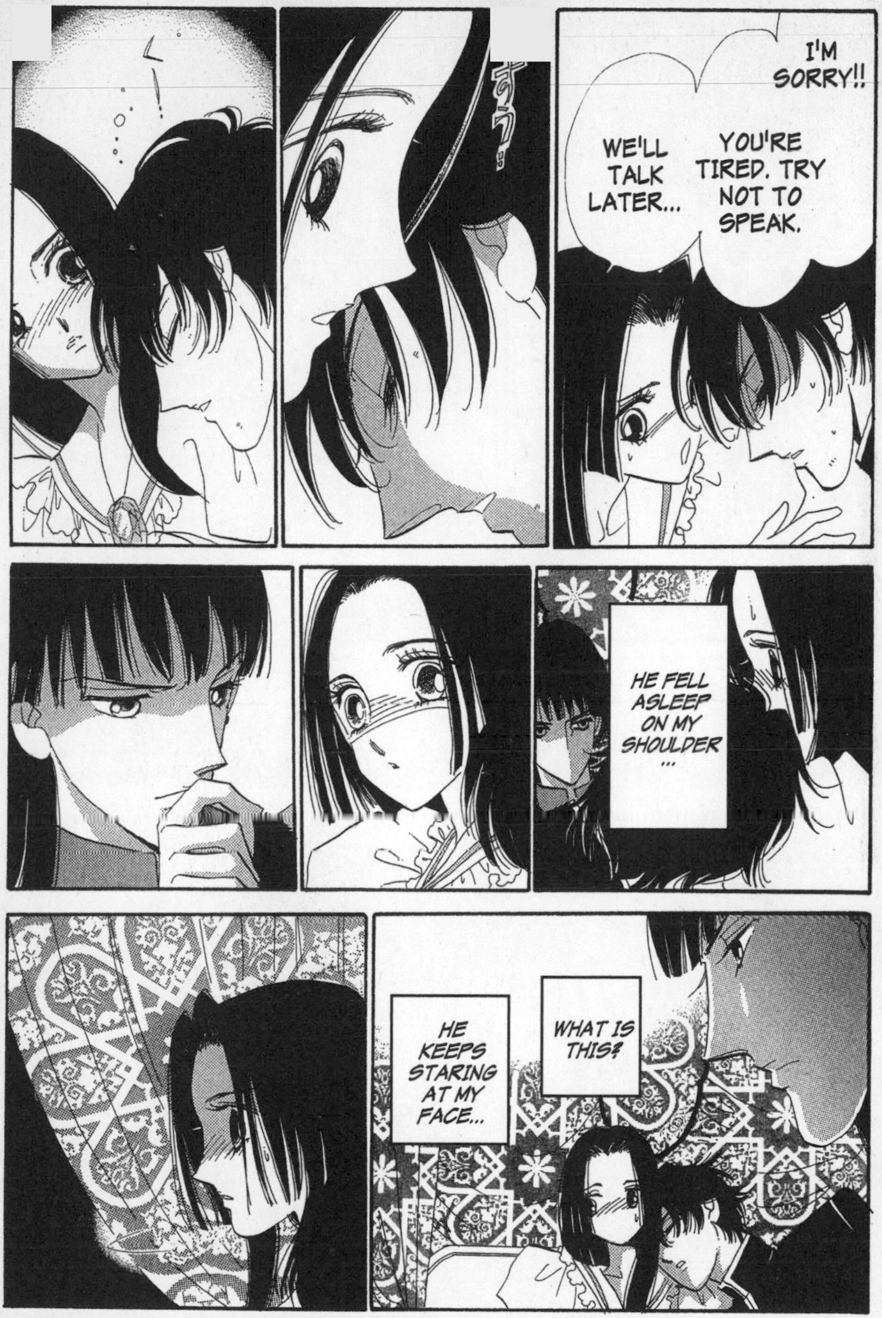
I'M SORRY!!
YOU'RE TIRED. TRY NOT TO SPEAK.
WE'LL TALK LATER...
HE FELL ASLEEP ON MY SHOULDER ...
WHAT IS THIS?
HE KEEPS STARING AT MY FACE...

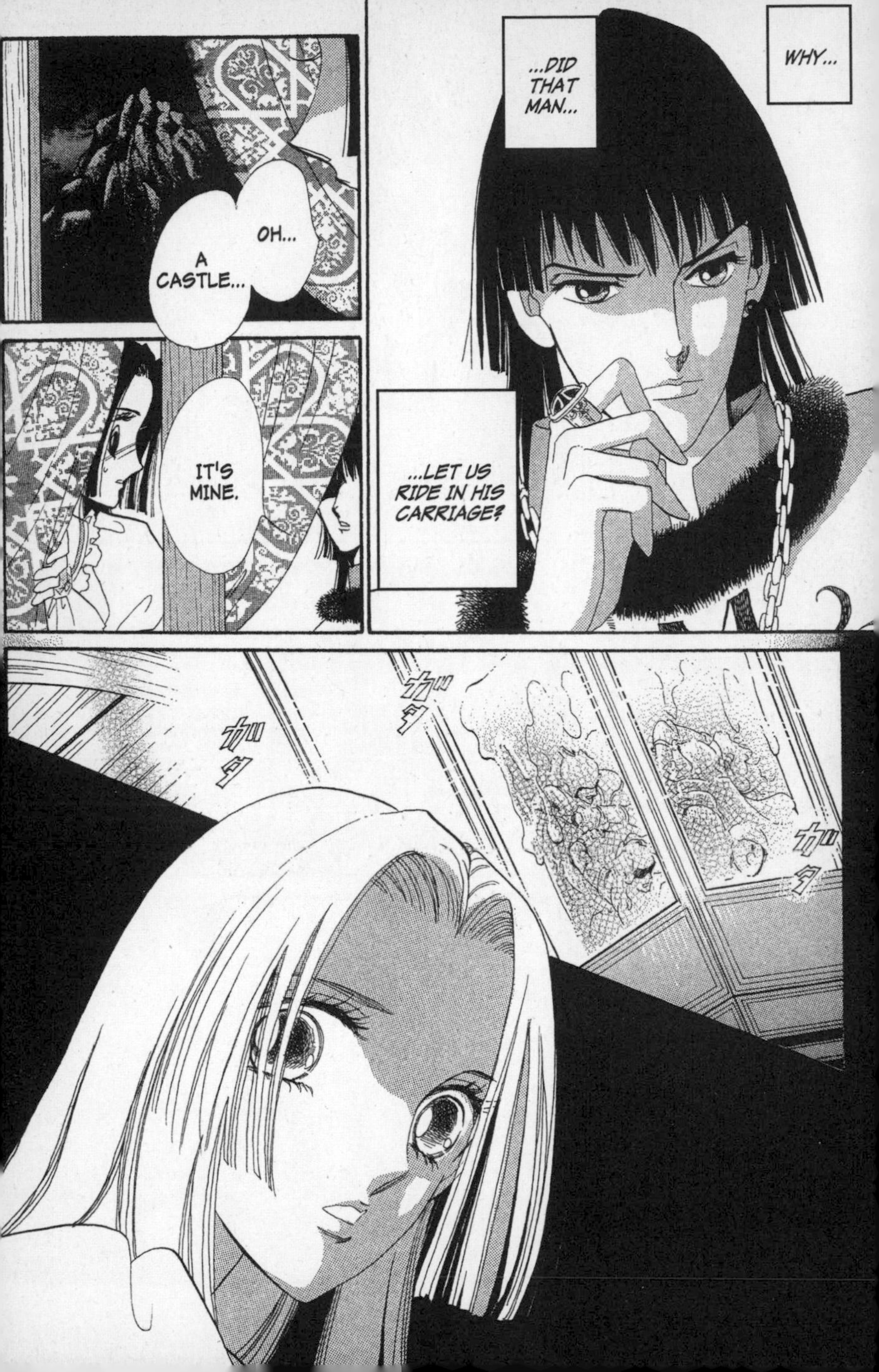
WHY...
...DID THAT MAN...
...LET US RIDE IN HIS CARRIAGE?
OH... A CASTLE...
IT'S MINE.
ガタ
ガタ
ガタ

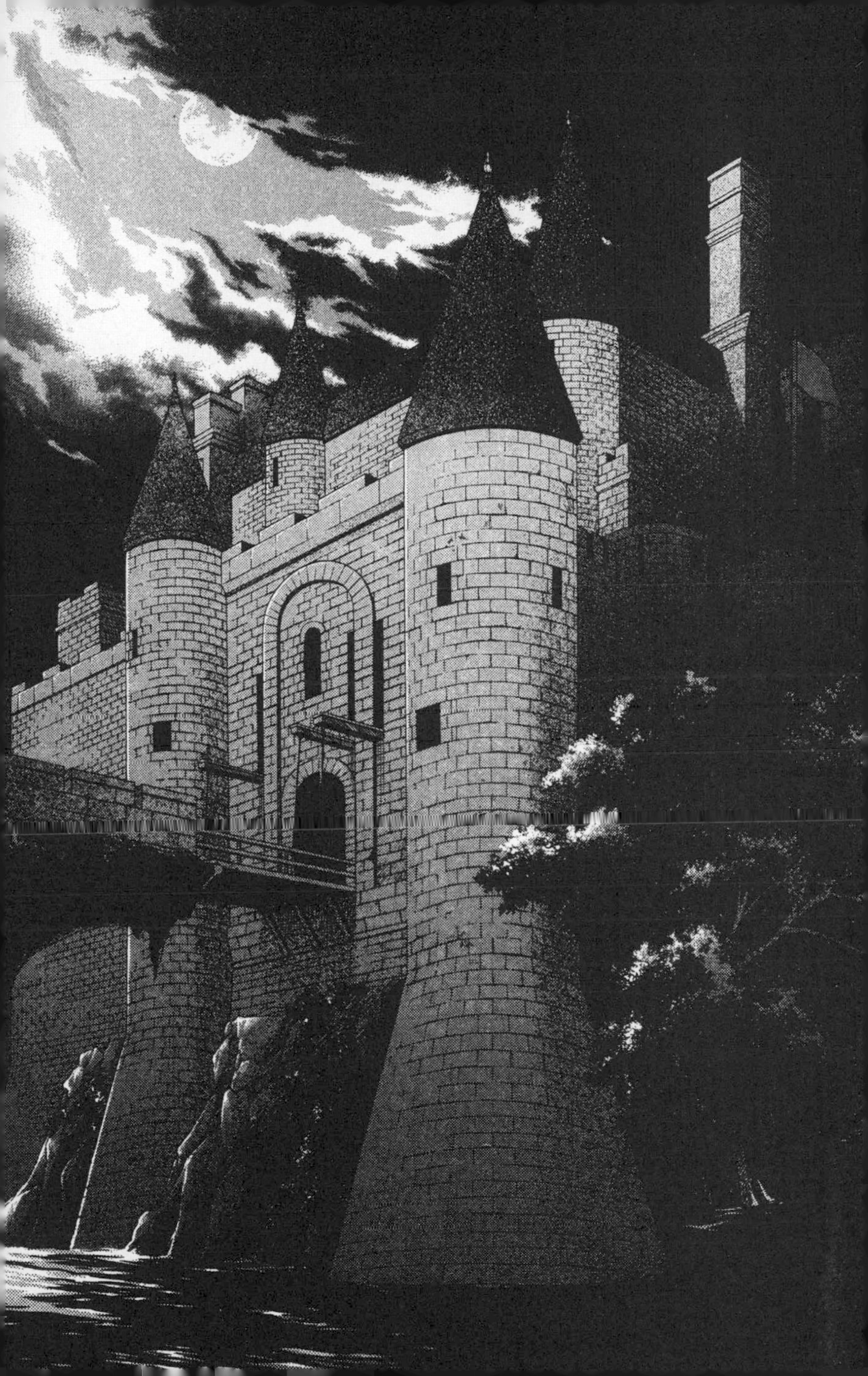

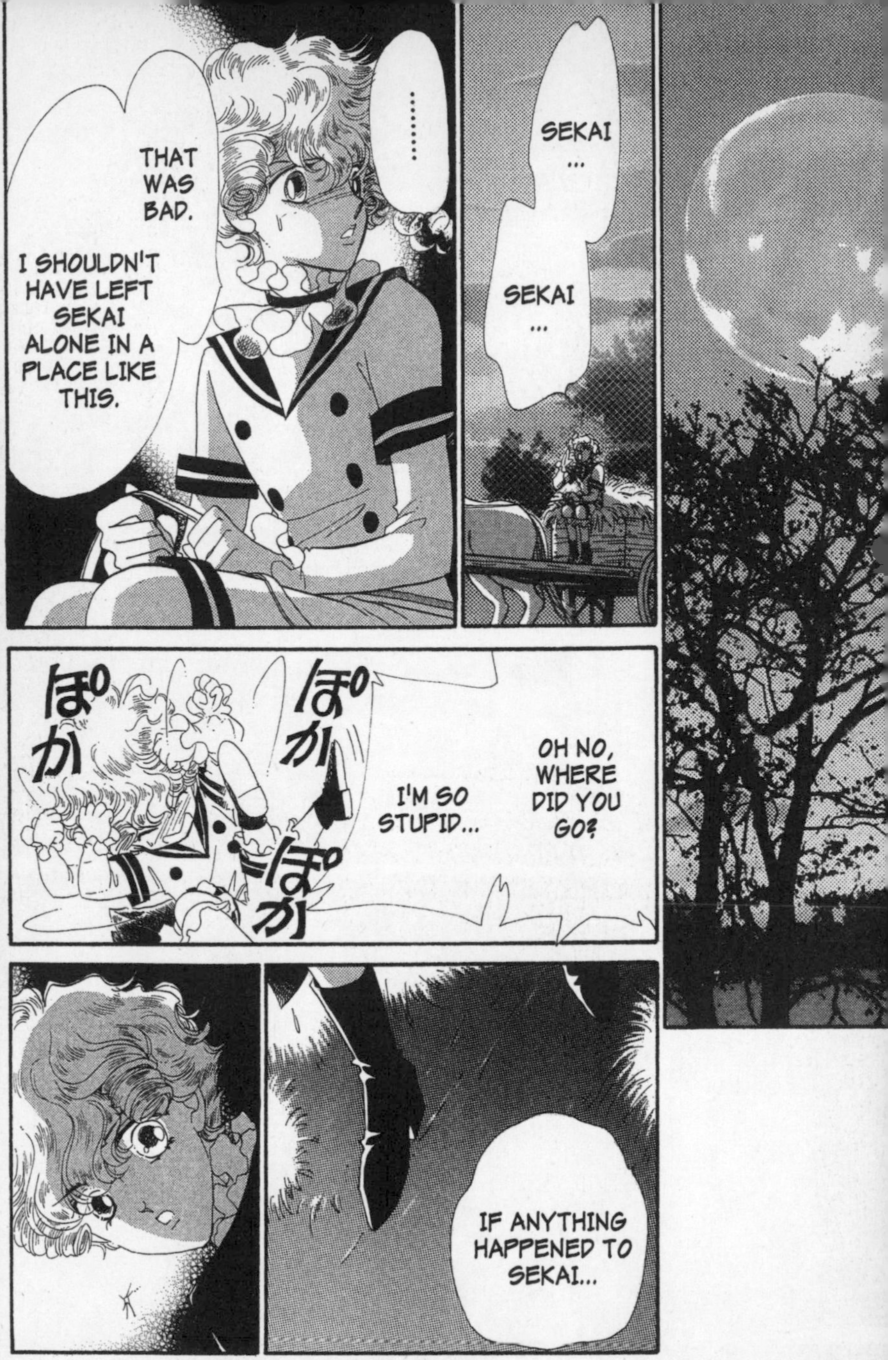
SEKAI ...
SEKAI ...
......
THAT WAS BAD.
I SHOULDN'T HAVE LEFT SEKAI ALONE IN A PLACE LIKE THIS.
OH NO, WHERE DID YOU GO?
I'M SO STUPID...
ぽか
ぽか
ぽか
IF ANYTHING HAPPENED TO SEKAI...

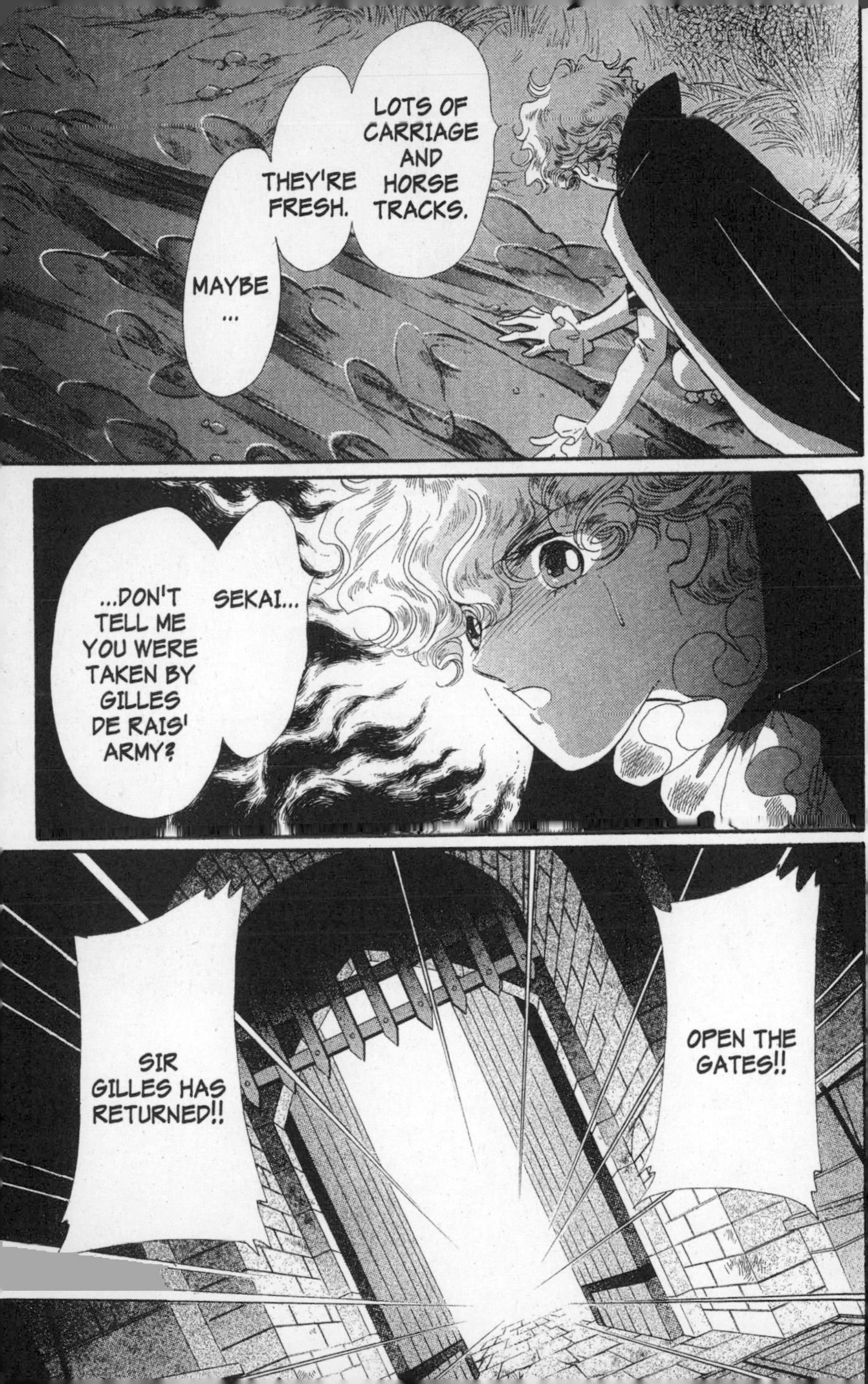
LOTS OF CARRIAGE AND HORSE TRACKS.
THEY'RE FRESH.
MAYBE ...
SEKAI...
...DON'T TELL ME YOU WERE TAKEN BY GILLES DE RAIS' ARMY?
OPEN THE GATES!!
SIR GILLES HAS RETURNED!!

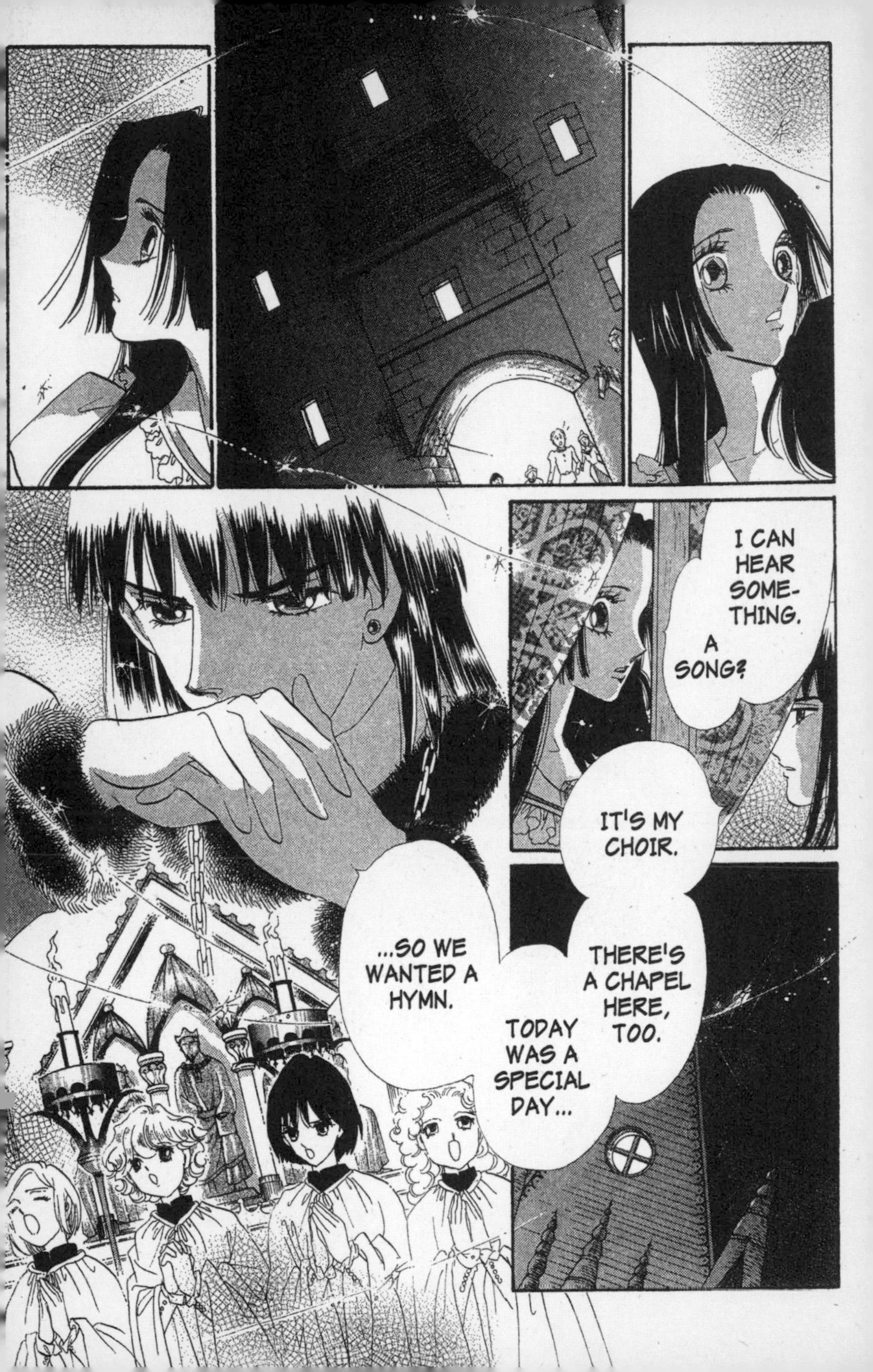
I CAN HEAR SOME-THING.
A SONG?
IT'S MY CHOIR.
THERE'S A CHAPEL HERE, TOO.
TODAY WAS A SPECIAL DAY...
...SO WE WANTED A HYMN.

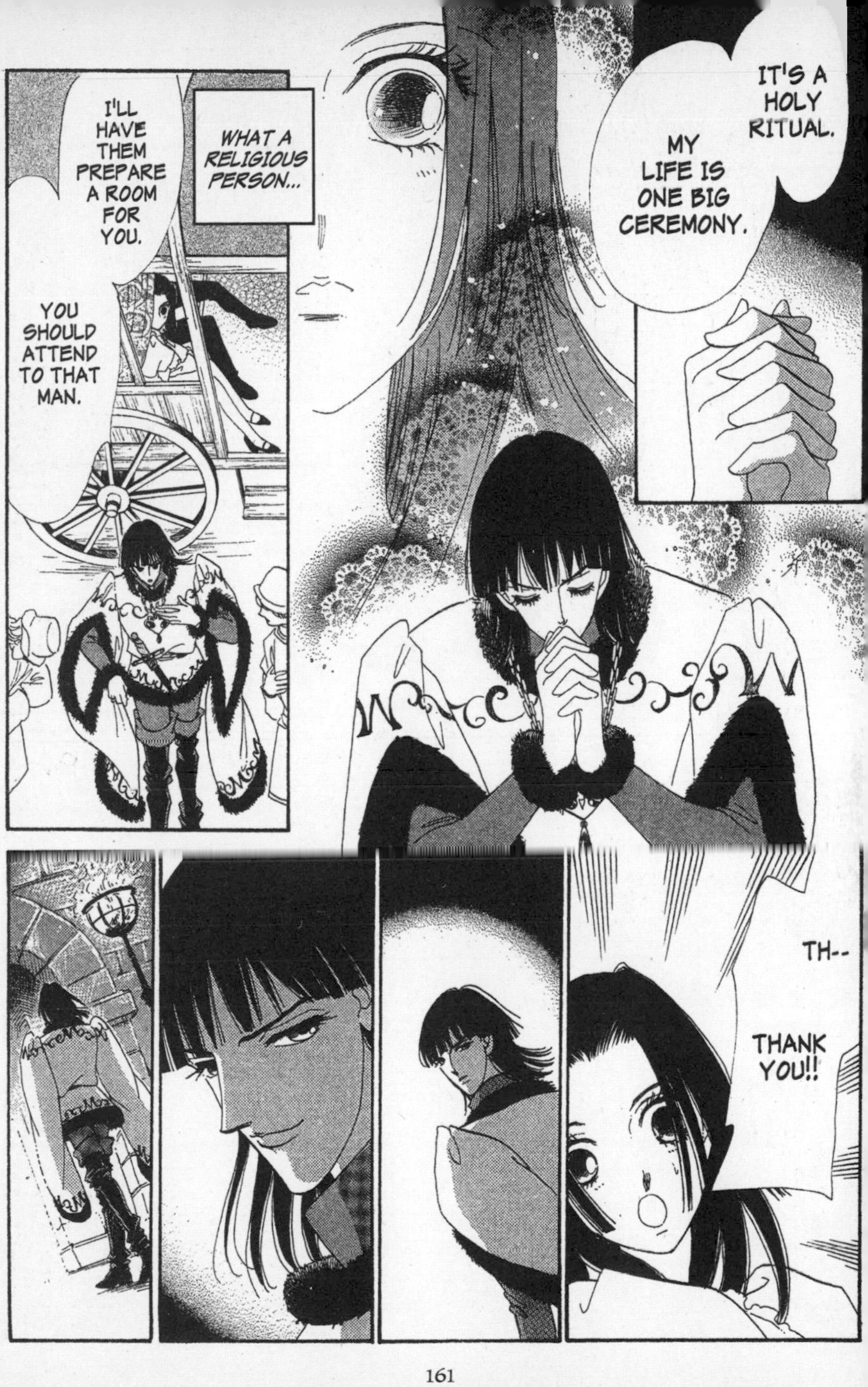
IT'S A HOLY RITUAL.
MY LIFE IS ONE BIG CEREMONY.
WHAT A RELIGIOUS PERSON...
I'LL HAVE THEM PREPARE A ROOM FOR YOU.
YOU SHOULD ATTEND TO THAT MAN.
TH--
THANK YOU!!

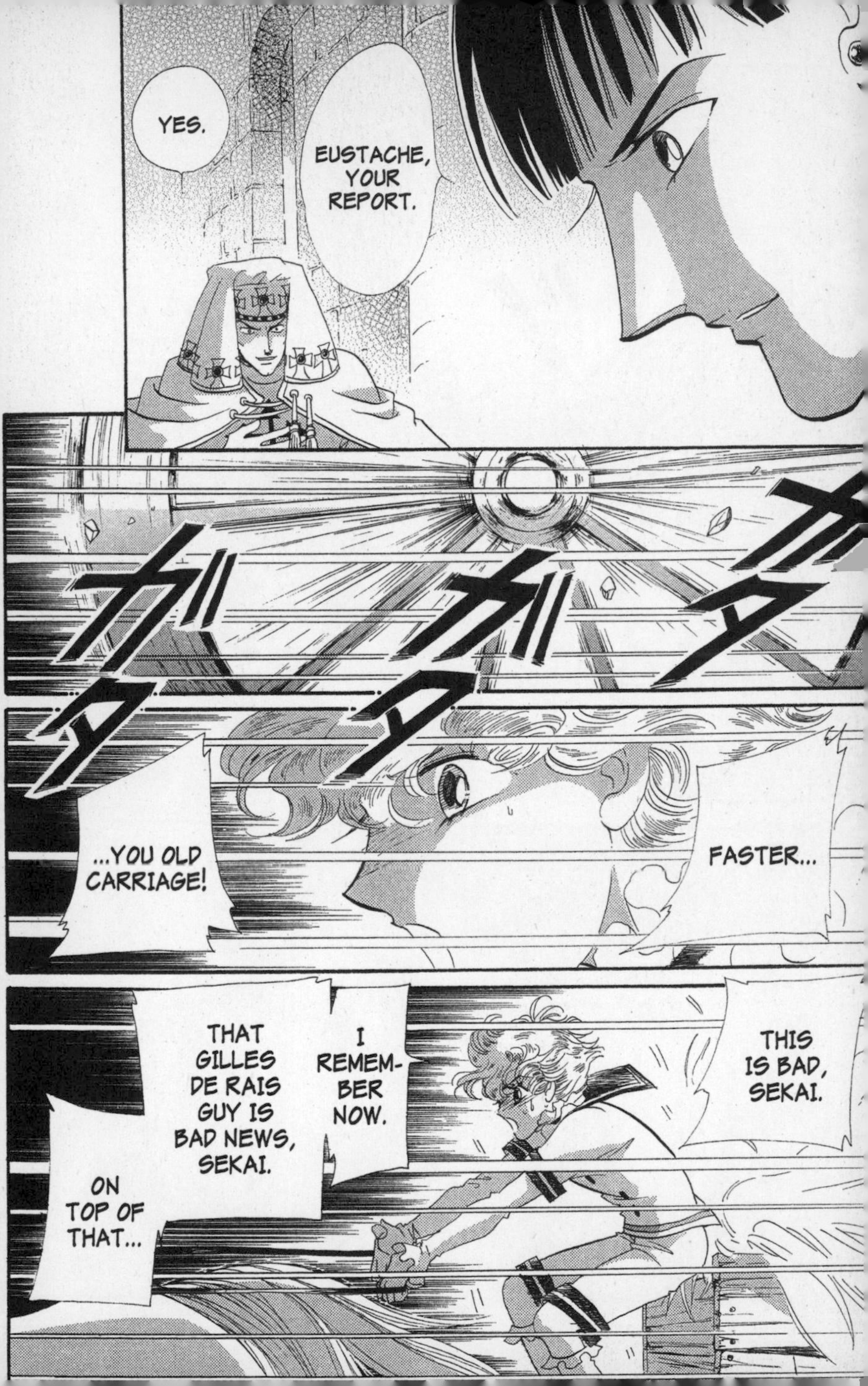
EUSTACHE, YOUR REPORT.
YES.
ガタ
ガタ
ガタ
FASTER...
...YOU OLD CARRIAGE!
THIS IS BAD, SEKAI.
I REMEMBER NOW.
THAT GILLES DE RAIS GUY IS BAD NEWS, SEKAI.
ON TOP OF THAT...

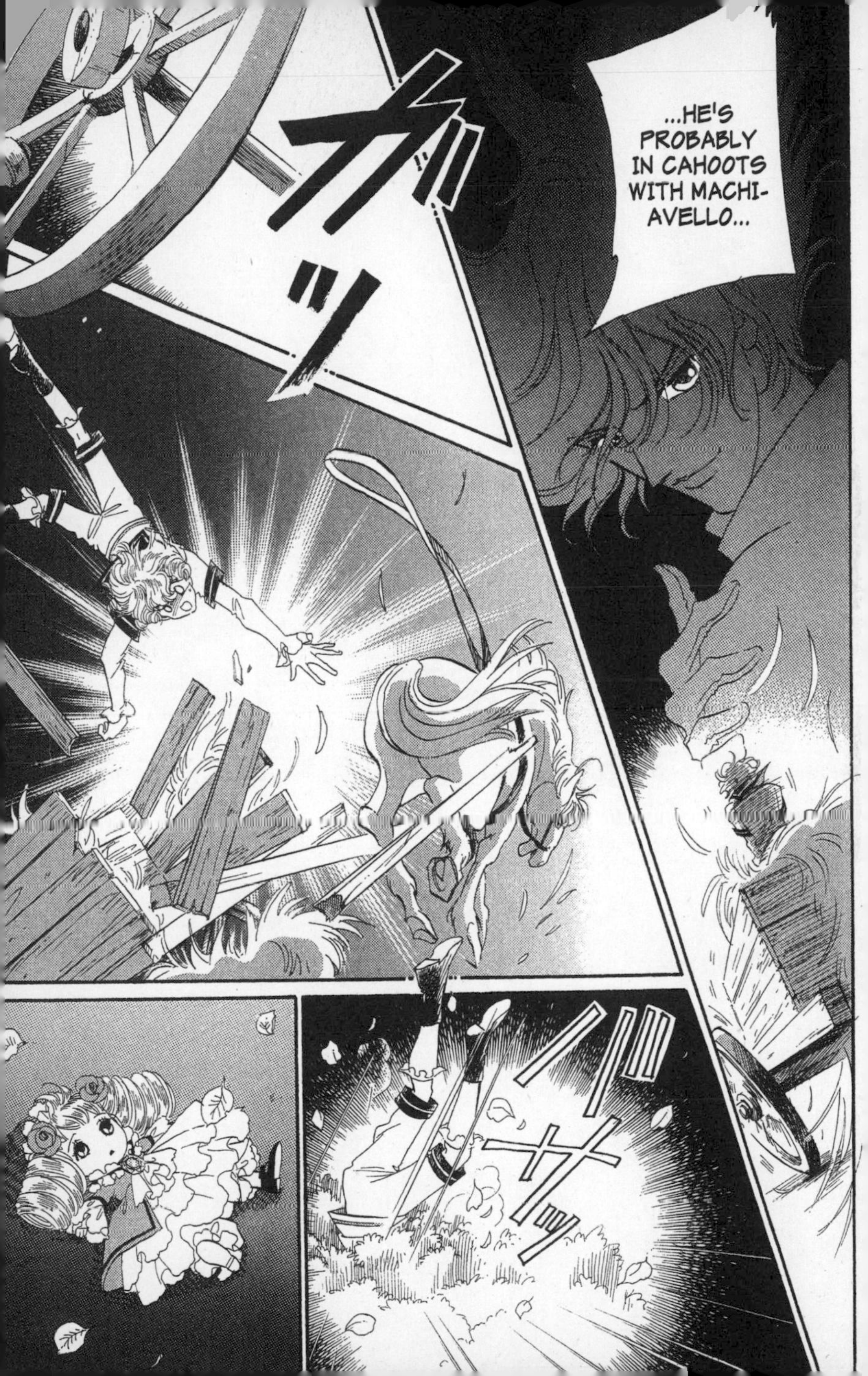
...HE'S PROBABLY IN CAHOOTS WITH MACHI-AVELLO...

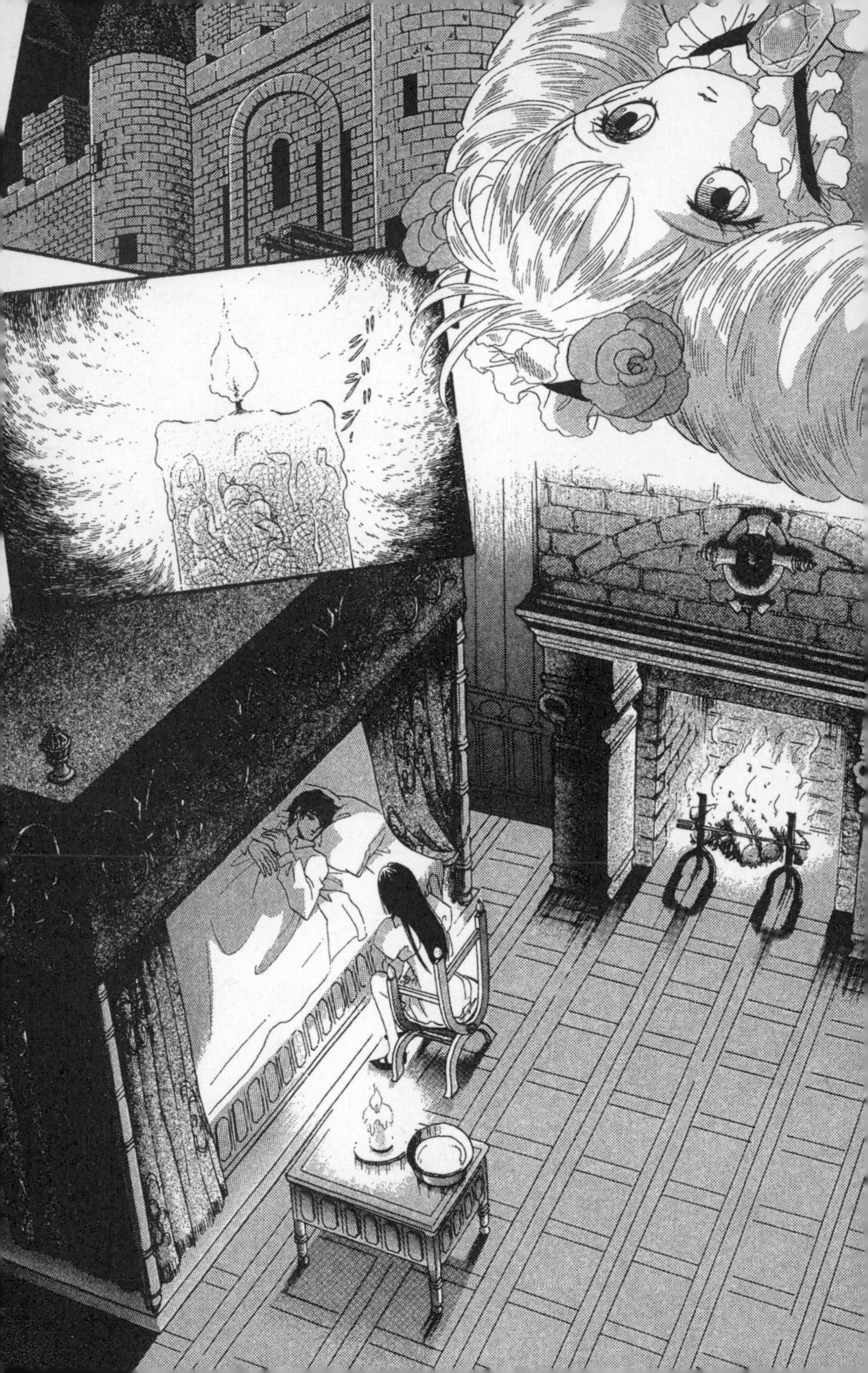

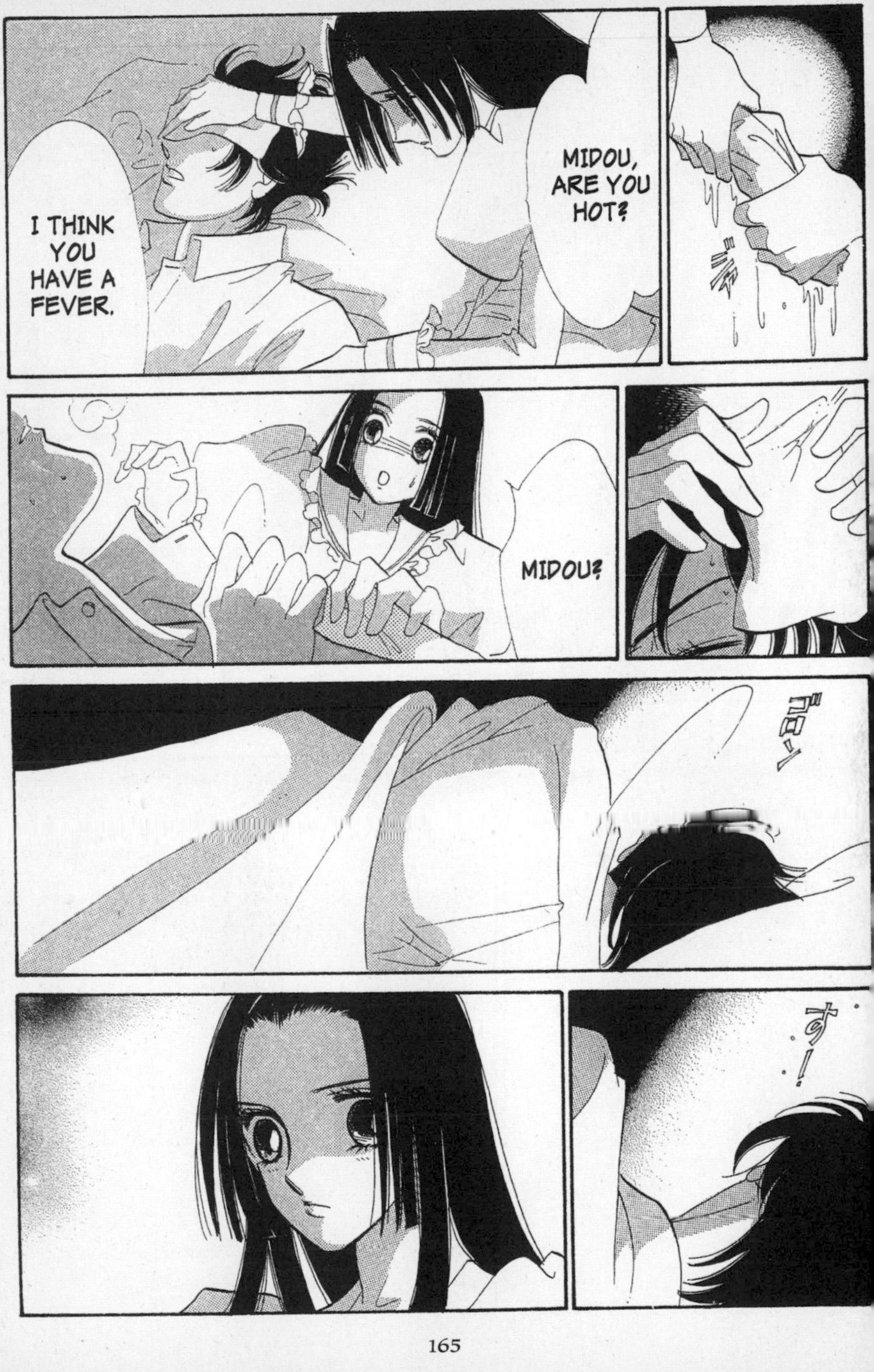
MIDOU, ARE YOU HOT?
I THINK YOU HAVE A FEVER.
MIDOU?
ゴロン!
すっ!

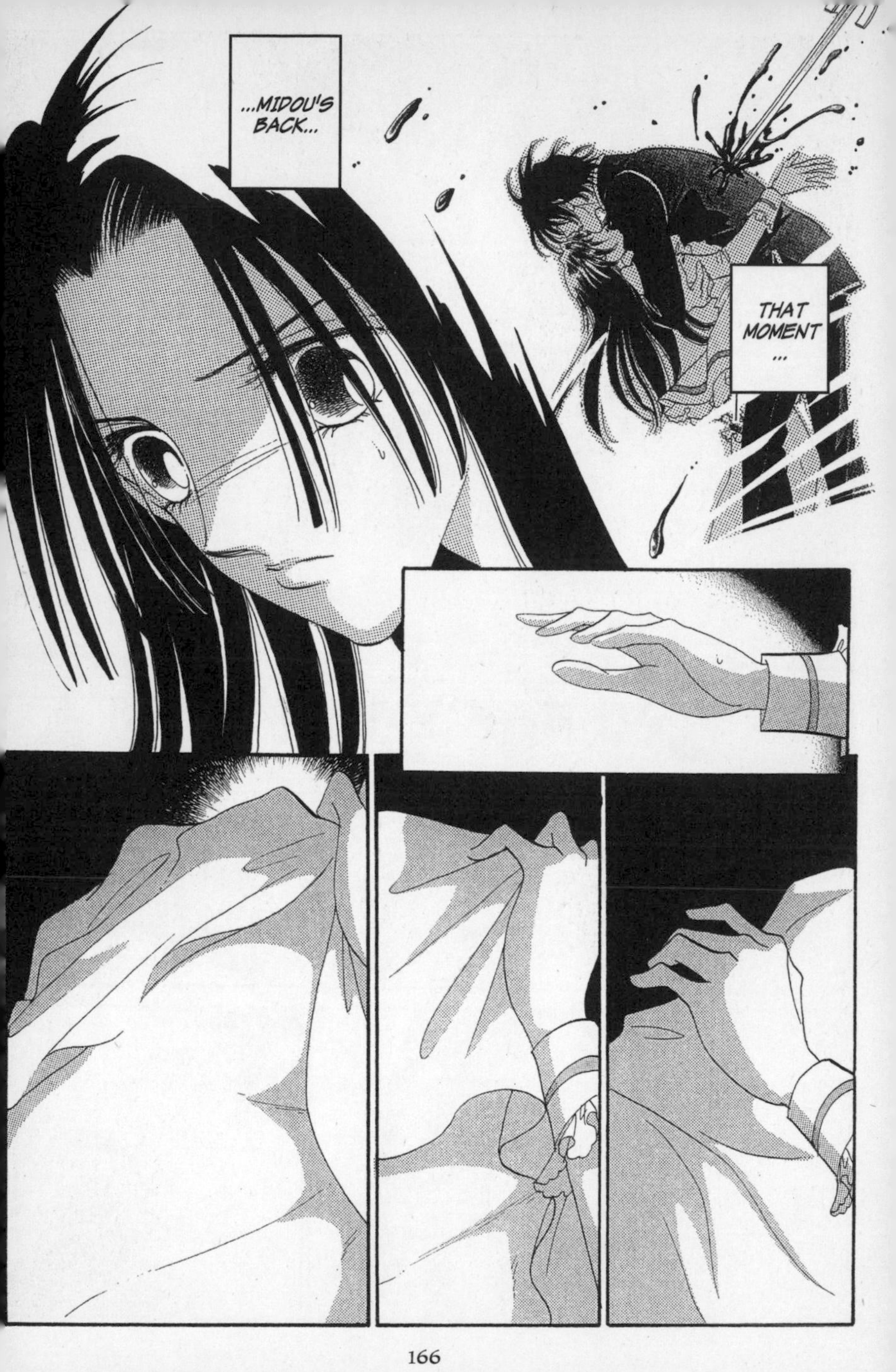
...MIDOU'S BACK...
THAT MOMENT ...

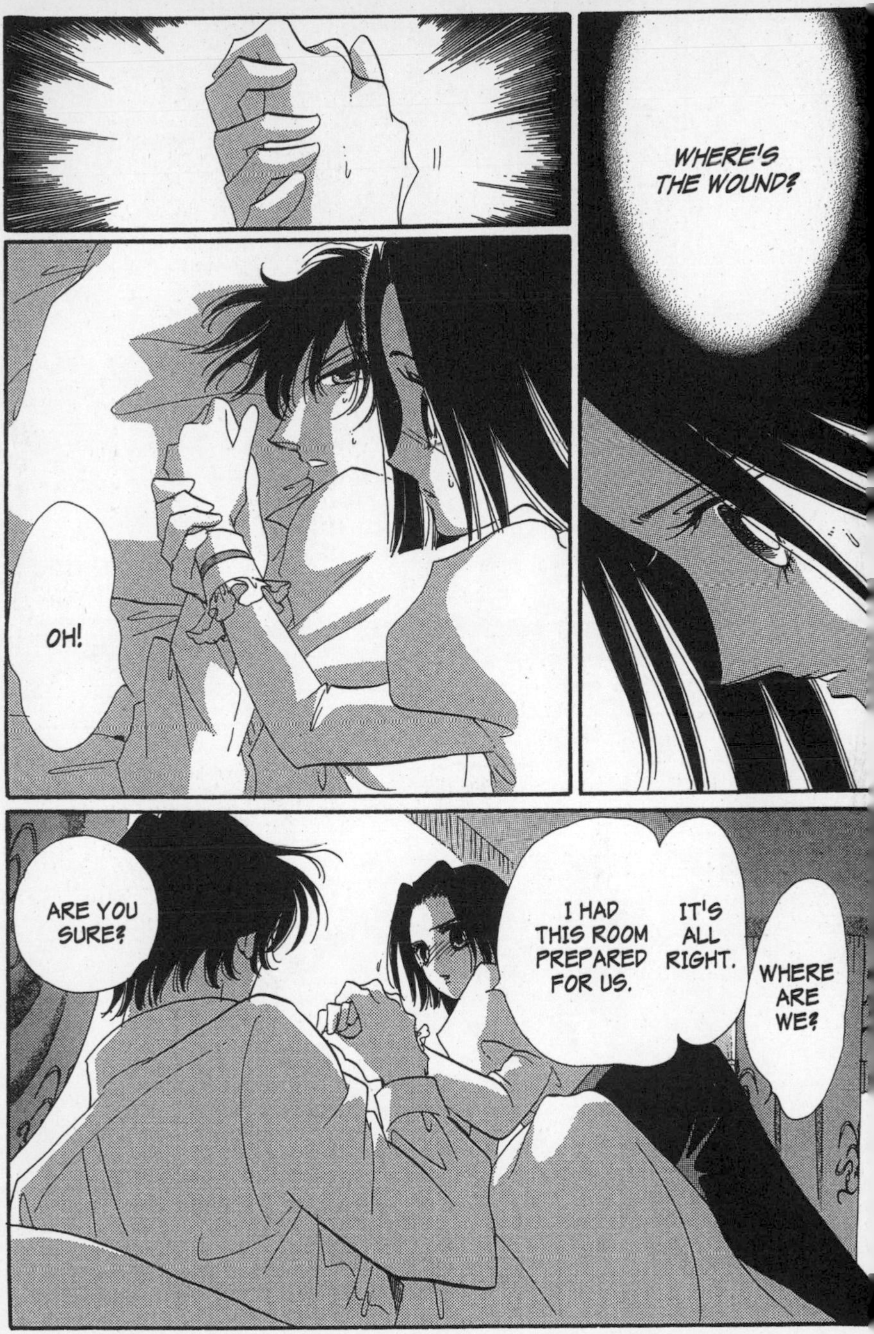
WHERE'S THE WOUND?
OH!
WHERE ARE WE?
IT'S ALL RIGHT.
I HAD THIS ROOM PREPARED FOR US.
ARE YOU SURE?

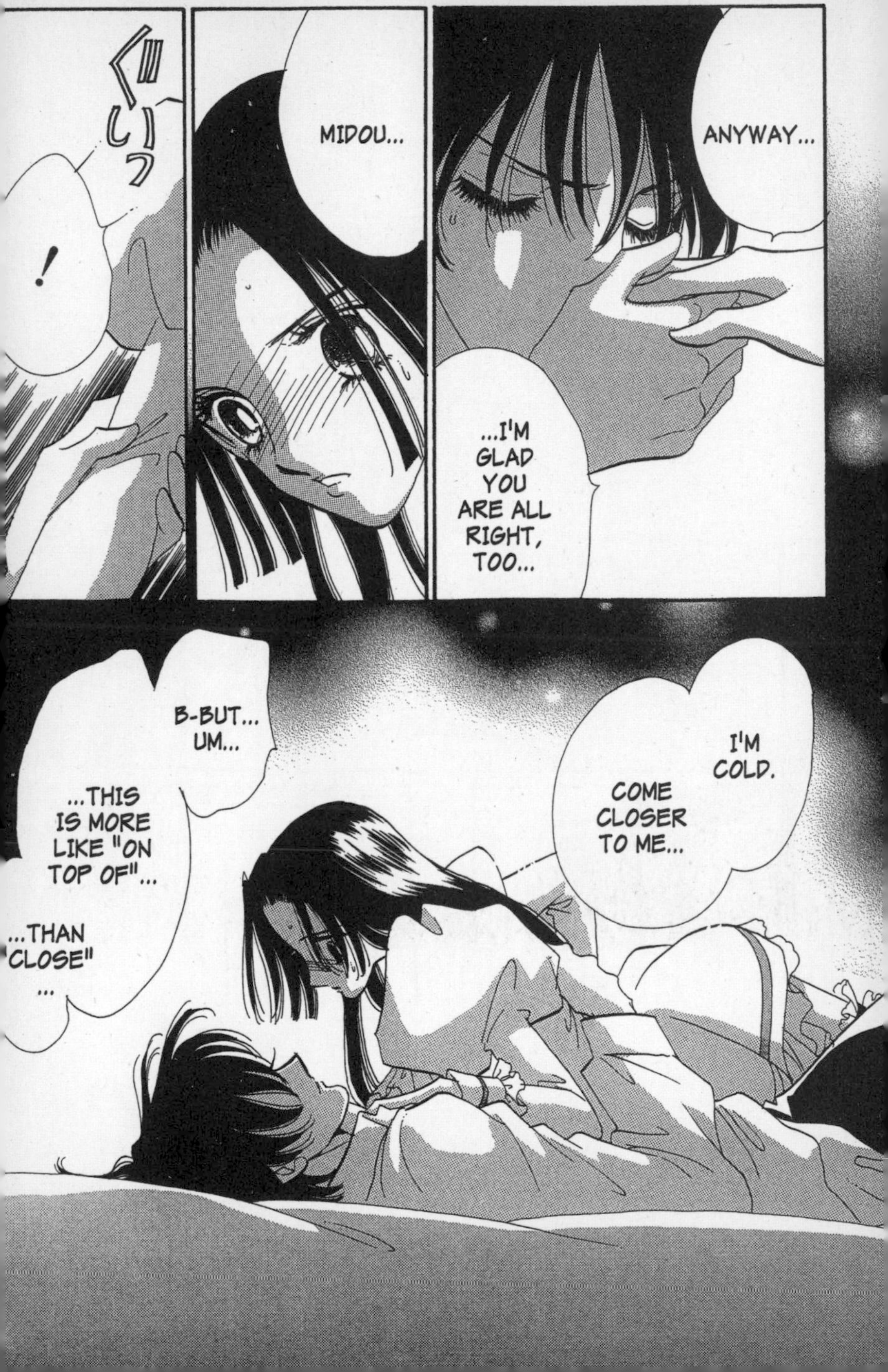
ANYWAY...
...I'M GLAD YOU ARE ALL RIGHT, TOO...
MIDOU...
くいっ
!
I'M COLD.
COME CLOSER TO ME...
B-BUT... UM...
...THIS IS MORE LIKE "ON TOP OF"...
...THAN CLOSE" ...

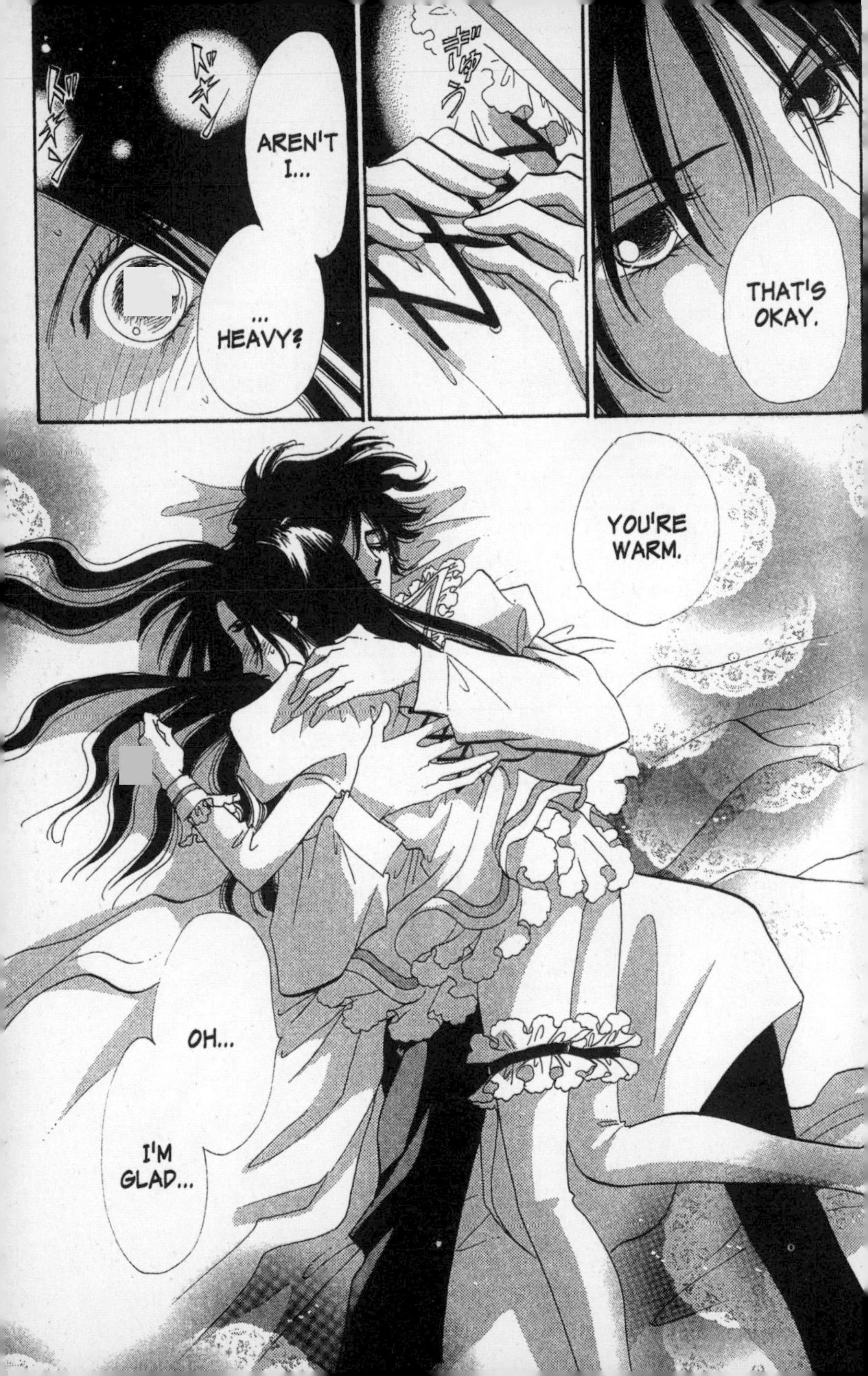
THAT'S OKAY.
ぎゅう
AREN'T I...
... HEAVY?
YOU'RE WARM.
OH...
I'M GLAD...

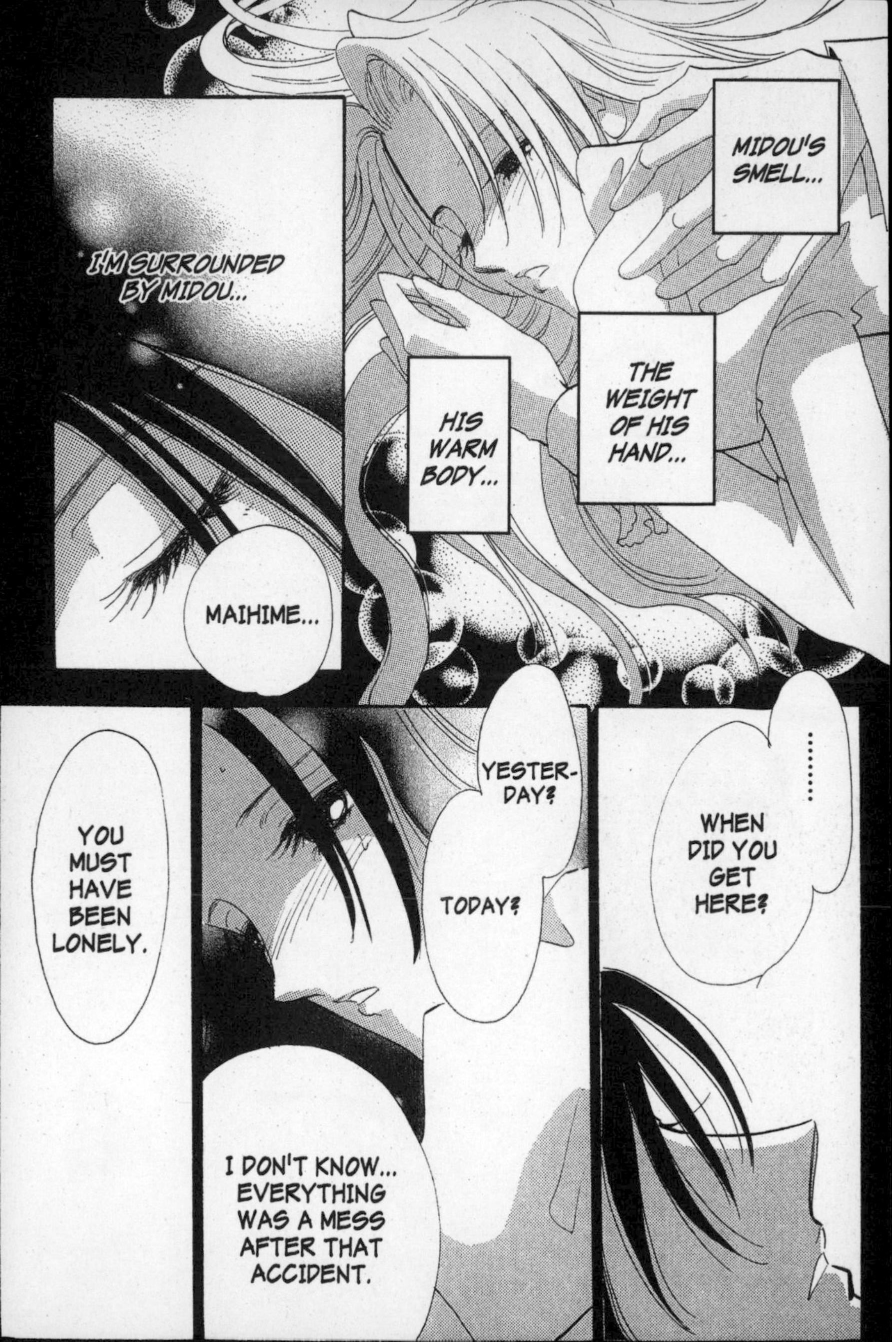
MIDOU'S SMELL...
THE WEIGHT OF HIS HAND...
HIS WARM BODY...
I'M SURROUNDED BY MIDOU...
MAIHIME...
......
WHEN DID YOU GET HERE?
YESTER-DAY?
TODAY?
I DON'T KNOW... EVERYTHING WAS A MESS AFTER THAT ACCIDENT.
YOU MUST HAVE BEEN LONELY.

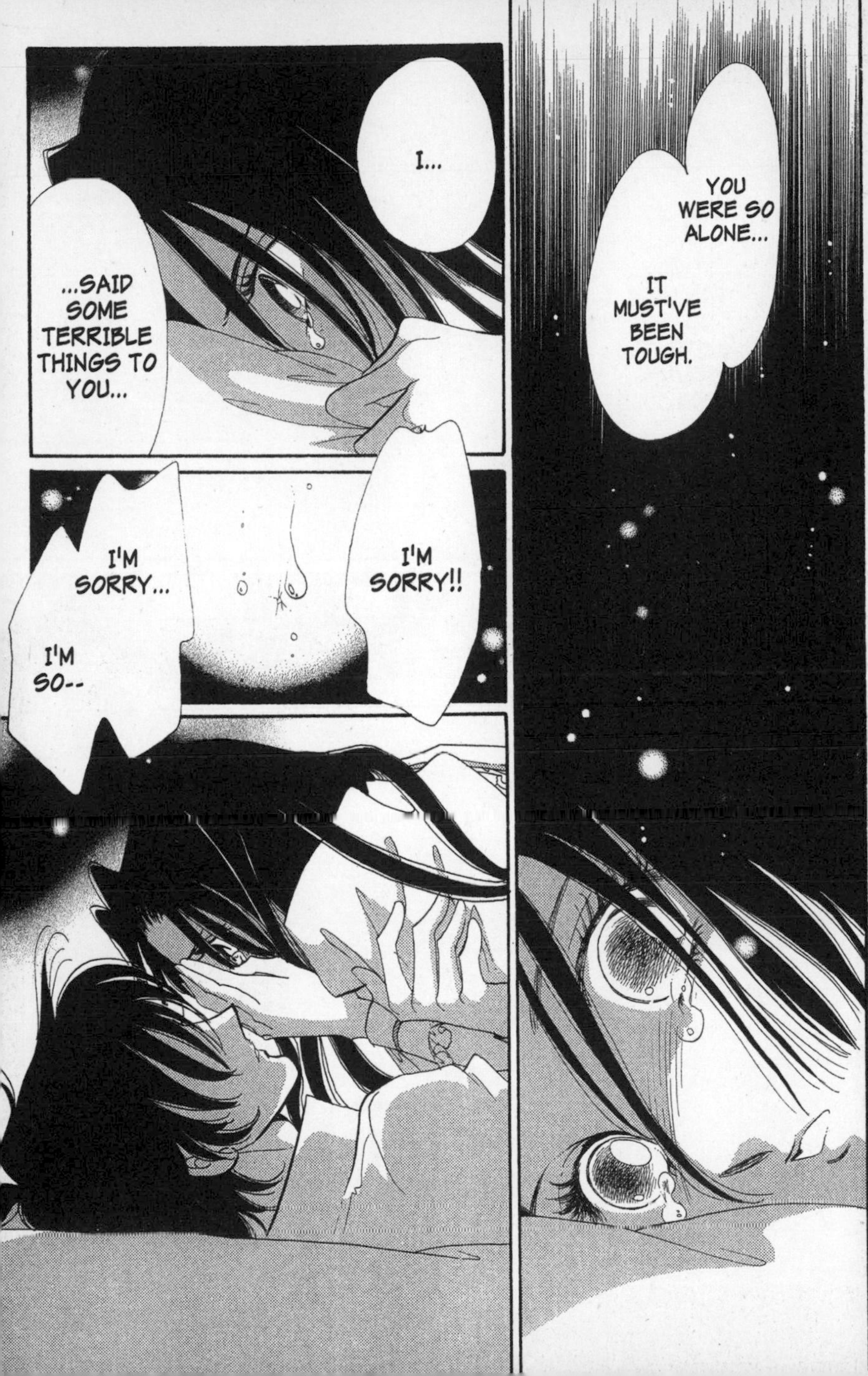
YOU WERE SO ALONE...
IT MUST'VE BEEN TOUGH.
I...
...SAID SOME TERRIBLE THINGS TO YOU...
I'M SORRY!!
I'M SORRY...
I'M SO--

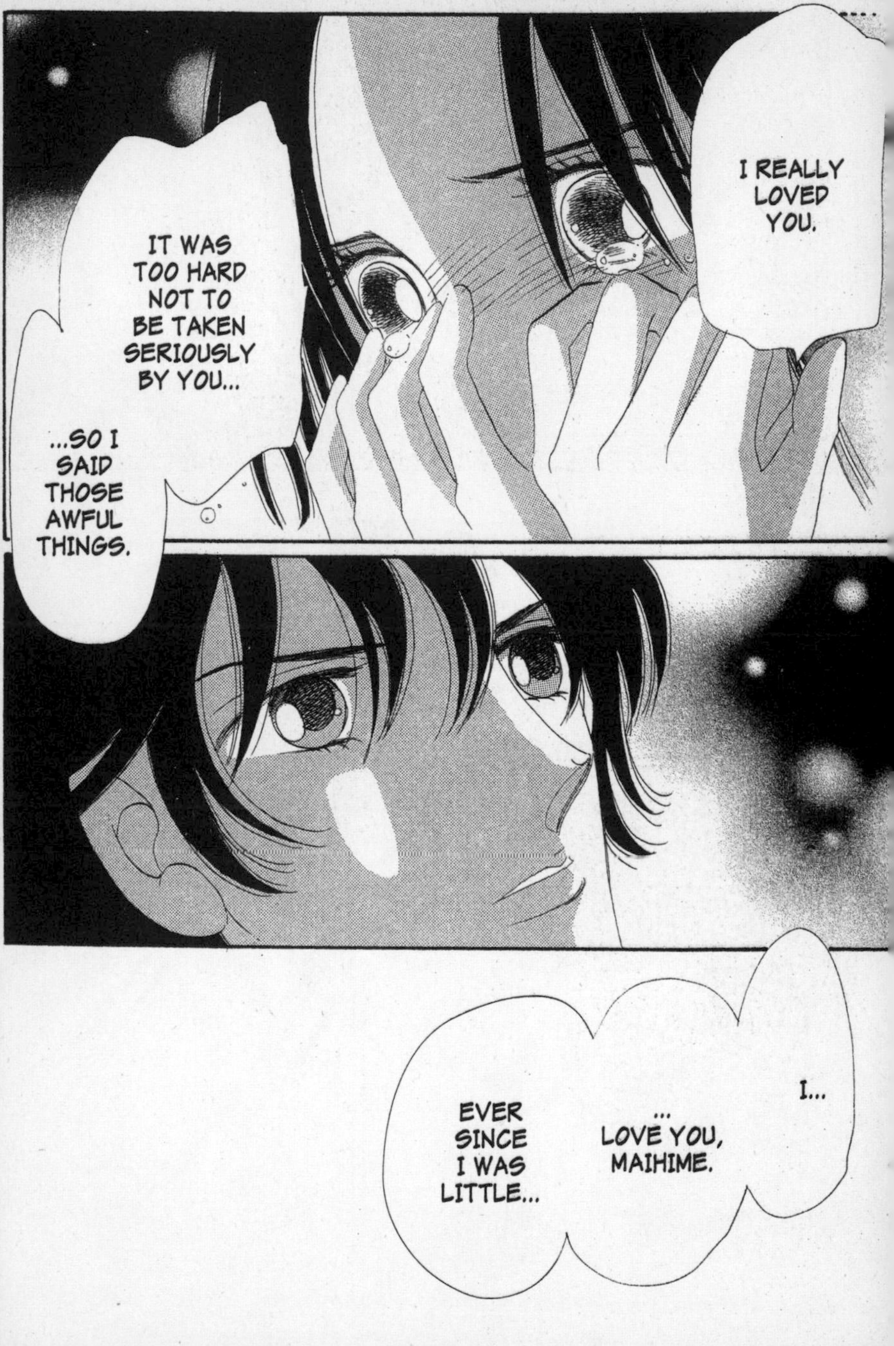
I REALLY LOVED YOU.
IT WAS TOO HARD NOT TO BE TAKEN SERIOUSLY BY YOU...
...SO I SAID THOSE AWFUL THINGS.
I...
... LOVE YOU, MAIHIME.
EVER SINCE I WAS LITTLE...

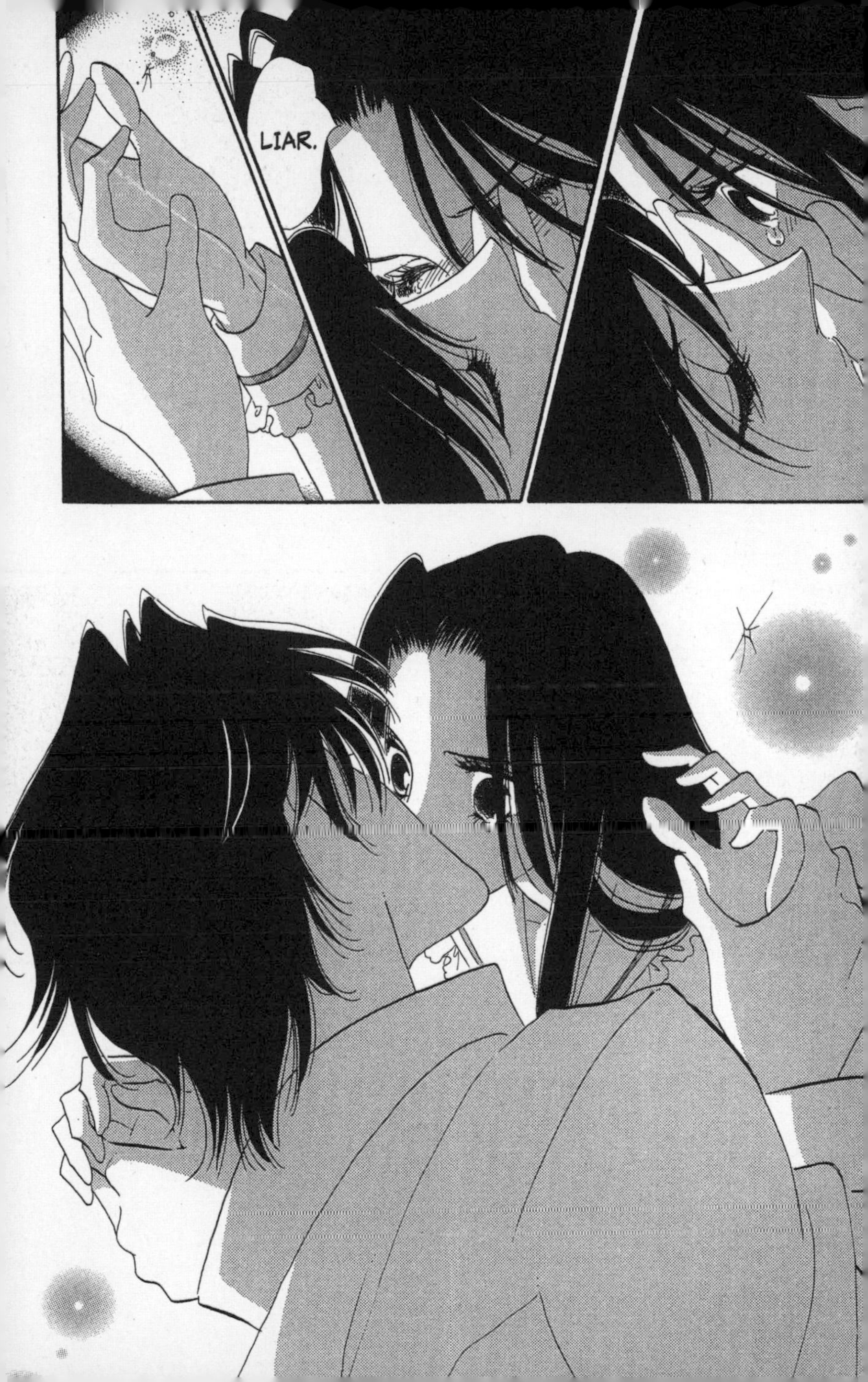
LIAR.

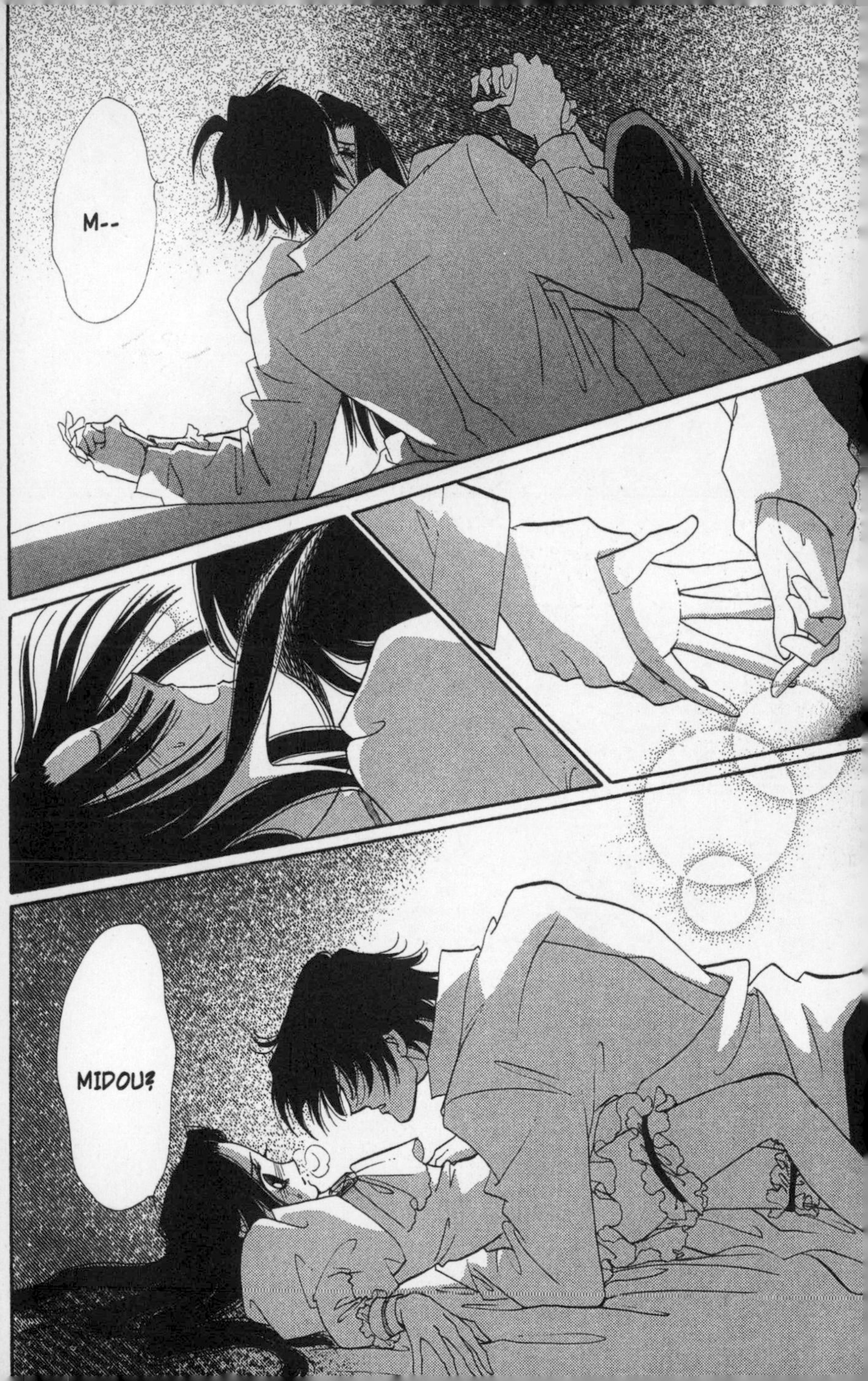
M--
MIDOU?

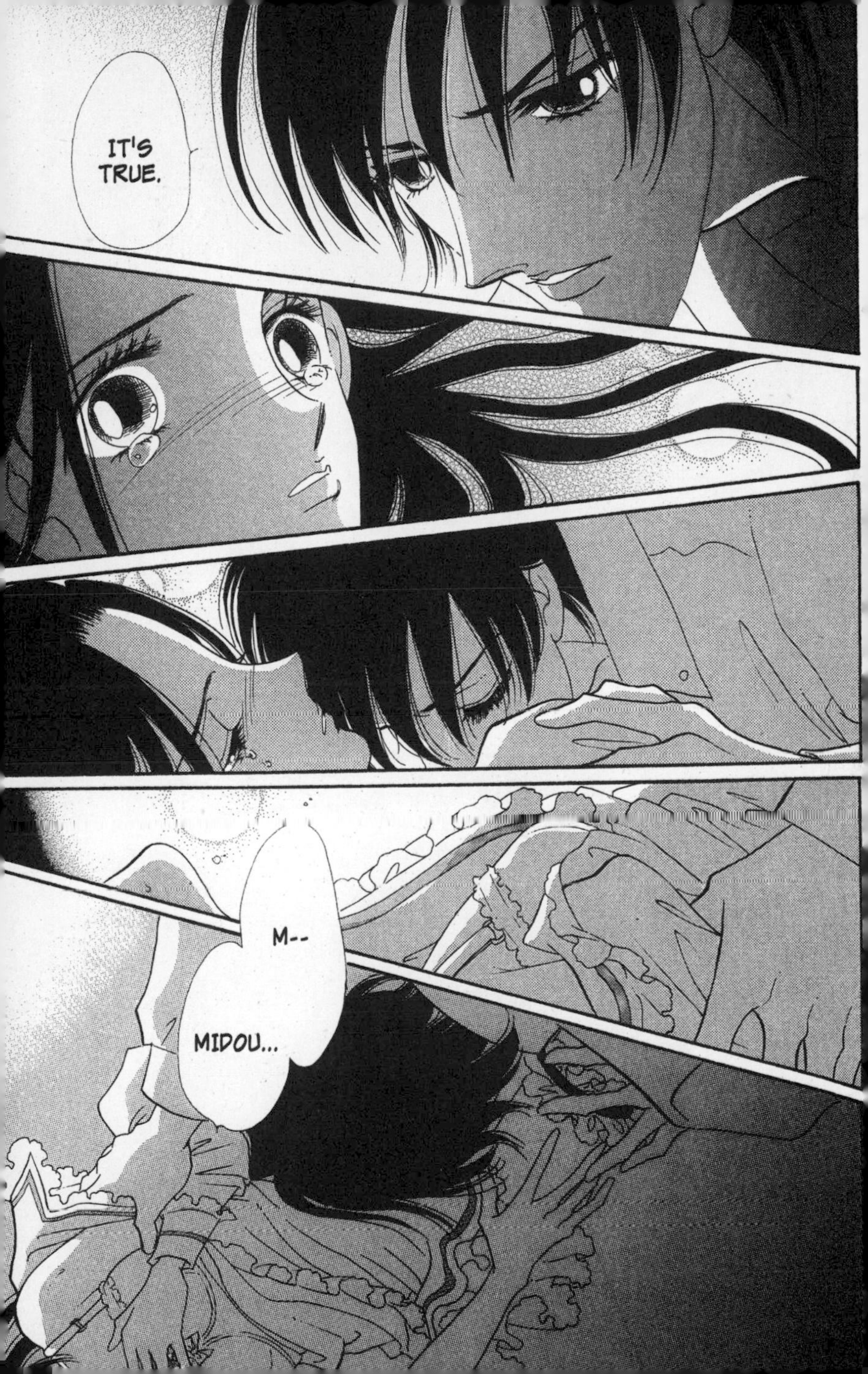
IT'S TRUE.
M--
MIDOU...

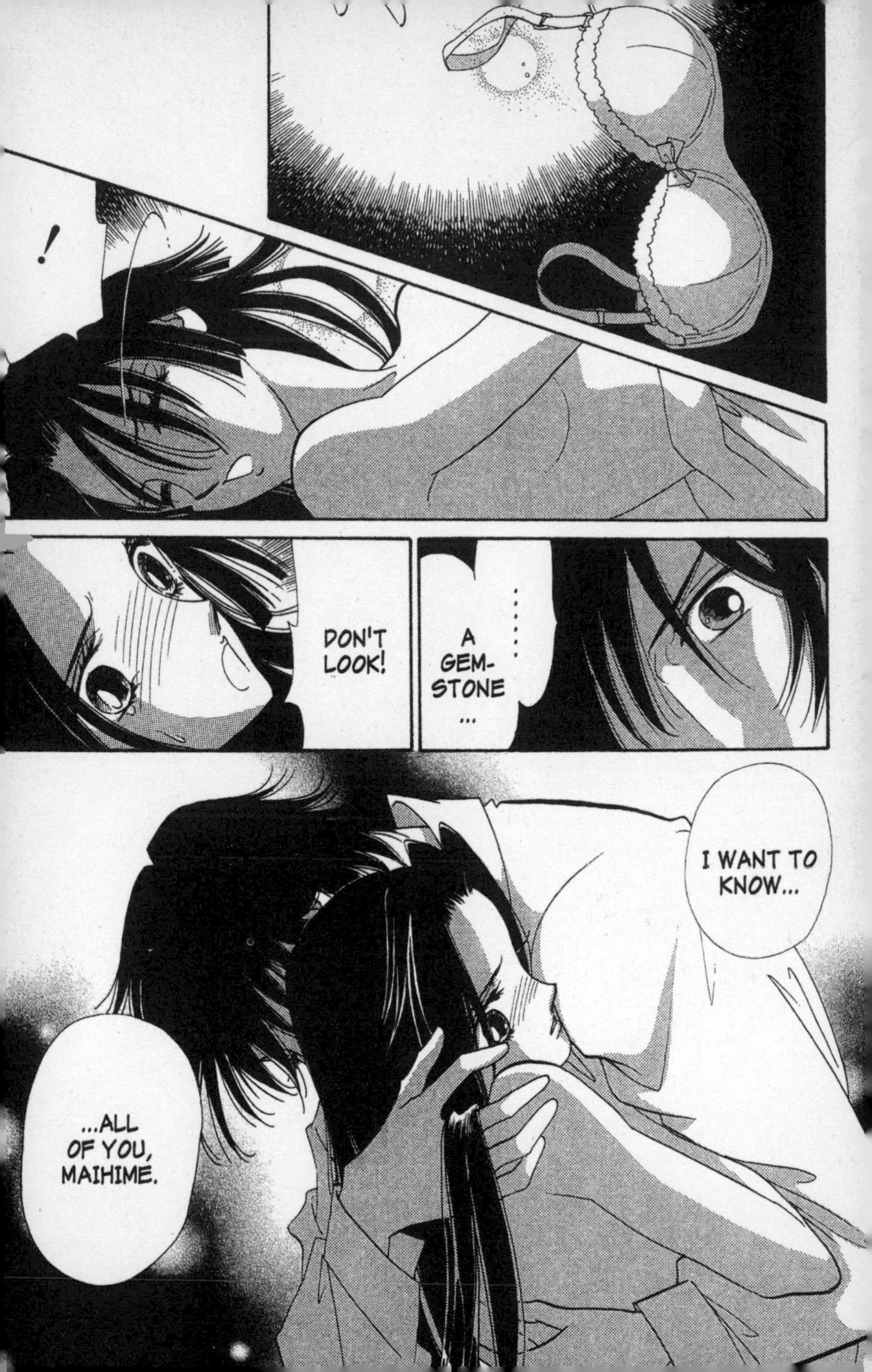
!
A GEM-STONE...
DON'T LOOK!
I WANT TO KNOW...
...ALL OF YOU, MAIHIME.

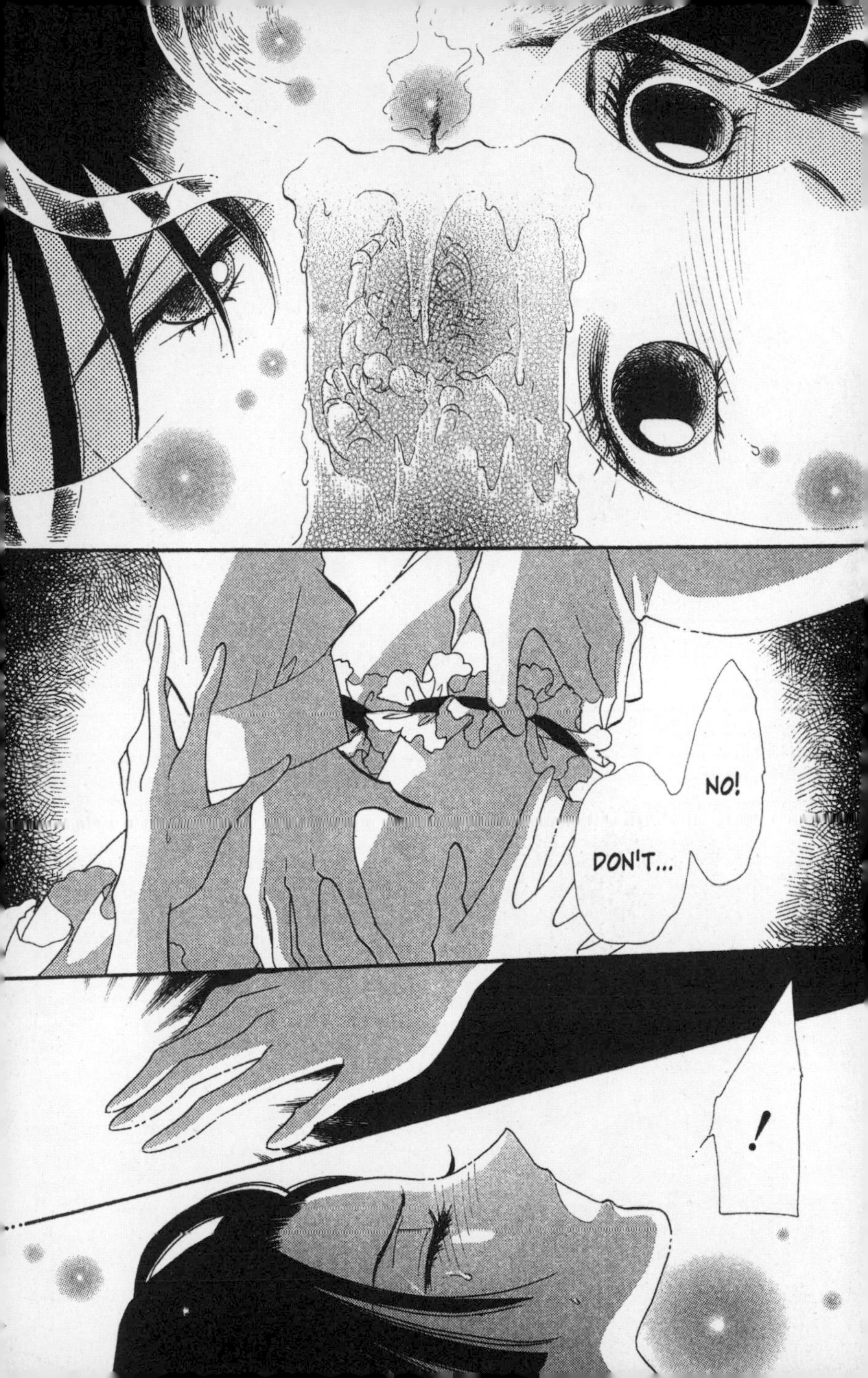
NO!
DON'T...
!

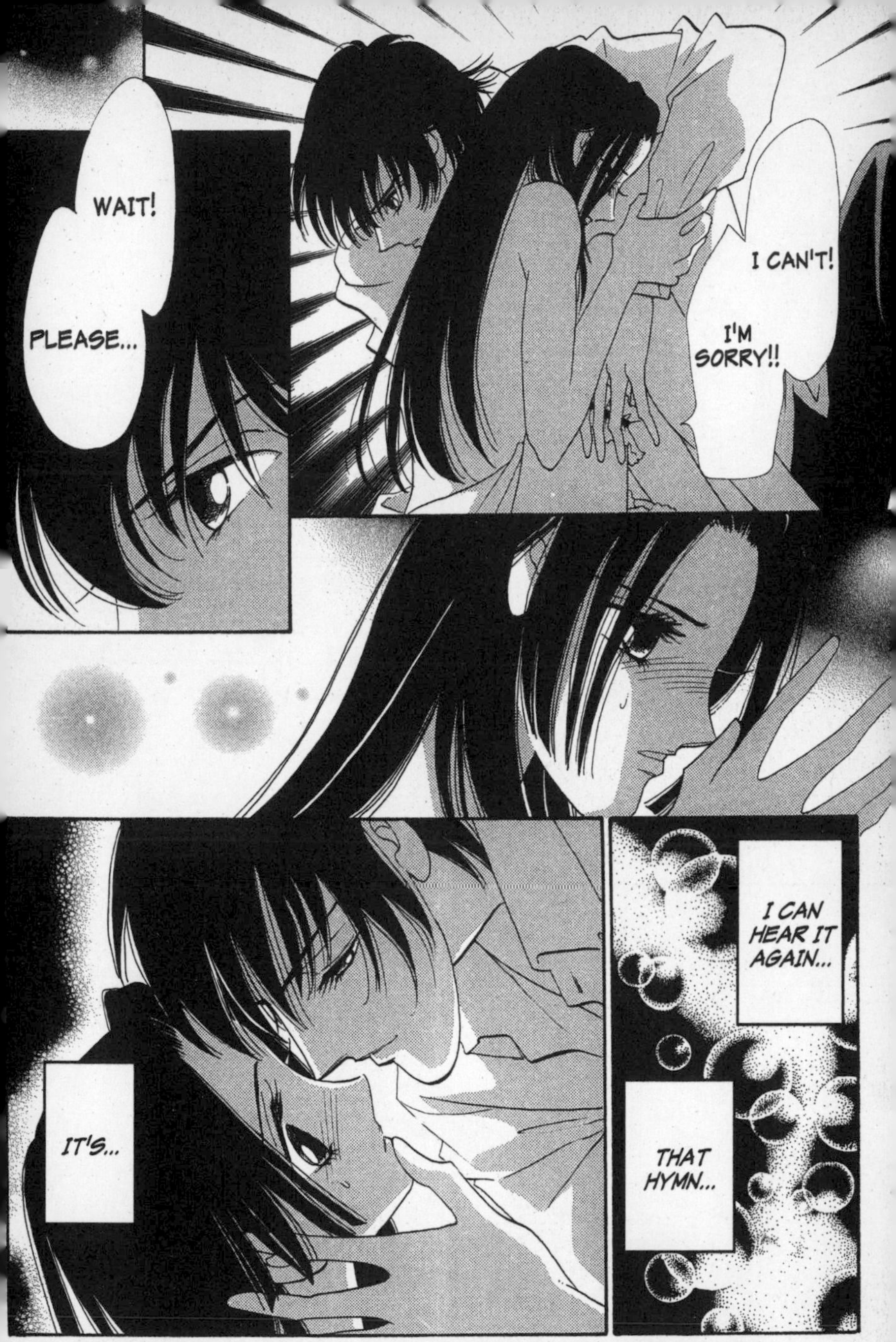
I CAN'T!
I'M SORRY!!
WAIT!
PLEASE...
I CAN HEAR IT AGAIN...
THAT HYMN...
IT'S...

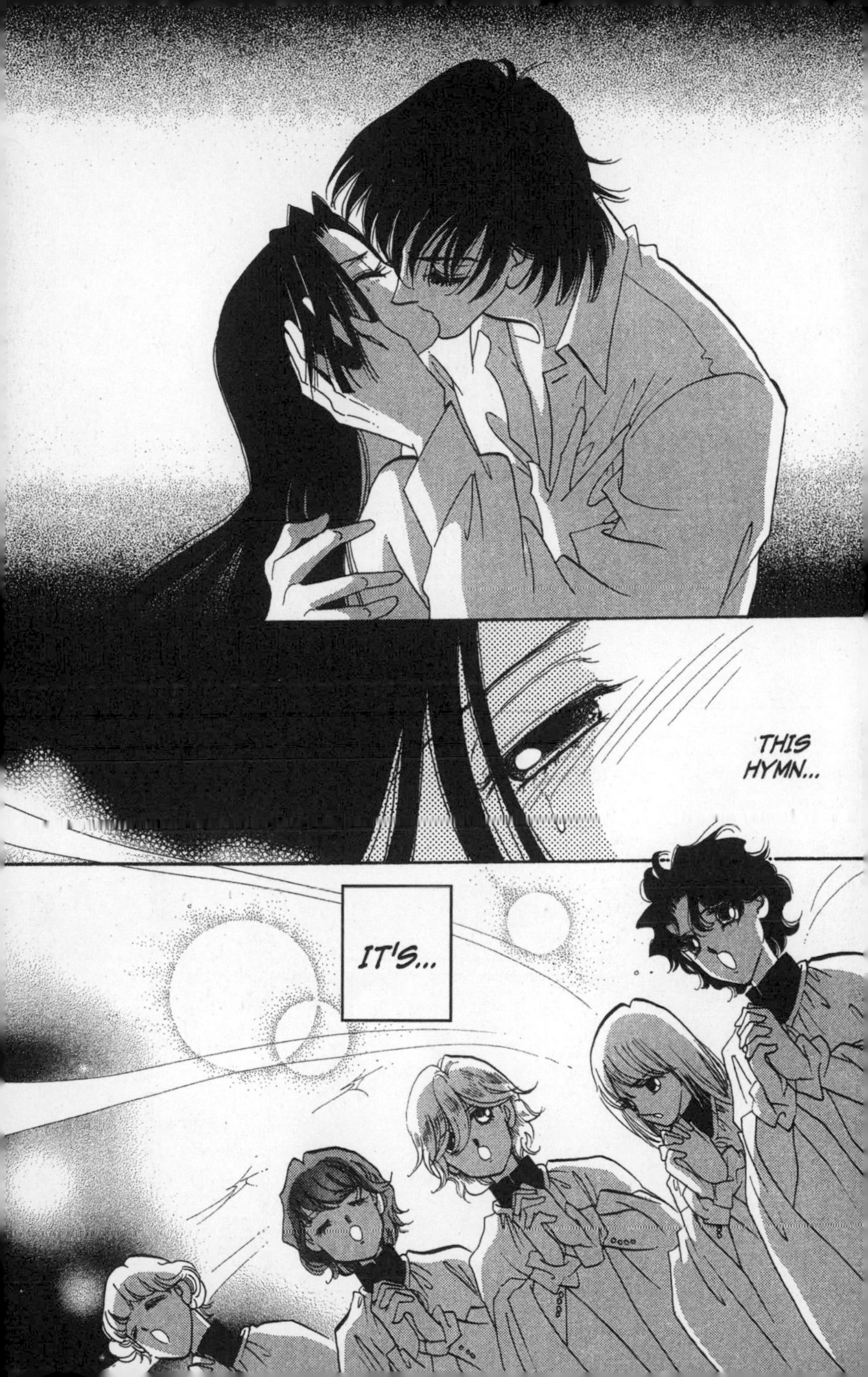
THIS HYMN...
IT'S...

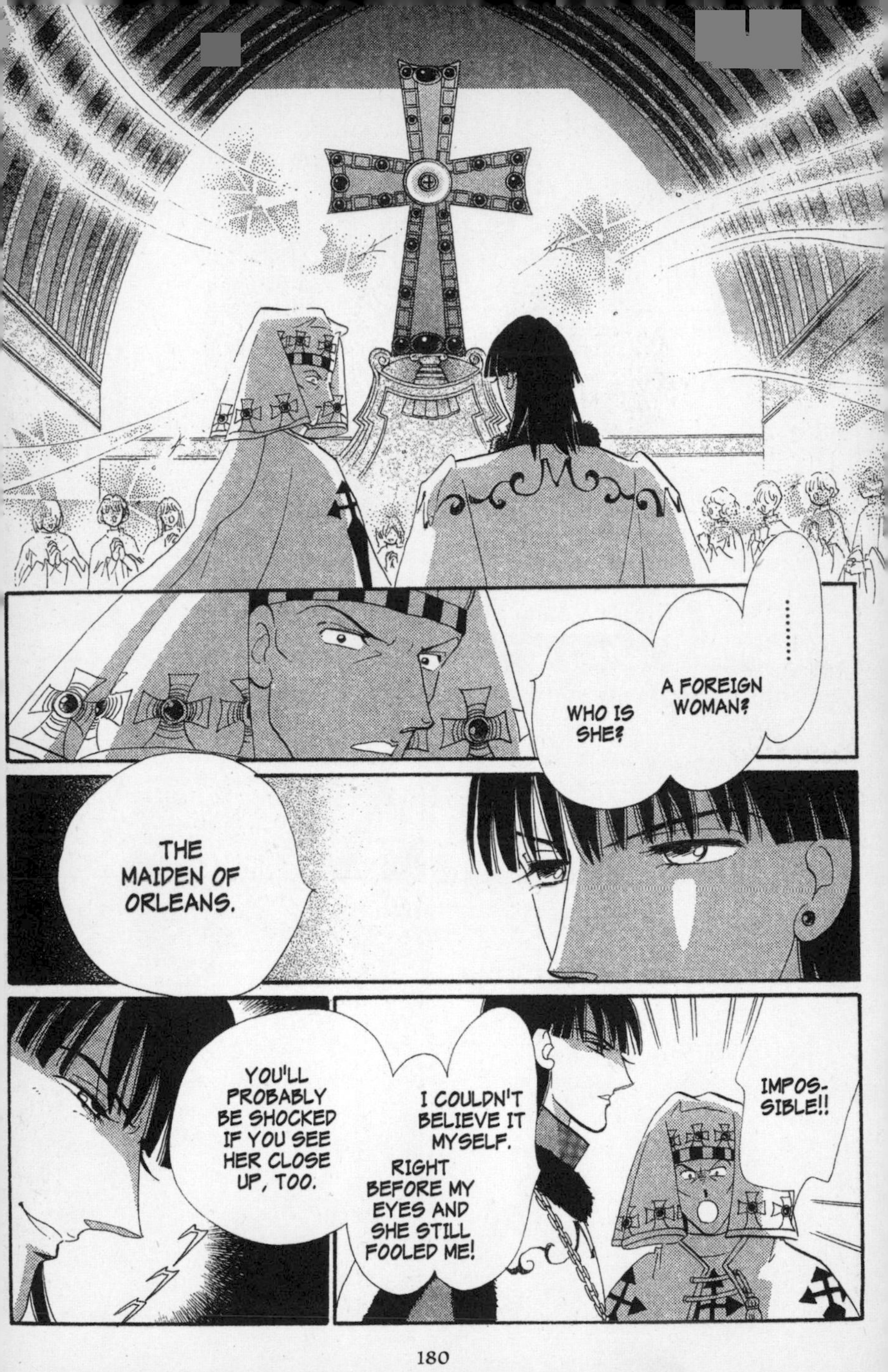
......
A FOREIGN WOMAN?
WHO IS SHE?
THE MAIDEN OF ORLEANS.
IMPOS-SIBLE!!
I COULDN'T BELIEVE IT MYSELF.
RIGHT BEFORE MY EYES AND SHE STILL FOOLED ME!
YOU'LL PROBABLY BE SHOCKED IF YOU SEE HER CLOSE UP, TOO.

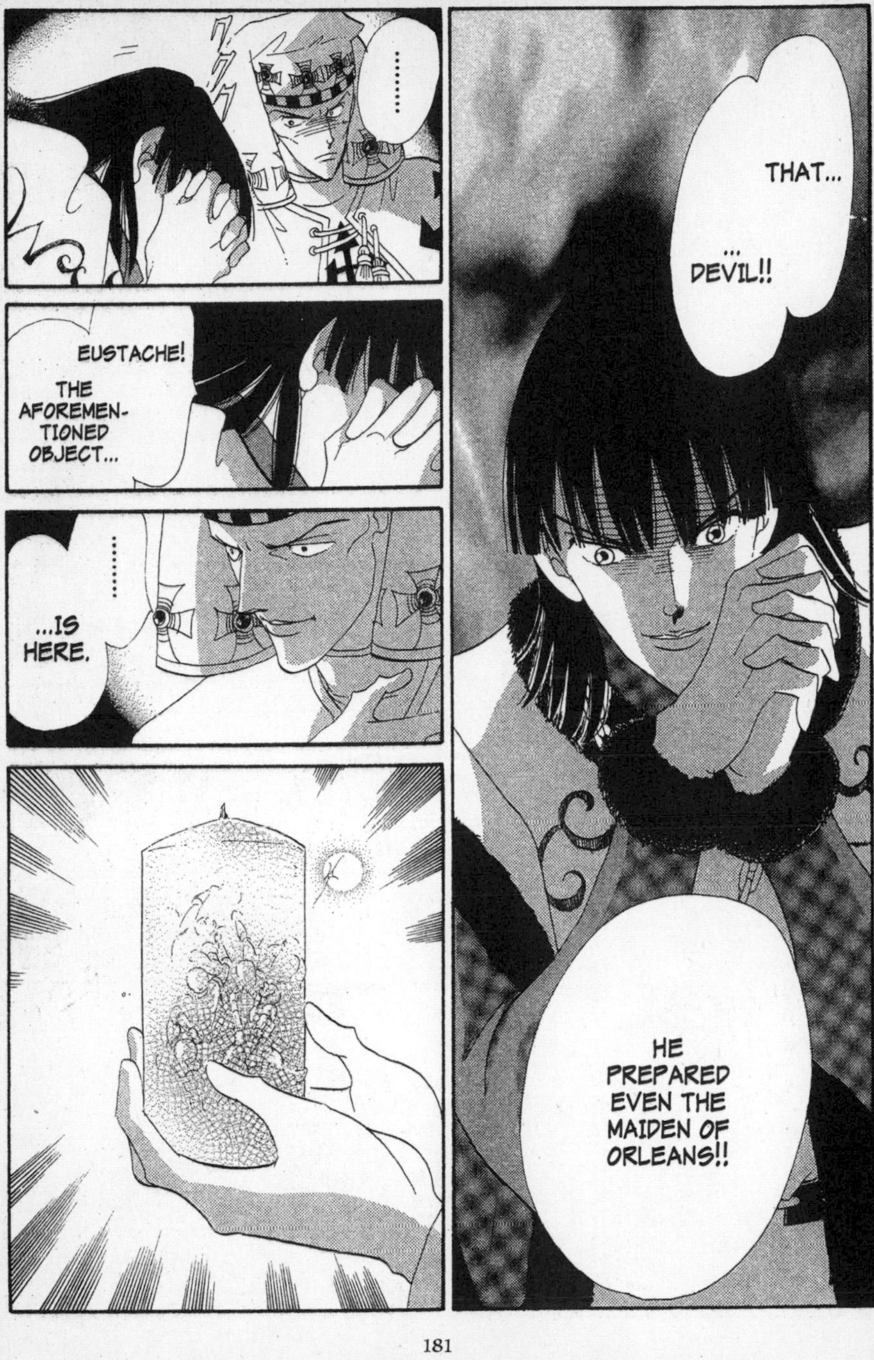
THAT...
... DEVIL!!
HE PREPARED EVEN THE MAIDEN OF ORLEANS!!
......
EUSTACHE!
THE AFOREMEN-TIONED OBJECT...
......
...IS HERE.

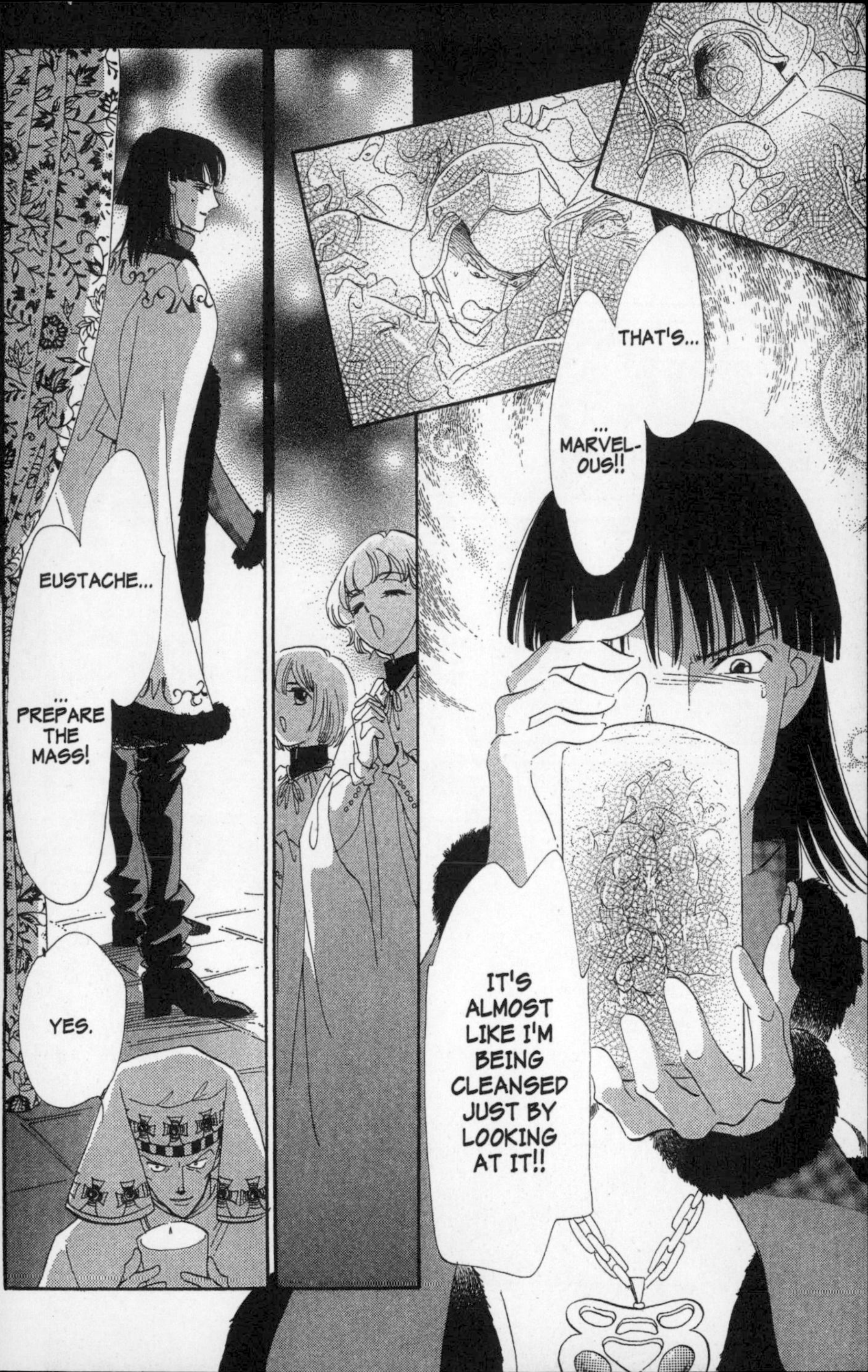
THAT'S...
... MARVEL-OUS!!
IT'S ALMOST LIKE I'M BEING CLEANSED JUST BY LOOKING AT IT!!
EUSTACHE...
... PREPARE THE MASS!
YES.

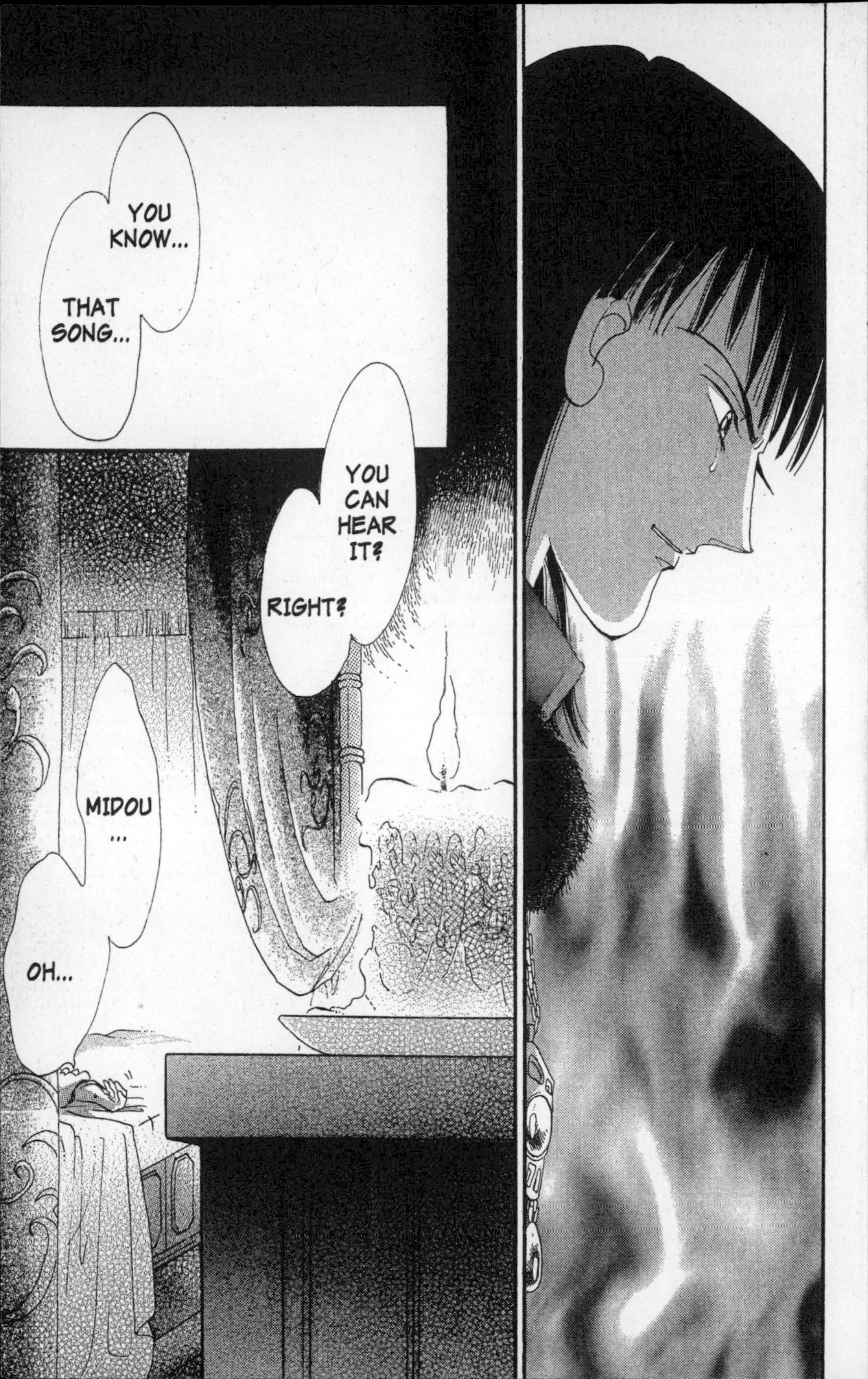
YOU KNOW...
THAT SONG...
YOU CAN HEAR IT?
RIGHT?
MIDOU...
OH...

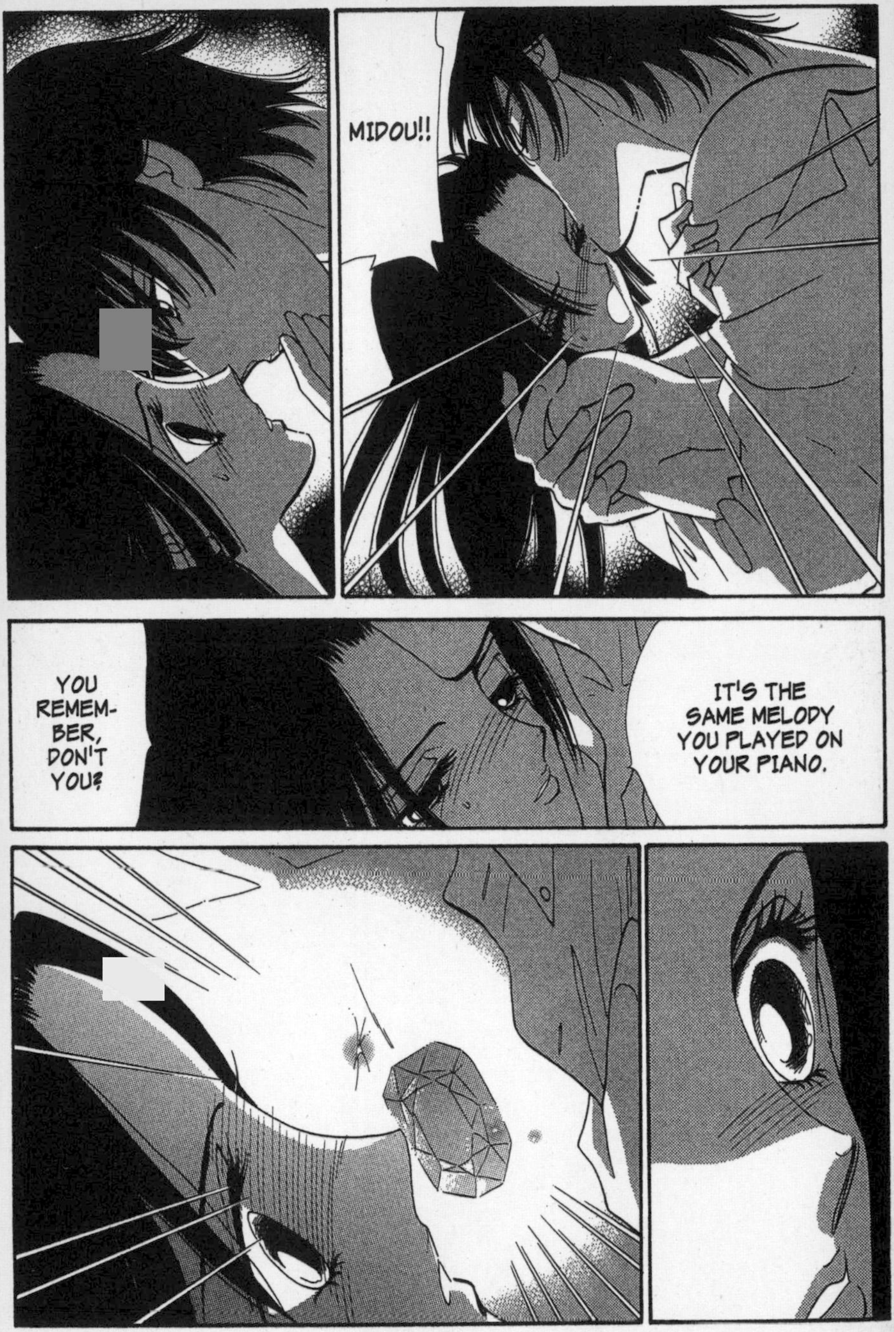
MIDOU!!
IT'S THE SAME MELODY YOU PLAYED ON YOUR PIANO.
YOU REMEMBER, DON'T YOU?

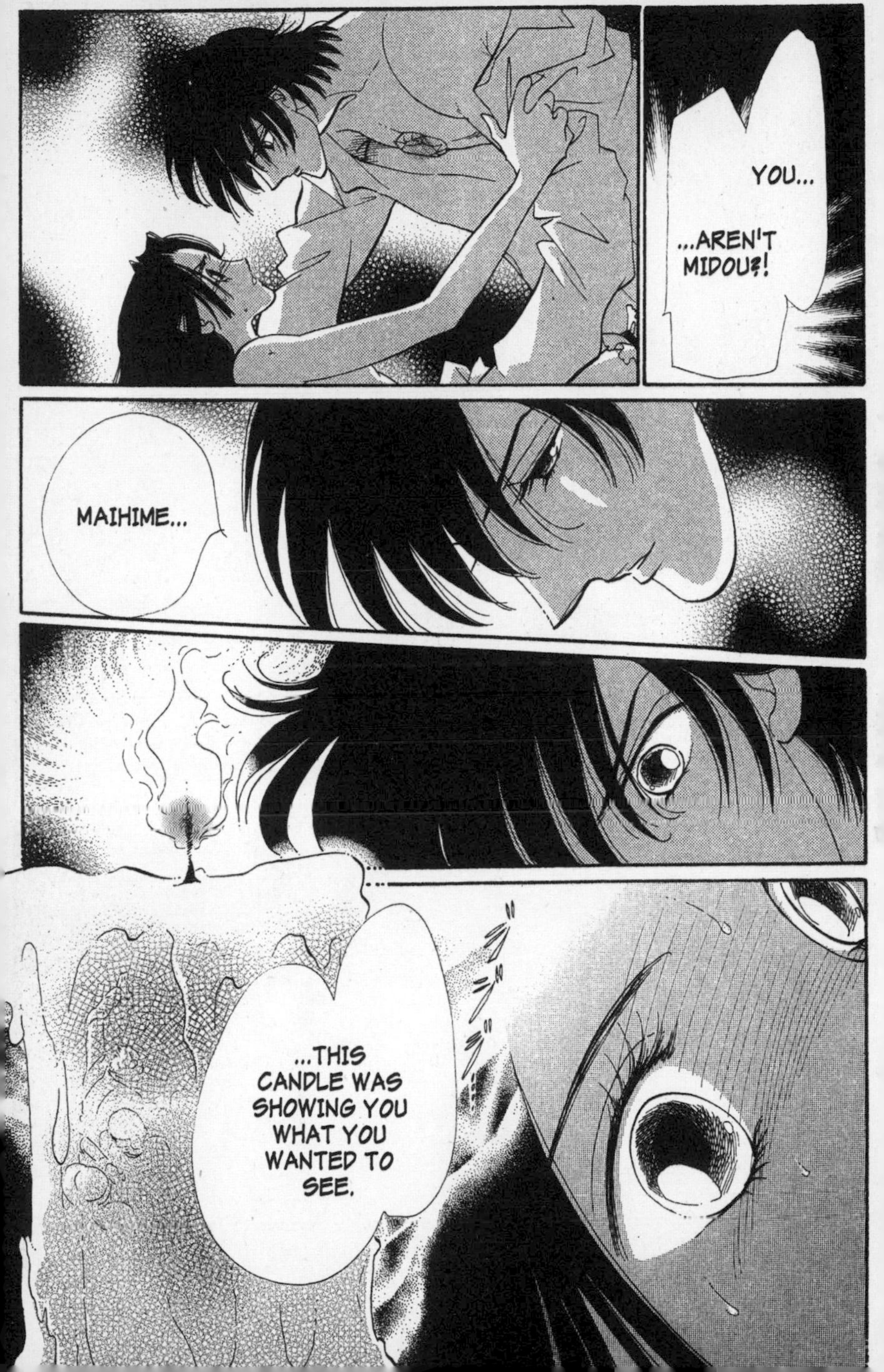
YOU...
...AREN'T MIDOU?!
MAIHIME...
...THIS CANDLE WAS SHOWING YOU WHAT YOU WANTED TO SEE.

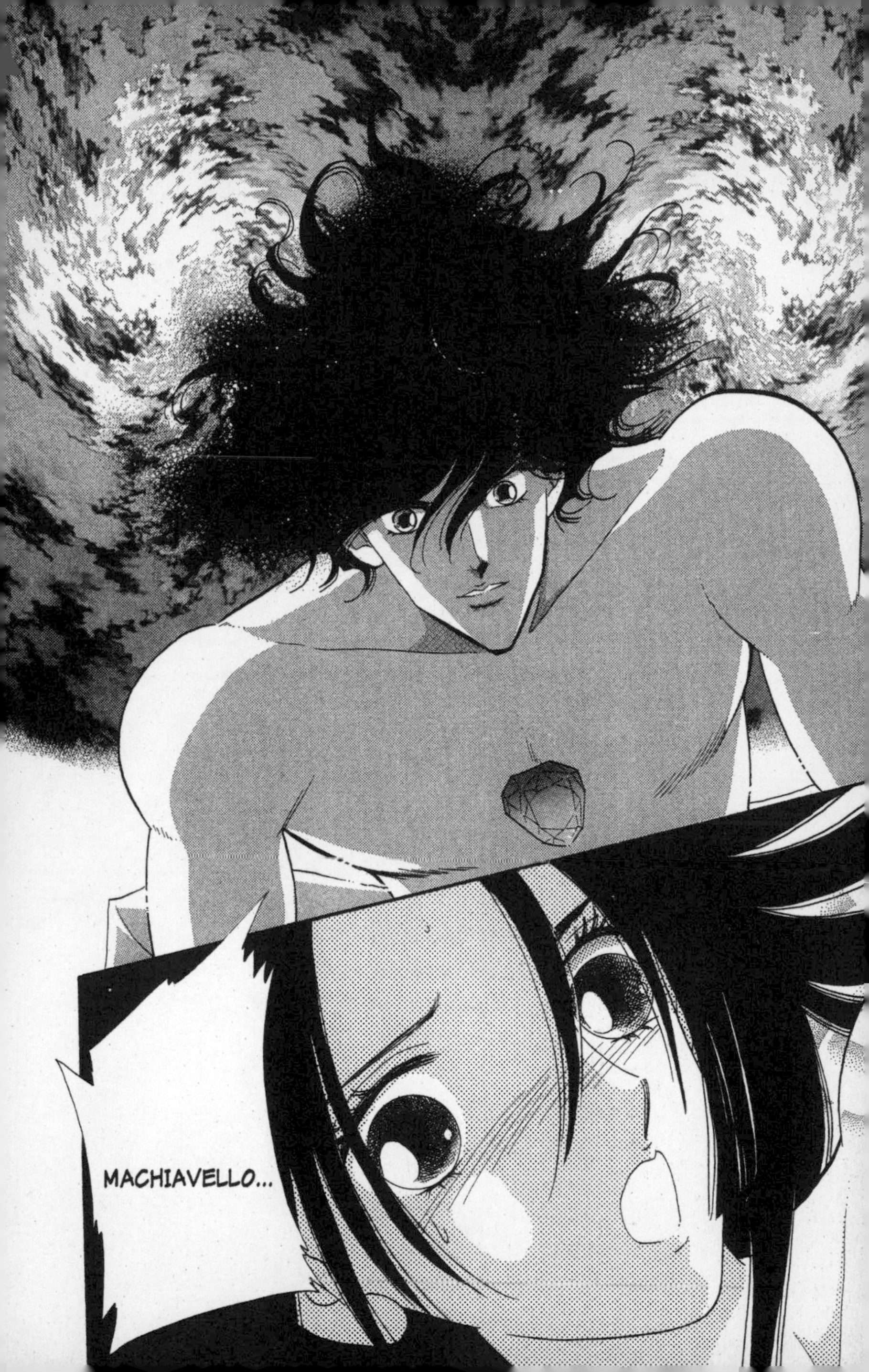
MACHIAVELLO...

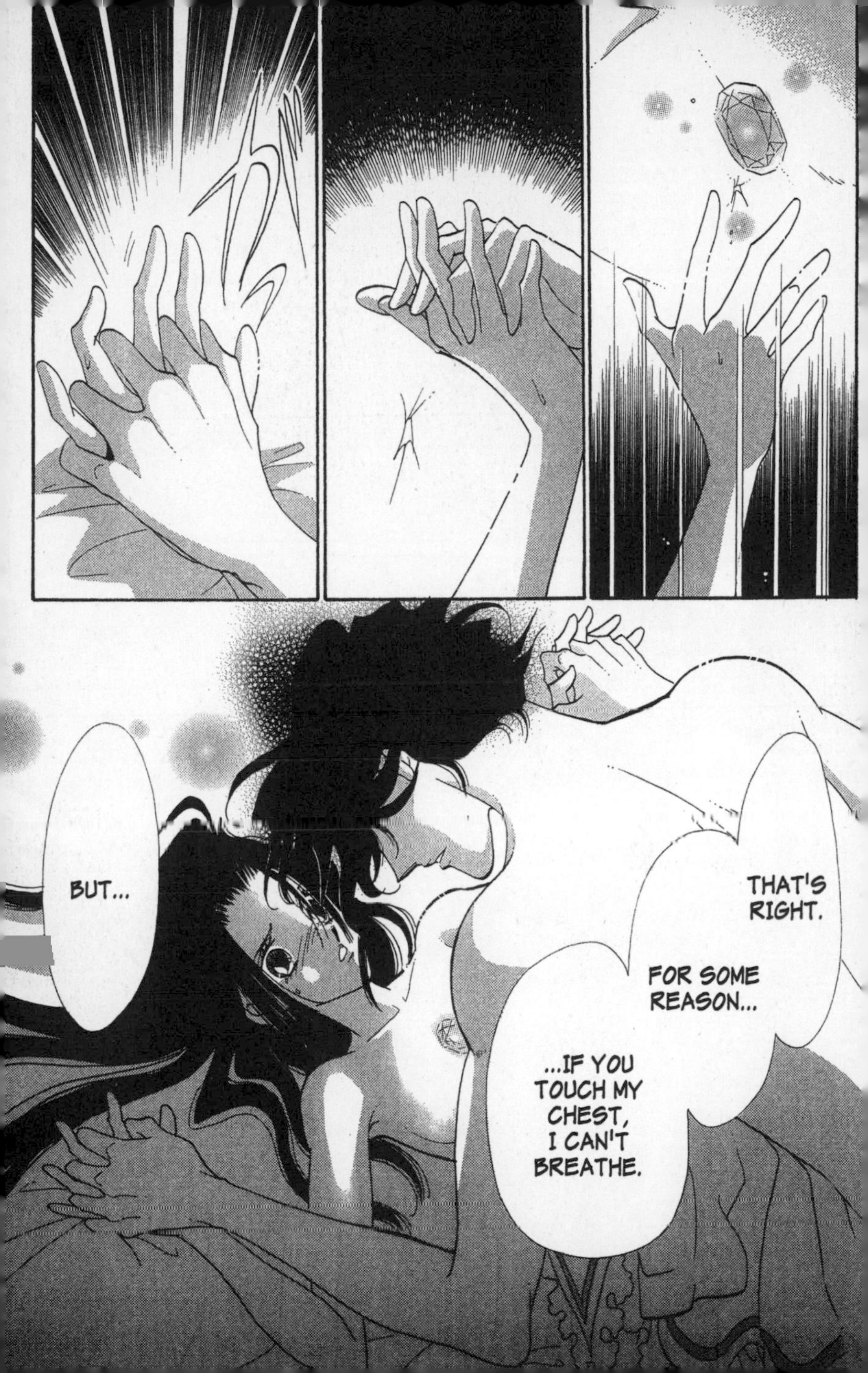
THAT'S RIGHT.
FOR SOME REASON...
...IF YOU TOUCH MY CHEST, I CAN'T BREATHE.
BUT...

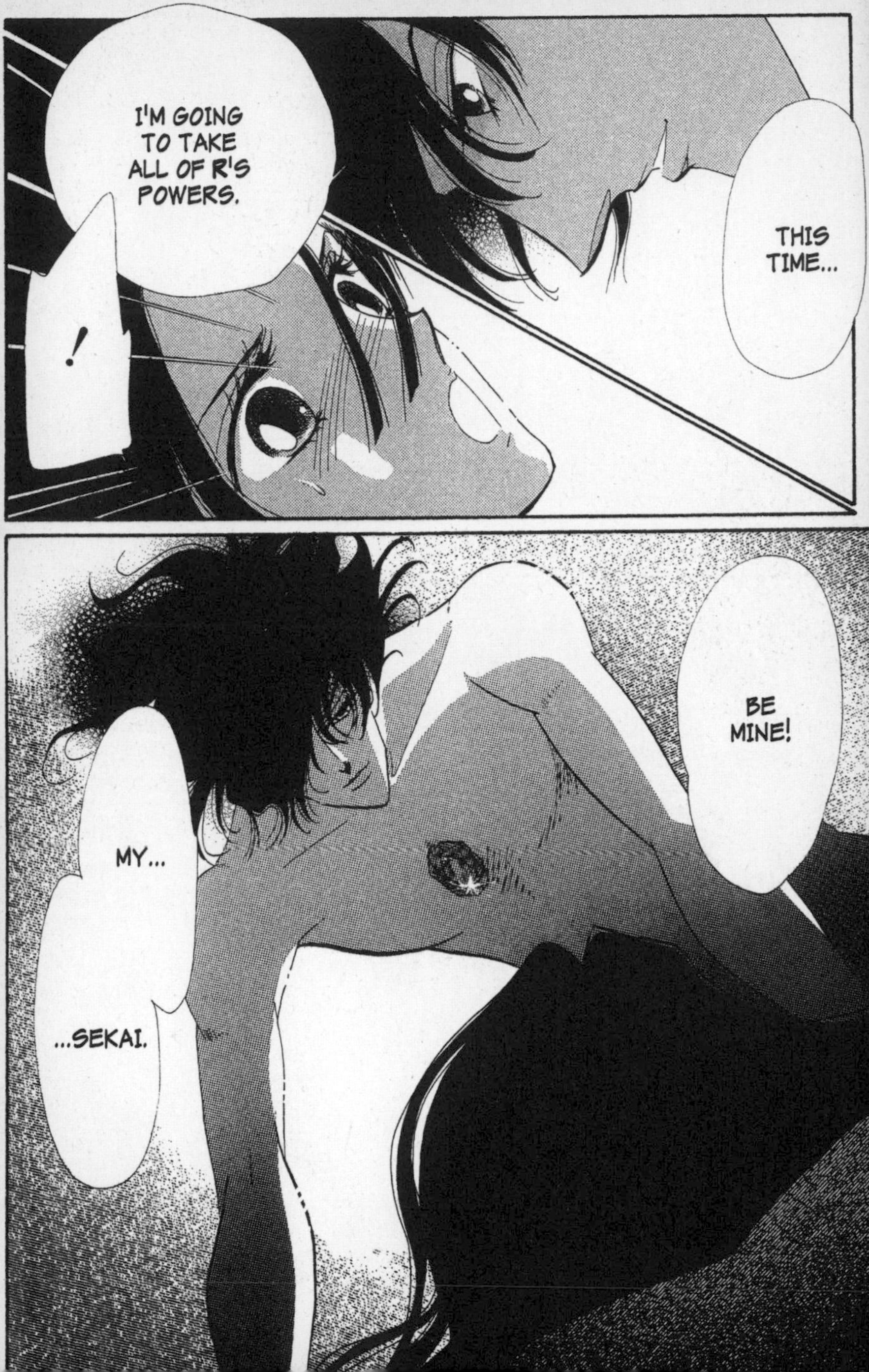
THIS TIME...
I'M GOING TO TAKE ALL OF R'S POWERS.
!
BE MINE!
MY...
...SEKAI.

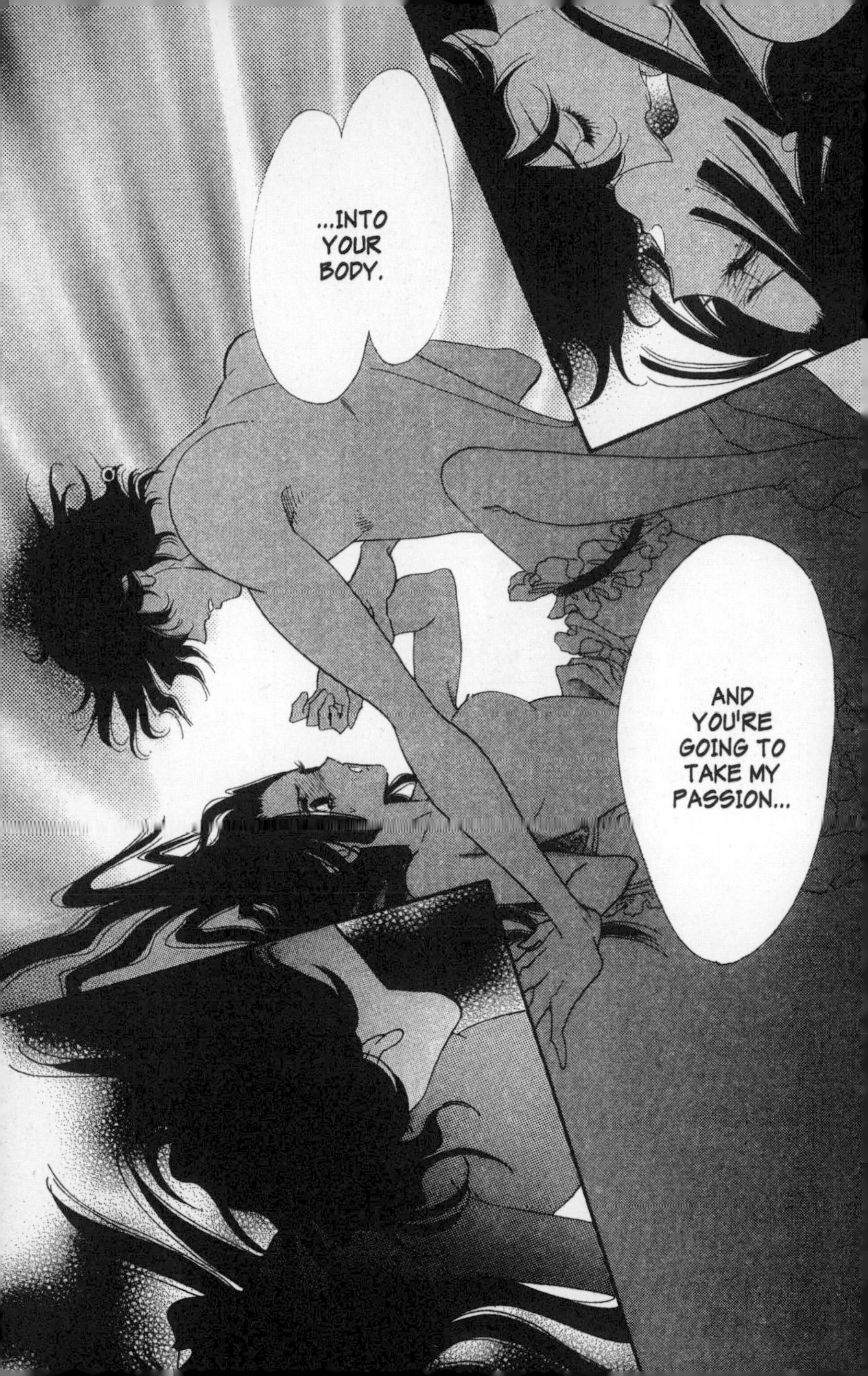
AND YOU'RE GOING TO TAKE MY PASSION...
...INTO YOUR BODY.

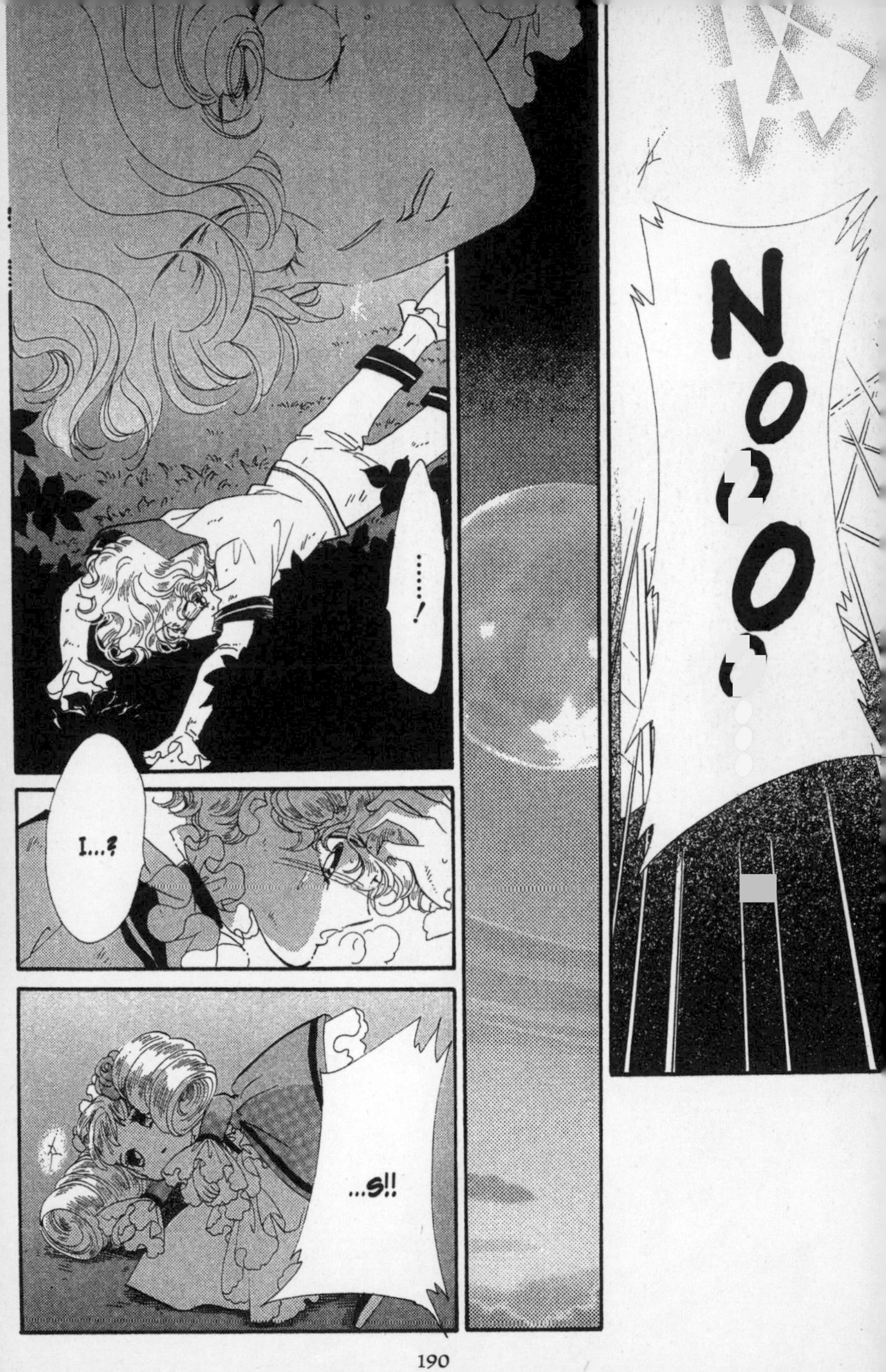
NOOOO...
......!
I...?
...s!!

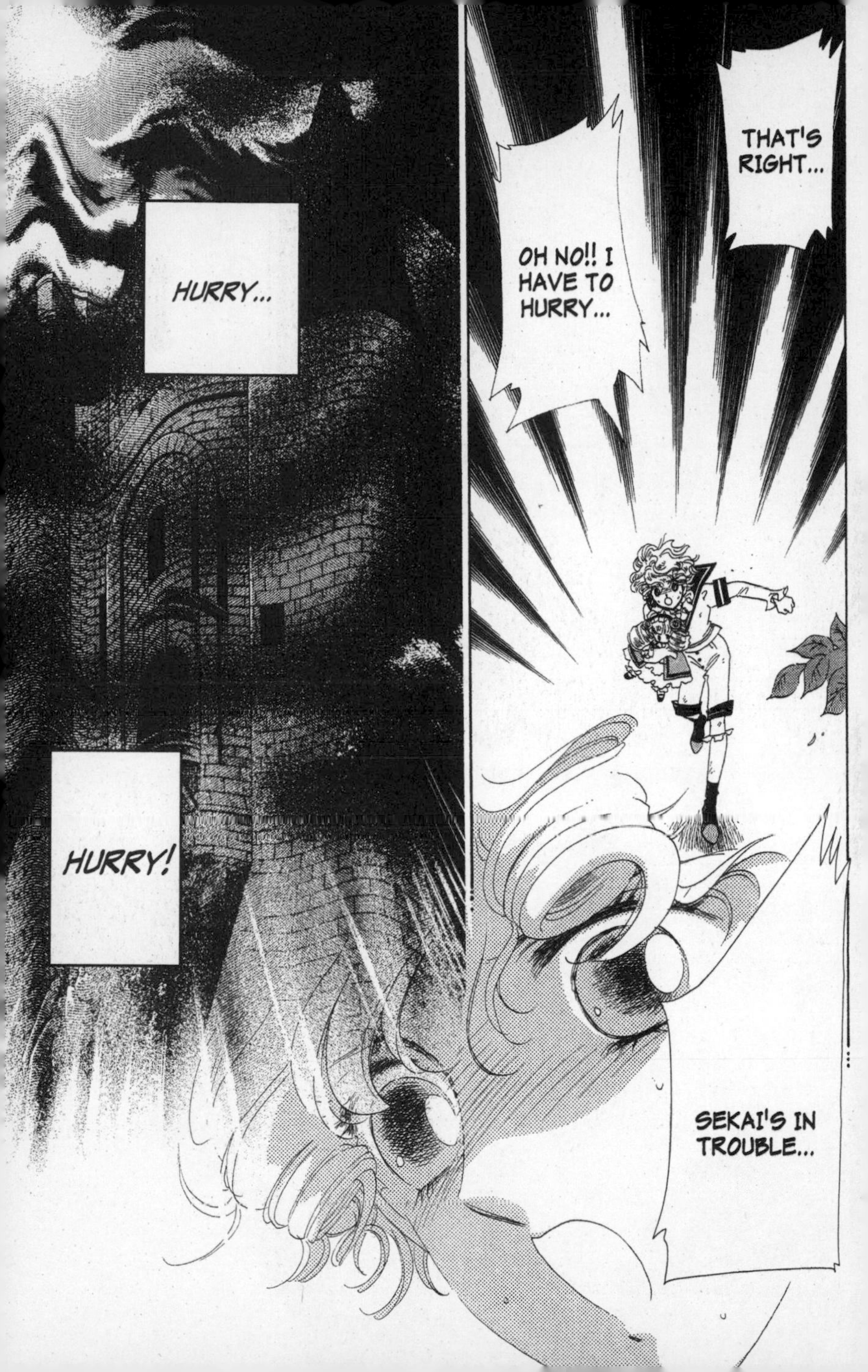
THAT'S RIGHT...
OH NO!! I HAVE TO HURRY...
SEKAI'S IN TROUBLE...
HURRY...
HURRY!

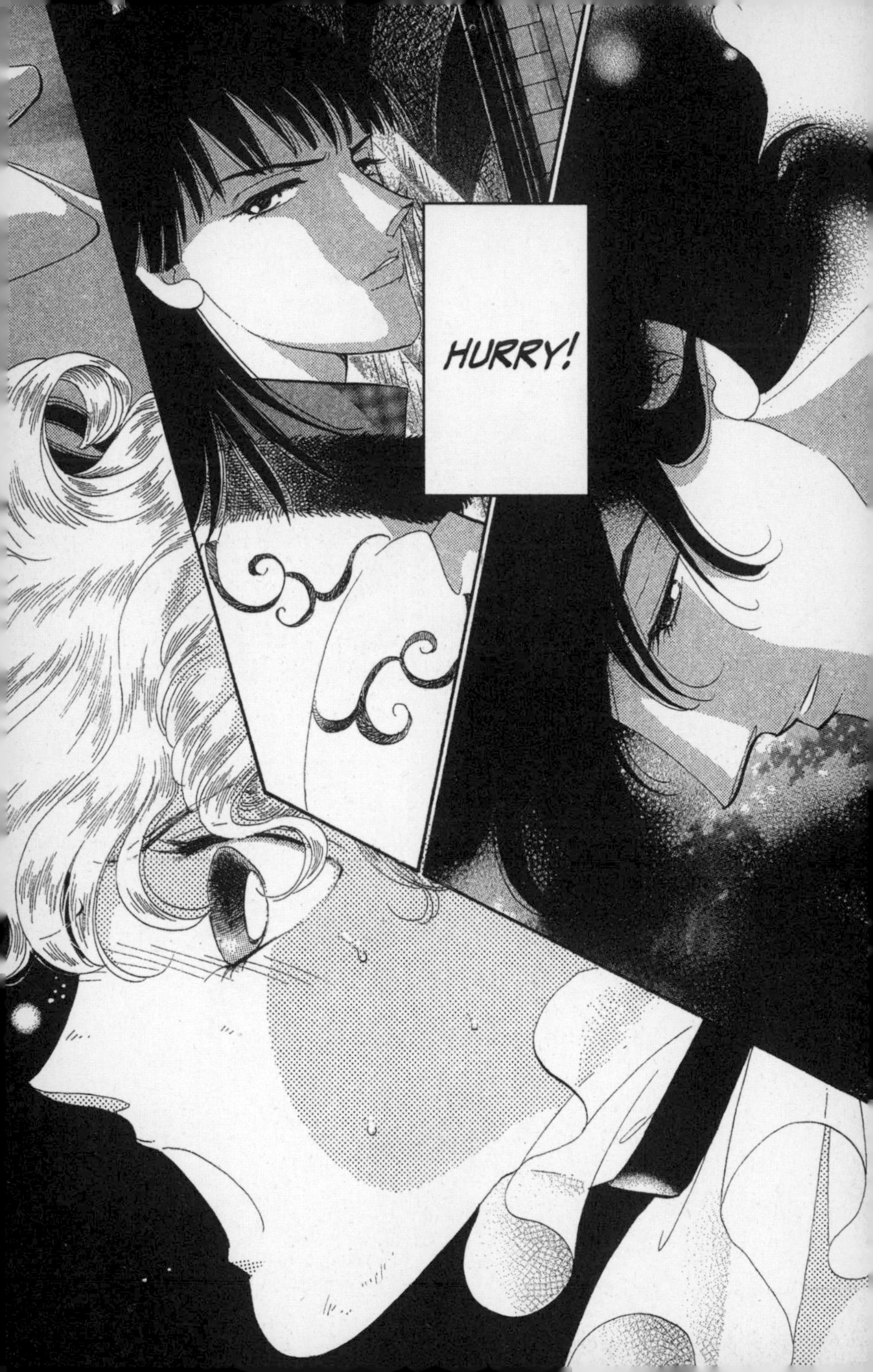
HURRY!

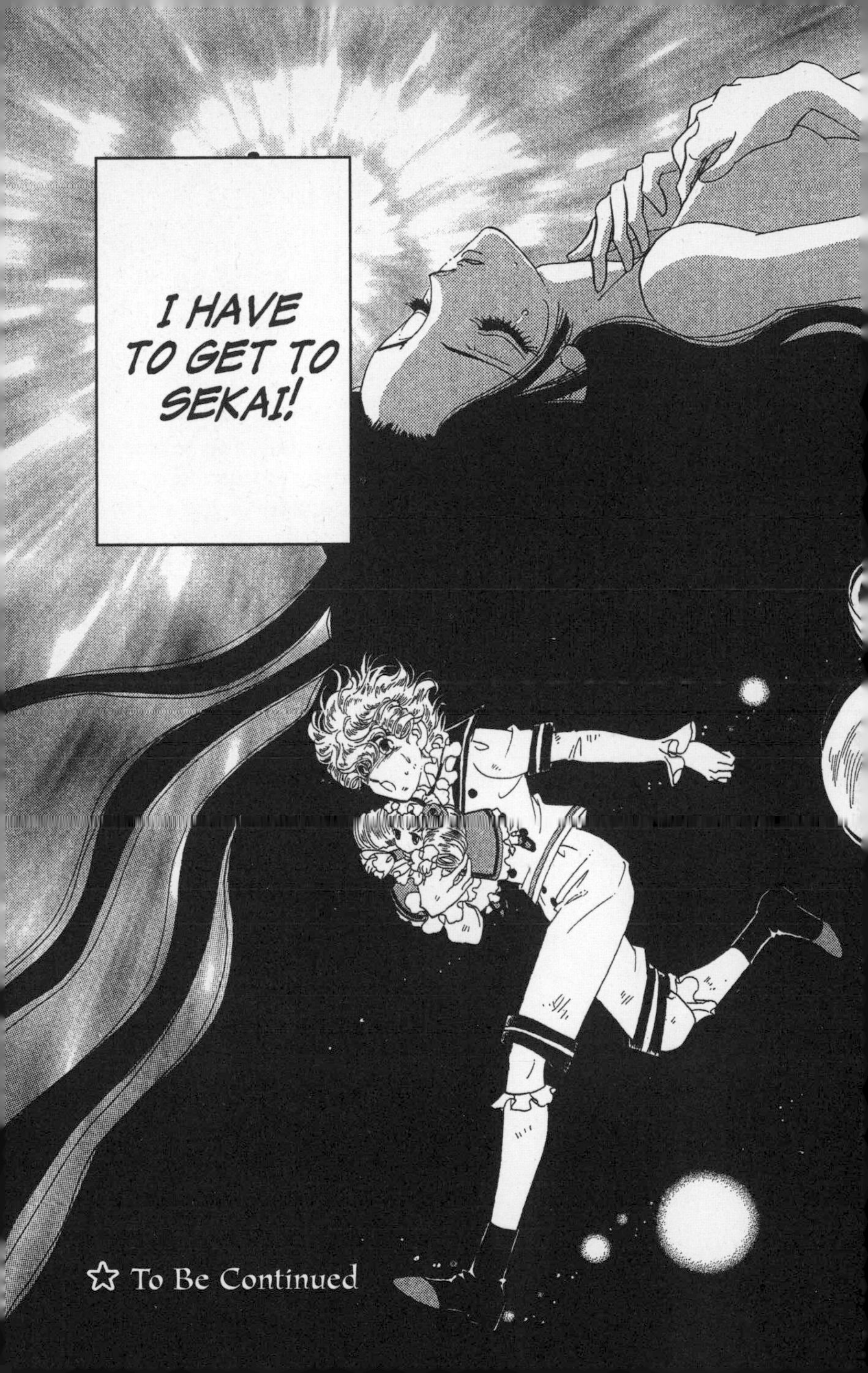
I HAVE TO GET TO SEKAI!
☆ To Be Continued

In the next

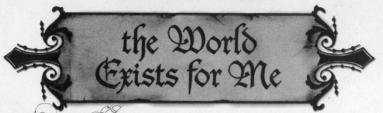

the World Exists for Me

Vol. 2

In 1431, France's General Gilles de Rais failed to rescue Joan of Arc before the Maiden of Orleans was burned at the stake. This could explain why de Rais suddenly becomes obsessed with Sekai...though it doesn't explain why de Rais believes Sekai is Joan of Arc!

Is Machiavello behind this latest deviltry or could there be other forces conspiring against Sekai and Sovieul? Don't miss the next volume!

the World Exists for Me.
TOKYOPOP
Volume 2

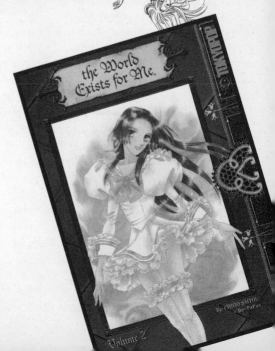

History of the World Exists for Me

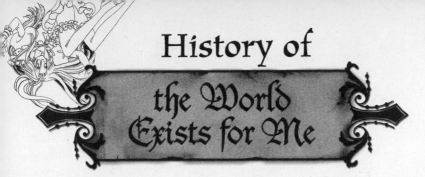

Montespan and the Affair of the Poisons

An historical perspective by Hope Donovan

Montespan--or Françoise-Athénaïs de Rochechouart, Marquise de Montespan--was a real person, as was Louis XIV. In 1667, she achieved her ambition of becoming the King's mistress. Their romance was the most enduring of Louis affairs, ending when the king's affections turned to the teenager Mlle. de Fontanges in 1679. Still, Montespan was a charming, intelligent woman, kept a place in court and had her seven children by Louis legalized as heirs. But she was also a heavy gambler with a short temper and a gift for making comedic impressions of other courtiers.

After a poisoning occurred in 1676 among nobles, fortune-tellers and suspected witches were rounded up and forced to confess and list their clients. This began the Affair of the Poisons, a three-year bubble of unease during the height of the Sun King's reign. One of these witches was la Voisin, also known as Catherine Monvoisin. She was an easy scapegoat--as a midwife, herbalist and fortune-teller, she was a remnant of early medicinal and spiritual practices being eradicated as France and the rest of the world moved towards science. Still, beliefs were up in the air. It was said at the time that every woman in the court had visited la Voisin at least once. La Voisin implicated several clients of hers while imprisoned in late 1680. To be an accomplice of la Voisin (as Sekai was accused), meant that Sekai was suspected of any number of behaviors, from getting or giving an abortion, having her fortune told, asking for poisons to kill family members, or for acting as a go-between for a wealthier aristocrat. One particular go-between, Mme. de Ouillet (who was executed herself), was instrumental in tracing Montespan to la Voisin.

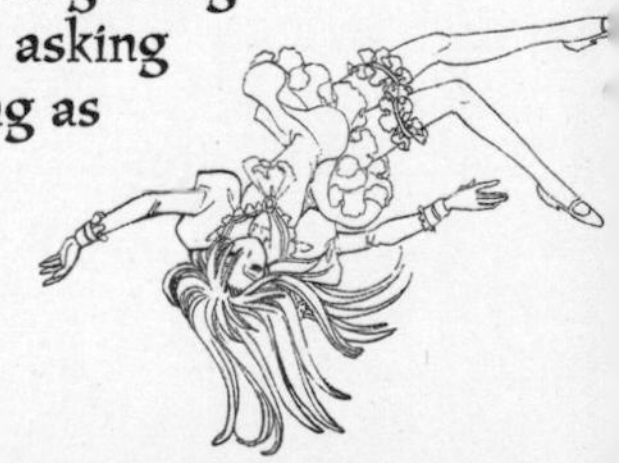

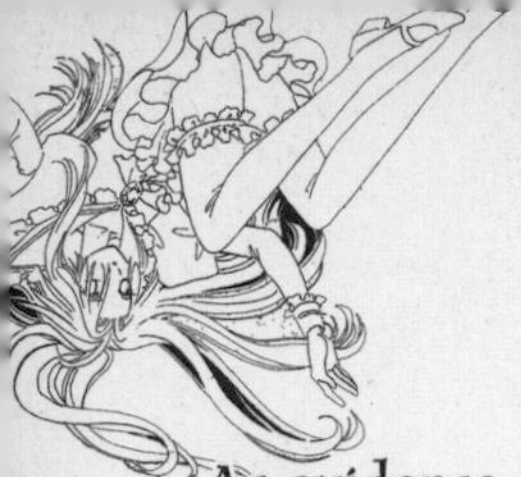

As evidence accumulated, Mme. de Montespan was linked with buying poisons and aphrodisiacs to make her way to Louis XIV's side, causing the miscarriage of Mme. de Fontanges' child and attempting to poison Louis XIV's first mistress, Louise. However, Montespan was never confronted about her activities by the court or the King, and indeed never had any awareness of the court proceedings, as Louis kept them a secret from her. Even though the two were no longer in intimate standing during the Affair, the king ordered the court proceedings burned. Her involvement in the Affair of the Poisons would have been forgotten entirely if the Paris Chief of Police, Nicholas de La Reynie, a leading force of justice in the witch-hunts, had not kept a copy that resurfaced a hundred years later.

While Montespan was never caught poisoning the King, as this manga portrays, the atmosphere of paranoia that pervaded the uppermost classes of society is depicted quite accurately. Montespan was not exiled, and she and her children lived on at Versailles until 1691, when Montespan unwisely asked to retire from the palace and was not invited back. She spent the rest of her life in Paris or traveling, dying in 1707. The events of Volume 1 of *The World Exists for Me* would most likely have taken place in February 1681, when Louis XIV was most doubtful of Montespan's innocence.

Aramis--the castrated swordsman--is conspicuously the name of one of the Three Musketeers. A fictional adventure story by Alexander Dumas, *The Three Musketeers* chronicles the escapades of three renegade musketeers. It is set in 1625 France, under the rule of the weak king Louis XIII and defacto ruler Cardinal Richelieu.

It is unlikely that Ikuhara intended his Aramis to be the musketeer--though the most pious of the musketeers, Aramis decided against joining the church. It's doubtful that the musketeer Aramis was castrated, as he had a mistress to satisfy. And of course, he would have been an old man or dead in Montespan's age.

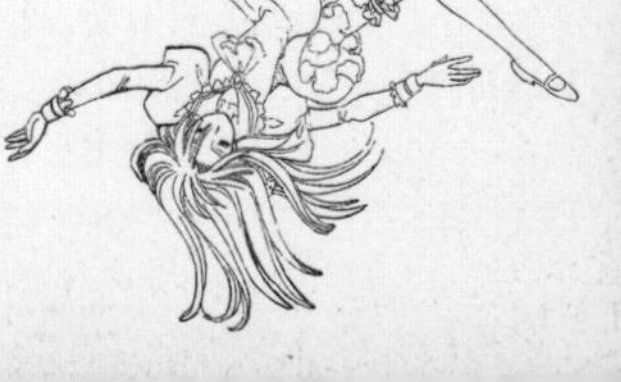

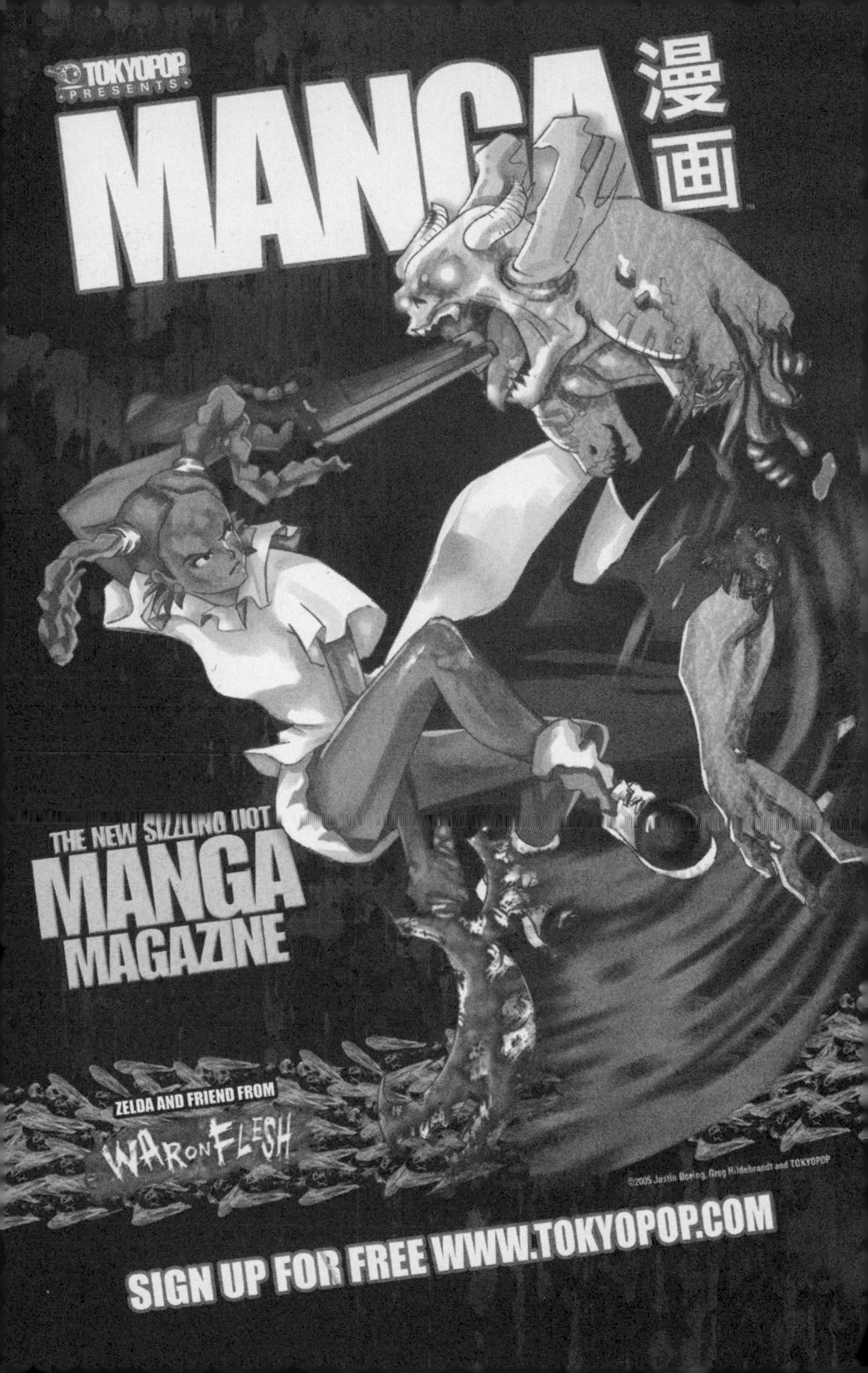
TOKYOPOP PRESENTS
MANGA 漫画
THE NEW SIZZLING HOT
MANGA
MAGAZINE
ZELDA AND FRIEND FROM
WAR ON FLESH
©2005 Justin Boring, Greg Hildebrandt and TOKYOPOP
SIGN UP FOR FREE WWW.TOKYOPOP.COM

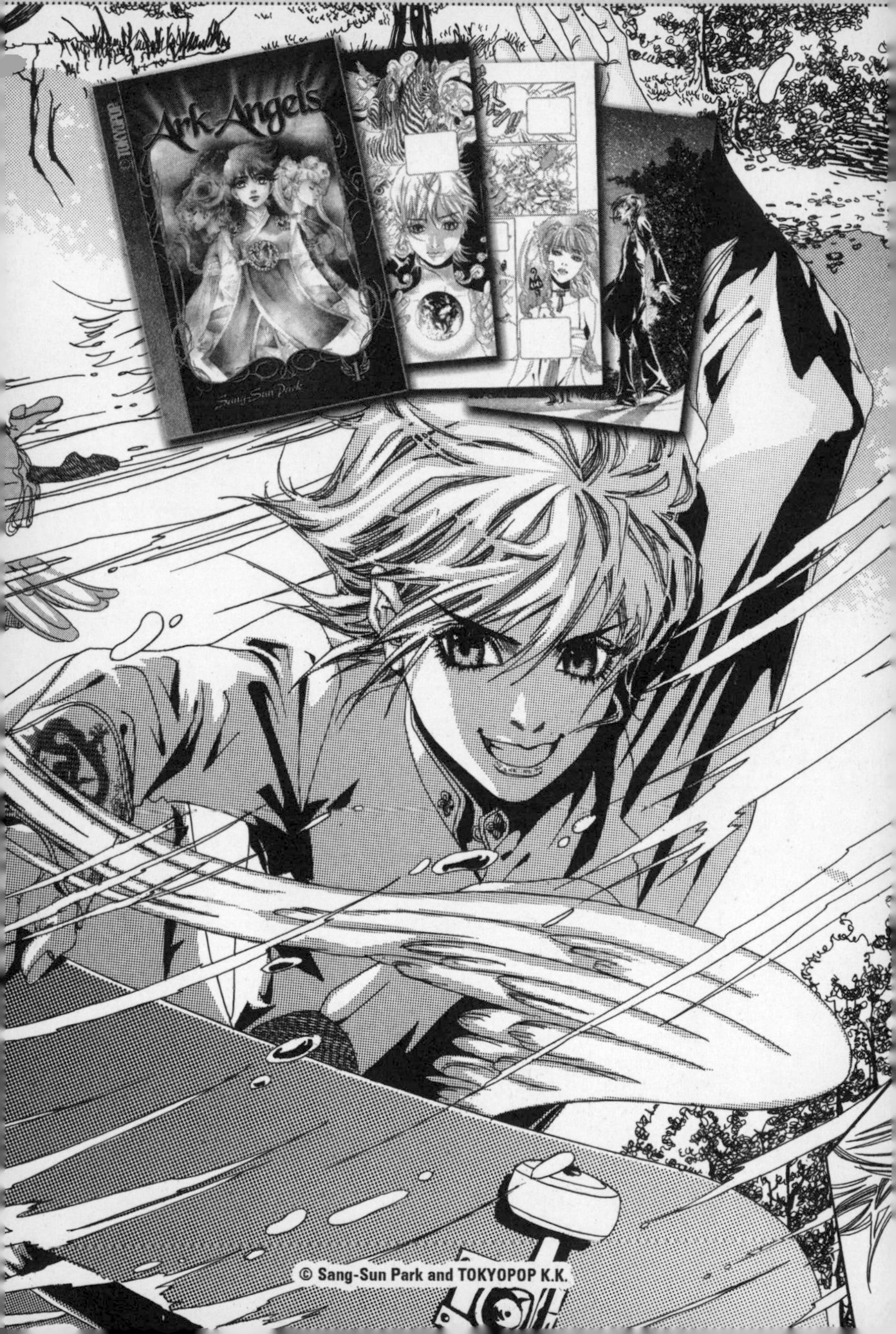
Ark Angels
Sang-Sun Park
TOKYOPOP
1

Ark Angels ™

Girls just wanna have fun— while saving the world.

From a small lake nestled in a secluded forest far from the edge of town, something strange has emerged: Three young girls— Shem, Hamu and Japheth—who are sisters from another world. Equipped with magical powers, they are charged with saving all the creatures of Earth from extinction. However, there is someone or something sinister trying to stop them. And on top of trying to save our world, these sisters have to live like normal human girls: They go to school, work at a flower shop, hang out with friends and even fall in love!

FROM THE CREATOR OF THE TAROT CAFÉ!

STOP!

This is the back of the book.
You wouldn't want to spoil a great ending!

This book is printed "manga-style," in the authentic Japanese right-to-left format. Since none of the artwork has been flipped or altered, readers get to experience the story just as the creator intended. You've been asking for it, so TOKYOPOP® delivered: authentic, hot-off-the-press, and far more fun!

DIRECTIONS

If this is your first time reading manga-style, here's a quick guide to help you understand how it works.

It's easy... just start in the top right panel and follow the numbers. Have fun, and look for more 100% authentic manga from TOKYOPOP®!